GENERATION MULTIPLEX

Generation Multiplex

THE IMAGE OF YOUTH IN
AMERICAN CINEMA SINCE 1980

Revised Edition

Timothy Shary

Foreword by Stephen Tropiano
Afterword by Catherine Driscoll

 UNIVERSITY OF TEXAS PRESS
Austin

Requests for permission to reproduce material from this
work should be sent to:
 Permissions
 University of Texas Press
 P.O. Box 7819
 Austin, TX 78713-7819
 http://utpress.utexas.edu/index.php/rp-form

♾ The paper used in this book meets the minimum requirements
of ANSI/NISO Z39.48-1992 (R1997) (Permanence of Paper).

Library of Congress Cataloging-in-Publication Data
Shary, Timothy, 1967–
 Generation multiplex : the image of youth in American cinema
after 1980 / by Timothy Shary ; foreword by Stephen Tropiano ;
afterword by Catherine Driscoll. — Revised edition.
  pages   cm
 Includes bibliographical references and index.
 ISBN 978-0-292-75662-5 (pbk. : alk. paper)
 1. Youth in motion pictures.   2. Motion pictures—United States.
I. Title.
 PN1995.9.Y6S53   2014
 791.43′652054—dc23
                                              2013030490

doi:10.7560/756625

This book remains dedicated to

CAROLYN ANDERSON

without whom this book
(and much of my career)
would not have occurred

and to the fond memory of

ANDY ANDERSON

beloved professor, colleague,
husband, and father

two great teachers who have inspired
countless young people like myself

This new edition is dedicated to

OLIVIA XENDOLYN

the greatest girl in the world

CONTENTS

Stephen Tropiano

FOREWORD

In Hollywood, certain film genres, such as the Western, the sci-fi film, and the musical, are cyclical. When Warner Bros. released *Unforgiven* in 1992, the revisionist Western was praised by critics, earned over $100 million, and won four Academy Awards, including Best Picture and Best Director for Clint Eastwood. Over the next few years, several of the major studios released big-budget Westerns: *Geronimo: An American Legend* (1993), *Tombstone* (1993), *Wyatt Earp* (1994), and *The Quick and the Dead* (1995). *Tombstone* turned a profit, but the rest were expensive flops. And so, once again, the Western genre disappeared into the distant sunset.

At the same time, there are some genres, like the Hollywood teen film and its various subgenres—the high school film, teen horror, sex comedies, and so forth—that never fade from view. What makes the Hollywood teen film so unique and differentiates it from other genres is that its target audience—teenagers—is also its primary subject. Teenagers make up a significant percentage of the ticket-buying audience, so there will always be a market for youth-oriented comedies and dramas—films that tell their stories, address their problems and issues, and express their joys and angst. Still, while they may repeatedly deal with certain subject matter and themes important to young moviegoers—coming-of-age, alienation, peer pressure, et cetera—teen films also have an expiration date. Consequently, in order to be relevant and "speak" to the experiences of a current young audience, the teen film, like any genre, must undergo some changes over time.

Thomas Schatz addressed this very issue in his influential essay, "Film Genre and the Genre Film" in 1981. Schatz defines Hollywood film genres as both "static" and "dynamic" systems. A film genre is "static" because "it is a familiar formula of interrelated narrative and cinematic components."[1] In other words, there are certain elements that films within a genre typically share. In the case of Hollywood teen films, the formula includes themes (e.g., coming-of-age, overcoming adversity), characters (e.g., the jock, the nerd, parents, teachers), and settings (e.g., high school, the home). At the same time, certain aspects of the genre are "dynamic" because "changes in cultural attitudes, new influential genre films, [and] the economics of the industry . . . continually refine any genre."[2] This is certainly true of the Hollywood teen film, which will reflect some of the obvious changes that occur with each new generation of teenagers in regard to fashion, slang, music, and technology. A comedy released in 2013 in which teen characters weren't talking or texting one another on their cell phones would likely be mistaken by a young audience for a vintage or nostalgia teen film. Since I published my own study of Hollywood teen movies, *Rebels & Chicks: A History of the Hollywood Teen Film*, back in 2006, the teen film has flourished, yet the "economics of the industry" have taken it in an entirely new direction.

The popularity of J. K. Rowling's *Harry Potter* and Stephenie Meyer's *Twilight* book series and the box office success of their respective film franchises can certainly account for Hollywood's renewed interest in youth-oriented films. Just as adult best sellers are likely to eventually find their way to the big screen (or get optioned by a studio and stuck in what is known in Hollywood as "development hell"), the studios are turning to young adult literature (YAL), popular novels and book series written for young readers, for source material. The list of 2012 releases included big-budget adaptations (Suzanne Collins's *The Hunger Games*, *The Twilight Saga: Breaking Dawn — Part 2*) and smaller, indie dramas (Judy Blume's *Tiger Eyes*, Stephen Chbosky's *The Perks of Being a Wallflower*). The list of 2013 releases is even longer. Like *Harry Potter* and *Twilight*, most are in the fantasy, horror, and mystery genres: Kami Garcia and Margaret Stohl's *Beautiful Creatures*, Cassandra Clare's *The Mortal Instruments: City of Bones*, Isaac Marion's *Warm Bodies*, Orson Scott Card's *Ender's Game*, and Suzanne Collins's sequel to *The Hunger Games*, *Catching Fire*. Other YAL adaptations in the works include Joseph Delaney's *The Spook's Apprentice* (retitled *Seventh Son*) and Joe Hill's *Horns*.

Television has also capitalized on the popularity of YAL. The latest trend on youth-oriented channels like ABC Family and the CW Network is to adapt popular teen book series into horror and mystery shows targeted toward a young female demographic: L. J. Smith's *The Vampire Diaries* (2009–) and *The Secret Circle* (2011–2012), and Sara Shepard's *Pretty Little Liars* (2010–) and *The Lying Game* (2011–). Certainly one important aspect of this trend in both film and television is that female characters are no longer relegated to the margins of male-centered narratives. Like Katniss Everdeen in *The Hunger Games*, these young women are not only at the center of the narrative, they are the narrative's driving force—the continuation of a trend that began on television with Buffy Summers in *Buffy the Vampire Slayer* (1997–2003). (Unfortunately, the same can't be said for Bella, the female protagonist of the popular *Twilight* series [2008–2012]. Instead of slaying Edward, the passive Bella literally gives her body and soul to him.)

Hollywood's preference for producing films based on existing material over original screenplays makes good economic sense, especially when it's time to market the movie. There is an assumption, and rightfully so, that young adult readers are likely to go see the film based on their favorite novel (if only to see how the two compare). Unfortunately, Hollywood's tendency to recycle what has already proved profitable has spilled over into teen movies. In addition to seeking out the latest YAL best seller, they are also going through their own video libraries, resulting in a string of remakes of popular teen films from the 1980s (some studios call them "updates"): *Fame* (2009), *The Karate Kid* (2010), *Footloose* (2011), *Red Dawn* (2012), and a second remake of Stephen King's *Carrie* (2013; the first remake, a made-for-TV movie, aired in 2002). Most but not all of them earned money at the box office (the *Red Dawn* remake was a bomb). If the profits from these films will make more screen adaptations of YAL possible, then Hollywood should continue to churn them out. Maybe it's time for a remake of *The Breakfast Club* (1985)? Or a sequel to *Ferris Bueller's Day Off* (1986)?

PREFACE

G*eneration Multiplex* was first published in 2002. The book was adopted by many professors teaching courses in the burgeoning field of youth cinema studies, and sold so well that the University of Texas Press produced a second printing in 2004. That allowed me to make a few minor changes (e.g., correcting some citations, adding some new film titles), but the past decade has been witness to such an expansion of the subject in the academy, and to changes in the industry's style and output of teen films, that a completely new, revised, and expanded edition is warranted.

The thesis from the first edition remains essentially intact here: American films about youth are dynamically and diversely representative of adolescents, to the point that these films constitute their own genre and have engendered individual subgenres with particular and often consistent codes for that representation. For instance, films set in or around a school environment tend to employ one to five recognizable character types, while teen horror films tend to care less about characters and focus more on the types of abuse and murder portrayed in their stories. Teen films about juvenile delinquency have a similar method of focusing on the crimes and misdemeanors of youth, and their etiology, while films about young people having sex and falling in love deliver moral messages about the perils and pleasures of romance, and hence, adulthood. These four subgenres are analyzed in single chapters of this edition, covering releases from 1980 to 2013.

One change from the first edition is the elimination of the chapter on science. That subgenre certainly rose to prominence in the '80s, but was already fading by the '90s, and despite the ongoing use of technology by children in real life, the topic is now almost entirely elided by Hollywood. The most likely cause for this is that youth do not find science and technology as dramatic or fearful as they were presented in the past. After all, kids today use computers and other machines in a seamless, confident connection to their personal lives.

A few sections of chapters have been reconfigured or excised, such as the "Patriotic Purpose" study, which, like the science chapter, was devoted almost exclusively to films and concerns of the '80s. Conversely, I have expanded on the sections about queer youth, whose films have become voluminous, and about athletes in school films, especially girls, who have gained refreshing prominence. The horror chapter now devotes a substantial section to fantasy films, and the romance chapter has a section on prom movies.

Other changes in this edition include the addition of relevant films and research since 2002, and corresponding commentary by critics. As previously noted, the outpouring of other academic studies on the topic over the past decade, as well as the further proliferation of teen cinema, has been incredibly rich. Accordingly, I have removed some less valuable citations and expanded on some that have proved more germane over time.

My greatest gratification in studying youth on screen has been in lending to the genre some semblance of legitimacy. While I do argue for the quality of certain films over others, teen films in general have given us an opportunity to appreciate a large section of the population that has been gaining authority yet still relies on adults to speak for them in most cases. In fact, the politics of age representation demand further study overall, because the young *and* old, while very influential, creative, talented, and vocal, are still continually disenfranchised.

In my own high school graduation speech, I told my fellow students, "Your youth is the single most valuable asset you have, and as you grow older, you may find that it was the only asset you ever had." Nearly three decades later, I recognize how that affected attitude infused my fascination with films about youth, while I also understood that such zeal for being young was rather cynical—especially now that I am moving into my later years with a perhaps predictable ambition to study geriatric roles in cinema.

I hope many more studies of aging politics will emerge, and that the various depictions of youth and the elderly will continue to evolve with sensitivity, insight, and appreciation.

Timothy Shary
June 2013
Millsboro, Delaware

ACKNOWLEDGMENTS

This book began as my doctoral dissertation at the University of Massachusetts at Amherst in 1998, so first and foremost, I express my deep and gracious gratitude to my committee—Carolyn Anderson (chair), Martin Norden, and Catherine Portuges—who were encouraging, informative, and inspiring during the early production of this work. I owe Carolyn a special debt of appreciation, for her lessons have been indescribably valuable in shaping me as a film scholar, and her teaching has been invigorating: she is wise, witty, dedicated, ambitious, and endlessly energetic.

My senior editor at the University of Texas Press, Jim Burr, had faith in this project back in 1998 when I sent my unwieldy dissertation to him. Jim maintained his support through the subsequent years as I developed that manuscript into the first edition, and ten years later he again supported its revision into the current second edition. Jim has further advocated my work on other publications, and has connected me with other editors and other presses. I give him my highest thanks and appreciation. Further thanks go to my copyeditor, Nick Taylor, and my manuscript editor, Lynne Chapman, who did so much of the real work in the final production of the book.

So many friends came forth to help me with this book that I cannot name them all, but in one way or another all of the following people offered me advice, ideas, data, hope, sympathy, and/or willing viewing of teen films I watched during the course of my analysis. I don't think it's too tacky to say *don't you forget about me* to: Richard Brown, Chris Boucher, Anne Ciecko, Darci and Rich Cramer-Benjamin, Susan Ericsson, Chris Goodwin, Devin and Rachel Griffiths, Perrin Harkins, Sara Hunicke, Katie LeBesco, Nancy Inouye, Jon Kitzen, Chris LeBel, Gary Marcus, Mark Mierswa, Carolyn Moore, Kelly Mullaly, Diane Mullins, Nicola Paterson, Jesse Rossa, Tom Scully, John Shields, Mike Wolpe, Zach Woods, and Zsofia Zvolensky. I also want to note that significant contributions were made to this book by two of my former students at the University of Massachusetts, Jon Lupo (who helped me work out the title) and Louisa Stein. Further, I offer universal thanks to the hundreds of students at UMass, Clark University, and the University of Oklahoma who took any of my youth cinema courses and offered numerous insights on the genre, as well as comments on the first edition of the book.

The Higgins School of Humanities at Clark University provided me with three grants between 2000 and 2005 to conduct research on youth cinema and to present my work at various conferences. The Higgins School further funded a special seminar on French and American youth film and literature in the spring of 2004 that I had the pleasure to teach with my colleague Beth Gale. My thanks to Higgins School directors Janette Greenwood and Virginia Vaughan, and their assistant Lisa Coakley. Two of my program directors in Screen Studies at Clark, Marvin D'Lugo and Marcia Butzel, prompted me to develop a youth course for the curriculum, which I was happy to teach numerous times from 1997 to 2006.

I also benefited from a grant endowed by the Hillery Charitable Trust at Clark University in 2005, which supported my research on youth cinema.

Angela Bazydlo at Clark worked most diligently to provide me with dozens of media appearances in the press and on radio from 2001 to 2007, each of which promoted my work to wide audiences. I owe her immense credit for boosting my career.

Research from this project has been presented at four groups' conferences, those of the Society for Cinema and Media Studies, the University Film and Video Association, the International Association for the Fantastic in the Arts, and the Popular Culture Association, as well as thematic conferences such as "Postmodernism and Cinema" (Kent State), "Intellect and Ideology in Media Culture" (Ryerson Polytechnic University), and "Children and War" (Rutgers University). Specific articles related to this project have been published in many anthologies, journals, and encyclopedias, including: *Virgin Territory*, ed. Tamar Jeffers McDonald; *American Cinema of the 1990s*, ed. Christine Holmlund; *Popping Culture*, ed. Murray Pomerance and John Sakeris; *Where the Boys Are: Cinemas of Masculinity and Youth* and *Sugar, Spice, and Everything Nice: Cinemas of Girlhood*, ed. Frances Gateward and Murray Pomerance; *Film Genre Reader IV*, ed. Barry Keith Grant; *The Journal of Popular Culture*; *Interdisciplinary Humanities*; *The Journal of Film and Video*; *Post Script*; *The Journal of Popular Film and Television*; *Telemedium: The Journal of Media Literacy*; *The Encyclopedia of Children, Adolescents, and the Media*; and *The Schirmer Encyclopedia of Film*.

The first edition was shaped and influenced by the careful critiques of David Considine at Appalachian State University and Kathy Merlock Jackson at Virginia Wesleyan College; their suggestions for revision in the early editing process were vital. For help with specific research on that first edition, I thank Brian Taves at the Library of Congress. Jon Lewis gave a helpful critique of my 2005 book at Wallflower Press, *Teen Films: American Youth on Screen*, and I thank Yoram Allon for motivating that publication. Alexandra Siebel and I coedited *Youth Culture in Global Cinema* for Texas in 2007, which substantially broadened my horizons on the field.

Academic colleagues, all of whom have become friends, have also shared provocative ideas with me on issues of youth representation over the past decade: Christine Holmlund at the University of Tennessee, Ilana Nash at Western Michigan University, Amanda Ann Klein at East Carolina University, and Murray Pomerance at Ryerson University, who first published my work on this topic. And in the greatest spirit of collegiality, Stephen Tropiano and Catherine Driscoll accepted my invitation to provide the foreword and afterword for this volume, lending their expert perspectives on teen cinema, notwithstanding our different publishing efforts. I hope their generous contributions will be an example that other academics with compatible interests will follow.

Back in the twentieth century, movie researchers like me often relied on what were then called "video stores" to rent and buy movies. While almost all of them have long since vanished with the advent of newer technologies, I'd still like to point out that one of these stores supplied the majority of movies that I screened for the first edition of this book: Video to Go in Amherst, Massachusetts. And just as each visual technology seems to become obsolete on an annual basis, so did the software containing the original texts for this manuscript, which I had to entirely retype, aided by Laptop and Computer Solutions of Millsboro, Delaware.

Two teachers in my precollege years had perhaps the most profound effect on my early education: Ty Walker, who taught me into my teenage years, and Lee March, who taught me out of them. Mr. Walker was the first teacher who demonstrated to me the legitimacy of studying movies as well as enjoying them (he had seen *Star Wars* seventeen times when I first met him), and Ms. March sparked my early academic film interests, pushing me to write my first essay on a movie, which prophetically turned out to be *The Breakfast Club*. These two teachers provided the foundation from which I pursued cinema studies, and for that I am forever grateful.

I have lived with my parents while writing this new edition and my mother passed away during that time. They always promoted my education and encouraged my work, and of course I owe my entire life to them.

GENERATION MULTIPLEX

One   I N T R O D U C T I O N

The Cinematic Image of Youth

The 2012 film *21 Jump Street* depicts two rookie cops posing as high school students to break up a drug ring. Much to their surprise and chagrin, popularity among teenagers has changed radically since they graduated in the previous decade: traits that had made students seem square and unattractive—studying for classes, caring for the environment, being politically sensitive—now make them appealing and cool. Such is the nature of adolescence, fluctuating on a continual basis with the various whims of time, which vividly illustrates how difficult understanding youth culture can be because it is so mercurial and fleeting.

These aspects of youth have led American cinema into a curious and often inconsistent fascination with stories about and images of young people, a fascination that became abundantly manifest in the last decades of the twentieth century. Various film trends catering to young audiences had emerged over past generations, but movies since the 1980s have appeared almost fixated on capturing certain youth styles and promoting certain perspectives on the celebration, and survival, of adolescence. Many arguments persist as to why teenagers have been targeted by both Hollywood studios and the American independent movie market: youth have disposable incomes that they like spending on entertainment; today's children are inculcated by media to be the consumptive parents of tomorrow; filmmakers engage in the vicarious experiences of their own lost youth; and young people make up the largest percentage of the movie-viewing audience. All of these points are valid, yet this book argues not as much for the reasons behind youth representation as for the issues and trends that representation engenders. Evident from the contemporary outpouring of American movies about youth, and the parallel production of teen-oriented television shows, magazines, and multimedia outlets, as well as the cultural attention paid to youth attitudes and behaviors in the wake of various scandals, crimes, and accomplishments, the imaging of youth has become indicative of our deepest social and personal concerns.

Consider, for instance, the most successful recent young adult phenomenon, the *Twilight* books and subsequent movies, which covered the years 2005–2012. The revenue generated from just these two media—not including subsequent products such as clothing, music, and ancillary texts—has been in excess of $5 billion, and while their number of readers and viewers is impossible to determine, their audience is unmistakably enormous. The stories about and images of the teenage characters in *Twilight* spoke to fantasies of the supernatural as well as romantic destiny, sexual development, and family politics, utilizing native and ancient mythologies, exotic regional locations, brutal violence, and myriad other dramatic elements within an otherwise conventional struggle between right and wrong. Further, the sensation spread beyond teens to adults, and beyond the target demographic of American youth to a global scale that extremely few stories have enjoyed with such speed and success. Through this universalization, the tormented love triangle of a girl with a vampire and a werewolf presented an incredibly satisfying journey that revealed our cultural appreciation of youth itself.

All dramas thrive on conflict, and the process of maturing is a natural conflict familiar to everyone by their teenage years. While many filmgoers freely participate in screen fantasies about the possibilities of life as a secret agent or of saving a loved one from the clutches of death, most of our lives are filled with less spectacular phenomena, such as how we come to be accepted by society, discover romance, have sex, gain employment, make moral decisions, and learn about the world and who we are in it. Most of us first encounter these phenomena in our adolescence, and how we handle them largely determines how we live the rest of our lives. The gravity of adolescence thus makes for compelling drama, even if many of us would rather forget those trying years. Understanding how we learn and grow in our youth is integral to understanding who we become as adults.

Since the 1950s the American movie box office, with varying interests, has been relying on people under thirty to pay for movies about their daily dramas and fantasies.[1] Of course, one of the telling dilemmas of youth films since cinema began is that while they address young people they are not produced by young people, for children and teens are effectively restricted from the filmmaking process. Thus, screen images of youth have always been traditionally filtered through adult perspectives. As a result of these commercial and political conditions, teen films have evolved into a visible and often coherent genre that has thrived for over half a century.

That genre has generated films as complex and sophisticated as many adult dramas, and in recent decades its patrons are no longer content with the rebellious posturing of 1950s hot rod races, the trite frivolity of 1960s beach parties, or the cheap tricks of 1970s drive-in dreck.

Since the 1980s a number of distinct subgenres and character types within this genre—call it youth, teen, and/or young adult—have emerged and have offered richly provocative images that question the changing concepts of youth in the United States. The specific number of these categories is arguable, and surely too large to detail in one volume, so I offer here an analysis of four subgenres—containing seventeen of the most significant youth film styles and movie roles—to demonstrate the changing nature of teen representation in American media since 1980.[2]

Young people have always been a concern in American film history, both in terms of their images on screen and their reception of films as an audience. In the earliest days of cinema there did not exist a distinct youth genre, nor for that matter much of an agreed social sense for what constituted youth. Children in the early twentieth century often left school by the age of fourteen to begin jobs (only 6.4 percent of young Americans completed high school in 1900) and many were married and having children by eighteen, a condition that kept the state of "youth" limited to just a few years between childhood and adulthood.[3] Government had just begun to formally distinguish youth from adults through legislation involving delinquency, when Illinois became the first state to do so with the Juvenile Court Act of 1899, which gave the court jurisdiction of children under the age of sixteen.[4] The reception of movies at that time was also affected by social fears about their corruptive potential, especially regarding their influence on children. Many moral guardians of the early 1900s preached about the dangers of exposing children to typically adult-oriented dramas, and rather than make films that specifically catered to a young audience, the fledgling movie industry tended to side with concerns over propriety.[5]

By the 1920s, Hollywood formed the Hays Office and began formal evaluations and restrictions on the moral content of American films, and despite a choice few popular films that featured young characters of the time—Lillian Gish in *Broken Blossoms* (1919), Mary Pickford in *Pollyanna* (1920), Jackie Coogan in *The Kid* (1921), Baby Peggy in *Captain January* (1924)—the industry took a steady position on youth films by the '30s: children were either pre-adolescent (such as Shirley Temple or the kids in *Our Gang*) or were stunted in their early adulthood (as in the musical films of Deanna Durbin or in the delinquency franchise that began with the Dead End Kids). In either case, young people did not routinely have on-screen discussions about otherwise typical developmental issues like sexuality, drug or alcohol use, or family dysfunction.

The notable youth films that followed in the years after the Great Depression tended to be optimistic and endearing fables starring the likes of Elizabeth Taylor, Judy Garland, and/or Mickey Rooney (who played the enduring teenager Andy Hardy for a decade), but these films were directed at and most often seen by an adult audience, or by a family audience consisting of both parents and children. Hollywood studios promoted these small troupes of young stars (also including Frankie Darro, Bonita Granville, Freddie Bartholomew, Dickie Moore, and Joyce Reynolds) who came to represent the contemporary ideals, if not the realistic conditions, of youth.

With the resolution of World War II, however, a distinct population in the United States began to emerge: teenagers. Gradually the age between childhood and adulthood came to be codified, debated, commemorated, and perhaps most significantly, elongated.[6] More young people stayed in and graduated from secondary school, and with the arrival of postwar prosperity, more began attending college. Other factors contributed to the burgeoning presence of the teenager in the 1950s: the greater availability of automobiles which allowed youth to travel and thus achieve a certain independence; the recovering economy that gave many teens extra money for entertainment outside the home; the popular reception of rock and roll music, which clearly flew in the face of previous standards; and the permeation of television, which, while giving all Americans a new common entertainment medium, also kept more adults at home.

In terms of the U.S. film industry, two landmark legal cases set the stage for the eventual proliferation of young adult fare. The "Paramount Case" was adjudicated by the Supreme Court in 1948; soon thereafter began the process by which major movie studios divested their holdings in theaters, giving rise to more small independent studios that would take advantage of their increased theatrical access by catering to niche audiences like teenagers. Then the important "Miracle Decision" by the Court in 1952 ensured selected First Amendment protections for films, thereby opening the door for a wider range of moral issues on screen; this development attracted young people to theaters where they could engage in mature topics and view more "adult" dramas than were available on television.[7]

However, Hollywood studios did not suddenly bank on hedonistic teen roles in the 1950s: the process of introducing the postwar teenager was careful if not apprehensive, as they gradually exploited the ephebiphobia—fear of teenagers—that was seeping into popular culture and politics. After

Jim (James Dean, center) is literally surrounded by peer pressure as he deals with his archetypal teen angst in Rebel Without a Cause *(1955).*

a few notable "clean teen" performances in the 1940s by Jimmy Lydon (the Henry Aldrich series, 1941–1944), Jeanne Crain (*Margie*, 1946), and Jane Powell (*A Date with Judy*, 1948), the archetypal '50s teen performer did not appear until mid-decade. That would be James Dean, whose performance in *Rebel Without a Cause* (1955) is probably the most influential demonstration of pure teen angst in American cinema. Marlon Brando had already showcased the young rebel image in *The Wild One* (1953), but Dean's affected demeanor was more penetrating, and his legend only grew due to his eerie real-life death mere weeks before *Rebel* opened.[8] Hollywood then continued to mold other performers into troubled youth, as in the milder but still afflicted roles of Natalie Wood (in *Rebel Without a Cause*, *Marjorie Morningstar* [1958], and *West Side Story* [1961]), John Saxon (in *Rock, Pretty Baby* [1956], *The Unguarded Moment* [1956], and *The Restless Years* [1958]), and Brandon De Wilde (in *Blue Denim* [1959], *All Fall Down* [1962], and *Hud* [1963]).

Perhaps a more notable trend than the emergence of these new young performers was the film industry's fresh confrontation with the conditions of youth. *Rebel* showcased the high school outcast who couldn't fit in (while also considering alcoholism, family dynamics, juvenile crime, and in more concealed terms, homosexuality); *Blackboard Jungle* (1955) dramatized the potentially violent conditions of urban high schools and tangentially introduced rock music to American cinema, giving rise to the teen "rock movie" that would become common thereafter; and *Peyton Place* (1957) and *Splendor in the Grass* (1961) demonstrated the supposed dangers of teenage sexuality.[9] Each of these films dealt with issues important to young adults, but now that Hollywood was finally making films about the difficulty of being young, a reactionary movement began, as usual in the film industry, in binary form: films were made that avoided or toned down the dilemmas of youth for the sake of celebrating its carefree aspects, or films were made to further exploit and enflame the dangers of teen delinquency and decadence. In other words, good kids were divided from bad kids.

Thus appeared a wave of inane beach films in the '60s (many featuring Frankie Avalon and Annette Funicello after their well-attended *Beach Party* in 1963) as well as the popular *Gidget* series (starting in 1959), alongside a lesser-seen but nonetheless visible output of youth exploitation films, a style that emerged as early as 1936 with *Reefer Madness* and was carried on by *City Across the River* in 1949 and sustained in such productions as *Teenage Devil Dolls* (1952), *Teenage Crime Wave* (1955), *High School Confidential!* (1958), *This Rebel Breed* (1960), *Teenage Strangler* (1964), and *The Wild Angels* (1966).[10] As my study shows, this reactive and divisive pattern of the movie industry is a trend that remains in effect to this day.

By the early '70s, after the implementation of the Motion Picture Association of America's ratings system (in 1968) and the national suffrage of eighteen-year-olds (in 1971), not to mention the young ages at which boys were being enlisted to fight in Vietnam, American youth began to have a different sense of their identity than that which had been provided for them in so many of the happier, hipper '60s films. The dark and more rebellious aspects of youth that had emerged in the '50s teen films continued in counterculture productions like *Wild in the Streets* (1968), *Easy Rider* (1969), *R.P.M.*, and *The Strawberry Statement* (both 1970). As was the case with films of the previous generation, most of these films were not about adolescents but rather young adults, just leaving high school or in college. In fact, Hollywood abandoned its practice of promoting teenage performers in the '60s and certainly had very few to account for in the '70s (the three prominent exceptions being Jodie Foster, Tatum O'Neal, and Robby Benson).[11]

After the dearth of teen stars and films in the 1970s, Hollywood could have maintained its lower output of youth films in the 1980s, but instead the industry concentrated more on young adult dramas than ever before. The most likely factor contributing to this was the emergence of another icon of youth independence, the shopping mall. The mall became a scene of teen congregation where arcades and food courts replaced the pool halls and soda fountains of the past. Further, since the '70s, following the dramatic decline of American movie theaters, Hollywood had come to rely on the centralization of multiple theaters in large retail centers to increase the number of screen venues and to offer moviegoers greater variety and convenience. Thus the multiplex was born. With the relocation of most movie theaters into or near shopping malls in the 1980s, the need to cater to the young audiences who frequented those malls became apparent to Hollywood, and those audiences formed the first generation of multiplex moviegoers.

The clearest result of the multiplex movement was a voluminous outpouring of films directed to and featuring teens, but in order to avoid a stagnating homogenization of the teen genre, Hollywood revised its '50s formula by intensifying the narrative range of youth films through placing teenage characters in previously established genres with more dramatic impact (gory horror, dance musicals, sex comedies), and as a result, a new variety of character types grew out of this generic expansion. Given the categorical choices offered by the multiplex theater, teens in the '80s were then able to go to the mall and select the particular youth movie experience that most appealed to them, and Hollywood tried to keep up with changing teen interests and styles to ensure ongoing profits. This led to constantly evolving efforts by the film industry to sustain the youth market through further generic expansions and revisions; more significantly for the audience, teens were then exposed to a wider range of characters and situations that directly addressed their current social conditions, even if many of the films that did so clearly had puerile provocation as their motive. Unlike the '50s when screen teens were steered down relatively rigid, righteous paths, the '80s teens encountered a complexity of moral choices and personal options on which the multiplex movies thrived. This gave teenage movie audiences at the end of the twentieth century a greater sense of presence in popular media, a deeper potential to be influenced by the films they saw, and a wider range of options from which they could construct and compare their sense of self.

The late '70s suggested the teen trends to come, as the popularity of such films as *Saturday Night Fever* (1977) and *Grease* (1978) with John Travolta — both of which combined music, dance, and sex (or its repression) — created a segue to the more dynamic stories that young audiences would soon demand. A handful of other films truly inaugurated new cycles: two 1978 American films, the low-budget horror sensation *Halloween* and the college farce *Animal House*, as well as two unassuming Canadian films, *Meatballs* (1979) and *Porky's* (1982). These were the starting guns of the new youth subgenres of the '80s, leading to an era of teen cinema that came to be appreciated by future critics more than any time before or since, as confirmed by the numerous studies that followed. *Halloween* was a simplistic but effective thriller about an apparently indestructible killer who stalks horny teenagers, although the purest of the group is spared. *Animal House*, *Meatballs*, and *Porky's* were raucous comedies featuring goofy and/or hormonal youth pursuing pleasure at college, summer camp, and a '50s-era high school, respectively, and their successes spawned numerous imitations over the next few years that featured desperate variations on this story line (with such suggestive titles as *Goin' All the Way!* and *The Last American Virgin* [both 1982], *Losin' It*, *Getting It On*, and *The First Turn On!* [all 1983], and *Gimme an F!*, *Hot Moves*, and *Joy of Sex* [all 1984]).

The new abundance of teen sexuality on screen also coincided with an increasing social awareness that the age of first intercourse was dropping for American youth, and the few earlier films that solemnly featured teens losing their virginity—such as *Rich Kids* (1979), *The Blue Lagoon* (1980), *Endless Love* (1981)—faded into the new appeal of carnal comedies about the plight of sexual pursuits.[12] At the same time, *Halloween* and similar films like *Friday the 13th* (1980) and *Slumber Party Massacre* (1982) were capitalizing on the moralistic aspect of teen sexuality, slaughtering wholesale those youth who deigned to cross the threshold of sexual awareness, even though these films usually hinged on a major suspension of realism. The early '80s then witnessed a remarkable intensification in American youth movie production with the appearance of numerous popular teen horror films in 1981 and the release of *Fast Times at Ridgemont High* in 1982, the first commercially successful hybrid of the contemporary sex, school, and delinquency elements.[13]

Between 1980 and 1986, there were six major approaches to youth cinema offered by Hollywood, most revised from past trends in the genre: the science saga, the horror thriller, the romantic melodrama, the sex comedy, the juvenile delinquent film, and the school picture that often borrowed generic elements from the rest. The one approach to not endure past 1986 was the science film, which had its experimental trials during the moon exploration years with sporadic examples like *The Computer Wore Tennis Shoes* (1969) and *Escape to Witch Mountain* (1975). These movies and those that followed tried to simultaneously stimulate youthful excitement about technology and agitate cultural fears of invasion or corruptive intelligence. Such a strategy suited the Reagan '80s, the era of sci-fi blockbusters like *E.T. The Extra-Terrestrial* (1982) and *Back to the Future* (1985), when the nascent subgenre found its most formal coherence, with films like *WarGames* (1983), *Real Genius* (1985), and *The Manhattan Project* (1986) essentially inspiring and warning young people about the possibilities inherent to their explorations.

This omen became real when *SpaceCamp* appeared just months after the Space Shuttle disaster in 1986, retroactively confirming that children should avoid ambitions beyond the realm of adult approval lest catastrophe ensue. Thereafter, the subgenre dwindled as relatively few films about youth and science were made aside from weak exploitation attempts featuring teens playing corruptive video games (e.g., *Brainscan* [1994], *Stay Alive* [2006]); even recent efforts at capitalizing on social networks failed with *Afterschool* (2008), *@urFRENZ* (2010), and *LOL* (2012). Today almost all concepts of youth and science are subsumed in unrealistic fantasies, like the planetary parable *Another Earth* (2011), or doomed by attempts to revive past generations' interests, as in the *Space Camp* cover *Space Warriors* (2013), while most realistic stories quite conspicuously minimize the presence of technology in teens' daily lives. Thus, while this subgenre was the subject of a full chapter in the first edition of this book, it is omitted here.

The horror film tended to offer the biggest grosses (literally and figuratively) and often showed the least knowledge of true youth conditions. Unlike infrequent teen horror hits in earlier decades such as *I Was a Teenage Werewolf* (1957) and *Carrie* (1976), these films were a runaway success in the early '80s and may in many ways be responsible for bringing a new image of youth to American cinema, however incomplete that image was. Within the new youth horror subgenre, teenage nudity and brutal violence had come to be expected, showing teens not only as sexually active but as morally culpable for their adultery, then paying with their lives for these transgressions. The youth horror film—especially in the "slasher" category so easily parodied by 1981 in *Student Bodies*—thereby brought attention to teen sexuality and responsibility, and other issues, by the most dramatic means possible.

While the subgenre apparently lost its prominence at the multiplex by the end of the '80s, its popularity was elevated through the home video market for much of the next decade, in cheap sequels to previous hits, and in less brutal supernatural stories like *Christine* (1983) and *Night of the Demons* (1987). Following this trajectory, teen horror found rejuvenating attention in self-conscious postmodern productions of the late '90s such as *Scream*

(1996) and *The Faculty* (1998). And a more certain sign that the previous appeal of simplistic teen homicide was waning in favor of scary cerebral schemes emerged with the flourishing trend of youth fantasy films in the '00s, which often relied on respected literary pedigrees and enticed wider audiences through tepid violence and virtually subconscious sexual tension. Primary influences were the British series of *Harry Potter* (2001–2011) and *The Chronicles of Narnia* starting in 2005, leading to *The Twilight Saga* (2008–2012) and *The Hunger Games* trilogy starting in 2012.

The sex comedy and romantic melodrama are companions, for despite the often gratuitous content of many of these films, they all consider the trial by fire that is the discovery of young lust and love, usually in that connected order. Youth romances, unlike sexual exploits, have a timeless quality, going back for centuries and arguably reaching their pinnacle with Shakespeare's *Romeo and Juliet*, which is built on the most common device of family conflict. In fact, all young love stories can be categorized by identifying the obstacle to the protagonists' romance: class, race, age, distance, and so forth. Youth cinema in the post-WWII era moved beyond chaste tales of innocent romantic struggle toward more mature consequences of love gone wrong, resulting in pregnancy (*Blue Denim*, 1959), date rape (*Where the Boys Are*, 1960), and mental illness (*Splendor in the Grass*, 1961). By the '70s, Hollywood viewed young love through a nostalgic lens and avoided these grave tensions in films such as *Summer of '42* (1971) and *American Graffiti* (1973), and that avoidance worked again for the '80s audience in cheery contemporary stories like *Valley Girl* (1983), *Sixteen Candles* (1984), *Secret Admirer*, *Seven Minutes in Heaven* (both 1985), and *One Crazy Summer* (1986). All the same, the conflicts of young romance continually captured audience imaginations for further generations, as with the murder-for-love plot in *To Die For* (1995), the cross-class clash of *Titanic* (1997), the transgendered taboo of *Boys Don't Cry* (1999), the international intrigue of *What a Girl Wants* (2003), the cultural dissention in *Towelhead* (2007), and the barely pubescent peregrinations in *Moonrise Kingdom* (2012).

Throughout the early '80s, the depiction of teens' sexual pursuits had become primarily ribald and explicit, as in *Private Lessons* (1981) and *Risky Business* (1983), but by the mid-'80s a distinct shift took place toward more serious and sensitive representations of teen relationships. The specter of AIDS had become a widespread heterosexual concern, as did the increasing teenage pregnancy rate, so John Hughes films like *Sixteen Candles* (1984) and *Pretty in Pink* (1986), as well as such softer tales as *Can't Buy Me Love* (1987) and *Say Anything . . .* (1989), were welcome antidotes to the increasingly delicate debacles of youth sex at the time. Then by the mid-'90s, films about youth having sex returned to a greater diversity of issues that sometimes accompany these practices, as with the three topics I address extensively hereafter: virginity (in *Kids* [1995], *American Pie* [1999], *Superbad* [2007]), pregnancy (in *Manny and Lo* [1996], *Riding in Cars with Boys* [2001], *Juno* [2007]), and queerness (in *All Over Me* [1996], *But I'm a Cheerleader* [2000], *Running with Scissors* [2006]).

The output of juvenile delinquent dramas was the most voluminous of youth subgenres until the early twenty-first century, when studios and audiences became especially uncomfortable with the topic after the Columbine murders in 1999. Such films have always been controversial, because they offer a rich appreciation for the aggressive expressions that teens most crave and parents most fear. The subgenre nonetheless persists with a clear range of immorality across its productions, which have become more refined since the older days of gang fights (*West Side Story* [1961], *The Warriors* [1979]) and drug trips (*Wild in the Streets* [1968], *Beyond the Valley of the Dolls* [1970]). This range now runs from harmless mischief that youth enact in daily life—such examples as *Adventures in Babysitting* (1987), *Snow Day* (2000), and the *Diary of a Wimpy Kid* films (2010–2012)—to life-threatening criminality of teen thugs in films like *Class of 1984* (1982), *Boyz N the Hood* (1991), and *Loren Cass* (2006). I look at five specific delinquent styles that represent this spectrum, starting with movies about "deviant dancing" from *Beat Street* (1984) to *Footloose* (2011) and concluding with crime films after Columbine such as *Elephant* (2003) and *Gran Torino* (2008).

School films are probably the most foundational subgenre of youth films, yet they often consider teenage identities quite separately from other subgenres. In most school films, the educational setting becomes an index for youth issues, featuring a variety of youth culture styles and types, as best represented by *The Breakfast Club* in 1985. Five character roles played out in that film—the nerd, the delinquent, the rebel, the popular girl, and the athlete—are the roles most commonly seen in all school films, going back to examples such as *High School Confidential!* (1958), *Billie* (1965), and *Grease* (1978), and thus my study examines the impulse of smart students to transform, the impact of delinquents on school order, the liability of conformity to rebels, the effects of popularity on teen girls, and the sensitive depiction of athletes. The cycles in school films are best revealed through tracing the characters that embody those cycles, from the nerdy outcasts of *Lucas* (1986) and *Dear Lemon Lima* (2009) to the tormented clique queens of *Heathers* (1989) and *Mean Girls* (2004) to the jock heroes of *Vision Quest* (1985) and *Coach Carter* (2005).

These subgenres remained in place into twenty-first-century American cinema, and with the further development of fantasy films within the horror realm, they form the frame in which youth films are made and marketed to this day, even as a number of the particular styles within the subgenres fade or change. Looking back, after the boom in the early '80s, the output of successful American youth films began to decline by the late '80s, as the "Brat Pack" of popular teen stars in the mid-'80s began taking adult roles and Hollywood moved away from the limited market of teen stories. Many little-seen youth films did continue to be made at this time, and while many were quite good, most were by small studios and thus had restricted releases. With the exception of a few notable films, such as those about African American crime in the early '90s, Hollywood did not demonstrate a refreshed interest in youth films until the mid-'90s, which once more ebbed in the early '00s only to rise again a few years later with teen fantasies. Part of the reason for this cycle is the cyclical nature of genres in general, and the short-lived recycling of teen films in particular. As the media industries have been merging and consolidating their products during this time, the movie market inevitably works to synergize its influences with teen-oriented TV shows and Internet sites as well.

This strategy certainly appeared to be working at the turn of the century, since the Internet had established its prominence as a means of two-way youth communication, and television networks expanded with more channels carrying teen shows that often found synergistic cult followings with movies, music, and fan blogs, as with *Buffy the Vampire Slayer* and *Dawson's Creek*, and later *Veronica Mars*, *Friday Night Lights*, and *Glee*.[14] Further, the industry discovered the financial advantages of making big-budget films about youth—such as *Titanic* (1997), *Spider-Man* (2002), and *Transformers* (2007)—while enjoying more modest profits from less expensive productions like *She's All That* (1999), *Napoleon Dynamite* (2004), and *Precious* (2009). The youth population by this point was clearly witness to another wide wave of films that catered to their interests and surveyed their images, films that were undoubtedly influenced by and built on the evolution of cinematic youth representations in previous decades.

The rich and compelling history of films about youth informs us of more than the changing social conditions and perceptions of young people; it gives us a special appreciation for how successive generations have endured the conflicts of claiming identity and seeking recognition for their actions. This endurance was seen most visibly in the post–World War II teen films as young people restively entered the Cold War era their parents created, and then again in the '60s counterculture films, through the falsely liberatory sex romps of the '80s, and in the current abundance of teen fantasies.

This study examines American youth films since 1980 to determine how recent generations of young people have been represented in American cinema and what that representation tells us about the various phenomena that constitute the contemporary coming-of-age process. Through this examination I demonstrate not only that youth films constitute a legitimate genre worthy of study on their own terms, but that they are imbued with a unique cultural significance: they question our evolving identities from youth to adulthood while simultaneously shaping and maintaining those identities.

SOCIAL REPRESENTATION AND GENRE THEORY

This is a work of film criticism based on the analysis of hundreds of films that are my primary texts, and my method employs genre theory to study social representation. Social approaches to film seek an understanding of cinematic images of groups and individuals under the tacit assumption that films are both aesthetic and cultural documents produced by an industry whose aim is to appeal to populations that will find the films worth seeing. Genre analysis considers patterns, motifs, and trends across a spectrum of films that share a commonality, usually subject matter and theme (such as melodrama, science fiction, and horror), and further explores how the elements of a genre are manifested and change over time. My study considers how American films about teenagers have utilized different techniques and stories to represent young people within a codified system that delineates distinct subgenres and character types within the "youth film" genre. Unlike other genres that are based exclusively on subject matter, the youth genre is based on the ages of the films' characters, and thus the thematic concerns of its subgenres can be seen as more directly connected to specific notions of different youth behaviors and styles.

Pioneering cinematic image studies include those of women (*From Reverence to Rape* by Molly Haskell, 1974), African Americans (*Slow Fade to Black* by Thomas Cripps, 1977), Native Americans (*The Only Good Indian* by Ralph Friar and Natasha Friar, 1972), Jews (*The Jewish Image in American Film* by Lester Friedman, 1987), and the disabled (*Cinema of Isolation* by Martin Norden, 1994).[15] The authors of these studies employ various approaches to their investigations, all of which are built on the belief that films are cultural artifacts revealing much about not only the people who are depicted in them but also those who make and view them. These approaches can be primarily interpretive, utilizing a subjective understanding of the films and the population in question, or more quantitative, attempting an objective "content analysis" to disclose various features of the films.

I study the images of youth in American cinema by combining both of these approaches. I feel that in any social study of cinema one cannot and should not rely solely on quantitative and statistical information, and an "objective" study of a medium as personal and social as film would not be effective in such matters as attitude, nuance, and style. However, I also feel that relying solely on inferential readings of films is problematic, for such a study can become so subjective as to be indifferent to other perspectives. I therefore aim to understand the subtleties and possible interpretations of youth films while also understanding the social and industrial contexts of the films' productions; I try to identify and analyze the "image" of youth with as much information as possible about what inspired and manifested that image and how that image developed over time. The films are thus my primary texts, while broader studies of youth cinema provide my theoretical and historical foundation, supplemented with current perspectives from critics who reviewed the films in their time of release. I do not study the reception of youth images however, and leave such a study to those who can pursue thorough audience research.

Genre theory has been developed alongside social analysis methods. While many critics observed the social influence of movies on viewers from the earliest days of cinema, serious genre examinations did not proceed until after World War II. Paul Willemen in 1983 described the two functions that genre theory was then designed to fulfill: (1) "to challenge and displace the dominant notions of cinema installed and defended on the basis of the assumed excellence of the 'taste' of a few journalists and reviewers, appealing to the 'age-old canons and principles' of Art in general," and (2) "in the wake of the realisation that any form of artistic production is a rule-bound activity firmly embedded in social history, [genre theory] set about discovering the structures which underpinned groups of films and gave them their social grounding."[16] Thus, as genre theories were staked out, many scholars argued alternately for political, aesthetic, social, and industrial methods for studying genres.

Theoretical arguments abounded before and after Willemen's work, and these polemics continue to this day with no consensus in sight. As early as 1973, Andrew Tudor pointed to the "empiricist dilemma" of arbitrary definitions and post hoc descriptors that are often used to describe a genre, in which a genre is defined "on the basis of analyzing a body of films that cannot possibly be said to be [a certain genre] until after the analysis."[17] In

1981, Thomas Schatz took a more symbiotic view, arguing that "a genre represents a range of expression for filmmakers and a range of experience for viewers" as audiences shape genres by describing to the film industry what films should be made based on what films they go to see.[18] Steve Neale employed an even broader compass in 2000 by suggesting that genres are "ubiquitous, multifaceted phenomena rather than one-dimensional entities to be found only within the realms of Hollywood cinema or of commercial popular culture."[19] And in 2012, Barry Keith Grant deftly summed up the customary academic practice of viewing genres as "cultural myths serving similar social and ideological functions in that they tend to take social debates and tensions and cast them into formulaic narratives, condensing them into dramatic conflicts between individual characters, heroes and villains, providing familiar stories that help us 'narrativize' and so make sense of the large, abstract social forces that effect our lives."[20]

In the case of my study, I consider the image of the American youth population within evident ranges of experience that youth are afforded within the films themselves, such as the educational environment, relationships of family and friends, and types of deviance. These experiences are essentially what define the more precise subgenres within the genre of youth films. Because my study argues primarily from the point at which images of youth are produced—the texts of the films—and not their reception within a historical reality of youth, nor their stylistic components (e.g., lighting techniques, editing patterns, use of sound), I offer primarily interpretive arguments about the social milieu as well as about the industrial and narrative range of films themselves. While any study that deals with representation must necessarily consider the context of said representation, my study only occasionally incorporates box office results as a measure of films' success, as well as statistics about historical trends, film release patterns, and the number of films within certain subgenres over time, as far as this information is relevant to particular arguments. Otherwise, cultural conditions of learning and lifestyle among young people in "real life" are too complex to analyze within the scope of this study.

One of the conspicuous problems of genre analysis over the past generation has been the assumption by many scholars that a genre's characteristics and development can be discerned by exclusively studying the most popular and "meaningful" examples of a genre or else a random sample of its offerings. Obviously this approach presents a number of dilemmas: how the determination of "importance" is made for the sample selected, what is lost in the films not studied, and how claims about the genre may not apply to every film that can be argued to fit the genre's code. Yet a methodology in which all the available films within a genre, and its respective subgenres, are addressed in order to ensure complete knowledge of that genre is untenable. Many films may be unavailable for viewing; the restrictions of space do not allow for ample discussion of all films; and some films that are only partially germane to a genre may not contribute to an understanding of the genre as a whole.

The first problem cannot be avoided: there are simply many films that are so obscure as to be inaccessible, and a scholar is left with the faulty option of making comments on these films based on plot descriptions. The second problem is unfortunate, demanding that some valuation be placed on films and styles that do warrant more extensive commentary, while others are given shorter coverage or omitted altogether. This and the third problem are symptomatic of the inevitably judgmental nature of generic definition: the author must determine which films are significant, as well as how they operate within a genre. I argue that most youth films fall into one of four subgenres as of 2013, but not all portray youth in such a way that lends deeper insight to the patterns and operations of those subgenres. Thus I have had to select the films that are most germane to these subgeneric categories, and I have needed to eliminate a number of valuable films and important issues for the sheer sake of concentration and demonstration. I thus apologize for the marginalization of numerous teen classics in the otherwise endearing cult of personality which they have fostered.

That films about youth actually constitute a genre has rather recently been identified in film studies. After the pioneering work of David Considine and a few other authors in the 1980s, two catalogs offered codifications for the youth genre. In his massive compendium *Films by Genre: 775 Categories, Styles, Trends, and Movements Defined, with a Filmography for Each* (1993), Daniel Lopez identifies the "Teen Movie," which has also been called the "'Juve' Movie," "Teenage Movie," "Teenpic," and "Youth Picture," placing undue weight on the exploitative nature of many films since the 1950s that have featured teenagers.[21] He then divides the Teen Movie into subgenres, while cross-listing other relevant genres such as the "Exploitation Film," the "Juvenile Delinquency Film," the "Motorcycle Movie," the "Rock Film," and the "Youth Film." Of Teen Movie subgenres, Lopez offers the divisions of "Beach Films," "High School Films," "Teen-Violence Films," and "Teen Comedies," the latter of which he distinguishes from "Teen Sex Comedies."

His further distinction of the "Youth Film" appears a matter of historically specific semantics, because he cites examples only from 1967 to 1972 and claims that these films "highlighted the concerns of young people querying the Establishment, society and its values," as if films before or since this time frame had failed to do so.[22] Such a dubious category exposes the difficulty of finding accurate descriptors for generic styles and movements, when Lopez would have done better to label the Vietnam-era films to which he was referring by their thematic concerns, calling them perhaps "Anti-establishment Films," or placing them in a temporal subgenre such as the "Vietnam-Era Youth Film." Lopez's attempt to define and divide films about youth is still significant, for he locates Teen Movies as a genre unto itself, and sees the necessity of making subgeneric distinctions.

In 1995, the Library of Congress commissioned its Motion Picture/ Broadcasting/Recorded Sound Division to study the cataloging of films by types, and by 1997 the group produced *The Moving Image Genre-Form Guide*, which relies on the work of archival sources (such as the *Film Literature Index* and the *American Film Institute Catalog of Feature Films*) to construct a descriptive structure for the various genres and forms of film.[23] This guide locates one comprehensive genre it labels "Youth," which comprises "fictional work portraying aspects of the trajectory through adolescence, including high school years, peer pressure, first love, beach parties, and initial attempts at adulthood, along with strains in the relationship with family."[24] The emphasis in these films is on teenaged characters, and the guide thus subsumes the distinction of "Teen" films within this category, moving films about characters aged twelve and younger to "Children," and films set in a collegiate environment to "College." These are essentially the same distinctions that I make (although I do include twelve-year-old characters) in delimiting the genre that is the youth film.

As Janet Staiger and other theorists continued to argue, many films do not easily conform to manufactured categories: some films may simply not fit into a discrete (sub)generic classification, or may cross over so many themes and styles as to defy any single (sub)generic location.[25] This is a dilemma of which I am keenly aware, and I attempt to address it by always foregrounding the existence of youth cinema as a genre itself, which has a relatively reliable denotative frame—that is, films in which youth appear. Then within that frame, I allow for much categorical interplay and cross-generic influence. Yet because not even all "films in which youth appear" can properly be identified as youth cinema (as when young characters are negligible to the story), the larger generic frame under which I work is still contentiously constructed. This is a dilemma that I do not feel disrupts the process of examining how youth have been represented in cinema because so many youth images are still being studied; yet from a methodological standpoint it does bear reminding, if only to argue that a truly reliable, consistent, internally and externally integrated model of genre study by

Adult actors representing teenage characters—such as Jonah Hill (age twenty-nine) and Channing Tatum (age thirty-two) in 21 Jump Street (2012), who play adults posing as teens within the story—are not contemporary contrivances. Mickey Rooney was twenty-four when he made his seventeenth film as famous teenager Andy Hardy in 1944, and Catherine Burns was twenty-five when she earned an Oscar nomination for her debut role as a teenager in Last Summer (1969).

social types may be an impossible goal. I believe that this book employs the paradigm that is best suited to the study of cinematic social representation through generic analysis, however incomplete and arguable it may remain.

What delimits youth in this context? For the purposes of my study, I consider the youth population to be between the ages of twelve and twenty. This represents a range of years that includes the actual teen years as well as the traditionally recognized entrance into adolescence (or at least in the United States, the beginning of middle school, or junior high school), as well as late adolescence and entry into the post–high school world. This is the same age range that David Considine analyzed in his foundational work *The Cinema of Adolescence.*[26] It is also the same age range used by Mark Thomas McGee and R. J. Robertson in their study of juvenile delinquency in movies, *The J. D. Films: Juvenile Delinquency in the Movies.*[27] The same upper limit of age twenty is used by the Young Artist Foundation in their selection of performers for the annual Young Artist Awards, which began in 1978.[28] However, I do not analyze films that are about characters in college — who tend to be between eighteen and twenty-four years old — because the college genre itself has been extensively covered in other studies, and further, because the majority of college films do not concern the same issues about youth as do teen and high school films.[29] Therefore, the chapters on delinquency, horror, and romance consider films about characters aged twelve to twenty, while the chapter on school covers characters in junior high or high school (generally twelve to eighteen years old). Using these parameters allows for a clear demonstration of the diverse and yet confined images of youth that the industry produces.[30]

I further delimit my study by concentrating on feature-length films, although I do consider many straight-to-video movies that achieved recognition outside of theatrical release. I do not examine films that, despite the presence of young performers or their appeal to young audiences, are not about the youth experience. As Thomas Doherty and other critics have argued, Hollywood "juvenilized" its films after WWII to such an extent that virtually all movies can be said to appeal to youth. Thus, given the comprehensive reach of what can be labeled "youth" films, I am not only concentrating on those films that are relevant to the dominant subgenres of youth cinema since 1980, but I am excluding films that just tangentially or incidentally depict youth. This study is designed to consider as many pertinent perspectives about these films as possible, without being indebted to any specific authors' theoretical arguments about youth films, youth culture, or film representation at large.

Assembling the filmography for this analysis proved to be an arduous task, and the process evolved considerably in the years between the first and second editions. Many of the so-called indexes of genres are incomplete or, as is the case with many generic categories, based on ambiguous or arbitrary judgments of what constitutes relevant films in the "youth" genre. Back in the mid-'90s, I began to create the filmography from scratch by consulting topical film guides and movie review collections, eventually generating a list of just over one thousand films. When *Generation Multiplex* first appeared in 2002, I was confident that my filmography was the most complete and refined list of American youth films since 1980 that could be compiled. For this edition written in 2013, I was able to further employ the Internet Movie Database and other Internet sites in building the filmography over another decade. Using the keyword search function of IMDb—adolescence, adolescent, coming-of-age, high-school, junior-high-school, juvenile, middle-school, school, teen, teenage, teenager, teen-angst, tween, twelve-year-old, youth—I added another 650 films to the study and removed some erroneous titles from the previous list, so the filmography now stands at approximately 1,700 titles, all of which are listed in appendix A. I remain confident in the exactitude and extent of this list.

A note on terminology: I use the label "youth cinema" to refer to the entire sphere of films made about young adults, a population that I may refer to as "teens" when accurate, and dub "youth" in general. "Children" are the offspring of parents, and thus youth may be included under this label in reference to families and adults. "Adolescence" is ambiguous in terms of precisely defining age, so I reserve use of the term for when I specifically discuss the social or psychological process of entering adulthood and leaving childhood. For the sake of classification, each chapter is about a *subgenre* of the youth film genre, and within each subgenre I identify and analyze *categories*, and when a category is prolific enough to create clear and consistent distinctions within its examples, I further distinguish *varieties*.

THE STUDY OF YOUTH,
IN AND OUT OF MOVIES

A study of cinema and youth offers an interesting historical parallel: motion pictures were invented in the 1890s and "youth" as an area of academic research emerged less than twenty years later in 1904, when social psychologist G. Stanley Hall wrote his pathbreaking *Adolescence: Its Relations to Physiology, Anthropology, Sociology, Sex, Crime, Religion, and Edu-*

cation, which may be credited as the beginning of youth studies.[31] That the proliferation of cinema and the founding of youth studies coincide within the same historical generation may not be indicative of a cause-and-effect relationship; however, the relationship between cinema and youth is significant. The twentieth century produced a series of "moral panics" around young people and social behavior, and the cinema—both as a gathering place and as a site of stimulation—has been a perennial source of those panics.[32]

Of course children and teenagers existed before the twentieth century began, but the social perception of the pre-adult population was considerably different before the early 1900s, and certainly before the Industrial Revolution. Many girls and boys abandoned school at preteen ages in the nineteenth century and started families soon thereafter, often entering the labor force in their early teen years or younger. As the modern era took hold, renowned researchers like Hall (and later Havighurst, Piaget, Winnicott, Erikson, and Anna Freud) began recognizing a distinct age of specialized development between childhood and adulthood that had been initially described through characteristics of sexual development and was then later examined as a more complex sociopsychological manifestation of cultural and internal conflict.[33] This age of development was adolescence, and its study by researchers (including Keniston, who even divided adolescence from youth) and its acceptance by society during the progressing twentieth century resulted in a new notion of youth, if only to distinguish a crucial transitional period during the teen years between childhood and adulthood.[34]

Until the 1960s the study of youth remained largely a discipline within the behavioral sciences as researchers studied the changing attitudes and "pathologies" of youth during the various cycles of twentieth-century life. Then in the '60s, certain global political events brought about a visible change in the activities of young people, not the least of which were the escalating war in southeast Asia and the student revolts in France in 1968. During this same decade Philippe Ariès wrote the next paradigmatic study of youth, shifting attention away from behavior and toward history in *Centuries of Childhood: A Social History of Family Life* (1962).[35] Throughout the 1960s and the 1970s, the new research on youth history was taken up by the growing field of cultural studies, which eagerly considered how the youth uprisings of that era could be representative of previously repressed or diffused class, gender, and race conflicts. First appeared the work of James Coleman in his 1961 book *The Adolescent Society: The Social Life of the Teenager and Its Impact on Education*, after which British scholars in the 1970s, among them Stuart Hall, Angela McRobbie, and Dick Hebdige, studied patterns of resistance and revolt within what was now called "youth culture."[36] By the 1980s, as the Reagan/Thatcher era brought about a series of new moral panics based on the vision of the New Right, the trend in youth research shifted back toward studies of youth "pathologies" (e.g., teen pregnancy, unemployment, crime) within a cultural studies method.[37]

One of the first such studies was *Hooligan: A History of Respectable Fears* (1983), in which Geoffrey Pearson claimed that essentially the same moral accusations about youth had been recycled for the past 150 years. A subsequent study in this vein was *The Road to Romance and Ruin: Teen Films and Youth Culture* (1992), in which Jon Lewis relied much on the observations and opinions of Hebdige and Hall as he studied various teen "vices" in cinema.[38] The influence of British cultural studies remained evident in further youth studies, such as *Teenagers: An American History* (1996), by Grace Palladino, who examined the emergence of the American teenage population in terms of its institutional identification through the rise of high schools in the early twentieth century, and its economic identification through the greater consumptive capacities that teenagers developed in the years after World War II.[39] Another notable study of youth culture from a perspective on power was *Freaks, Geeks, and Cool Kids* (2006), in which Murray Milner argued that the regimentation of schooling induces students to find meaning in forming their own subcultures of high and low status, yet this supposedly empowering effort is to the detriment of their own personal progress.[40] Regardless of how youth studies have focused on deviance and development (psychology) and/or resistance and economics (politics), one theme of youth studies has been undoubtedly clear since the 1980s: youth culture is not homogenous.

The 1980s thus became a time of distinct change in youth studies as the trajectories of sociology, history, and cultural studies merged over concerns about refreshed conservative attitudes that were broadly vilifying youth.[41] These concerns may have been legitimate given conditions of the time; however, these conditions were not necessarily being visibly addressed in the American cinema of this period. Most Hollywood films about youth in the 1980s relied on formulas that exploited youth issues, specifically sexual development, while gradually revealing an increasing tension and confusion about the roles of contemporary youth. By the early '90s, in the wake of the Reagan and Thatcher years and under the patriotic swell of the Gulf War, teens in American films had been entirely reconfigured, if not often extinguished, as increasing emphasis fell on portraits of the post-teen generation in movies after *Slacker* in 1991 (examples include *Singles* in 1992 and *Reality Bites* in 1994). Popular studies of youth thus shifted their attention: in July 1990, *Time* magazine published an extensive and influential article titled "Proceeding with Caution," which debuted the skeptical "twentysomething generation"; over the next few years more magazines followed suit (including dueling cover stories in the *Atlantic Monthly* and the *New Republic* at the end of 1992) with studies of young adults now labeled "Generation X" after Douglas Coupland's eponymous 1991 novel.[42] "Youth" by the mid-'90s then covered a wider age range than ever before, spanning the first year of post-elementary education (usually the age of twelve) to the first few years after college (or, considering that the majority of young people do not complete college, at least the mid-twenties).[43]

This perception had already been supported in Susan Littwin's *Postponed Generation: Why America's Grown-Up Kids Are Growing Up Later* (1986), in which she argued that adolescents required ten years after the onset of puberty (usually the early teens) to become adults.[44] Further evidence of this widening age range and the tensions about young people prolonging their youth came from more demographic studies like *Marketing to Generation X* by Karen Ritchie (1995) and *Welcome to the Jungle: The Why Behind "Generation X"* by Geoffrey T. Holtz (1995).[45] These studies argued that "youth" had been realigned as a specialized and crucial age group for American commercial marketing, and they showed how certain youth attitudes—notably cynicism and narcissism—had been amplified and exploited by advertisers, corporations, and even politicians. Arguing from an earlier historical assessment in *The Rise and Fall of the American Teenager* (2000), Thomas Hine actually located this identification of teenagers in the desires of post-WWII businesses that wanted to capitalize on the burgeoning youth population, and he went on to further indict schooling practices for stifling youth ambitions.[46] And demonstrating that this issue did not fade with the close of the last century, Christina Lee published *Screening Generation X: The Politics and Popular Memory of Youth in Contemporary Cinema* in 2010, which addressed the insecure economic, social, and even spiritual conditions under which youth had been living while witnessing their own tenuous identities reified in the cinema.[47]

Sustaining the consumer market for youth became no less crucial for commercial forces in the new millennium, just as other adult forces continued to exploit the perceived weaknesses of young people. New tags for teens emerged, such as "Generation Y" and "Millennials," and youth studies remained fixated on establishments that threatened young people—especially the media, advertising, and education. Thus appeared books such as *Branded: The Buying and Selling of Teenagers* (2003), by Alissa Quart; *The Corporate Assault on Youth: Commercialism, Exploitation, and the End of Innocence* (2008), edited by Deron Boyles; and *Youth in Revolt: Reclaiming a Democratic Future* (2012), by Henry Giroux.[48] Yet alongside these critical concerns, the field still welcomed work that handled youth from a more holistic view, such as *Youth Cultures: Texts, Images, and Identities* (2003), edited by Kerry Mallan and Sharyn Pearce; *American Youth Cultures* (2004), edited by Neil Campbell; *Understanding Youth: Perspectives, Identities, and Practices* (2007), edited by Mary Jane Kehily; and most recently *Youth Culture and Private Space* (2012), by Siân Lincoln.[49] Comprehending young people, as these numerous volumes have repeatedly proved, is a laborious and disconcerting endeavor, more so when undertaken by adults.

The shifts in youth studies and the cultural perception of youth over the past generation thus makes for intriguing research, but studying how the image of youth has changed, and further how it has diversified into a heterogeneity of styles, attitudes, and ages, offers insight into the significant and often contradictory notions of who young people are. The cinema, with its limited range of products with unlimited ranges of meaning, is a system of representation that provides a useful inventory of issues about various conditions, especially those of youth, its most vital audience. Yet general studies about youth in cinema did not emerge until the 1980s with Considine's *Cinema of Adolescence*, which had a lasting impact notwithstanding its rather limited release.[50]

Considine employs a method that many other studies omit or minimize: he provides narrative descriptions of virtually all the films he discusses within the context of a thematic examination of the history of a population he calls "screenagers." His overall argument is that American youth films over the course of the century have lacked verisimilitude because "the American film industry has been spectacularly unsuccessful in realistically depicting adolescence," and thus the image of youth in films has been distorted.[51]

Considine proceeds chronologically (up to the early 1980s) through chapters divided into sections on family, school, delinquency, and sexuality, and thereby lays out a structure that other critics and I have followed. (I do not locate "family" as an individual subgenre of the youth film since 1980: few recent youth films actually concentrate on family issues — indeed, much of Considine's examination of family is from pre-1970 films — or the family issues are contained within dramatizations more relevant to other subgeneric qualities.)[52] *The Cinema of Adolescence* strikes the best balance between historical and narrative analysis of any study I have found (with emphasis on the sociological), and his study demonstrates quite well the ways in which Hollywood had portrayed youth until the early '80s, predominantly in negative images. I proceed from this representational model and analytical method with a deeper consideration of how youth themes have become subgenres and how individual movies themselves became the paradigms for those subgenres.

The less sympathetic *Road to Romance and Ruin* by Jon Lewis preserves a thematic approach similar to Considine's, although with a perspective that is often pessimistic and occasionally condescending. He proceeds through various forms of teen vice to support his ultimate thesis that "despite stylistic, tonal, industrial, and by now even generational differences within the genre, teen films all seem to focus on a single social concern: the breakdown of traditional forms of authority."[53] Lewis is rather selective with the films that demonstrate his argument, and ultimately he is more concerned with teen films' audiences, moving away from film analyses to incorporate ideas on youth movements (mods, rockers, punks), music, and to a lesser extent, sociopsychological commentary. This could have resulted in a study that would have cast new light on the conditions of contemporary youth culture, yet so much of what Lewis says about young people is recycled from notions that are two or three generations past. When he concludes, "For this [current] generation of teenagers, the present is dominated by images and narratives of their parents' youth," his overall approach is revealed as exaggerated and lacking in serious study of teen films after the early 1980s, which are much more occupied by a nostalgia for the present—the instant recycling of, and ironic longing for, contemporary phenomena—than they are by scenes of an extinct parental history.[54]

A waggish yet surprisingly comprehensive analysis of teens in '80s films appeared in 1997, when Jonathan Bernstein published *Pretty in Pink: The Golden Age of Teenage Movies*, an often rousing if largely frivolous set of ruminations, because Bernstein only briefly mentions the many significant social, political, and economic conditions of the time, a shortcoming that is more glaring when he then attempts to study the representations of youth in films.[55] An immediate liability, as Bernstein admits, is that he does not intend to examine an "exhaustive collection" of these films, and even though he does address about 120 examples, his review process is rather skewed to easily fit his blanket remarks about the hedonism and angst portrayed in the films he describes. This yields sentimental reflections that can be amusing, while Bernstein's arguments remain self-fulfilling and lacking in much depth.

Perhaps the surest sign that the teen genre had achieved academic legitimacy by the '00s was the publication of numerous anthologies on the subject. Murray Pomerance and John Sakeris were among the first to bring together a diverse range of scholars to discuss youth culture and screen media, and coedited a collection of articles based on their 1996 conference, *Pictures of a Generation on Hold*.[56] Pomerance then joined Frances Gateward in editing two distinctive anthologies dealing with youth movies in terms of gender: *Sugar, Spice, and Everything Nice: Cinemas of Girlhood* (2002) and *Where the Boys Are: Cinemas of Masculinity and Youth* (2005).[57] Even more encompassing compendia appeared later in the decade, as Alexandra Seibel and I turned to an international scope in coediting *Youth Culture in Global Cinema* (2007), and all manner of media were considered in *The Changing Portrayal of Adolescents in the Media Since 1950* (2008), coedited by Patrick Jamieson and Daniel Romer.[58] Evidence of the continuously increasing array of interests and authors around the topic came in 2009 with the publication of conference proceedings from Wake Forest University, titled *Coming of Age on Film*, which was hosted by their Romance Languages Department.[59]

Stephen Tropiano and I published books within a year of each other that evaluated the emergence of youth cinema in addition to the greater prominence of the genre since the 1980s. My own *Teen Movies: American Youth on Screen* (2005) traced images of youth back to the silent era, but Tropiano's *Rebels & Chicks: A History of the Hollywood Teen Movie* (2006) agrees with my approach, and that of many others, in tracing the foundation of the genre to the 1950s.[60] Tropiano admittedly strikes a lighter tone than my writing, yet he is no less thorough in his research, providing a thoughtful consideration of the post-WWII era and its movies, moving through the counterculture years that he broadly identifies as 1965–1980, and celebrating films of the past three decades. Lamenting the extremes to which so many movies carry their representations of youth, Tropiano idealistically concludes, "It would be refreshing to see a film about an ordinary teenager, who, in the final reel, is still ordinary, yet happy."[61]

Most recently, Catherine Driscoll took on the genre in *Teen Film: A Critical Introduction* (2011), which offers a generally more theoretical approach beyond concerns about character representation and social developments.[62] Driscoll is clearly influenced by postmodernism, a popular school of thought in recent years that has often been applied to youth culture in terms of consumption, reproduction, identity, and the loss of history. While the book moves toward a stimulating argument about the classification of teen cinema and its location in the realms of commerce and globalization, her historical analysis is more expansive than most, elabo-

This text-heavy advertisement from a trade publication for The Perks of Being a Wallflower *(2012) indicates the interest that current studios now have in legitimizing serious teen movies, a phenomenon the genre did not enjoy until recent years.*

rating on teen images before the 1950s and also incorporating an appreciation of teen television into her account. Driscoll offers spirited challenges to past research, taking Doherty to task for focusing on teen movies as exploitation fare, and questioning my own focus on youth as teens rather than in the broader social perception of young people as pre-adult.[63]

Arguments regarding the generic formation and conditions of youth films have persisted since 2000 in such works as *Genre and Hollywood* by Steve Neale, who made the judicious observation that the myriad movies he identifies as "teenpics" tend to "testify to the complexity and interest of a genre which has for years been important to Hollywood, but rarely, it seems, to genre critics, theorists and historians."[64] Pam Cook employed Neale's work in her encyclopedic tome *The Cinema Book* (2008), giving a significant identification to "teenpics" that indicated how the film field was taking the genre seriously.[65] Amanda Ann Klein took an alternate look at the genre as part of compound cyclical developments in *American Film Cycles* (2011), exploring the effect of youth subcultures on film releases. She argued that "fragments" of these subcultures—such as hot rod racing, drug use, teen sex—"are eventually conventionalized by their appearance in film cycles, spreading out through mainstream culture and exposing a broader public to styles and images that were once contained within a small, isolated subculture."[66] (Richard Nowell maintains a similar cyclical discourse about the horror subgenre in *Blood Money: A History of the First Teen Slasher Cycle* [2011].)[67] Such arguments continue to illuminate the nature of the youth film genre as a product of both industry and culture, and suggest the further range of research that has yet to be written in the effort to understand the genre.[68]

In their 1980 reference catalog *The Screen Image of Youth: Movies About Children and Adolescents*, Ruth Goldstein and Edith Zornow describe a 1972 article by *New York Times* film critic Vincent Canby titled "Stop Kidding Around," in which he portrayed a ten-year-old boy who was so angry about the "lies" that films told about children that he was going to write a corrective book, "The Image of the Child in Film."[69] Neither Canby nor the mythical boy ever produced such a book, although the critic did indeed recognize a significant need for research, revision, and appreciation for the ways in which young people are represented in cinema. Most of the authors above, knowingly or not, have participated in fulfilling that need articulated by Canby over thirty years ago, and my goal is to augment that tradition by examining young adult films in this book.

Two

YOUTH IN SCHOOL

         Academics and Attitude

You see us as you want to see us, in the simplest terms and the
most convenient definitions. But what we found out is that each
one of us is a brain, an athlete, a basket case, a princess, and a
criminal.
BRIAN (ANTHONY MICHAEL HALL) TO HIS PRINCIPAL
IN *THE BREAKFAST CLUB* (1985)

You got your freshmen, ROTC guys, preps, JV jocks, Asian
nerds, cool Asians, varsity jocks, unfriendly black hotties, girls
who eat their feelings, girls who don't eat anything, desperate
wannabes, burnouts, sexually active band geeks, the greatest
people you will ever meet, and the worst.
JANIS IAN (LIZZY CAPLAN) DESCRIBING HIGH
SCHOOL STUDENTS IN *MEAN GIRLS* (2004)

The three keys of coolness in high school. . . . One, don't try
hard at anything. Two, make fun of people who do try. Three, be
handsome. Four, if anyone steps to you on the first day of school,
you punch them directly in the face. Five, drive a kick-ass car.
THE ADULT GREG (CHANNING TATUM) TO HIS POLICE
PARTNER IN *21 JUMP STREET* (2012)

The school film is perhaps the most easily definable subgenre of youth films because its main plot actions focus on the setting of
high school and junior high school campuses. The vast majority of school
films present the educational building as a symbolic site of social evolution,
with young people learning from and rebelling against their elders (and
each other) in the ongoing cycle of generational adjustment and conflict.
In certain instances, school films have actually considered how the design

and structure of the educational facilities of a school affect the students and teachers, but often the school itself is an indifferent location wherein various gender, race, class, and above all, popularity issues are contested among students.

School is also a site of individual growth through not only educational achievements but also the earning of social acceptance. Young people learn very early that specific traits—good looks, money (in the form of nice clothes or cool toys), intelligence, athletic skills, toughness—yield special attention from their elders and their peers. The struggle for gaining attention in any school system is a complex contest for recognition of genetic privilege and negotiation of social status, for young people without naturally attractive traits must learn to cultivate whatever characteristics will most successfully earn them acceptance, unless they can deny the process of acceptance and adopt an alternate means of gaining self-identity and esteem. Yet by the teen years, with the onset of puberty and adolescent angst over conforming to the adult world, all young people are faced with even larger confrontations about acceptance, and their physical placement in the school environment becomes a visible reminder of their plight. School may be a land of opportunity to demonstrate one's worth or a locus of oppression where one's attempts to gain worth are met with resistance or ridicule.

Much of American teens' socialization takes place at or around school. (Most school districts offer junior high school, or middle school, to students between the ages of twelve and fourteen, and high school to students age fourteen through eighteen.) The school is thus a prime location for a wide range of youth development, and movie studios have capitalized on the variety of applications to which the school setting can be utilized generically; all of the other subgenres in this study contain some films in which schools are used as various narrative devices. What makes the school film a specific subgenre is its focus on the actual socialization process at the school, as opposed to other youth issues that are less integral to the school setting, such as crime, sex, or terror. This chapter examines the American school film as a subgenre dependent on the social recognition of junior high and high school as contained milieux for the educational development and cultural disciplining of youth, where youth are most often clearly divided into distinct types with certain levels of achievement and acceptance according to that development and disciplining. In environments of such change and containment, conflicts are inevitable; because such containment is rendered upon a population teeming with physical energy, sexual curiosity, and psychological tension, the dramatic potential of those conflicts, and their resolutions, seems limitless.

CONTEXTS AND TRENDS
IN THE SUBGENRE

The school film as a subgenre has moved through discernible waves of popularity. From the debut of postwar high school discontent in such teen trouble films as *City Across the River* (1949) to the more celebrated image of tense school conditions in the two 1955 classics, *Rebel Without a Cause* and *Blackboard Jungle*, both major studios and smaller independents tapped into (or exploited) the burgeoning cultural anxiety about reckless youth. With the rapid proliferation of multiple teen subgenres, the school film became only one avenue for representing teens, and as tensions of the 1960s shifted to college campuses, fewer high school films were made. While the youth film market boomed in the 1980s after the tamer 1970s, the school film did not maintain any consistent popularity of its own.

The film that perhaps presaged the '80s high school cycle (while openly borrowing from the '50s crime dramas) was *Over the Edge* in 1979. The film features a young Matt Dillon as a James Dean–style rebel who galvanizes a small group of suburban tough kids to fight for a tentative liberation from their alcoholic parents and misguided school system. In one of the most extreme teen fantasies ever filmed (although the film's premise was based on a true story), the students ultimately lock their parents and teachers in the high school and terrorize them. The film may now be viewed as an examination of social anxieties about delinquency and discipline in the late '70s; however, according to Jonathan Bernstein, the film was in fact kept from public release for a few years as the studio feared copycat violence.[1]

The next major school film of the era took a decidedly different approach. *Fast Times at Ridgemont High* (1982) arrived just as the new trend in teen sex films was developing (notable examples included *Foxes* and *Little Darlings* [both 1980], *Endless Love* [1981] and *Porky's* [1982]), and while the film was at once a lighthearted portrait of suburban youth making their way through the curricular and extracurricular maze of high school life, it also gave viewers a full array of sexual melodramas, complete with titillating nudity and sex talk. Many other school films of the early '80s also incorporated the same attitudes and themes about young sex, although the novelty quickly wore off as popular films such as *Teachers* (1984) and *The*

Breakfast Club (1985) offered more focused interrogations of schools and their effects on students.

The later '80s marked a decline in the overall number of successful school films (nonetheless, as is the case with some other youth film subgenres, the number of school films in total increased, even if many of these were barely seen by audiences). After the previous movement from sexual themes to character dramas based on school and family problems, the school films of the late '80s covered a range from such tasteful coming-of-age comedies as *Lucas* (1986) to more tasteless attempts to exploit teen interests like *The Principal* (1987) and outright attempts to reproduce previous hits as with *Hot Times at Montclair High* (1989). With the exception of *Stand and Deliver* in 1988, which concentrated on the role of an inspirational math teacher, there were no school films between the formative *Breakfast Club* in 1985 and *Heathers* in 1989 that matched their popularity.[2]

Such a cycle would soon repeat itself, for after the release of a few more successful school films in 1989 and 1990 (*Bill and Ted's Excellent Adventure*, *Dead Poets Society*, *Lean on Me*, *Pump Up the Volume*), the school film again declined in recognition through the early '90s. As if the genre were on a prescribed cycle, it returned in 1995 with *Clueless*, *Powder*, *Angus*, and *Dangerous Minds*, and then again in the late '90s with *Can't Hardly Wait*, *The Faculty*, and *Rushmore* (1998), and *She's All That*, *Varsity Blues*, *Election*, and *10 Things I Hate About You* (1999). The new century did not disrupt this ongoing pattern: school films customarily waned for another few years before gaining a revival after the unexpected followings motivated by three distinctly different 2004 releases: *Napoleon Dynamite*, *Mean Girls*, and *Friday Night Lights*. Then, once again, the subgenre retreated at the end of the decade.

The reasons for the alternating wavelength of popularity in the contemporary school drama may be deceptively easy to explain. As with all genres, new styles and approaches to the same subject matter appeal to audiences for only a short time. The sexual and narcotic hijinks of the early '80s films may have at once been an initial reaction to the Reagan era's puritan ethic for youth (movies were at least a safe site where teens didn't have to "Just Say No"), but declining box office returns for the ongoing imitations of *Fast Times* (e.g., *Private School* and *Losin' It* [1983], *The Wild Life* and *Joy of Sex* [1984]) indicated that interest in rowdy teen sex stories was waning. Likewise, the escalating violence of '90s films that gradually infiltrated real-life education for teens late in the decade was no longer welcome in an '00s era concerned about school shootings, bullying, and stalking.

Another definite factor is the short-lived viability of young actors, most boldly witnessed with the emergence of Hollywood's teen screen casting machine in the '80s known as the Brat Pack. From 1984 to 1986, photogenic young performers such as Molly Ringwald, Anthony Michael Hall, Andrew McCarthy, Judd Nelson, Ally Sheedy, and Emilio Estevez found themselves in a series of successful teen dramas. Their appearance in the teen market was built on wistful, tormented, and ultimately clean images of mid-'80s youth who proffered occasionally sincere questions about sex and drugs as they engaged less in these practices (on screen, at least) than their previous counterparts. The success of this troupe was still inevitably limited, and by the late '80s the performers had either gravitated toward adult roles or faded into obscurity. As has been the case with child and teen performers before and since, the aging process swiftly carries young actors out of their original personae, and few are welcomed into more assertive adult roles.

Trends in American schooling and social fads are further factors in the oscillating popularity of school films. Each high school "generation" itself lasts for only three or four years, and these rapidly sequential generations do not want to be associated with the outmoded styles and fashions of the groups that preceded them, lest they be perceived as unoriginal and conformist. Thus, the glamour of certain types of music, styles of dress, ways of speaking, and even attitudes is bound to be restricted to relatively short lifespans among youth, especially those in school who are constantly monitoring the changing cultural landscape. The same phenomenon applies to films about school: with the exception of the rarely successful period film (e.g., the abiding *Mr. Holland's Opus* in 1995), young viewers pay to see their current conditions celebrated and exaggerated on the screen, and the conditions of 2003 are simply not as interesting as those of 2013 (or perhaps even 2010).

Another point may explain the highs and lows in school movie production and/or success. Given the critical acuity of youth audiences, studios must understand the hit-or-miss dilemma of marketing films about youth to a young audience. Whereas adult films that appeal to youth may at least draw a wide audience, contemporary teen dramas have a more finite allure, and a financial investment in a school picture (unless it has the adult crossover potential of *Dangerous Minds* [1995], *Finding Forrester* [2000], or *21 Jump Street* [2012], each of which featured major adult stars) is a considerable gamble for a studio. Even the mid-'00 resurgence in school films was brought on by relatively low-budget hits like *Napoleon Dynamite*, *Mean Girls* (both 2004), *Brick* (2005), *Half Nelson*, and *Step Up* (both 2006). The industry thus finds itself subject to the same fickle inconsistencies as students themselves, and despite its research and records the system is always indebted to the erratic interests of youth, as proved by the bombing of seemingly sure bets like *Assassination of a High School President* (2008), *Fame* (2009), *High School* (2010), *Prom* (2011), and *Struck by Lightning* (2012).

And as previously argued, the spreading synergy of media outlets for youth influences the fluctuation of school representations. Where youth in earlier decades were drawn to teen trends on television that at least took weeks to develop, today's digital youth communicate in an immediate world of information and influence, affecting and effecting their senses of reality in increasingly spastic ways. This development has predictably changed the nature of learning itself, because knowledge and myth can be circulated so quickly and extensively, and school has become just one of many sites for socialization among peers. Movies, which typically need many months or years for their gestation, are a medium that is now preciously slow in keeping pace with youth in school who can navigate their entertainment choices and gravitate toward or away from trends in mere seconds.

SCHOOL KIDS

All of these conditions explain why there has always been an effort by filmmakers to experiment with or change the types of characters featured in school films, regardless of how much the conditions of school environments and the context of youth images have continued to evolve. Most school films before the 1980s focused on one type of school character and his or her relation to others, such as the misunderstood rebel played by James Dean in *Rebel Without a Cause*, the sexually curious but nonetheless repressed virgins played by the popular Natalie Wood and athlete Warren Beatty in *Splendor in the Grass* (1961), or the outcast nerd played by Sissy Spacek in *Carrie* (1976). But by the 1980s, many school films began showcasing an ensemble of school characters, as was shown in *Fast Times at Ridgemont High*, based on Cameron Crowe's "exposé" investigation of real school life, and reaching an apex with the "experiment" of (stereo)type casting in *The Breakfast Club*.

Both *Fast Times* and *Breakfast Club* feature the five basic characters of school films that permeate the subgenre: intellectual and essentially repressed (and thus occasionally aggressive) nerds; delinquent boys and girls "from the wrong side of the tracks" who either pay for their crimes or learn to reform; psychologically distraught rebels who may dabble in crime but are usually looking for a more acceptable outlet for their mal-

The Breakfast Club *(1985) presents the five types of characters who populate schools in American youth films, and this publicity still demonstrates some of their traits. Delinquent John (Judd Nelson) lurks behind shades and working-class garb, rebel Allison (Ally Sheedy) is coiled up and nonconforming in the shadows, athlete Andy (Emilio Estevez) is tensely wrapped in his wrestling jacket, popular Claire (Molly Ringwald) exudes an elite nonchalance, and nerd Brian (Anthony Michael Hall) is drably trying to blend in on the edge. (Autographed image of Ally Sheedy, author's collection.)*

aise; "popular" types whom everyone at school knows and who support their status through fashion, appearance, and attitude; and athletes, usually shown as physically focused and prouder than their counterparts, dedicated to a given sport yet surprisingly emotional as well. These stereotypes can embody different ages, races, classes, and genders, but as my study shows, there are indeed not only codifications for the behaviors of each type but also certain patterns that reveal narrative modes of acceptance within each type. The ways in which school characters are portrayed may offer an index of identifiers and signifiers for the young viewers who are presumably meant to relate to one or more of these types, and thus the films can be seen to "teach" the proper mannerisms of each school persona. This chapter then analyzes the five basic character types in school films through an evaluation of their primary conflicts: the ways nerds seek to transform, the means delinquents use to express anger, the actions rebels take to resist conformity, the efforts popular girls make for notoriety, and the signals athletes use to show their sensitivity.

There are crucial characters within school films that I do not analyze in this survey for obvious reasons: teachers.[3] Despite their age disqualification, their influence is worth mentioning, especially when they have a profound impact on children. Going back to at least *Goodbye, Mr. Chips* (1939) and *The Miracle Worker* (1962), movies have presented inspirational teachers alternately as saviors of troubled youth, replacements for ineffective parents, and visionaries who motivate learning and success within diffident teenagers. Since 1980, there have been at least twenty such films, with popular examples including *Dead Poets Society* (1989), *Mr. Holland's Opus* (1995), *The Emperor's Club* (2002), *Freedom Writers* (2007), and *Detachment* (2011). And there are indeed films about corrupt teachers and administrators, who in recent years are eventually reformed, as in *Mr. Woodcock* (2007) and *Bad Teacher* (2011), whereas previously they were subject to proper punishments, as in *Foxfire* (1996), *187* (1997), and *Wild Things* (1998). According to a study by Katy Wolfrom, since the '00s, school films have moved to replace incompetent leaders with more "democratic" principals: visible in the school, firm on discipline, effective at communication, knowledgeable about curriculum and instructional practices, seeking input from stakeholders, and nurturing positive relationships, as seen in *Mean Girls* (2004), *Dear Lemon Lima* (2009), and *Terri* (2011).[4] Yet far more beloved are the films featuring those dedicated souls who endure the numerous challenges of teaching young people, and whose value is almost always underestimated during the actual time of schooling. After all, teachers play a significant role in determining what kinds of characters their students become.[5]

TRANSFORMING THE NERD

The roles of intellectually ambitious school characters in youth films since 1980—who are portrayed as socially inept and uncouth—indicate that nerds lack the respect of their teen counterparts, but most films featuring nerds (who are also called dweebs, geeks, dorks, brains, and whizzes) reveal that they, like other school characters, are simply struggling to be understood and accepted in the face of social oppression. The paradox of nerds' oppression is that they excel at the very practice that school is designed to promote—learning—but such a blatant conformity to institutional expectations gives nerd characters a reputation for being unoriginal and excessively vulnerable. Further, their capacity to excel is viewed with jealousy by other students, who occasionally exploit nerds' skills (many nerds in school films are used to help struggling students overcome academic obstacles). Nerds most often attain their liberation through some abandonment of academics—joining a sports team, falling in love, committing a crime—but they always reaffirm the value of learning as a way of life. In many ways, nerds face the greatest struggle of all school characters because they must make the most forceful denials of their true nature, but this often gives them a distinct sense of accomplishment and respect. In his 1986 review of *Lucas*, Joseph Gelmis noted, "The nerd is to the high school movies of the '80s what the rebel without a cause was to the high school flicks of 30 years ago: an unlikely hero."[6]

The heroic nature of most nerds is also based in class backgrounds that are poorer than those of their school counterparts (as in *The Breakfast Club* [1985], *Lucas* [1986], *Angus* [1995], *Powder* [1995], *Napoleon Dynamite* [2004], and *Just Peck* [2009]). Due to nerds' tendency toward ambitious career goals, their financial disadvantage fuels a professional drive that is inspired by a desire to rise above the low-income conditions they were born into, a trait embodied by the smart boys in *October Sky* (1999), who are not nerdy in appearance but in spirit. Nerds' exaggerated lack of acceptance for other reasons is also augmented by their poverty, as they are unable to purchase the clothes, cars, and other commodities that foster fashion sense, freedom, and the coveting of wealth. Thus nerds need to fight and struggle for acceptance on many levels.

Nerds in school films from 1980 to 2013 were usually male (who did occasionally find nerdy girlfriends; *My Science Project* [1985], *Lucas* [1986], *Heathers* [1989], and *No Secrets* [1991] also contained small but significant roles by female nerds). In 1996, *Welcome to the Dollhouse* offered the first extended portrayal of a female nerd in junior high school, and *She's All That* (1999) presented the female high school nerd as yet another compromising conformist. Some nonschool films, such as *A Nightmare on Elm Street 4: The Dream Master* (1988) and *She's Out of Control* (1989), portray female nerds, but in the case of the horror film the character is killed, and in the romantic comedy she is transformed into an attractive socialite. This seems to be the option for all nerds: change or perish.

Save such exceptions, which nonetheless employ many of the same stereotypes that are used for male nerds, the reasoning behind this gendered portrayal of nerds may arise from the more compelling tensions generated by bookish boys compared to girls—smart boys are generally portrayed as tormented by their lack of physical presence in relation to their athletic peers, and are further ridiculed for their assumed lack of social skills, whereas girls are shown to use their intellect to their advantage. Nerds are also either virgins or sexually inactive, a condition that most films attempt to eradicate through the transformation of nerds into other school types (but nerds who remain nerds almost never have sex). Given the sexualized imaging of female characters in Hollywood history, the neutered role of the nerd does not comply with the traditional vision of screen "girls." In fact, in many other films that depict particularly smart female teens, such as *Pretty in Pink* (1986), *Say Anything . . .* (1989), *The Crush* (1993), *10 Things I Hate About You* (1999), *A Walk to Remember* (2002), *Saved!* (2004), or *Easy A* (2010), much effort is taken to make the characters appear attractive and stylish and thus avoid stereotypically nerdish markers, although the intimidation of female intelligence to male characters is alleviated through other liabilities, respectively: poverty, shyness, psychosis, feminism, religion, pregnancy, and virginity.

Boy Nerds

Even though its characters are in college, the film that has offered perhaps the most dominant image of male nerds is *Revenge of the Nerds* (1984), about a group of outcast freshmen who are ridiculed by popular campus characters such as jocks and party girls until they form their own fraternity and ultimately exact a very clever series of pranks to retaliate against their tormentors. In the process, the nerds show not only their ingenuity but also, somewhat ironically, their common interests with their college cohorts in having a good time. The nerd transformation that is common to virtually all other such depictions is thus somewhat challenged, because the characters achieve pleasure, power, and popularity without shedding their nerdy images, which may seem more legitimate in a college setting as opposed to high school.[7]

Like *Revenge*, many school films feature nerd characters as part of an ensemble depiction of various school stereotypes. In these films, nerds tend to fill background roles, clustering together in tribes, awkwardly bumping into one another, and speaking with big words. Most ensemble films tend to focus on another type of school character, leaving nerds to be less developed and therefore more easily viewed with pity and occasional contempt. For instance, the main nerd character in *Fast Times*, Mark Ratner (Brian Backer), is chastised by his best friend, the lubricious Mike Damone (Robert Romanus), for his lack of sexual prowess. Mark is thus seen as timid and immature; however, his patience in waiting for sex does afford him the film's one lasting romantic relationship. The nerds in *Heathers* are more extreme caricatures, assembled at a table in the opening cafeteria sequence, with their hallmark pocket protectors, eyeglasses, and braces. They shudder at the fleeting attention of the popular Heathers, and then are oddly absent from much of the rest of the film.

A more complete picture of the nerd type in an ensemble film is Brian (Anthony Michael Hall) in *The Breakfast Club*, who is portrayed with a tentative pathos that points to the alienation of nerds in school films. Brian wears khaki slacks and a bland sweatshirt, signifying his lack of class, plus he has "pale skin, pale-blue eyes, and almost milky blond hair; he's bodiless, almost translucent," as David Denby observed.[8] This lack of corporeality causes Brian to be constantly shut down in conversations with his fellow students, and they don't even learn his name until many scenes into the film. The story's premise is quite simple: five students, three boys and two girls, spend an entire Saturday in detention and systematically open up to one another about their personal problems. By the end of the film, after Brian has confided the dark secret that he is failing a shop class (his recognition that he's not so smart after all, as well as his badge of communal tribulation), the other students take advantage of his usually boastful academic skills in asking him to write their assigned "punishment" essay for the whole group. As Brian is writing the essay, the two remaining couples pair off, leaving him as the only character without a partner, except of course for his studies: in virtually parallel sequences, the other couples exchange first kisses while Brian, alone in the library, kisses the essay he has so proudly rendered on their behalf.

While the role of Brian in *The Breakfast Club* may be more complete than many other nerd characterizations, it supports as well as defies some of the usual nerd typings. Brian is indeed ostracized, ridiculed, physically and socially inept, and desexualized, but his yearning for a transformation from his nerd status to a more acceptable or dramatic personality is minimal. Unlike most nerd characters in school films, Brian ultimately appears to accept his nerd labeling, and his peers eventually show some sincere appreciation for the difference he represents (Brian is especially funny when he smokes pot with the others, and he's the only one who admits to contemplating the classic teen temptation of suicide). When the students leave school at the end of the day, Brian may be alone unlike the others, but he has thus quietly maintained a certain independence that is not afforded to them. His resistance to romance and to changing himself to look like or act like the others—something the rest do—indicates that he is the least conformist of the bunch. As other school films show, nerds must either aspire to homogeneity with their peers to gain acceptance or endure a compromised acceptance that consequentially preserves their individuality.

Anthony Michael Hall also played a nerd in *Weird Science* later in 1985, which, like many nerd stories in the '80s, took a somewhat endearing perspective on its two nerds. The same applied to *Class* (1983), *Real Genius* (1985), *Can't Buy Me Love*, *Three O'Clock High* (both 1987), and *The Beat* (1988), but such sweetened portrayals became rare by the '90s, after the torment of teen intellect began to take more serious turns in the late-'80s films. The goofy protagonist in *Three O'Clock High* eventually turns to violence to prove his worth, *The Beat*'s enigmatic nerd kills himself, and even a college comedy like *Real Genius* shows that its hero's premature sapience is easily manipulated by nefarious adults. These films did entertain positive nerd fantasies of achieving love and popularity through "self-improvement," and in all cases they came with a price: broken friendships, family crises, social disappointment, or literal money in the case of *Can't Buy Me Love*, wherein a nerd pays his pretty neighbor to date him and fails to see what a jerk his resulting fake status makes him.

The most earnest nerd depiction of the '80s is *Lucas*, whose plot sounds familiar even though its story is actually unique among nerd films; as David Edelstein observed, the film is different from other teen romances in that it "strolls up to each of the genre's clichés, sniffs it, and makes a gallant show of casting it off."[9] The title character, played by Corey Haim, is a bespectacled and undersized freshman overachiever who gains the attention and sometimes affection of everyone at his high school—a shy classmate longing for him is Rina (Winona Ryder)—when what he really wants is the love of a junior named Maggie (Kerri Green), who enjoys Lucas's friendship but is more attracted to football star Cappie (Charlie Sheen).

What makes *Lucas* shine is its sincere (almost saccharine) handling of Lucas's coming-of-age, and its earnest refusal to elevate him from his otherwise lowly nerd position. David Denby called *Lucas* the first high school film "told from the point of view of the nerd," a strategy which "might have been disastrous, but Lucas's being a bit of a pain, as well as a bright boy, absolves the movie of self-pity."[10] For all of his quirks and embarrassing demonstrations, Lucas remains proud of his intellect and still wins favor among many at school (even Cappie befriends and defends him, because Lucas helped him study once when he was injured). However, given that Lucas's romantic conquest of Maggie is still the film's central plot, and that even the most tame sexualizing of his innocent desire would disrupt his secure status as a nerd, the film uses Lucas's failed and ultimately dangerous attempt to play on the football team as a device to display both his lack of virility and his abundance of heart. In the end, Lucas still doesn't win Maggie (a rare romantic comedy in which the lead character is left alone), but he's still desired by Rina, who is implicitly a better match, being closer to his age, size, and intellect. When the guys on the football team give him a varsity jacket in the last scene, he proudly dons it to signify his triumphant ascent to a potentially new level of masculinity in which he may gain both physical and sexual confidence. This notion that a better life is waiting for the nerd is common to most of these films, a suspended promise of success in a world where intelligence and sensitivity are valued, a world unlike school.

The major male nerd roles in the '90s—*Class Act, Angus, Powder*—eschew easy categorization, although each typically advocates a transformation from the shyness associated with intellect and difference to characteristics that offer greater social acceptance, even if that acceptance isn't achieved. *Class Act* (1991) is the only one in which real acceptance for the nerd is gained, using an interesting variation on the switched-identity theme by crossing a street hood with a nerd. *Angus* (1995) compassionately endeavors to show how an overweight ninth-grade pariah achieves pride through standing up against the popular jocks in his class, placing its emphasis less on his social integration than on his gaining self-respect. *Powder* (1995) presents its superintelligent albino outcast as more cosmically mysterious than simply shy, a portrait of the nerd as alien life-form, with his cosmic qualities never explained and never appreciated either, a condition that many prodigies must feel.[11] And while it isn't a school film *per se, Can't Hardly Wait* (1998) does feature a prominent nerd daydream, with a boy becoming a party animal and a sex machine for the evening thanks to a low dose of alcohol; in the end, after his temporary acceptance, he is again rejected by the popular school jocks, yet a closing credit tells us that he went on to become rich through the computer industry, signaling his eventual true revenge.

Class Act teams up African American rappers Kid and Play (real names Christopher Reid and Christopher Martin) as Duncan and Blade; these names already foretell that Duncan is a smart and humdrum nerd who, as signified by his high-top haircut and glasses, is dramatically different from Blade, a bad boy with attitude who is fresh out of prison and ordered by the court to return to high school. By chance their files are switched at the beginning of the school year, and because Blade wants to avoid the derision of being placed in the "delinquents" class and Duncan is susceptible to his pressure, the two decide to let the school continue believing that they are each the other, resulting in Duncan being feared by his classmates as a criminal and Blade being placed in a special class for gifted students. The different treatment that the two receive, and the way each changes in relation to that treatment, demonstrates the film's central message, which David Denby describes well: "Teenagers, particularly black teenagers, get typed early on in life and then act in ways that fulfill the expectations placed on them. Change the circumstances and expectations and—presto!—you get a different teenager."[12] The racial and class commentaries of the film further call attention to the differences that *Class Act* attempts to highlight in its portrayal of nerdy and criminal youth: very few smart teens in films before the '90s were nonwhite, and Duncan is the sole nerd since *My Bodyguard* (1980) who comes from a financially prosperous background.

Nonetheless, the film preserves much of the explicit moralizing that many African American youth films contain: crime does not pay, staying in school is better than being on the streets, true success is measured in respect and not dollars. Or as Jami Bernard saw it, "The movie manages to keep to today's requisite anti-drug, pro–safe sex agendas without getting too bogged down in do-goodism, and gently mocks the stereotypes of uncool intellectuals and idiot homeboys."[13] Duncan is able to make an initially slow but ultimately complete transformation from unhip nerd to stylish dude thanks to Blade's training and the school's attitude toward him, but he thus achieves a certain balance with Blade, who softens some of his toughness and negativity to enjoy the admiration that comes from being (perceived as) cool but smart. By the end of the film, the two opposing types meet at the center of a fulcrum of teen acceptability: Duncan will always be smart but can now be appreciated by his peers as also being cool, and Blade will always be cool but can now be appreciated by his superiors as also being smart.

After the minimal presence of nerds in youth films of the '90s, they regained some notoriety in the '00s, only in less extreme roles than they played in the '80s. Epitomizing this contrast was *Love Don't Cost a Thing* (2003), a loose remake of *Can't Buy Me Love* recast with African American teens that manages to dilute the cheery, if optimistic, messages of *Class Act*. The familiar ploy, in which a nerdy boy makes a financial deal with a popular girl to pretend they're dating, again leads to the nerd gaining

The title character played by Jon Heder in Napoleon Dynamite *(2004) exhibits the trademark glasses and eccentric dress of nerds while his friend Pedro (Efren Ramirez) is awkward without such visible markers.*

school status and a cool set of duds, although he is afflicted with relatively few of the visibly uncouth symptoms past nerds have suffered. As a result of its milder manner, the film is surprisingly ineffective in portraying the tensions nerds endure as the two films to which it is indebted. The nerd transformation was also enacted in *Spider-Man* (2002), with its fantasy of a nerd becoming the title superhero; *The New Guy* (2002), whose title describes a nerd posing as a hoodlum after transferring schools; *Thumbsucker* (2005), in which the title affliction is overcome by a nerd through psychiatry; *Harold* (2008), with an oddly aging nerd as the title character who wins favor at his school by defeating a delinquent in a go-kart race; and *Kick-Ass* (2010), whose title nerd has typical teenage ambitions until he becomes a brazen and bungling comic book hero.

Another mild nerd, yet by far the most influential of any during the 'oos, was the hero of *Napoleon Dynamite* (2004), played with virtually flat affect by Jon Heder. Napoleon lives in a nondescript Idaho town with his older, aimless brother, thereby suggesting his meager background; his drab clothes and gangly stature induce his middling classmates to dismiss his presence at school. Napoleon befriends the mutually unemotional Pedro (Efren Ramirez) and graceless Deb (Tina Majorino), forming a threesome of outcasts who nonetheless are not determined to change for mere acceptance. In fact, their passing ambitions are in self-fulfillment, because Napoleon wants to master martial arts, Deb wants to go into fashion work, and Pedro wants to be class president, all goals they seem unlikely to achieve. And none of them is particularly smart or talented, although they live under pitiful beliefs that they are, which is especially mortifying alongside Napoleon's delusion that he is a skilled illustrator. Rather than intelligence, it is their delusions that make them so nerdy, for they do not seem to realize how peculiar they appear to everyone else, as is the case when Napoleon tells Pedro what girls seek in guys, "like nunchaku skills, bow hunting skills, computer hacking skills, girls only want boyfriends who have great skills."

The story proceeds through quirky episodes with Napoleon collecting tater tots and trying to feed the family llama, and his brother discovering a rather extravagant love interest through online dating. Then the climactic school election pits Pedro against a girl who had already rejected his affections, in a cheerless contest lacking all relevance, which Pedro surprisingly wins after Napoleon desperately performs a terribly befuddling dance in front of an assembly, and the students are inexplicably impressed. Napoleon later makes an overture to Deb by remarking on a delicious bass he caught for her, intimating that the two of them may become more than friends. The film ends just as uneventfully as it began, with no dramatic speech about students accepting each other nor any heartfelt messages about the importance of individuality, and in that way the story suits the cultural pathos of the 'oos educational setting. Nerds may be recognized as such in school, but they are not as insulted as before, now that this era has become hypersensitive to bullying, and lessons about tolerance have already been taught and learned. *Napoleon Dynamite* is not so much a revision of past nerd depictions as it is a darkly comic celebration of being strange in the contemporary educational venue, where all students know that everyone is subject to the spotlight of lurid and instant mass communication. The film's success primarily derives from the irreverence it has for social sensitivities about acceptance, and its exposure of the absurdity typified by school popularity.

The film industry's waning enchantment with traditional nerds was evident in *I Love You, Beth Cooper* (2009), a surprisingly dull version of the "wild night" story common to many comedies. Denis (Paul Rust) is the valedictorian of his class, and utilizes his graduation speech to confess his affection for the popular title girl (Hayden Panettiere) he has crushed on since seventh grade. More compelling are his further confessions about other students in the class: a conceited rich girl who is really insecure, a neurotic girl with an eating disorder, a bully who was sexually abused, and even his best friend Rich (Jack Carpenter), whom he knows is gay. Unfortunately, all these characters are so thinly drawn, and the ensuing plot is so inane, that the film has very little to say about school, romance, or acceptance.

The three lead characters are joined by two of Beth's female friends in an aimless evening of escalating indulgence meant to reveal the nerdy charisma of Denis and the untested homosexuality of Rich. The results are insulting in both cases, because Denis subjects himself to recurring abuse at the hands of Beth's military boyfriend (and Beth clearly enjoys the sadistic validation of her importance), while Rich persists with denials about his sexual preference through ongoing flirtation with the two other girls, leading to an absurd threesome that miraculously confirms his queerness. Denis is marginalized by his peer group like most nerds, and loaded with the clichéd signifiers of inapt clothes and physical weakness, yet his intelligence is rarely displayed and his long-standing longing for the insipid Beth is barely explored beyond her cute appearance and cheerleader charm. His graduation revelations about his other classmates are confirmed throughout the course of the night, which could have highlighted his insight and sensitivity, but these qualities are left uncelebrated. The story does not give Denis enough time to face the transformative pressure that so many nerds in other films face, and makes no suggestions about what he would do even if he had such time. This is most evident in the conclusion, when Denis returns home the next morning with Beth, and while they have kissed, he plainly has little motivation to pursue their relationship any further. In that way, Denis does maintain some integrity with his nerdy image intact, yet seems indifferent to it at the same time, with no expression of pride and certainly no salvation.

Nerdy Girls

More than twenty years after *Revenge of the Nerds*, a similar but critically different story about nerds in college played out in *Sydney White* (2007), meant to be a postmodern commentary on *Snow White*, in which a boyish girl starts college with the plan of joining a sorority, just to be turned away. Instead, she decides to live with seven male nerds, all of whom have humorously distinctive qualities that predictably serve well in helping her to secure a popular boyfriend while she helps them to gain visibility on campus. Again the nerds preserve their original attributes while achieving value, yet in this case the girl must discard her tomboy image to appear more feminine and attract a boyfriend who is not a nerd. As previously noted, maintenance of gendered image standards usually trumps girls' resistance to transform, even when they associate only with nerds.

Fairy tales like *Snow White*, and more so *Cinderella*, speak to the classic expectation that women need to change to find proper liberation from their gloomy circumstances, and that their makeover must be recognized by men who sweep in to take them away from the troubles around them.[14] Girls' nerd stories operate under virtually identical conditions, with a further emphasis on validation in addition to escape. In the very visual medium of youth films, this means that boys must realize that nerdy girls are in fact pretty after all. Hence, the adherence to a beauty standard explains the less common depiction of female nerds in youth films, as the industry promotes appearance over intelligence, and conformity over individuality, much more for girls than boys. The fact that nearly no female nerds were the protagonists in youth films until the mid-'90s supports this argument, as does an early example like *The Sterile Cuckoo* (1969), in which the quirky heroine loses her sanity in a failed effort to simultaneously keep her boyfriend and her gawky image. Time and again, nerdy girls usually pay a price for being exceptional: scorn and alienation from their peers, or their own damaging self-contempt.

After smaller girl nerd roles in '80s films mentioned before, *Welcome to the Dollhouse* (1996) became the first full portrayal of a female nerd in American school films. Dawn Weiner (Heather Matarazzo) is a seventh-grade target of ridicule, which is assured by her dressing in tacky clothes and wearing the trademark thick glasses.[15] What makes Dawn a nerd to be reckoned with is her intense anxiety about her awkward image, something she recognizes but cannot seem to change. The other girls at school obviously dress differently and aggressively intimidate Dawn, as when one even forces Dawn to defecate while she watches, a complex psychological degradation that other films have never risked depicting. Her peers make clear that it's not her intelligence they envy (for Dawn is the rare nerd who's not book-smart), but her sheer appearance that they so easily abhor. Dawn asks the girl who taunts her in the bathroom, "Why do you hate me?" Her flat response: "Because you're ugly."

Rather than cower into shyness, Dawn has learned to fight back or, more often, to vent her anger in other ways (such as her active disgust for her younger sister). Dawn doesn't crave acceptance by the social order at large, and initially doesn't seem to crave acceptance at all, until she develops a crush on her older brother's friend Steve (Eric Mabius). This crush makes Dawn consider her image even more seriously, as does the violent interest a class delinquent, Brandon (Brendan Sexton Jr.), shows toward her. Brandon threatens to rape Dawn, but in an unexpected revelation, he shows Dawn that he's more innocently attracted to her, even if he doesn't want anyone else to know. Brandon's sensitivity thus becomes an interesting foil to Dawn's: both students want the affection of someone who cannot provide it (Dawn tells Brandon she's in love with Steve, but she still wants to be friends), and both face the embarrassing discovery that the images they've cultivated deny them both acceptance and security. Brandon ultimately runs away from home and Dawn tries a similar tactic, albeit with the purpose of finding her younger sister, who is temporarily kidnapped, and thereby steals more attention away from the long-suffering Dawn.

Dawn realizes in the end that, rather than finding a way out, she must endure five more years of school, and one can only hope "that Dawn Weiner—and Heather Matarazzo—will one day soon bloom into talented and beautiful young women," as Lisa Schwarzbaum wrote in her review.[16] Indeed, the film proposes that Dawn can only wait and hope for nature to bring better options, and perhaps this powerlessness is integrally linked to her gender positioning: unable to capitalize on her smarts and savvy, the nerd girl must hope for change from without to gain a respectable place in society, while the changes she has made or will make from within are basically not recognized by those around her. After Dawn's crush rejects her and Brandon runs away, she is really left alone, more so than the many male nerd characters in earlier films, who had at least won their crush's attention if not some friends.

She's All That (1999) offers a more insidious depiction of a teenage female nerd, in a plot that revises *My Fair Lady*, with a creative girl transformed into a desirable figure by a popular jock on a bet. Once again, an already-pretty performer simply needs to doff her glasses to start looking attractive, and she gradually gives in to the lure of being accepted, despite the fact that the popular crowd still resists her. In this way, the film is harsher than many of the previous nerd tales, for she so openly compromises her sense of identity despite herself (setting aside her dedication to political causes as well as her expressive artistry) that her embarrassing efforts at gaining acceptance become more self-deprecating than socially integrating. Jane Ganahl expressed a common sentiment among critics: "Just once, I'd love to see a teen flick that doesn't send out a message to young girls that to be acceptable, you have to conform."[17] The true deception of *She's All That* is that it suggests its heroine is indeed all that—smart, comely, talented, caring, resilient—and concludes that such great qualities do not guarantee happiness without social and, more strikingly, masculine endorsement.

Such a sexist attitude toward girls was at least challenged that same year in *Never Been Kissed*, about an adult journalist who infiltrates a high school for a feature story and ultimately disrupts the pecking order of acceptability by criticizing the intolerant students. While this twentysomething protagonist was rather nerdy herself, most other depictions of smart girls in the '90s continued to represent them in captivating and even erotic modes, automatically vanquishing their nerdy qualities, as in *The Incredibly True Adventure of Two Girls in Love* (1994), *Hackers* (1995), *Wild Things* (1998), and *Election* (1999). Nonetheless, these characters were also disparaged for their morally questionable behavior, raising another suspicious set of consequences for female intelligence, and promoting another sexist double standard, which became so ludicrous that it was easily parodied in *Not Another Teen Movie* (2001).

Transformation of the nerdy girl was still an appealing topic in the '00s given the success of *The Princess Diaries* (2001), in which Anne Hathaway's insecure teen is shocked to learn she is an imperial heir to the throne of a small country. Her ensuing change is thereby motivated not by personal desire but by familial obligation, which is tested by friends who merely like her newfound fame, and by the burdens of regal decorum, yet of course she ultimately decides to accept her calling. In the sequel, *Princess Diaries 2: Royal Engagement* (2004), the post-teen protagonist is tested by more adult mysteries such as seduction and marriage, only without the same requirement of metamorphosis, so she is able to disrupt the chauvinist traditions of her new nation *and* still find a boyfriend. The sequel is compelling for this contention that once the nerdy qualities of the girl are gone, she is no longer daunted by the torments she endured during her formative years, confirming that her sloppy comportment and slovenly looks were far greater liabilities than her inexperience with leadership and propriety.

The nerdy girl was treated to a markedly alternative resolution in one of the most noteworthy youth films of the decade, *Dear Lemon Lima* (2009). Vanessa (Savanah Wiltfong) is a slight, shy, and bright half-Yupik girl in Alaska on scholarship at her new exclusive high school. She is somewhat conflicted about her heritage, because her Eskimo father is absent, her paleness is in stark contrast to her other native classmates, and she is pressured by condescending administrators to represent the conspicuous local minority. As Christopher Campbell points out, the story "tackles a common issue for teenagers of fitting in and parallels it smartly but delicately with the history of Native Americans adjusting to their forced assimilation into white culture."[18] Vanessa expresses her own assimilation angst in a series of letters she writes to "Lemon Lima," an alter ego presumably derived from her last name of Limor, recounting such humiliations as her snobby boyfriend breaking up with her, and her exile to a secluded exercise room for the school's athletically impaired students. She is not afraid to tackle some muscular questions about life, though, such as, "Why do I question what God thinks when I'm an atheist?"

Vanessa encounters common dilemmas associated with nerds until she begins allying with the other castoffs in the exercise room, who form a team to take on the more popular and skilled students in a ballyhooed field day contest based on actual Eskimo games. In the process, Vanessa and her fellow outsiders gain confidence and support one another to prevail, even after the suicide of a boy whose overbearing parents are threatened by his revolt against their expectations. The tragedy slightly disrupts their shaky unity, although his memory rejuvenates their determination as they gain solidarity in taunting the social order, leading them to give their team a profane name in protest. When the crew wins the competition at the climax, they only momentarily bask in their glory, saving their bragging rights to ride away in a limousine provided by one of their parents.

This final status statement notwithstanding, *Dear Lemon Lima* is a refreshingly realistic and sincere portrait of the nerdy girl with an understanding of her marginal place in the communal structure; and despite her discontents, she does not long to gain authority through conformity. Rather, Vanessa is balanced without being boring, and smart without being a smartass. Unlike Dawn in *Dollhouse*, her self-preservation is actually fulfilling, and unlike so many boy nerds, she does not need good looks, trendy clothes, or even a romantic conquest to feel triumphantly accomplished. To that end, the film delivers one of the most positive images of—and messages to—girls in the early twenty-first century.

The main emphasis in the majority of nerd films has alas been on transformation, on changing from someone who is brainy and physically awkward to someone who is merely clever but popular and sophisticated, and this emphasis became more complicated in recent years as nerdy teens have been increasingly portrayed as smart enough to realize the fallacy of this expectation. *Can't Hardly Wait, Napoleon Dynamite,* and *Dear Lemon Lima* may indicate that nerds will continue to be ostracized as teenagers, but will have the last laugh as they become successful and contented with their images. Or, in even more progressive ways, nerds like the protagonist in *The Perks of Being a Wallflower* (2012) will actually reach some kind of catharsis in working through their needs for acceptance. At least most youth movies continue to acknowledge this, even if other films in the mold of *She's All That, The New Guy,* and *I Love You, Beth Cooper* are likely to also continue the stereotypical depiction of smart youth as inherently conflicted by their intellect, a conflict that, after all, grants nerd characters an elevated dramatic interest.

DELINQUENTS AND THEIR AVENUES OF ANGER

The delinquent character has long been a staple of school films, and was certainly a common screen image of youth in the '80s and '90s. (I analyze the larger topic of teen delinquency in the next chapter.) Like their roles in films since the '50s, delinquents are used to demonstrate that crime is not a proper means of acceptance, and unless the delinquent reforms, he or she is destined for a life of misery (or else the delinquent dies before the end of the film). Delinquency in school films is portrayed through characters who not only violate the moral code of the school, but who also usually carry their troubling behavior outside of school, and thus often use the school as a refuge from even greater repercussions for their acts. Delinquents sometimes act aggressively toward other students, but often teachers are the targets of their anger, and in the case of a specific type of delinquent film, the teachers' reformation of delinquents is the focus of the plot. Acts of delinquents' aggression range from simple teasing and taunting to fistfights and gun battles, and because delinquents have what they perceive to be valuable territory and/or a reputation to uphold, they often launch their attacks against defenseless victims, inadvertently demonstrating their false sense of power.

Like the "inspiring teacher" character, some school films feature a "reforming teacher" variety, who sees a school as exigent from the start, either due to the presence of a few particularly bad students or, in more dogmatic dramas, due to inept management on the part of the school administration. A few school films in the early to mid-'80s portrayed reforming teachers working against small groups of troublemakers—such as *Up the Academy* (1980), *Class of 1984* (1982), *Teachers* (1984), and *Tuff Turf* (1985)—but after the late '80s, most films either dealt with delinquent school characters as a large group, as in *The Principal* (1987), *Lean on Me* (1989), and *The Substitute* (1996), or in smaller roles beside other school types, as in *Three O'Clock High* (1987) and *Class Act* (1991). After the increasing media attention to school violence in the late '90s, films have depicted fewer delinquents altogether (the "bad boys" of *The Faculty* [1998], *A Walk to Remember* [2002], *Step Up* [2006], and *Prom* [2011] all show softer sides and at worst commit petty crimes, revealing that they aren't inherently dangerous).

As with nerd characterizations, the great majority of delinquent characters are male and from low-income backgrounds. The Hollywood rationale for this pattern may be clearer than it is for nerd roles: males are responsible for the vast majority of violent crimes in the United States and poverty is a dominant factor in most criminality. Delinquent characters in past decades of school films nonetheless evolved from the reckless abandon they displayed in early '80s films like *Class of 1984* and *Tuff Turf* to more sensitive portraits of misunderstood underachievers who really want to succeed, from *Stand and Deliver* in 1988 to *Dangerous Minds* in 1995. Again, even this positive turn subsided in the '00s; despite the cultural efforts to curb teen crime, Hollywood was apparently more willing to avoid the topic altogether rather than more carefully examine its causes. On the other hand, as I demonstrate in the next two chapters, there is still a sensational aspect to portrayals of teen fighting, be it with realistic people or fantasy figures, which remains quite appealing to audiences, especially when the conflicts are outside of school settings.

I divide delinquent school roles into two styles of conflicts, which essentially correspond with the changing views on delinquency over the past generation: conflicts with other students and conflicts with the school. While there is some overlap in this division, the films that feature conflicts with the school tend to focus equally on teachers and administrators, and films that feature delinquents fighting other students tend to be less political and more personal, with the menace of bullying always being a hazard. Students fighting teachers has been an essentially extinct plotline since 2000 because youth are no longer granted the audacity to fight their elders; students fighting other students in the past decade has declined but not disappeared altogether.

Students Versus Teachers

Most films focusing on youth with disciplinary problems take themselves quite seriously, as in the ham-fisted *Class of 1984*: the prologue states that the events depicted in the film are "partially" based on actual scholastic incidents, a tactic that highlights the film's occasionally prophetic realism but also makes its excessive depictions somewhat dubious.[19] The story revolves around a gang of punks led by talented but violent Peter Stegman (Timothy Van Patten), who clashes with new music teacher Mr. Norris (Perry King). The school itself is under the grip of Stegman and his cronies: graffiti is everywhere, the extensive school security is nonetheless rendered inadequate, and one teacher even resorts to pulling a gun on his class to keep them in line. Norris attempts to turn the drug-running Stegman over to the police, but he is told that prosecuting juveniles is next to impossible. With the law thus rendered impotent, and the school administration looking the other way, Norris abandons his originally altruistic efforts at reform. After the delinquents attack and rape his wife, he lowers himself to their level, killing three of them and letting Stegman fall to his death.

Class of 1984 is the first film of the 1980s to depict an American school as overrun by delinquents, a drama that has been nonetheless extant since the late 1940s. Many of the earlier examples, such as *Blackboard Jungle*, also featured a tough and idealistic teacher who was attacked by his students outside the classroom as well as at school. However, this film does draw attention to two opposite shifts in the depiction of "bad" students and "good" teachers: Stegman is clearly shown to have a potential for success that he denies for a criminal lifestyle, and thus he is portrayed as more culpable for his acts than many of his predecessors who were "victims" of society who lacked opportunities; and Norris does not prevail with his educational ideals but instead resorts to killing off the delinquents. The film's blurring of responsibility for delinquency—everyone is at fault, and worse yet teachers become delinquents themselves—is a theme that saw further manifestation in *Teachers* in 1984 and was maintained in virtually all the reforming teacher films of the '80s and '90s.

The next three such films in the late '80s showed students under further difficult conditions. In *The Principal* (1987) and *Lean on Me* (1989), urban schools have become cesspools of corruption, with helpless teachers unable to control their wayward students until a new administrator arrives to shake things up. The featured delinquents in *The Principal* are African Americans, while the Latino students, who obviously maintain an uneasy distance from the black gang, tend to ally with the castigating white principal. These two groups never actually fight or even talk much to each other, and the film has little to say about the implicit tensions between them, but the fact that earlier delinquent films in the '80s didn't even point to racial issues gives *The Principal* some relevance, primarily because race is a prominent topic in most depictions of delinquents that followed. This was certainly the case in *Stand and Deliver* (1988), where the school conditions aren't quite as bad, and the Latino teacher takes on a smaller portion of the population to enforce his reform, turning his math class from potential street hoodlums into calculus geniuses, and later defending them against racist charges of cheating on tests. Delinquent students abound in all three films, but each film goes out of its way to demonstrate that at least some (if not all) young people really do want to learn and be successful, and given the success of students in the latter two films, this message represents some sense of hope compared to the fate of previous delinquents.

Stand and Deliver and *Lean on Me* derive similar bold messages from their true stories: students need leaders who exemplify the discipline and dedication they preach, and hard work must be done to reach tangible goals as well as more philosophical ideals. *Stand and Deliver* is a rare depiction of delinquents who not only learn to "behave" but who also work toward lasting educational results. The delinquents in *Lean on Me* aren't given quite such a chance. The film chronicles the reforming efforts of Joe Clark (Morgan Freeman), who is appointed principal at a run-down urban high school. Clark's first executive act is to gather up all of the "miscreant" students and summarily expel them, and he thereafter makes vocal and stern demands of his faculty and staff, in whom he tolerates no questioning of his authority as he oversees the transformation of the school from its drug-infested and decaying, dismal state into a bright and cheerful environment. Only one of the expelled delinquents appeals to be readmitted, and Clark agrees to give him one more chance—but not until he stands the student on the school roof and challenges him to jump off if he doesn't want to learn.

There is a glaring flaw with the reform that Clark brings to the school, which Charles Epstein has well identified: "His 'unconventional' tactics, brutal in any other context, are made acceptable, even heroic, by the nightmarish universe he attempts to subdue, affording us ample opportunity to let loose with a few cathartic cheers—and to suspend judgment. But ques-

Lou Diamond Phillips portrays one of the Latino students in Stand and
Deliver *(1988) whose assumed delinquency casts doubt on his ability to
excel in calculus.*

tions persist. Clark's methods did produce short-term results, but the ends,
as they say, don't invariably justify the means, especially if those means
border on the fascistic."[20]

The film does offer a running criticism of Clark's actions by his staff and
the students' parents, but despite this and the emotional appeal that Epstein
points out, the film has a distinct lack of sympathy or understanding for
the students. While simply casting the "bad apples" out to society and away
from the students who use school for an education more than a drug opera-

tion is a way to promote a serious attitude for the school, it also begs the question of how secondary education, specifically in urban areas, can afford to ignore the very serious problems that produce delinquency in the first place. A film like *Lean on Me* is deceptive in a way that *Stand and Deliver* is not: the kids obviously need help and get it, but their achievements are less the result of their dedication than of their dodging delinquent influences that are supposedly chased away by their dictatorial principal. The film thus ends appropriately with students receiving their diplomas at graduation, a proud accomplishment indeed, yet also a symbol of passage to even more difficult adulthood, a treacherous state that this film, and all films about school delinquents, safely avoid confronting.

The school films of the '90s featuring the delinquents-versus-teachers plot are wildly different from one another, from the cute humor of the tame *Sister Act 2: Back in the Habit* (1993) and the dark comedy of *Teaching Mrs. Tingle* (1999) to the curiously apocalyptic *Class of 1999* (1990), a "sequel" to *Class of 1984* in which the real villains are cyborg teachers who carry out their violent discipline against unruly youth gangs until a proletarian student uprising brings down the greater adult evil.[21] Each of these depictions points to interesting adult dilemmas in handling contemporary school delinquents, yet only one, *Dangerous Minds* (1995), can be viewed as a realistic story. Here Hollywood banked on another urban student transformation tale, although this time based on the true story of high school teacher LouAnne Johnson (Michelle Pfeiffer). Johnson is an ex-marine (three of the teachers in delinquent school films of the '90s had some military background, as if that was a requirement), and after initially failing to reach her unruly English class with poetry, she shows her street cred by teaching them karate skills. The film proceeds to develop a few student characters in Johnson's class, which is composed of "crucially challenging" delinquents, most of whom are African Americans or Latinos in contrast to Johnson's suburban lily-whiteness; she takes on a saintly concern for all of them, trying to turn them away from the criminal lifestyles that they all seem to lead. Johnson shows an amazing acuity for understanding their concerns—death, survival, fighting, and pride are more important to them than grammar and punctuation—and she works these issues into her lesson plans.

The racial tension between Johnson and her charges still pervades the film, irrespective of her efforts to mollify it. Jeannette Sloniowski points out that Johnson "implies to minority teens that they, too, can fit into the 'normal' world of white society—a world that both the teacher and the film tend to portray as more legitimate than the world that the teenagers inhabit."[22] This sense of white legitimacy is embodied by Johnson bribing her students to learn by passing out candy bars, taking them to an amusement park, and even treating one student to a fancy dinner. Perhaps these "bribes" are effective inducements, for many of her students do come to appreciate poetry—the film oddly uses Bob Dylan and Dylan Thomas in place of the rap songs that Johnson used in real life—but *Dangerous Minds*, like virtually all delinquent dramas, does not offer a clear vision of a better future through education, and Johnson's tactics seem like placebos designed to promote high graduation numbers rather than dedicated learning skills.

The film shows that the delinquents in Johnson's class can indeed be calmer citizens if they are faced with friendly leadership and visibly gratifying rewards, and perhaps in that way it is offering a suggestion to American educators. Yet unlike *Lean on Me*, the film must struggle to depict learning and reform as good for their own sake, and similar to *Lean on Me*, the film only implies the long-term results of education, opting to end—like *Teachers* and *Stand and Deliver*—with the teacher's decision to stay and teach future classes of delinquents, so she can make a "difference." *Dangerous Minds* thus lays bare a myth more applicable to adults than to youth: by winning over delinquents, the reforming teacher finds her purpose, regardless of the fact that her students may still lack direction.

The few ensuing school delinquency films of the decade did little to advance the issues of previous films, although they did escalate the amount of violence before vanishing after the late '90s. *The Substitute* (1996), like *The Class of 1999*, is another school-as-battle-zone film, with a mercenary posing as a teacher to systematically expose a school's drug-running students as pawns of the principal, yielding another vision of youth delinquency turned back on more corrupt adult forces.[23] A more deliberately ridiculous delinquent student film that appeared in 1996, *High School High*, parodied these films, making jokes about drug abuse, violence, and undereducated youth, and in the process foretelling that these stories had exhausted their severity. Such was the case with the farcical *Teaching Mrs. Tingle* that had its title changed from *Killing Mrs. Tingle* in an attempt to ease concerns about its story of three students (hardly the deviants of past films) executing an ultimately effective kidnapping of a mean teacher. The box office and critical failure of the film proved that the mere threat of student-teacher violence was no longer a welcome subject.

The film *187* (1997) had already been testament to this in its slick style and animalistic imaging of delinquents, but it ventures into further excess with its reforming teacher who secretly begins to maim and kill his most troublemaking students. The criminal youth are themselves so homogenous that they become caricatures of adolescent menace wallowing in an environment of urban violence that makes the deviant teacher's actions appear almost justified. The film actually seems to propose murder and suicide as the existential solutions to the cycle of school crime, especially after the teacher and his last student nemesis each end up killing themselves in an absurdly macho game of Russian roulette, an ending that loses its pathos by leaving no viable alternative to the crisis. Hollywood by this point seemed to have no reasonable way of dealing with the very complex topic of school violence—*187* appeared at the start of the late-'90s wave of student mass murders, and given the standard of irresponsibility it represents, the film industry was smart to steer clear of further school violence parables, which is a much better option than further promoting such inflammatory, unsympathetic images of difficult teens.

Just as there are two conflicts that school delinquents engage in—against other students and/or against teachers—there were two images of delinquents that school films of the '80s offered: they were either irresponsible and unreformable truants who were the cause of the social decay of high schools, or they were misunderstood and simply defensive adolescents seeking identity in the face of serious struggle. By the '90s, after the supposedly successful reforms brought about by teachers and administrators in late '80s films, depictions of delinquent school kids retained this division yet more thoroughly implicated teachers in students' behavioral problems, and the adults' utilization of their disciplining power—and capacity to educate—became more suspect.

Students Versus Students

While some delinquents in '80s movies were busy fighting with their teachers, there were other examples of school kids taunting, harassing, and hurting their classmates, such as films early in the decade like *Rivals* (1981), *Christine* (1983), *The New Kids* (1985), and *My Bodyguard* (1980), a searing study of school bullying and retribution. Two films from 1985 that considered how students handle one another's delinquency (with minimal input by teachers) also feature delinquent characters confronting their peer reputations. In *The Breakfast Club*, John Bender (Judd Nelson) gains the most attention of his detention-hall colleagues through his endless rants and rowdy actions, even though he seems to be undoubtedly disconnected from them socially. Bender initiates the dialogue on personal terms, and takes an early stand for his authority in a brief showdown with the principal. This begins to galvanize the group, as David Edelstein observed: "When they realize they're united against a common enemy—the teacher, their parents, adults in general—they begin to open up, confessing sins and fears and telling stories. And all, in their way, feel trapped by their images."[24] Despite the students' initial disdain for Bender, they recognize that his lack of concern for social acceptance is not genuine but is indeed demanded by his image—after all, he works incredibly hard to gain their attention—and as he reveals more of his sensitivity to being understood if not accepted, they come to appreciate and envy his capacity to express his feelings. During the film's climactic set piece, Bender has the least to reveal because he has already exposed so much of himself earlier, throwing Andy's earlier accusation back at him: "I could disappear forever and it wouldn't make any difference. I might as well not even exist at this school, remember?" Bender is the classic delinquent, disgusted with his place in the world but unsure of what place would be better, taking on a demonstrative toughness to shield his vulnerable desolation.

Bender's toughness can also be displayed without his resorting to violence. This is not the case in *Tuff Turf*, where Morgan Hiller (James Spader) has come to a new suburban high school after being expelled from prep school. However, Morgan isn't guilty of the usual delinquent crimes: he simply finds himself dealing with the violent thugs at his school (a gang plainly called the Tuffs), and struggles to escape his middle-class family values to achieve his own identity. Morgan's own rebellion takes the form of taunting the Tuffs and openly romancing their leader's girlfriend, Frankie (Kim Richards). The premise is clearly lifted from *Rebel Without a Cause*, complete with an overbearing mother who wears down Morgan's financially struggling father, and with Morgan's fawning friend Jimmy (Robert Downey Jr.).[25] This updating includes far more fighting, swearing, and some sex, and it raises the stakes for its reluctant rebel—Morgan's father is shot by the leader of the Tuffs—before resorting to a happy ending in which Morgan beats the Tuffs' leader to death, sees his father recover, and wins Frankie's affection.

What makes *Tuff Turf* more a study in delinquency than rebellion is the fact that Morgan's rebellion is so underdetermined (he lives in the shadow of a successful older brother and the threat of losing class status, but that doesn't explain why he actively aggravates the dangerous Tuffs), and the film ultimately supports the message that might makes right. Or, as Michael Wilmington remarked flatly, "The basic problem with *Tuff Turf* is a question of values. *Rebel Without a Cause* had them, dealt with them. This movie doesn't."[26] While Morgan has every opportunity to ignore the Tuffs or to at least call the police when he witnesses their crimes (which include street robberies, car stealing, vandalism, and attempted murder), his deliverance comes not from a stand of individuality but from using a dart gun and two-by-fours to beat up the Tuffs. *Tuff Turf* shows its delinquents in a world practically devoid of authority and identity because they have only one another to fight, and as other school films in the '80s and '90s would demonstrate, a sharp force of authority is exactly what supplies delinquents with their identity.

Dangerously Close (1986) and *The Beat* (1988) also featured delinquents in conflicts with other students, although the plots of these films contain the weakest examples of delinquent psychology and contemporary school conditions, and they can largely be dismissed as attempts to capitalize on teen tensions portrayed in earlier films. The emphasis on sensationalism in these films did carry over from films featuring conflicts between students and teachers, but students did not fight one another like they had before. Youth cinema of the '90s was essentially devoid of such plots, and the fighting among students in '00s films was just as psychological as it was physical. Even the post-Columbine tales of school shootings and bullies (discussed in the next chapter) were often built on the anticipation of menace rather than the enactment of violence, as schools had become safer bastions of teenage protection.

An odd episode of this menace, and a stunning entry in the dwindling depictions of school delinquents during the '00s, was that of Kimberly (Evan Rachel Wood) in *Pretty Persuasion* (2005), the rare girl villain determined to hurt not just teachers or fellow students but almost everyone around her. Kimberly's motivation arises not from the pent-up anger or neglect of past delinquents, for she comes from privilege; rather, she has a desire to be even more elite, aspiring to gain media fame through an escalating series of evil acts. Her initial target is a smarmy English teacher whom she fraudulently accuses of sexual harassment, and she enlists two friends to promote the ruse with her. Roger Ebert wryly pointed out what Kimberly knows, "that sexual molestation, especially against attractive, articulate students in rich neighborhoods, is a publicity magnet."[27] So as the local news and authorities descend on her school in efforts to promote their own celebrity, Kimberly begins exploiting the exploiters, who trumpet the girls' victimization while enjoying so much attention for themselves.

The story proceeds with Kimberly revealing more of her despicable tactics, which include intimidating her friends, one of whom is an otherwise obedient Arab girl, and boldly lying to the press and the courts. To that end, the film builds downright contempt for Kimberly and those who fall prey to her, because her duplicities have no apparent boundaries. This is demonstrated when the sexually precocious fifteen-year-old seduces a female news reporter and blackmails her with a recording of the statutory rape, revealing her brashly sexist insensitivity by telling the lesbian, "I could never give up men. I like cock too much. But sometimes, I just need a woman's touch." The lingering quandary is that all this contempt is never alleviated by vindicating any of the characters—her Arab friend is so ashamed that she commits suicide—and Kimberly herself wallows in such pride at her own brutal power that her slight comeuppance at the end of the film is insincerely caustic. Granted, none of Kimberly's actions is categorically violent, making her delinquency perhaps the most vile kind, being so effective at destroying people without appearing to do so, and at evading punishment that may be reciprocal to her own cruelties. Removing the physical weapons of delinquents may only make them more sinister, for no metal detectors or security guards can protect against plain old-school malevolence.

RESISTING REBELS

The distinction between delinquents and rebels may seem superficial, given that every school delinquent is rebelling against something or someone. The difference for the rebel type in school films of the past generation is in the sophistication of the rebellion. Where fighting and crime are dramatic and dangerous forms of rebellion, the rebellions waged by some school kids are not so visible or even consequential. Thus, the rebel type is more heterogeneous, ranging from undisciplined revelers who have more interest in socializing than learning to neurotic youths who aggressively confront their own complex psychologies. Most youth rebellion in school films is founded on an angst generated by the social and/or physical tensions of being in school, but not all rebellions point in the same direction: some rebels become heroes, some become enigmas, and some remain troubled young adults. Rebels are best defined by what they do not want to do—conform—but if they are to make it in society (or school) they must find some means of surviving with their adamant individuality intact, which necessitates the sophistication of their techniques.

Rebels are often male but there have been a number of female rebels, in strikingly different roles (e.g., *The Breakfast Club* [1985], *Heathers* [1989], *Just Another Girl on the I.R.T.* [1993], *The Faculty* [1998], and *Tart* [2001]). Rebels also come from a rather wide class range, incorporating the toughness associated with low-income conditions—as in *Scent of a Woman* (1992),

Light It Up (1999), and *Pay It Forward* (2000) — or the demonstrative anger that seems to come from the ignorance of wealthy parents, as in *Heathers*, *Pump Up the Volume* (1990), and *Chasing Holden* (2003). Rebels do tend to be white (at least until *Light It Up*), which is interesting in comparison to the number of black and Latino delinquents who populate the school and delinquency subgenres after 1987. Certainly nonwhite students have plenty to rebel about, but Hollywood shows little interest in accommodating those voices of rebellion unless they are heard through crime on the streets and not in school classrooms. One enthusiastic anomaly arrived with *Kids in America* (2005), showcasing a mixed-race cast of students who unite in protest against the draconian policies of their school, and successfully quash the candidacy of their principal in her bid for superintendent.[28] Alas, even in the Obama era, nonwhite students remain rare as rebel characters, in or out of school.

Offering an ordered chronology of rebel students in films of the past generation is particularly difficult given the variety of roles. Even within ensemble casts — such as *Fame* (1980), *Fast Times at Ridgemont High*, and *The Breakfast Club* — the rebel students are dramatically different. In *Fame* the students' attitudes are fueled by their intense drives to succeed in the performing arts; the rebel of *Fast Times* is a generally harmless pothead surfer; and *The Breakfast Club* offers a reclusive "basket case" who seems to be on the verge of suicide — thus demonstrating that stereotyping rebels may be fruitless, a dilemma that would make most rebels proud. As this analysis shows, not only are rebels diverse and diffuse (they tend to not travel in gangs like many delinquents), but they face the losing proposition of either accepting a rebel identity that no one challenges or denying the rebel attitude that has ostracized them. In just a few instances, such as *The Chocolate War* (1988) and *Pump Up the Volume*, does a rebel character maintain his distinctive identity and become accepted for it.

One pre-1980 school rebel worth mentioning is Riff Randell (P. J. Soles) from *Rock 'n' Roll High School* (1979). The film is a fusion of past rock music rebellion movies and the classic fantasy of students taking over their school: Riff plays rock on her school's small radio station against the orders of the stuffy principal, and eventually the administration orders all of the school's rock music to be burned, resulting in Riff's friends — and her favorite band, the Ramones — blowing up the entire school. Unlike the shocking ending of *Over the Edge* from that same year, the climax of *Rock 'n' Roll High School* is set within a hyperbolic comedy, and the film is meant as a parody of the exploitative school films of the '50s and '60s (e.g., *High School Confidential*, *The Cool and the Crazy* [both 1958], and *Platinum High School* [1960]). Riff's ability to rally her peers around the power of rock music to declare that they'd rather have no school than a dull school was a refreshing (if still not serious) image of youth taking control of the educational environment, and that attitude would permeate many school films of the '80s, up to and particularly including *Pump Up the Volume* in 1990. Oddly enough, that spirit was completely truncated in the film's sequel, *Rock 'n' Roll High School Forever* (1991), which is evidence of the awkward shift that took place in school films from the late '70s to the early '90s, as screen students not only became less visible but largely lost their sense of purpose.

Two other rebels became archetypes of their generation, from dramatically different positions yet for equally intriguing reasons. Jeff Spicoli (Sean Penn) in *Fast Times* is an unlikely rebel because his rebellion is very casual and even pleasurable. Spicoli spends far more time catching waves and smoking pot than he does studying, with his only visible resistance coming from his history teacher. Otherwise, his schoolmates know Spicoli as a mellow stoner dude, radical for his disinterest in social acceptance and school achievement, yet no upholder of ideals (or even ideas). As the end credits tell us, Spicoli goes on to continue his wayward ways of surfing after graduation, so while he may indeed reject social conformity, the rejection is founded more on hedonism than anxiety.

Anxiety has become a lifestyle for Allison (Ally Sheedy) in *The Breakfast Club*, as she embodies the neurotic girl rebel of the late twentieth century. Allison wears black makeup and clothes (a "goth" look that would become more popular in the '90s) and doesn't speak to her detention-hall peers until the day is half over. Unlike rebels who wear their woe on their sleeve, Allison's problems demand to be unearthed, which she invites the others to do late in the film by dumping the contents of her very full bag on a couch and lying that she's a nymphomaniac. However, the students around her are too busy with themselves to be shocked much, and Allison's only solid quality is her nihilism: when another student wonders if they'll grow up to be like their parents, Allison delivers the memorable mantra, "When you grow up, your heart dies." Her supposed psychological tribulations are revealed to be a tactic directed at her parents' ignorance of her—and all the students in the film indicate that their parents are the roots of their torment. Allison's role, however, is compromised the most of any character when Claire (Molly Ringwald), the popular prom queen, convinces Allison to let her change her into a more common-looking girl. This wins Allison the attention of Andy (Emilio Estevez), the attractive wrestler, but it also superficially makes her a more acceptable member of the group, thereby diminishing her previous rebel status and providing simply another facade behind which she can hide her anxieties. As in virtually all films featuring psychologically disturbed young women—going back to *David and Lisa* (1962), *Last Summer* (1969), and *I Never Promised You a Rose Garden* (1977)— *The Breakfast Club* doesn't offer the means for its subject to overcome her troubles, and thus perhaps Allison is ironically the ideal rebel, destined to remain excluded even when she looks included.

Prep School Rebels

The prep school environment would seem particularly fertile for producing rebels, with its orderly traditions and high expectations that readily invite challenges. A number of youth films since 1980 have presented the rebel character in prep school, although many of them have shifted their focus away from actual school activities. In most cases, the prep school drama is set in the past to emphasize the rebellion of earlier youth resisting traditions that have become even more archaic from a contemporary perspective. This is the case in at least five examples: *Heaven Help Us* (1985) is about a group of Catholic school boys in the 1960s who continually find themselves vexed by the morally rigid priests running their school. More famously, *Dead Poets Society* (1989) portrayed the classic inspiring teacher role within a 1950s prep school where a group of boys is forever changed by the lessons of their English teacher. The first film is about modern notions of adolescent mischief running into old traditions of Catholic discipline, and the latter film focuses more on the ideals of discovering individuality and unlocking creative potential. The main student character in *Dead Poets* rebels by pursuing his interest in acting, and faces such stifling opposition from his strict father that he eventually kills himself, the ultimate act of passive-aggressive rebellion. *School Ties* (1992) is another prep school period film, about a Jewish football quarterback in the McCarthy-era '50s who stands up to the anti-Semitism he encounters at school after trying, unsuccessfully, to hide his ethnicity. *Outside Providence* (1999) tells the story of a free-spirited teen in the '70s whose father sends him to prep school in an effort to keep him away from turmoil. *All I Wanna Do* (2000), which was originally called *Strike* during its limited theatrical release in 1998, is about a group of prep school girls in 1963 resisting their school's conversion to co-ed status. This unfocused but enjoyable film failed to achieve the notoriety of similar films about boys, perhaps because the image of young female rebellion is not as compelling or appealing to young audiences, and such disinterest has also been common to the more prolific "tough girl" films, as described in the next chapter.[29]

Taps (1981) presents the most literal youth rebellion depicted in any film of the '80s: the cadets at a boys' military academy stage a takeover rather than allow the school to be closed. The narrative is a morality tale on themes of honor and duty, with the students defending their notion that the traditions of the school—training young men to become disciplined soldiers—are worth preserving over the changing times that have rendered their institution an anachronism. Brian (Timothy Hutton) is the highest-ranking cadet, and thus he organizes the students, coordinating their entrenchment and maneuvers with the high-strung David (Tom Cruise). Brian's roommate Alex (Sean Penn) has doubts about their success from the start, and even Brian is unsure of what they will achieve, but he knows its political import: "They want us to be good little boys now so we can fight some war for them in the future. Some war they'll decide on. We'd rather fight our own war right now." The cadets' initial demand is to communicate with their former headmaster, who unexpectedly dies, resulting in a growing number of students defecting to their parents, who are waiting outside the school's gates.

The story further changes course with the accidental shooting of a cadet by one of the adult soldiers who has been stationed nearby, a symbolic gesture of the warlike conditions that the students have brought on themselves. Brian, under the influence of Alex, resigns to declare their standoff a victory and to surrender, a decision that David cannot live with. David opens fire on the outside troops, drawing their fire in return, and as Brian tries to stop him, both are killed. *Taps* ultimately confirms what its characters so valiantly attempt to deny: that despite the aspirations to masculine pride upheld by the military, the manufacturing of soldiers has become a suspicious, and perhaps altogether unnecessary practice. Brian and the other cadets actually fail in their rebellion; in the process the school is destroyed, and they become the victims of the impractical ideals they sought to preserve.

The Chocolate War (1988) indicts the preparatory educational system's contradictions in a similar way to other prep school films, only suggesting that the rebels are lonely and forlorn. The story is set at a Catholic boy's school where Jerry (Ilan Mitchell-Smith) seems to want nothing more than to earn a place on the football team and get over the death of his mother. All of the students are coerced by a demanding teacher to volunteer for the school's annual chocolate sale, but the school's secret gang, the Vigils, gives Jerry the "order" to not sell the chocolates for a few days in an effort to irritate their teacher and force Jerry to be disobedient. After the Vigils nullify their order, however, Jerry continues his resistance to selling the candies,

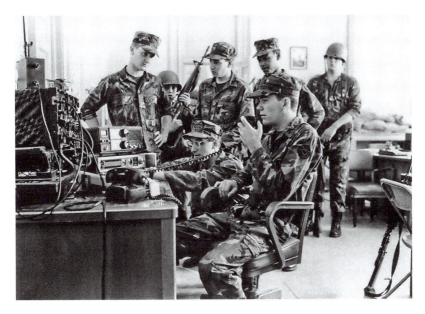

The teenage cadets in Taps *(1981), led by Sean Penn (far left) and Timothy Hutton (at radio), will not allow their military academy to be closed without a fight.*

even with the gang now pushing him to volunteer. Jerry's introspective sense of rebellion then is what begins to sway other students, who secretly join him in a passive strike against the chocolate sale, although the reasons for his fight are rather ambiguous compared to the motivations of school rebels in other films.

Jerry initially shows no clear resentment toward the Vigils until they begin physically harassing him to sell the chocolates, thereby making him realize how he has gained levels of attention and obstinacy that earn him a veiled respect among many of the students. The film concludes with a dramatic boxing match in which Jerry is set up to be beaten by a Vigil leader, only Jerry surprises them all by winning; after this, the defeated former leader is shown taking orders from a younger Vigil, with the continuation of prep school tyranny now complete. While Jerry's rebellion against the school's traditions—the candy sale and the Vigils—may appear unfulfilling, *The Chocolate War* offers a sympathetic parable about the defense of individuality without resorting to condescending sermonizing; as Hal Hinson said, it "is about the triumph of sensitive natures over the vulgar forces of power—it's kind of a revenge fantasy in which all the skinny kids who got kicked around by bullies at school get to replay the past and win."[30] Jerry, like most school rebels, remains the same confused kid at the end of the film, but the incidental testing of his identity by the school affords him a secure pride that many rebels do not achieve. This is the one instance in which a school itself is shown to actually *create* a rebel.

In *Rushmore* (1998), the suave fifteen-year-old Max (Jason Schwartzman) juggles an absurd amount of student activities at his private academy while becoming embroiled in a more pressing crush he develops on Ms. Cross (Olivia Williams), a first-grade teacher twice his age. Max is too hyperconfident and cocky to let his nerdish qualities get in his way, although his attraction to Ms. Cross throws him so badly that he is expelled from school for plotting to build an aquarium in an attempt to impress her. Max nonetheless reconstructs his overachieving identity at his new public school, showing that his drive and not his environment is his primary identifier, as the film proposes (through Max's fierce romantic competition with an older man who also desires Ms. Cross) that his creativity and ingratiating manner are rooted in his desperate longing to be treated like an adult. Yet where previous prep school rebels were motivated by sincere interests and admirable ambitions, Max is caddish and ultimately puerile, or as Kevin Courrier described him, "monotone and morose," adding, "We don't believe that this kid is dynamic enough to be writing numerous hit plays for the school, playing chess, and learning French and German on the side."[31] Indeed, Max is so focused on making a name and image for himself that his supposedly selfless efforts for his schools are exposed as egotistical, and his endless extracurricular activities betray his lack of interest in developing his academic abilities, and shield him from finding truly effective ways to channel his energies. He is a rebel with too many causes, none of which is consequential.

The film does introduce an interesting class issue, because Max attempts to hide his humble background through his private school pretense, but once he is expelled (and later drops out of school altogether) he comes to understand that his hard work ethic is more respectable than his previously pompous efforts to appear rich. Curiously, like *The Chocolate War*, *Rushmore* avoids markers that label its contemporary setting, relying more on '60s motifs and styles that hint at its spirit of assiduous determination, and reminding us that Max—who manages to win back favor from everyone by staging and playing the hero in a Vietnam War play—could pull off his sham revolt only in an era less cynical and disaffected than the '90s. Similarly, the academic traditions and ideals of prep schools themselves seem better suited to period nostalgia than current cinematic depictions of post-modern youth.

If not postmodern, the girls laboring to rebel against prep school customs in *The Smokers* (2000) and *Tart* (2001) can at least be called disaffected and detached, and all three of the lead characters in the Shakespearian adaptation *O* (2001) are caught in a triangle built on defying the social expectations of their elite academy. The protagonist in *Chasing Holden* (2003) clearly is quite affected, especially once he decides to leave his prep school to find J. D. Salinger, the reclusive author of the classic teen novel *The Catcher in the Rye*. And prep school rebellion continues to evolve, while simultaneously remaining tethered to archaic norms, in films like *Assassination of a High School President* (2008) and *Beware the Gonzo* (2010), each of which happens to feature an idealistic journalism student working for his school newspaper. *Assassination* was the more popular of the two, yet its star casting cannot save the film from its weak script and bitter tone.

The story takes place in another ambiguous period of the twentieth century, with students using 1980s computers while referring to their 1990s cell phones, taught in a building that looks like a 1950s warehouse and living in homes with 1970s decor. The ambitious reporter with the hackneyed name, Bobby Funke (Reece Thompson), is a sophomore who wants to attend a college journalism program for the summer, and to that end he is seeking his big break with an exposé about the theft of SAT tests. Using the school's woefully outdated broadsheet (which is implausibly supposed to be a daily), Bobby directs his suspicions at the student council—composed of four arrogant delinquents—who may indeed be behind the larceny. Yet Bobby soon comes to regret his implication of council president Paul (Patrick Taylor) in the crime, and moves on to the more likely culprit Marlon (Luke Grimes), who is assigned to take over for Paul. By this point, Bobby's energy is fully invested in solving the case, especially after he becomes romantically involved with Marlon's stepsister Francesca (Mischa Barton), and he is apparently determined to expose anyone in his school as the phonies they are.

Alas, the assassination of the title is a tease in both senses of the word, as when Paul stages a fake shooting of the council with a paintball gun, and the character assassinations of Marlon, Francesca, and Paul that Bobby enacts at the end of the film are entirely inane. It turns out that the council has been stealing tests for some time, in order to degrade the highest scores and induce the best students to take speed pills that Marlon supplies, yielding profits connected to Paul's illegal gambling debts, all of which is much too ludicrously contrived for anyone to really care. Thus, not only is Bobby's rebellion hollow, but his affection for Francesca is shattered when he learns she has been using him as a replacement for her former boyfriend Paul and a distraction from her ongoing consensual incest with Marlon. The film enjoys its snarky commentary on teen lechery so much that it vitiates the very passion Bobby feels in his quest to somehow flaunt the insincerity of these vile characters, and once again a prep school is shown to generate corruption in its members because its very nature is corrupt. At the same time, the film drops its obvious opportunity to comment on the moral hypocrisies of the Christian school, for the school itself is so mired in immorality that any Christian ideals are long since lost. With not a single inspirational teacher to guide the students and not a single student of integrity to foment meaningful change, the film fails to enlighten or even entertain. Prep schools, meanwhile, continue to paradoxically foster *and* stifle rebellion.

Lone Rebels

The disparity in representation among other school rebels is striking, demonstrating the diverse backgrounds and tactics of contemporary rebel types. For example, the rebellion of Bill and Ted (Keanu Reeves and Alex Winter) in their totally awesome odysseys, *Bill and Ted's Excellent Adventure* (1989) and *Bill and Ted's Bogus Journey* (1991), is not founded on any typical resistance to conformity; what characterizes these two heavy metal flunkies the most is their sheer lack of ambition, their utter revelry in middle-class suburban stupidity. The goofy plots of both films have the duo traveling through time, in the first film meeting important historical figures to gain their help with a school project, and in the second film going into the future to fortuitously save the world. The intended incongruity is that even sybaritic dolts like Bill and Ted become heroic (and wise) by maintaining their honor, however frivolous it may be. In that way, the two Bill and Ted movies offer a sustained fantasy for spoiled and laconic young men seeking identity through the least rebellious and laborious means possible.

Permanent Record, *Heathers*, and *Pump Up the Volume* appear to be more uniform depictions of high school rebellion, if only because their plots focus on otherwise well-to-do students who simply ask the usual adolescent questions and demand to be accepted on their own terms. Each of these films features teens committing suicide, and each depicts a rebel character trying to deal with his or her troubled surroundings, but each film approaches youth rebellion—and high school—from distinctly different perspectives. *Permanent Record* (1988) follows the confused friend of a suicide victim who becomes the conscience of his peer group, telling everyone that there's no sure way to find happiness as a teenager. The film is daring in that it leaves open the question that haunts these teens—why their friend committed suicide—but in lieu of providing answers it offers an artificial and temporary panacea for teen suicide: life is worth living when you have good friends and a good school. No one knows why their friend failed to recognize this, so he cannot be the martyr or rebel he might have been, and only students who actively fight their frustrations survive. High school itself must be survived, rebel characters tell us, not enjoyed.

Such is the message driven home by *Heathers* (1989) and *Pump Up the Volume* (1990), both of which star Christian Slater as a deviant out to expose various problems in his high school's social and academic systems. In the shamelessly sarcastic *Heathers*, Slater plays Jason Dean, aka "J.D." (his name is not far from its 1950s James Dean inspiration, and his initials remind us that he is indeed a juvenile delinquent), who becomes the boyfriend of Veronica (Winona Ryder) just as she is staging a revolt against "the most powerful clique in the school," of which she is a member along with a trio of her fellow rich friends who are all named Heather. In many ways, Veronica is the true rebel character of *Heathers*: she uses the popularity and attention she has gained from hanging out with the Heathers to forge her own confident identity, recognizing from the start that her friends are really conformist and superficial. Veronica actually talks to the school's outcast population, including J.D., whom she initially believes is a kindred spirit sharing her disdain for the school's social order, and whom she soon takes as her lover without question.[32] What Veronica does not anticipate in J.D. is the extreme to which he takes his disdain. Veronica and J.D. poison and kill one of the Heathers by devious chance, and later, in a prank that supposedly goes wrong, they end up fatally shooting two football players. (Veronica writes a line in her diary that would prove to be prophetically eerie by the late '90s: "My teen angst bullshit has a body count.") While Veronica is disturbed by this series of events, she agrees to cover up the crimes with J.D., disguising both as suicides and thereby marking suicide as a chic practice for the popular.

Heathers takes youth rebellion to its greatest extreme, climaxing in J.D.'s attempted bombing of the school, and Veronica's restoration of order by defusing the bomb and cornering J.D. into killing himself (although no typical popularity awaits him). Along the way, *Heathers* points accusations at all elements of the secondary educational system for why such strife exists among adolescents, placing responsibility on teachers and administrators who are sorely out of touch with their students, parents who are self-absorbed and as immature as their children, and the students themselves, who succumb too easily to the pressures of acceptance. J.D. is a failed rebel, one whose efforts to gain individuality lead to a psychotic inability to accept others, whereas Veronica finds a way to manifest her rebellion more successfully, disrupting the school's oppressive caste system and exposing, however briefly and unintentionally, the inability of high school to provide social acceptance at all.

Slater's performance in the more serious *Pump Up the Volume* reveals an honest appreciation for the desolation and confusion of teen rebellion. He plays Mark, a shy new kid at school who has trouble making friends but no problem communicating to his fellow students who listen to his clandestine low-band radio show every evening. During his shows, in which he calls himself Happy Harry Hard-On, Mark unleashes all manner of frustrations, be they sexual, parental, political, or simply musical. The world according to Mark has come to suck—"All the great themes have been turned into theme parks," he rants—and high school is only an enforced concentration of the commodification and sterilization that has disenfranchised young people. Mark does not realize the impact he has on the students at school until a fellow shy student calls in to ask if he should kill himself, and Mark, by not talking him out of it, becomes complicit in the suicide.

What began as Mark's attempt to alleviate his loneliness escalates into a call to arms among students: despite the suicide, other students take his advice to rebel, to "steal the air" and express themselves. Teachers and parents immediately try to quell the uprising. Authorities eventually apprehend Mark, but not before he publicly exposes the villainous actions of the school administration and goes live to inspire the students to form their own radio stations, a harbinger of the latent mass communication the Internet would soon provide for youth: "Listen, we're all worried, we're all in pain. That just comes with having eyes and with having ears. But just remember one thing: it can't get any worse, it can only get better. I mean high school is the bottom. Being a teenager sucks! But that's the point, *surviving* it is the whole point! Quitting is not going to make you strong, living will."

This character undoubtedly represents the most culturally commanding teen rebel in school films of the past generation. Mark's rebellion is not contained within his personal and familial environs, but rather it reaches out through its technologically sophisticated means and psychological simplicity: by describing to his listeners his most deeply suppressed emotions—fears, anxieties, perversities, fantasies, curiosities—Mark becomes a model for their liberation from the roles they endure on a daily basis. And the fact that he reaches so many of the students at school, from expelled delinquents to nerds to the popular types, prevails in contradiction to his continual anonymity. *Pump Up the Volume* supports a vision of teen independence and identity that is rare among all school films: it not only says that students should surrender their accepted images in order to end repression and oppression, but it demonstrates a practical method of achieving this supposed empowerment.

Pump Up the Volume also marks an interesting moment in the history of school films. After its premiere in August 1990, the only other notable school films in the next five years to even feature the contemporary white suburban population, which had been the staple of teen films through the '80s, were the farcical comedies *Buffy the Vampire Slayer* and *Encino Man* (both 1992). Perhaps the movie market had simply lost its demand for school films, but I propose that the level of political confrontation brought up by *Pump Up the Volume* essentially warned studios away from tackling further issues about the serious dilemmas facing contemporary students. Not only does *Pump Up the Volume* take a jab at the previously rebellious ideals of students in the '60s (who became the parents of the '80s), thereby further discomforting any adult audience, but the film features such potentially "controversial" youth issues—a pregnant student is expelled from school, a gay student comes out on the air, less intelligent students are exploited by the administration, wealthy students come to hate their parents' privilege—that any subsequent films would necessarily have to up the ante and confront even more sensitive and serious issues. Films about African American youth in the early '90s did do this, but outside the school setting and within the context (and generic traditions) of criminal action, offering compelling images of troubling youth conditions that were nonetheless centered on a small portion of the young population. Even the proud black protagonist of *Just Another Girl on the I.R.T.* was shown as a student in only a few scenes, and thus the film is discussed (in chapter 5) as a movie more about pregnancy than school rebellion.

Then in 1999 *Light It Up* finally did raise the stakes with its confrontation of contemporary conditions among a mixed-race group of school rebels, led by the pensive Lester (Usher Raymond), a black student who unexpectedly rallies a small group of his classmates in taking over their decrepit school to demand better conditions. Lincoln High is a prison vision of a school: dark, dank, and cold, and recently under the watch of an edgy cop who, in trying to detain the protesting Ziggy (Robert Ri'chard), is accidentally but not seriously shot. This is the match that lights Lester's incendiary anger at the school administration, and he and Ziggy take the wounded cop hostage in the school library with a group of variously dedicated peers, including Stephanie (Rosario Dawson), a smart Latina, and three school outcasts. Two of the students are white, yet racial tensions do not divide the group.[33] Rather, the broader conflict of racism is spoken by Lester's burning rage at the police who recently killed his unarmed father, a generational oppression which he screams at his cop hostage: "I'm sick and tired of being treated like a fucking criminal, of never being listened to." This frustration is exactly what fuels the efforts of the students to be heard, and perhaps not coincidentally, the students of color are the most vocal (the two whites may be token, but they may also be intended to diversify the students' cause, and to lighten the tone of black militancy).

The film's image of armed students in a library is eerily reminiscent of the confused cowards who killed their classmates at Columbine, only these teens are not hatemongers; they're simply trying to draw attention to their plight. That is exactly what they achieve by the end of the day, when media crews and the local community converge to watch Lincoln's fight for emancipation, as scores of police surround the barricaded building. The students realize they have a spotlight and, to their surprise, are asked by the authorities for a list of demands, giving them a false sense of confidence. They think that these adults might listen to them, and thus they begin making very reasonable requests for the school—better facilities, more books, the reinstatement of a fired teacher—which they convey most effectively by going online to news outlets. These rebels thus quickly find their causes, although they soon realize that none of the adults outside are actually interested in fulfilling these requests; they simply want to return to school to their own control. Mick LaSalle aptly points out a symptom of the film that explains essentially all youth rebellion: "The adults in power don't want to listen and don't want to know anything. They want to make assumptions and impose their authority."[34]

Despite the heavy media exposure, the students are unable to convince the authorities to meet their demands, and the group finds itself cornered in an attic where Ziggy has quite symbolically painted an urban homage to the Sistine Chapel. In this place of contemplation and artistry, the students realize they cannot escape, leading Lester to threaten killing the cop, a gesture that backfires, resulting in Ziggy being gunned down by police. The film's epilogue is quite telling, because all the students serve brief prison terms and get on with supposedly better lives, but only Lester and Stephanie go to college and retain their dedicated ways. In a solemn voice-over, Ziggy suggests that the protest was indeed successful (the school got its improvements), and that even two members of the "Lincoln Six" are enough to preserve their purpose. The rebels have thus achieved their respect, although again the film is careful to advocate for this respect to come from within, since no adult figures acknowledge their accomplishment. The very fact that students had to expose the terrible conditions of their own school, unlike the reforming teachers of earlier films who took matters into their own hands, indicates that rebellion has become even more solitary for youth. Given the lack of such rebels in school films since then, their rare actions thus appear even more courageous.

Rebels in school films since 1980 always think they have objectives, even if they can't articulate them, and this faith in individual purpose can make their self-dedication endearing to their elders, whose condescension and expectations are exactly what rebels require to know how *not* to be. The idea that teen discontent arises from predictable patterns in psychological and social development is endorsed in these films, as is the tradition of young people not going gently into adulthood. Among school characters, rebels fight the most emphatically for their understanding of self, even if sometimes their fights are directed more at themselves than at others, and they face the same inevitable realization that all teens must face: high school is just a proving ground for the greater challenges of adulthood. As long as young people continue to recognize these foreboding challenges, they will continue to resist them, and that dramatic conflict will permeate virtually all characterizations of high school students, even if relatively few of these roles offer the conflict *as* their character's identity.

THE LABOR OF BEING POPULAR

As with the struggle for identity, the struggle for high school popularity—in other words, maximum acceptance—is an enduring process. Perhaps incongruously, popularity among high school students is often determined by a fine combination of conformity *and* rebellion, as popular students must appear and act acceptable to a wide range of people while also staking out an individual identity that makes them special and desirable. Of course, physical attractiveness is a *sine qua non* for popular students, as is fashion sense, agreeable attitude, and normally wealth. Popular students find their acceptability bestowed on them at an early age—they are the most pretty and handsome, the most coordinated, the most endowed—and thus high school becomes an opportunity to demonstrate their privilege. In rare instances, popularity can be systematically learned and earned, usually through association with already popular students. Popularity and its concomitant acceptance are achieved only by a minority of fortunate students, who can hope that with popularity will come a lessening of the strife they would otherwise face in the social challenges of high school.

However, in many contemporary youth films, students who have embodied the popular image have been troubled by the tacit acceptability they otherwise relish, and those who have fought to become popular often find that the rewards of acceptance do not outweigh the costs of compromising one's individuality. Regardless of how effortless the lives of popular students seem, most school films focusing on popularity portray the great effort involved in maintaining it. Whereas high school is already a site of inconsistent endeavors, perhaps well-adjusted and widely liked students simply enjoying their educational experience would strike audiences as unrealistic, and thus school films depict the popular as having their own special problems, primarily related to the stress of supporting their fragile image.

Few high school films have been made about boys being popular for its own sake; at best, sports provide them with a different sense of popularity (as I discuss in the next section), so boys must earn popularity tactically. However, when boys do achieve popularity they are almost always confronted with contempt or controversy, because they tend to exploit their admiration in less subtle ways than do girls and thus more easily draw ire from the common kids, as with the title students of *John Tucker Must Die* (2006) and *Charlie Bartlett* (2007). Girls in high school films remain in the odd position of either being already popular or else denying their desire for popularity, resulting in a more sensitive attainment for girls than for boys.

The development of youth films focusing on popularity has been uneven over the past generation. Popularity is either studied within the context of other character types (after all, how do popular students know they are popular except by comparison?), as in *The Breakfast Club*, *Clueless*, and *Mean Girls*, or is used as a mere plot device to advance other aspects of the narrative, as in *Just One of the Guys* (1985), *Buffy the Vampire Slayer*, and *The Hot Chick* (2002). While the industry has not promoted popularity stories in any particular pattern, one consistency has persisted over time: popularity is always portrayed as a valuable commodity to those who have it.

Even popular boys labor at keeping or gaining popularity outside of sports, as in *Ferris Bueller's Day Off* (the title character enacts a clever mythology for himself that goes far beyond his school), *Encino Man* (in which two losers try to "create" a popular friend out of a caveman), and *The Brady Bunch Movie* (which flatly ridicules the elder brother's delusions of grandeur). One pedagogical yet predictable twist is offered in the somewhat surreal *Full of It* (2007), in which a boy's mystical wishes for popularity start to come true, leading to similar lessons that many girls learn when their popularity becomes too burdensome to bear. Aside from such erratic examples, girls still have a far more dominant relationship with popularity, and as the following review demonstrates, they have been shown cultivating similar notions of popularity over time, overcoming the changing environments and appearances that signify that popularity.

Popular Girls

The attainment of popularity for girls is highly complex. While maintaining a popular image takes considerable work—and as these films show, it induces considerable stress—it must nonetheless appear natural and effortless. Popular girls in school films are always pretty and well dressed and come from wealthy backgrounds; their parents' genetics and class status seem to ensure them a large measure of automatically acceptable features. Nonetheless, features alone are not enough to ensure popularity, for it must be agreed on in consensus by the school community, and as freely as it may be bestowed, popularity can be ruined by the slightest mishap or misunderstanding. Girls in most of these roles are at first devastated if their popularity is diminished (which is almost inevitable), yet come to learn that being popular was actually a greater liability than an asset.

Once again in *The Breakfast Club*, John Hughes provided an archetype for the popular American movie girl: Claire (Molly Ringwald). While the film actually limits the demonstration of Claire's popularity by confining her exposure, the four students who surround her are painfully aware of her highly visible image at the school, which they simultaneously acknowledge and detest. The wealthy Claire exhibits a snobbish attitude toward John and Brian, the working-class members of the group, and is initially only friendly with Andy, a jock made popular by his wrestling skills. However, as the students move through their therapeutic afternoon, Claire reveals two unexpected aspects of her personality: she is attracted to John's delinquency because she longs to be deviant herself, and despite her privilege, Claire is just as unhappy at home as the other students.

Claire openly protests the special treatment she receives for being popular, which keeps her restricted to the very expectations and standards of acceptance that have ensured her popularity. Claire clearly uses her attraction to John as her declaration of deviance *and* acceptability—at one point she even smokes pot with him and Brian, leading her to candidly comment, "I am so popular. Everybody loves me so much at this school." She ultimately preserves the privilege of her popularity in the face of her complaints against it, and when she hands John one of her diamond earrings at the end of the film, the gesture is as much an example of her pity on him as it is her appreciation for his reciprocal affection.[35] Claire, like the rest of these students, may also return to ignorant parents, but back at school on Monday she will still be the prom queen who does not need the rest of the school to understand her like these few students do, as the majority will still honor her superficial status. *The Breakfast Club* reminds us that while acceptability comes from privilege, there is no greater venue for popularity than the rarified milieu of high school.

Further sardonic commentary on high school popularity lies at the heart of *Heathers*. The three Heathers who rule over Westerberg High are pretty, porcelain, and prosperous, with a bitter sense of confidence: one of them looks down on the other students and proclaims, "They all want me as a friend or a fuck." The Heathers' invitation to Veronica to join their clique is contingent on her not only having the same traits but also rejecting her past affiliations with the "losers" of the school, something that she refuses to do. Veronica sees beneath the artificial acceptance that the Heathers have carved out for themselves, even though she initially wants to be a part of it: she tells J.D. early on that the Heathers are "like these people I work with and our job is being popular and shit." As Veronica gets involved with J.D. and loses interest in being inducted by the clique, the Heathers begin to realize that their popularity is threatened the moment that any guy doesn't want them and any girl doesn't want to be like them. At one point, after overweight outcast Martha "Dumptruck" (Carrie Lynn) attempts suicide, one Heather tells Veronica that the losers at school are only trying to imitate the deaths of the popular students.

Heathers thus uses its dark comedy to exploit the ignorance and conceit of these popular students, who achieve their greatest popularity through death; unlike Claire in *The Breakfast Club*, the Heathers never come to a profound realization of their tenuous position. In the end, Veronica offers the most critical commentary on school popularity through demonstrating the reincarnating nature of acceptance: even though she supposedly comes to freshly appreciate the losers of the school, when she tells a dejected Heather that she's the "new sheriff in town," Veronica is simply staking out her final achievement of the authority she desired in the first place. Of course, the

Clueless *(1995) celebrates the highs and lows of being popular for Cher (Alicia Silverstone, fourth from left): juggling a crush on a gay classmate (Justin Walker, far left), maintaining fashion sense with her best friend (Stacy Dash, third from left), transforming a misfit (Brittany Murphy, fourth from right), and falling in love with her stepbrother (Paul Rudd, far right).*

popularity that she now proposes—which would include the previous un-desirables of the school, as evidenced by Veronica's invitation to skip the prom with Martha—is a popularity that could not hold up under the con-ditions of contemporary teen acceptance, and the *possibility* of such popu-larity, while promising, is only a mirage itself.

Heathers turns the otherwise serious high school business of popularity into a farce, and that is exactly what films of the '90s continued to do with the roles of popular female school characters. *Buffy the Vampire Slayer* (1992), *Clueless* (1995), *Jawbreaker*, and *Election* (both 1999) all feature popular school girls who are at once dedicated to maintaining their accepted image but who struggle (or fail) to recognize the contradictions and abuses of their position. The films thereby become parodies of popularity, although *Clueless* and *Election* also offer the same wide social scope as *Heathers*.

Clueless is a more complex and more humorous examination of the same Southern California high school scene that is staked out in *Buffy*. The film is a loose adaptation of Jane Austen's *Emma*, in which Cher (Alicia Silverstone) attempts to use her good fortune to discover the supposed joys of selflessness. Cher and her friend Dionne (Stacey Dash, playing a rare popular African American character in a mixed-race school film) share more than their pop-singer names: both come from conspicuous wealth and maintain a high-profile elite image at school. "What matters to the kids in *Clueless*," Owen Gleiberman astutely claims, "is looking good and hanging out with other kids who are looking good."[36] Therefore, when they spot the less attractive but friendly Tai (Brittany Murphy), they decide that they can transform her frumpy image and make her an acceptable member of their clique. This process reveals the classic standards of school acceptability: first Cher and Dionne work on Tai's appearance, giving her a makeover and changing her wardrobe, and then they inculcate her to their ways of speaking and dealing with boys. While many at school notice Tai's changes, she nonetheless fails to gain the affection of her snobbish crush (he tells Cher that Tai is simply beneath his class status), which would have signified her attainment of equal popularity. Ultimately, Tai directs her attention to a more appreciating, if less popular, rebel skateboarder, thereby confirming the same statement on popularity that is preserved in virtually all school movies: acceptance is given, not earned.

Cher, on the other hand, does not question or concern herself with her own acceptability except when she doubts her ability to win favor with it. After receiving lower grades than she expected on her report card, she makes variously smarmy appeals to her teachers, all of whom agree to raise her grades except for her debate teacher. Upset but not undaunted by this, Cher softens him by matching him with a spinster teacher, and Cher eventually persuades him to raise all of his students' grades, thereby gaining further popularity for herself. Cher later encounters another lack of acceptance when she pursues a good-looking guy whom she quite slowly realizes is gay; more telling is Cher's eventual coupling with her college-aged stepbrother—which makes for a rather strange statement on the "safe" acceptability afforded by finding romance close to home. These relational conditions are all in contrast to Cher's confident social status, symbolized by her stylish clothes, high moral standards (she smokes pot only at parties and is waiting for the "right guy" to lose her virginity), and buoyant but refined personality. Popularity comes easily for Cher, but she must ultimately struggle to help others, finding her calling through raising money for a "beach relief"; her fulfillment in self-sacrifice rather than enjoying her usual constant consumption is an ironic discovery, which her narcissistic ways had previously concealed.

Three 1999 films also examined school popularity in farcical and often dark tones: the *Taming of the Shrew* adaptation *10 Things I Hate About You*, *Jawbreaker*, and *Election*. The first film is more of a romantic conflict based on family tensions, although it does examine numerous contemporary school issues: a popular girl's father won't let her date until her uptight firebrand sister also dates, setting in motion a morality play about contemporary teen acceptability in the age of desperate consumerism (the popular girl) and tough-girl chic (her feminist sister). The risible *Jawbreaker* is no less critical in its examinations, reaching for a *Heathers*-level satire in its portraits of popularity. After three girls accidentally kill one of their friends, they decide to cover up the death rather than face the possibility that their image at school could be tainted. This film also sets up an intriguing duality, showing that a popular girl who is focused on maintaining her status rather than being a responsible friend is ultimately cast out of social acceptance altogether, while the girl who endures shows that she can properly manage being attractive, smart, and caring, the qualities that mark *lasting* popularity.

In many ways, *Election* presents an even more menacing portrait of popularity, further showing the increasingly sophisticated characterizations of '90s school films. The story begins with Tracy Flick (Reese Witherspoon), an overambitious student who doesn't want popularity in the traditional sense — through acquiring elite friends — but through the more formal process of being elected student council president. As Cindy Fuchs wittily observed, Tracy is "the girl everyone admires and despises, the model student and scary Heather (without a posse, because who could hang with her? she's far too self-involved), the delectable Lolita and the don't-fuck-with-me chick."[37] Such qualities earn Tracy the scorn of her adviser Mr. McAllister (Matthew Broderick), who fears not only that her winning the election would wrack him (his love/hate feelings for her stem from a disastrous affair she had with his colleague), but that Tracy's implicit lust for power would just grow more monstrous if she won. She even exposes her own counterfeit naïveté: "You see, I believe in the voters. They understand that elections aren't just popularity contests." As McAllister tries to thwart her efforts, using his social savvy to encourage an athlete and a lesbian rebel to join the race, Tracy engages in her own unethical conduct, raising the stakes of the generally inconsequential election to a validation of all her dreams and desires.

Unlike most other screen girls, Tracy wages her war of acceptance in rather solitary terms, losing sight of the very people whose approval she needs to secure, for she has taken popularity to an altogether new level, where it is not simply granted by informal recognition but enforced through political structure, a critique of the '90s mania for litigious revisions of reality. The film mainly focuses on McAllister's blithe torment: not only does Tracy win the election but he loses his job after rigging the ballots, thereby showing how his own irrational immorality (wrought most poetically by his failed affair with his fired colleague's wife) arose in response to Tracy's dominating influence. The mildly gynophobic ending suggests that girls like Tracy, who is shown rising in the ranks of the federal government, do indeed carry their drive for acceptance to potentially destructive levels, and given the film's plausibility, this is a harrowing scenario compared to the popularity parodies that came before.

The state of popularity for female high school students, as films since the '90s tell us, has become increasingly suspect, despite the ongoing value placed on being popular. Characters like Cher and Tracy are popular in the face of their visibly selfish goals, and even *The Brady Bunch Movie* (1995) lampoons the older-sister popularity bestowed on Marcia (Christine Taylor), showing the oblivious enjoyment of her scholastic and familial acceptance. Popular girls are enterprising at earning social value but most have become intellectually or morally deficient because their acceptability usually comes without question, unlike the more troubled depictions of characters in *Just One of the Guys*, *The Breakfast Club*, *Can't Buy Me Love*, and *Confessions of a Teenage Drama Queen* (2004). Stephen Holden questioned this backlash against popular girls in late-'90s films like *Cruel Intentions* (1999) by pointing out that "the beautiful are the bad": "The underlying message seems to be that teenage girls, having finally been given license to swear like truck drivers and sleep with whomever they want, deserve to be punished. Being born beautiful means being born bad. Only ugly ducklings who have turned themselves into swans have a right to be happy."[38]

The recent harsh depiction of popular teenage girls may thus be a symptom of reactionary Hollywood sexism and broader fears of women's authority, permeating an array of films such as *The Faculty* and *Disturbing Behavior* (1998), *She's All That* and *Never Been Kissed* (1999), *Saved!* (2004), *Bad Girls from Valley High* (2005), *Bratz* (2007), and *Slap Her, She's French* (2002), with the most misogynist and xenophobic title outside of the horror subgenre. More sympathetic popular girls have certainly been less visible: *Can't Hardly Wait* and *Mean Girls* (2004) offer the only prominent examples since the mid-'90s.

The first *Mean Girls* movie was a devious proclamation of the supposed corruption inborn to popular girls. Cady (Lindsay Lohan) is new to her high school, and to schooling in general, after being educated at home since childhood. Thus, she is the perfect slate on which rules of social politics can be written, as she takes up with two slighted but shrewd friends—an apparently queer boy and girl—before falling under the spell of a clique duly called the Plastics. The clique and their queen, Regina (Rachel McAdams), take Cady into their trust, showing her the literal catalog of wrath they have collected about every girl around them, an odious tome they call the Burn Book. Through this device the film scrutinizes the "acutely hilarious sociology" of "nailing the servile malice of 15-year-old girls [and] the voodoo art of sparkly-eyed mindfuck," according to Jessica Winter.[39] Indeed, Cady soon finds herself subject to this malice when she develops a crush on Regina's ex-boyfriend, and thereafter a war ensues wherein Cady and her two displaced friends strategize to learn enough about the Plastics so that they can be publicly humbled. Yet in trying to disempower the popular poseurs, Cady slowly becomes just like them: while she makes a reckless play for Regina's ex she enlists another Plastic to divulge Regina's secrets, and even slanders her favorite teacher in foolhardy revenge for her failing grades. Cady tries to rationalize her immoral behavior by illogically excusing its appearance, explaining in voice-over, "I know it may look like I was being like a bitch, but that's only because I was acting like a bitch." When Regina turns over the Burn Book to the school principal, and effectively the entire student body, a scandal erupts not just about the existence of the book, but over the cruelty that all of the school's girls impose on one another.

Mean Girls is atypical in dramatizing its central conflict as a particularly gendered issue, with the girls working against one another, and themselves, in trying to achieve or maintain their beloved popularity. However, after Holden's anecdotal argument about girls in the late '90s, the quantitative research of Elizabeth Behm-Morawitz and Dana Mastro in 2008 revealed that female characters in teen movies are more likely to be portrayed as socially aggressive than male characters.[40] Boys are indeed part of the system, but unlike most movies about popular girls where boys' lust provides validation, their influence here is actually less potent than the backstabbing dishonesty wielded by other girls. Worth noting is that the film was based on one of the cautionary self-help books for parents of teenage girls in the

'oos, so there's no surprise that the Plastics' scandal prompts the principal
to round up all the girls for a mass purging of their guilt at treating one another so badly.[41] Yet the story itself offers its own dual deceit when Regina
appears to be killed, and this visual illusion gives way to a social delusion
in which Cady makes still another Hollywood plea to celebrate the beauty
of *all* girls—even if they are overweight, disabled, foreign, or suspected
of being queer—thereby condescending to all those girls who do not retain her more acceptable image.[42] The utopian coda of the story, in which
all the previously contentious clans of the school congregate in harmony,
compromises the film's idealism, as the less popular girls do not elevate
themselves to acceptability on their own terms; rather, the more popular
girls allow those beneath them to be accepted based on *their* interests.[43] This
hegemonic structure thrives in high school perhaps better than any other
human environment, where the commodity of power is intangible and is
determined by the arbitrary standards of those with authority.

Perchance by the mid-'90s Hollywood filmmakers simply found a way
to balance the appeal of popular girls with the evolving skepticism of teen
audiences, producing the many bold critiques of these characters that resulted in condemning depictions such as those in *Election, Jawbreaker, Saved!,*
and *Assassination of a High School President,* or even less partisan depictions as
in *Can't Hardly Wait, Mean Girls,* and *I Love You, Beth Cooper.* In more recent
years, the industry has largely avoided making distinctions about popular
girls altogether, a trend that may be due to the assumed sensitivities that
all girls face in contemporary culture. Popularity remains coveted and yet
rare, while its intricacies appear increasingly difficult to manage and simply
not worth the risk of compromising one's sense of self.

THE SENSITIVE ATHLETE

For many boys (and an increasing number of girls) in
American schools, athletic ability is a more important asset than intellect, looks, or wealth. Athletes are thus often stereotyped as being stupid
and preoccupied with their sport, because their abilities in that sport may
be their main means to success at school, or even later in life. Nonetheless, school movies featuring athletes in leading roles have, for the most
part, offered rather sensitive portraits of them as very ambitious, determined, and sometimes smart. Of course, any film can be difficult to sell
with an unappealing lead character, which may explain the added depth
that these films provide their leads, and the films that feature so-called

jocks in supporting roles often do resort to the common notion of athletes as dumb or mean (as in *Fast Times at Ridgemont High, Lucas, Heathers,
The Faculty, Can't Hardly Wait, Election, Napoleon Dynamite,* and *Dirty Deeds*
[2005]). Popular attraction may nonetheless favor these stereotypes, which
Jason Beck argued in his 2011 thesis: the highest-grossing teen films from
the '80s through the '00s (not necessarily focused on sports) portrayed male
athletes as more physically or verbally aggressive, and less intelligent, than
their peer counterparts.[44]

The sports movie, while a genre unto itself in terms of professional athletes, has been surprisingly tepid for school films since 1980, contrary to the
overwhelming popularity of school sports in American communities.[45] Of
the many movies since 1980 that have focused on an athlete and his or her
role in school, few were popular successes. In the '80s, athletes were usually
featured in common high school sports — football, basketball, wrestling —
while in the '90s, otherwise unsung school kids began to find pride in their
more daring mastery of martial arts, and more traditional sports remained
the subject of only a few films. The trend of the '90s was incredibly interesting given the nation's unwavering interest in traditional sports and the
number of sports films that focused on college students at the time, such
as *The Program* (1993), *Rudy* (1993), *Blue Chips* (1994), *The Sixth Man* (1997),
and *The Waterboy* (1998). Martial arts became increasingly popular, both as
a form of self-defense for youth and as a new holistic form of fitness in
the healthy '90s, but I still cannot explain the lack of otherwise traditional
teen jock movies through the decade.[46] The '00s most positively gave much
needed attention to female athletes after they had been all but invisible in
youth cinema, and further revealed an implicit racial and communal tension in male team sports.

The Emergence of Female Athletes

Remarkably, there have been extremely few films focusing
on female athletes, in school or out, despite the fact that in real life girls
participate in sports almost as much as boys. Before the '00s, girl athletes
were protagonists in only a handful of movies, including *Billie* (1965) and
The Bad News Bears (1976).[47] Presumably the industry and the culture were
simply too influenced by sexist attitudes that dismissed women as physically weak or fragile, or at least applied this thinking to girls in their school
years. Because many girls' sports that have been organized for schools have
been kept different and separate from boys' sports — girls are relegated to
softball, field hockey, and tennis while boys participate in baseball, football,

and wrestling—the dichotomy in perceptions between girls' and boys' athletic abilities endures, even though today women have formed professional leagues in football, basketball, soccer, and boxing.

The one prominent example of an athletically proficient girl in youth films between 1980 and 1999 is the eponymous *Next Karate Kid* (1994), the fourth in the *Karate Kid* series.[48] (The first three [1984, 1986, 1989] starred Ralph Macchio as a growing boy finding pride—and plenty of fights— outside the confines of his oppressive high school.) The female role in *The Next Karate Kid* was essentially a *raison d'être* for expanding the series, yet the "jock" in this case is not only excluded from any school sport, she doesn't even formally compete against her peers—something the male martial artists in the previous *Karate Kid* movies, as well as *Sidekicks* and *Only the Strong* (both 1993), are afforded. The film stars Hilary Swank as Julie, a distraught senior whose parents have died and who finds purpose and self-esteem through Mr. Miyagi (Noriyuki "Pat" Morita), a martial arts instructor who volunteers to babysit her for a few weeks. Julie initially wants nothing more than to get through her bizarre Boston school, where teachers are all but absent and a paramilitary gang of students called the Alpha Elite roam the halls to enact "discipline" under the excessively aggressive orders of Dugan (Michael Ironside), their drill sergeant instructor. Julie is stalked by Ned (Michael Cavalieri), the leader of the group, who implicitly threatens to rape her—that is, until she develops her martial arts skills and prepares to defend herself against him.

While the plot then becomes a classic tale of finding inner strength through athletic development, Julie's transformation from a sad brat to proud young lady is indicative of Hollywood's awkward handling of female muscle. Julie is despondent at school and home until Mr. Miyagi shows up and takes her away for her training; then, upon her return to school, Julie agrees to go to the prom with Eric (Chris Conrad), the one nice guy at school who's ever spoken to her, who's also an Alpha Elite defector. Mr. Miyagi buys Julie a sexy prom dress and approves of her date, but she and Eric are harassed at the prom by Ned and his gang, who lure the two into a climactic showdown. After the gang beats down Eric, Julie takes on Ned and soundly beats him *with her eyes closed*, until Dugan orders the rest of the gang to fight her, which they refuse to do. Mr. Miyagi then fights Dugan into submission, and Julie walks away with him and Eric. The film clearly demarcates traditional masculine roles while questioning Julie's capacity to maintain her tomboy image, even after she has become a better fighter than the guys. The fact that Julie comes to the rescue of her boyfriend may seem to be a progressive twist, but Miyagi is the ultimate

The Next Karate Kid *(1994) was groundbreaking in its depiction of an athletically proficient high school girl, played by Hilary Swank, who would go on to win two Oscars for other roles as physically strong characters.*

victor in the film, as his fighting skills have defeated the most evil character and his parenting skills have directed Julie out of her asexuality and toward a "healthy" heterosexuality. Even Julie's convincing fight with Ned is diminished by its location—on a dark pier—thereby excluding the school from witnessing her defeat of its fascist oppressors. The athlete role in films about boys is considerably different, as the male jock achieves victory and increased masculinity, usually with hundreds of people watching. *The Next Karate Kid* shows that while increased athletic ability cannot be equated to increased masculinity for girls, the obvious solution is to win the fight and a more pronounced "feminine" pride, at least as determined by males.

However, the new century yielded many films that offered positive changes in the roles of girl athletes, in terms of quantity and quality, as sexist attitudes at large continued to ease somewhat, and the Title IX legislation of 1972 that was intended to provide equal treatment for male and female students (in terms of participation, benefits, and discrimination) at last began to have a more visible effect on bringing some previously lacking equity to athletic programs. Three films in 2000 alone made inroads to changing girls' depictions in sports films, albeit each with some level of compromise. *Love and Basketball*, which focuses on the post-teen lives of two African American athletes who become romantically involved, at least features a section showing how the boyfriend and girlfriend develop their basketball skills in high school. In terms of girls' team athletics at school, *Bring It On* was something of a turning point: the plot revolves around competing cheerleaders who are the main attraction at school games (because the football team is so weak), and makes a clear statement that the girls' (and boys') routines are indeed athletic contests. More prominent and challenging to past norms was the independent film *Girlfight*, about a teenage female boxer who not only gains impressive fighting power as she redirects her frustrating home life into the ring, but who defeats her boyfriend in a title bout. The story is somewhat similar to *The Next Karate Kid*, with its featured athlete overcoming family trauma and finding a love interest in the course of developing her sporting agility, one whom she ultimately surpasses in brute skill as she learns to accept him in her private passions.

After this trio of girls' athletic films in 2000, the industry unaccountably dragged its feet in making further comparable stories (the soccer skills of the protagonist in *10 Things I Hate About You* [1999] are only present to suggest her insolence), although they did begin to finally appear with some consistency, if not more popularity, in the mid-'00s. Nonetheless, as with *Girlfight*, many of the contests had little connection to actual school sports. *Stick It* (2006) revolves around an elite gymnastics academy; *Her Best Move* (2007) and *16–Love* (2012) portray budding soccer and tennis stars, respectively, both in private clubs; *Whip It* (2009), while mildly with-it thanks to the presence of Oscar nominee Ellen Page, takes place in the dodgy world of roller derby; *Ice Castles* was remade from the 1978 original to coincide with the 2010 Winter Olympics, the tale of a small-town Iowa skater overcoming tragic blindness; and most improbably, two 2011 films boasted surfing, *Beautiful Wave* and *Soul Surfer*, the latter a famous story about a girl who rejoins competitive surfing after losing her arm in a shark attack.

A more popular skating film, *Ice Princess* (2005), also takes place outside of school, with its title portending that the protagonist becomes a regal figure skater, even though she is brilliant at physics and her entrée to the sport is through a science project. This promising depiction of a smart female athlete is unfortunately compromised by her preposterously fast rise to expertise in the sport and her rejection of a chance to attend Harvard so she can pursue the far more fanciful dream of a career as a professional skater. Other dream-chasing scenarios play out in films about girl athletes, with more justification than contemporaneous films about boy athletes, as if girls can better withstand the likely disappointment they will encounter, and do not suffer the same pressures as boys in facing the practicalities of adulthood. Girls' fears of loss are then fittingly unfounded, as volleyball players go on to win Olympic gold medals in *All You've Got* (2006), the title soccer players in *She's the Man* (2006) and *Gracie* (2007) compete on the boys' teams at their schools, and the maladroit girls' teams in three basketball movies of the late '00s all go on to play the "big championship game," the first two of which were based on true stories: *Believe in Me* (2006), *Tournament of Dreams* (2007), and *The Winning Season* (2009).

None of these movies was a notable success, and so Hollywood is still waiting to take the step of commonly showcasing teenage female athletes in established school sports like soccer and basketball; after all, martial arts, gymnastics, boxing, ice skating, roller derby, and surfing are uncommon in scholastic programs, and are much more within the province of private clubs and gyms. Despite the increasing number of girl athletes, they still remain strikingly scarce in youth cinema compared to real life, and their sports remain primarily outside the domain of publicly funded and locally supported schools. One possible benefit of this restriction in representation, however, may be that females in sports movies are generally less homogenous than males, making them more individualized characters. Further, because girl athletes are still less familiar than boys, their increasing success is viewed as more monumental and praiseworthy.

The Emotional Male Athlete

Issues around masculinity abound in films about male athletes, especially in leading roles. The jocks in ensemble casts have fewer opportunities to consider their virility, save a rare exception like Andy

(Emilio Estevez) in *The Breakfast Club*. The football hero in *Fast Times at Ridgemont High* vocalizes more grunts than words; the leading football stars of *Heathers* are nothing more than abusive and stupid (although their pronounced homophobia connects them with a jock conflict that was somewhat developed in earlier films); Cappie in *Lucas* is a football player of some integrity, yet he's also not very articulate and he bluntly lures Lucas's crush away from him. Even the basketball players of the nostalgic hit *Hoosiers* (1986) were secondary to the film's focus on its adult characters, which was also the case in *Reggie's Prayer* (1996), *He Got Game* (1998), *Remember the Titans* (2000), *The Slaughter Rule* (2002), *Friday Night Lights* (2004), and *Coach Carter* (2005), preserving the belief that boys need father figures to show them how to be men.

Evidence of a crisis in masculinity within jock roles of the '80s is provided by films addressing the very physical sport of wrestling, which was disproportionately prominent in youth films relative to its popularity in real life vis-à-vis football or basketball. Three teen wrestling characters were portrayed in 1984 and 1985, the first in *Hadley's Rebellion* (1984), about a churlish boy who goes to an uppity boarding school to pursue his wrestling ambitions. A more notable wrestling role that was also a dramatic exception to the usual jock ensemble typecasting is Andy in *The Breakfast Club*, a wrestler with classic jock traits—he has an enormous appetite and wears a muscle shirt—who is also at odds with his demanding father. Andy immediately comes to blows with John, who has disarmed Andy's assumed sense of control, and thus they vie for the most masculine role (Brian is eliminated due to his nerd status). Andy later reveals that he earned his detention by beating and wrapping tape around the butt of a smaller student, an act that he claims was inspired by his father's attitude to be a "fighter." Like the other students, Andy wears his identity (literally on his sleeve, in the form of a wrestling patch), and he desperately wants to break free of its confines, which he unveils when he says, "We're all pretty bizarre. Some of us are just better at hiding it, that's all." While his wrestling abilities secure him an equal physical position against the larger John, he realizes that his instilled antagonism comes from his father, and he expresses a vulnerability that would otherwise seem rare for his toughness. His most sensitive side is brought out by the distraught Allison, for whom he shows concern and to whom, after her transformation by Claire, he becomes attracted. Andy is the jock as conflicted masculinity, determined to maintain his brawn but desiring to explore his more emotional—if not intellectual—dimensions.

The third teen film of this brief period to feature a wrestler was *Vision Quest* (1985), in which Louden (Matthew Modine) is more concerned with his sport, and one particular competition, than his larger life goals. For Louden, defeating his wrestling rival—Shute (Frank Jasper), the best wrestler in the state—will secure his manhood, and in the course of training for the big match, Louden is able to confront his other obstacles: he cannot achieve success until he loses his virginity, which will chase away his tacit confusions about his sexuality, and he needs to secure a college athletic scholarship to rise above his low-income background. However, he needs to lose twenty-three pounds to qualify for Shute's weight class, and his brutal training regimen brings on nosebleeds and fainting spells that threaten to thwart his chances. Most of the film is then taken up by Louden simply fighting his own body, an appropriate metaphor for a young man who has no secure career or life ambitions, as he has to become as strong and lean as he possibly can to even compete against the best. (The homoerotic overtones of the film are rich, beginning with a gay man's pass at Louden, his own excessive attention to his thinning body, and his passionate desire to physically dominate a better-looking young man. The film both alleviates and enhances these tensions through Louden's daydreams of becoming a gynecologist so that he can "look inside women to discover the power they have over me," and through his eventual loss of virginity to a slightly older woman who's boarding at his house, while his greatest fulfillment still comes through his conquest of the slyly named Shute.)

The idea behind Louden's "vision quest" is to find some Emersonian self-reliance that will emerge from his dedication to perfection (he knows this through an English teacher), a lofty ideal to which David Edelstein responded, "This is the stuff of adolescent epics, and *Vision Quest* brims with portents and seizures and mystical tussles."[49] However, the film offers a notion of masculine fulfillment that is narrowly focused on sexual and physical achievement, a jock fantasy sustained through getting the girl and beating the guy. As in all school jock roles, the protagonist seems to have some greater potential lurking beneath his temporary goal of victory—and because Louden *is* victorious in the big fight his goal is fulfilled—but he is ultimately neither smart nor sensitive enough to understand the necessity of achieving larger goals, a supposedly noble quality of athletes that is just as limiting as the image of manhood to which Louden aspires.

The tough-but-vulnerable jock is also featured in two early-'80s football stories, *Choices* (1981), about a teenage football player denied a role on his team due to a hearing impairment, and the more popular *All the Right Moves* (1983). Like *Vision Quest*, *All the Right Moves* examines the search for manhood identity that is an inherent obligation of boys' varsity sports, and shows the serious meaning that sports represents to its protagonists, low-income students who are just looking for a way out, if not a way up. *All the Right Moves* offers a gritty realistic image of high school life: Stef (Tom Cruise) is a senior cornerback on his high school football team in Ampipe, Pennsylvania, a fictional steel town based on the many such real towns spread across Appalachia. Like so many other jocks, Stef just wants his sport to carry him away from the depressing conditions of his hometown, but unlike other jocks, Stef does not exploit his popularity at school, and he sees football not as a ticket to fame and fortune but as a way of securing a college scholarship so that he can be an engineer. Stef has a pretty girlfriend and a rather supportive family (his father and brother both work in the town's steel mill), and he's a good enough player to be recruited by colleges, but his coach turns on him after Stef criticizes his play calling, kicking him off the team, and for the second half of the film Stef has to confront the loss of his life goal. Rather than resort to the jock mythology that would have Stef coming back to the team to save the season, *All the Right Moves* chronicles the lost dreams of Stef's fellow athletes: one is arrested for robbery, another loses his scholarship after getting his girlfriend pregnant, and most are destined to work in the steel mills. The same fate seems to befall Stef, who gives up on football to work at the mill, until his coach miraculously invites him to his new job at Cal Poly, with its football scholarship and excellent engineering program.

While the film thus recuperates a happy ending, *All the Right Moves* is the first film of the '80s to portray the teen athlete as talented but troubled. The dour conditions of Ampipe and the heavy criticism that Stef receives from locals—high school football is very big in this town—do not compose the glorious and rewarding environment of athletic success that so many jocks long for. Stef struggles with his girlfriend, who resents his ambitions since she cannot get very far with her musical talents, and who reminds him that while his best friend is becoming a father Stef is still a virgin. Even though Stef is an otherwise effective and valuable player to his team, once his coach cans him Stef is left with nothing but his family's heritage, of which he is not proud. The ascent to manhood that Stef was following is thus threatened to collapse into a manhood to which everyone else succumbs. High school sports in this instance are shown to be humbling rites of passage for young men who may not excel at much beyond their practical skills, but *All the Right Moves* also reminds us that what is gained from the jock image—strength, pride, determination—may indeed be more valuable than excelling at any particular sport.

The jock image offered in three '80s school comedies is just superficially different. The famously shoddy *Teen Wolf* (1985) replaces a macho attitude about athletic achievement with its supernatural conflict of pubescent development: the hero, who occasionally turns into a werewolf and saves his high school basketball team, learns to give up his popularity and ferocity as a wolf, just so people can accept him for who he really is. *Wildcats* (1986) is more a study of a female coach, who tests the masculine mettle of a ragtag football team. As a portrait of school jocks, the film is skewed toward the most stereotypical extreme, that of inconsiderate chauvinist beasts needing to be tamed, even if the taming does reveal that the beasts are not so uncivilized or untalented after all. *Johnny Be Good* (1988) begins to consider the corruptive potential of school athletics before becoming yet another message movie about male pride. The title character is a high school football star who is such an outstanding quarterback—he can pass, run, *and* kick— that college recruiters throw themselves at him, at least until he gives up his inevitable fame to live a more humble life. The film is unremarkable except for its excesses (it was desperately re-edited to an R rating for video release, adding nude scenes in an attempt to lure a wider male audience) and the fact that it was the last well-known film about a white teen athlete in a traditional school sport until 1999. There is no clear correlation between this hiatus and the release of *Johnny Be Good*, although the film does show the straining of believability required to watch a film in which a contemporary teenager rejects his chance to have a life of glory for the sake of the athletic pride and social morality connected to the noble jock image.

Team sports became rarer in student athlete depictions in the '90s, and a definite martial arts trend emerged. Three of the more obscure sports films featured solo athletes: *Diving In* (1990) is the story of a high school diver who becomes derailed by a fear of heights, *Windrunner* (1994) portrays a student who enlists the help of legendary Native American athlete Jim Thorpe from beyond the grave so that he can come to terms with his inadequacies on the football field, and *The Break* (1995) is about a failing teen tennis player who won't give up his dreams of becoming a professional.

As for the martial arts films, because the majority of American high schools do not have an organized program or competition in martial arts, these narratives portray their jock characters outside the school mainstream. (In fact, martial arts as a theme in youth films proliferated in the '90s, as in *A Dangerous Place* [1994], *The Power Within* [1995], *Tiger Heart* [1996], *Tiger Street* [1998], and the *3 Ninjas* franchise [1992–1998].) In the case of Julie in *The Next Karate Kid*, a lonely girl takes on and defeats the closest thing her school has to a team, its gang of oppressive thugs. *Only the Strong* (1993) uses the same premise, except here the evil gang is composed of older drug lords who intimidate the students. Once again, an ex-soldier has become a teacher, training his previously "troubled" students in *capoeira*, a Brazilian martial art that looks like acrobatic break dancing, and through honing their skills the students not only become better fighters but begin to take pride in the craft of their fighting and come to respect one another as well as their school, banding together to clean up their campus. The film's de-emphasizing of the usual violence in '90s teen gang films—few guns are drawn, no bullets are fired, and little blood is shed—shows a perhaps unrealistic but still optimistic perspective on effectively channeling the energy of angry youth into an athletic context. *Sidekicks* (1993) is a more conservative invention in which an underdog student uses the inspiration of his hero, Chuck Norris, to overcome his intimidation by the school bully and win a karate competition. In all three cases, school is merely the backdrop for an external contest of martial arts waged off campus, and unlike previous jock roles, these characters have to literally fight to earn their sense of pride and achievement.

Like *Wildcats*, another portrait of a determined woman coach helming a boys' high school sports team is *Sunset Park* (1996), which, unlike most '90s depictions of African American jocks, is not entirely aligned with the delinquency subgenre, even though the teens' behavior is an issue. The novice white coach stands out within a virtually all-black urban high school setting, where the basketball team has become undisciplined and unruly, if only due to their greater problems off the court. The film has the opportunity to play like *Dangerous Minds*, with its white woman leader ultimately showing her charges that their game is simply a metaphor for their progress through life—she persuades them to take their closing championship loss as a step in a larger struggle—and within the context of darker depictions of youth in films by the mid-'90s, *Sunset Park* suggests that life will indeed be more difficult for these student athletes than the game they play.

Varsity Blues (1999) harked back to a mythical image of high school sports, and became the first successful film in this category in many years.[50] The story itself is not very unusual: a dominant football team led by an overbearing coach begins to break down under his abusive pressure, and when the smart second-string quarterback takes over for the injured starter, dissension brews among the ranks. The film absolutely owed some of its profits to heavy MTV marketing and the casting of *Dawson's Creek* star James Van Der Beek as Mox, the new quarterback who initially cares more about getting into college and getting out of his small Texas town than he does about the team. Mox's early indifference to his role is what gives the narrative a twist: he's a casual hero, ambivalent about the town's attention to the game and everyone's artificial acceptance of him, even if it has advantages. As Owen Gleiberman pointed out, "The emotional hook of *Varsity Blues* is the way it presents Mox caught between his own sane vision of athletic elation and the revved-up dreams of victory his new status as a hero forces him to confront."[51] As he gains popularity and authority, Mox encounters a deeper connection to his teammates—who all have their personal fears and frustrations—and a deeper suspicion of the coach, whose zeal for winning blinds him to the torture he inflicts on his players' young bodies.

The story proceeds through various episodes in which the team parties and plays ever-bigger games, even losing one as a result of a drinking binge the night before, and meanwhile the sensitive, loyal Mox consoles colleagues ranging from an obese lineman to a passed-over African American receiver. When the big game arrives, Mox confronts his coach's practice of injecting injured players with painkillers, leading to a dual showdown, first of the team's solidarity against their failed father figure, and then of their insecurities out on the field. He trumpets the mythology so common for these moments: "If we go out and half-ass it 'cause we're scared, then we'll always wonder if we were really good enough. But if we go out there and give it all we've got . . . that's heroic." Of course they win the championship, but Mox's closing voice-over places an unexpectedly sober tone on the moment, reminding viewers that this was only one great night in these young men's lives before they faced their less exciting adulthoods, yet keeping intact the symbolism of athletic victory signifying the ultimate masculine achievement.

What perhaps makes the '90s jock images most different from those of the '80s is their emphasis on athletic development, in that the accomplishment of athleticism comes as much from work (easy as it sometimes appears) as it does from natural bodily qualities and talents. While all of the serious portrayals of athletic characters in school films hinge on a discovery of self beyond physical skills, and the resolution of a dilemma in which the characters must rely on their integrity and pride as much as their bodies, the trend in portraying jock characters has shifted away from organized team sports and toward even more intensively personal conflicts. The overlooked 1998 drama *He Got Game* further illustrates this, with its depiction of a renowned basketball star who must choose which college he will attend, who is then thrown by an unexpected visit from his convict father. The film contains virtually no scenes of the teen in school and few more of him with the team (even the climax is a one-on-one contest with his father), for the focus here is on his sense of familial and moral obligation, showing how the hard work ethic his father instilled in him and the solid values his mother gave him have made him not just a great athlete but a righteous man.

Athletic depictions of boys in the '00s did not deviate much from established formulas, despite offering a slight increase in films about team sports over individual competitions, which did not prevent another unexpected wave of martial arts and wrestling films by the end of the decade: *The Forbidden Kingdom* and *The Sensei* (both 2008), *Legendary* and the remake of *The Karate Kid* (both 2010), and *Win Win* (2011). A possible explanation for the proliferation of these films is the evolving respect for the sport of mixed martial arts, which is specifically featured in *Never Back Down* (2008) as an alternative to undisciplined street fighting. And while not a school movie *per se*, *Pride* (2007) offered the unique true story of an inspirational adult athlete forming an African American swim team at a municipal recreation center in the 1970s.

Pride is proof that the indisputable foundation for teen team films in the '00s was *Remember the Titans* (2000), the true story of an African American coach who was hired in 1971 to lead a football program as it is integrating an all-white school with an all-black school. Coach Boone (Denzel Washington) is careful yet forceful in capably unifying the two teams through a summer training camp before the start of their first season together, trying to defuse the obvious racial tensions of the players while under the shadow of the antecedent white coach. His efforts are successful, at least with the team, which must continue to win successive games to convince the surrounding community that racial harmony could prevail off the gridiron. The significance of the racial divisions in this film would not become evident for another few years, although its use of the traditional slow ascent to a last-second play in the championship game tactically displays its parallel between fostering social accord and forming team spirit. Coach Boone and his players are indeed championed for their dedication to the sport and to one another, extending a hopeful solution to strife in the populace even though the athletes themselves are only catalysts for this loftier progress.

Friday Night Lights (2004) was based on a true story as well, although it is in many ways more noteworthy for its cinematic style than what it says about its characters. Shot primarily in close-ups with handheld cameras and edited with jerky jump cuts clearly inspired by the polarities of documentary and music videos, the film intends to bring both a sense of immediacy and the thrill of sports action to its account of a Texas community in 1988 that is symbiotic with its high school football team. The form accordingly carries the content, with the subdued script doing little to convey the characters' emotions while the drama remains almost en-

tirely contained in the games they play. The narrative is thereby obliged
to operate on symbolism: images of pensive players awaiting each game
and wondering about their future; props such as beer cans, championship
rings, and varsity jackets used to describe player's relationships; an unre-
lenting music track that replaces dialogue with mood. In this way the film
mimics the very anonymity that so many athletes embody in team sports,
for they remain simple components of a machine that generates an ongoing
codependence between the community and the players.

The most developed character in *Friday Night Lights* is again the coach
of the team, who has the familial and financial commitments to make his
position consequential. The highest concerns of the players off the field
are their older relatives, who offer them varying levels of guilt, pressure,
and vacillation, as their life goals are understandably abstracted into vague
possibilities of attending college, or at the least leaving their sleepy town.
These conditions would be enough to make these teenage boys fertile candidates for compelling messages about life beyond school, yet such messages are left for the flatly impassive conclusion, in which we learn via cap-
tions that the defeated senior players went on to undistinguished careers
in Texas outside of football—insurance, truck driving, criminal defense,
surveying—while the remaining team came back the following year to
win the state championship. This closing by way of text is a subtle nod to
the core concept of giving one's all in a game regardless of the outcome,
because even if these students had won the championship game, their fates
would have likely remained the same. And in that way, as with the ending
of *Remember the Titans*, the athletes' temporary endeavors at accomplishment undergo the same erasure, whether they win or lose. The anticipated
fame and fortune from their efforts, and their very identities, are consequently erased as well, off screen, with the community prevailing in its
anticipation for further seasons while the players are denied their dreams
forevermore.

Coach Carter (2005) was another movie based on a true story that focused on a high school team's adult leader, in this case an African American
basketball coach played by Samuel L. Jackson. Unlike *Friday Night Lights* and
many other films about school athletes, the coach in this case places an emphasis not only on physical exercise and practice drills but on personal attitude and academic performance, and reinforces the point that their chosen
sport will not advance them in life as much as the benefits of a good education. By 2005, this point was supplementary to the previous warnings of
high school basketball movies like *Sunset Park*, *Above the Rim*, *He Got Game*,
and the 1994 documentary *Hoop Dreams*, where the sport's ethos worked

to steer African American teens away from crime, a danger that does not threaten white athletes in films like *All the Right Moves, Johnny Be Good, Varsity Blues, Remember the Titans*, and *Friday Night Lights*. Even though all of these football movies do feature black athletes, they are aligned with communities that support the players, whereas the basketball movies assume the athletes' struggles take place within shifty neighborhoods that leave the teens deserted. To that end, the far more aggressive, expensive, and physically damaging sport of football serves far greater public needs than does the less elaborate sport of basketball, and teen movies in recent years have propagated a fundamentally racist division between these games.[52]

The heroic mythologies of football were also endemic to *Hometown Legend* (2002), *The Blind Side* (2009), and *Touchback* (2011), with their commemorations of players who rose to prominence. Predictably, lesser notoriety was gained by the basketball players in *Rebound* (2005), *Home of the Giants* (2007), and *Hurricane Season* (2009), and the films themselves garnered far less renown. This ongoing disparity intimates that the male school athlete can remain a compelling and emotional character in teen cinema, yet he faces a definite risk of irrelevance if his sport does not import significant fulfillment to its audience. This readily explains the predominance of pugilistic contests and tackle football, with their bellicose gravity, compared to otherwise respectable school sports like basketball, baseball, and the many modes of track and field. The resolution of personal conflicts for athletes in youth movies has been of distinct interest in contrast to their formal contests for supremacy, yet increasingly these movies have made the satisfaction of group interests the dominant concern, to the detriment of students who have a sincere investment in achieving victory for themselves.

CONCLUSION

The school subgenre is a helpful starting point for the analysis of youth images in cinema: it provides the character codes with which most youth films portray their protagonists, and it demonstrates the classic conflicts that adolescents face in their ascent to adulthood. Because school is signified as such an official environment, unlike more variable teen settings such as home, hangouts, and places of employment, it offers to filmmakers a consolidated location against which to dramatize youth, and more so, it provides for youth a certified directory of accomplishments (popularity, grades, trophies, relationships) and thus of identity.

Unlike the other subgenres that follow in this study, the school sub-genre is virtually dependent on the sustained characterization of certain youth types to ensure the recognition of its styles and narrative interests. Other subgenres, while also employing these types, are more dependent on narrative devices themselves—obstacles to romance, techniques of terror, means of rebellion—to provide their senses of style and motivation. Youth in school films tend to declare and/or resist their identification through character stereotypes, yet remain identified accordingly. Youth in other subgenres are either less concerned with identity issues or, most often, find themselves struggling for identity more mightily within the context of such arbitrary and inconsistent experiences as love, fear, and delinquency.

Three

DELINQUENT YOUTH
Having Fun, on the Loose, in Trouble

Nobody puts Baby in a corner.
JOHNNY (PATRICK SWAYZE) REFERRING TO
HIS DANCE PARTNER IN *DIRTY DANCING* (1987)

*If you ever put your hands on me again, I'm gonna snip your
little nuts off with my toenail clippers!*
RITA (JENNY LEWIS) TO HER SEXUALLY HARASSING
TEACHER IN *FOXFIRE* (1996)

*No, bulls would gum it. They'd flash their dusty standards at the
wide-eyes and probably find some yegg to pin, probably even the
right one. But they'd trample the tracks and scare the real players
back into their holes, and if we're doing this I want the whole
story. No cops, not for a bit.*
BRENDAN (JOSEPH GORDON-LEVITT) EXPLAINING
HIS PLAN IN *BRICK* (2005)

Young people would seem to be natural candidates for
trouble, from mischievous misadventures brought on by playful curiosities to criminal acts induced by more violent and angry drives. Indeed,
the range of plots in films dealing with youth in trouble is quite wide.
Sometimes teens wander into their delinquency with little effort or intent,
turning a day off from school or a night of babysitting into a series of unexpected (and usually humorous) exploits; more often, however, teens approach their delinquency quite deliberately, rebelling against uncaring or
uninformed parents, against a misdirected society, or as demonstrated in
the previous chapter, against the educational system. Rebellion is thus the
usual inspiration for teens in these films, whether on a large or small scale,

and regardless of intent. Some teens are clearly out to just have fun while others envision themselves as crusaders bent on upheaval.

Teens in real life inevitably find themselves acting in deviant ways because they are beginning to learn the social codes of proper behavior and are learning how to test those codes. This is why delinquency covers such a broad spectrum of behaviors: what in one cultural setting or period is considered transgressive (say skipping school) may be more acceptable in other settings, in which teens would have to commit rather dramatic offenses (such as violent crimes) in order to demonstrate their deviance from the norm. Not all teens become deviant simply as a means of testing their social acceptability — the etiology of delinquency runs to class and race issues, family dynamics, genetics and psychology, and political conditions. Yet all teens find themselves accounting for their delinquent behaviors through the very systems that determine exactly what is delinquent: the family, school, society, and law. Teens' struggle to gain a sense of self and independence is most often wrought through their challenging of these systems and institutions, and thus delinquency becomes the means through which many teens not only achieve an identity (or at least a reputation), but a sense of who they are in relation to the structured world around them and the adult life ahead of them.

Films about delinquent teens thus make for great drama, and the subgenre of delinquent youth films has been quite voluminous for generations. Further, due to the diversity of deviant styles and themes in these films, the subgenre is perhaps the most broadly defined. Here the generic trends that are visible in each of the other youth subgenres (e.g., the cyclical prominence of school films, the rise and fall of the slasher cycle) are more difficult to discern. The commonalities among films about runaway teens, for instance, testify to the distinct sorrows of their protagonists, but from such different perspectives and within such different settings as to pull asunder any coherent argument about their chronological development, or even their influence on one another. More than any other chapter, this one is founded on an examination of youth representation through the characters' actions in the films, relying less on generic trends and thematic motifs. In that way, this chapter demonstrates the range of youth delinquency, but more significantly, the general inability (or lack of interest) of the film industry to codify any particular delinquent style for any length of time. Perhaps this is indicative of the ambidexterity and revolutionary nature of youth delinquency itself.

CONTEXTS AND TRENDS
IN THE SUBGENRE

Despite their diversity of delinquency styles, the number of teen delinquency films from 1980 to 2013 followed certain production patterns. Teen delinquency films became quite prolific in the mid-'80s, with more than fifteen in 1986, and then slowly declined until 1991. However, the uprising of African American crime films that year seemed to revive interest in youth delinquency dramas, even though other youth subgenres were still in decline at the time. Hollywood produced at least a dozen teen delinquency films each year from 1991 to 1996, raising their levels of violence and social consciousness. Then, in the late '90s, the youth delinquency film again declined in production, at the same time that increasing media attention was paid to high-profile school shootings by youth (when in fact the overall crime rate among teens was declining).[1] By the 'oos, juvenile delinquency was primarily relegated to independent companies that were still willing to experiment with the form and to take the risk of broaching the increasingly controversial subject.

Within the range of youth delinquency, various acts of rebellion became more and less notorious. For example, films in which dancing was portrayed as deviant and energizing essentially vanished in the '90s, after '80s dance films had so often attempted to connect themselves with perceived musical trends of the time: rap and hip-hop in *Beat Street* (1984) and *Fast Forward* (1985), or Latin routines in *Rooftops* (1989), *Lambada* (1990) and *The Forbidden Dance* (1990). Actually, the week-long phenomenon of "lambada" movies in early 1990 signaled the end of dance as a form of delinquency in teen films for many years. Likewise, films about teens frolicking at the beach—which in the '60s became a conspicuous alternative to the relatively troubling delinquent dramas about the suburban youth population—also lost their popularity after the '80s.

Meanwhile, other images of rebellious youth became more distinguished in the last two decades. Stories about wayward youth learning valuable lessons about themselves through their relationships with animals and/or nature, such as *Free Willy* (1993) and *Fly Away Home* (1996), were rather popular in the '90s after being little seen in the '80s. Another interesting pattern can be found in films depicting hardened teenage girls who rebel against their schools, parents, and/or society: many depictions in the '80s featured a lone troubled girl (*Angel*, 1984), whereas in the '90s these girls were usually operating in pairs or small groups (*Foxfire*, 1996), and in the '00s tough girl characters tended to act alone again (*Teeth*, 2007). Perhaps the most unsettling trend in delinquent depictions arrived after the Columbine murders in 1999, when films like *Home Room* (2002) and *Elephant* (2003) depicted disturbing mass murders of students by students.

Overall, teen delinquency depictions over the course of the twentieth century became increasingly confrontational about the source of their protagonists' rebellion, whether it was the typically unsatisfying home life brought on by inadequate parents or the more complex operations of social institutions. The earliest youth delinquency films—such as those featuring the "Dead End Kids" of the late '30s and the "East Side Kids" of the early '40s, and then the teen rebellion films of the '50s such as *The Wild One*, *Rebel Without a Cause*, and *Blackboard Jungle*—examined these sources as well, albeit under the guise of traditional moral values, which these films were just beginning to question on larger social and historical terms. The questioning of teen rebellion in films toward the end of the century was comparatively explicit, and often sided with the youth who ultimately wanted to achieve success and independence but simply chose impractical—not necessarily "wrong"—ways to proceed. At the turn of the millennium, this approach subsided as more films left the causes of youth delinquency ambiguous and problematized the sympathy for offenders so often promoted in the past.

In the case of youth films in which the rebellion is more subtle or less deliberate, the narratives do not explore the reasons behind the protagonists' activities as much as they *celebrate* rebellion, and this is a charge that can be levied against many of the "serious" films as well. As in the larger action/adventure genre, many youth delinquency films find their appeal in the raw exhilaration of danger and daring, and any excessive examination of the characters' motives within the film could distract from that essentially simplified sense of thrill-chasing and pleasure-seeking. Youth quite often think of themselves as fearless, if not invincible, and that notion of confidence and irresponsibility finds an audience in youth who long for creative means to express their courage and loose their frustration, and in adults who fondly remember (and may still relate to) those impulses. This dual attraction of delinquency to young and old was exceedingly demonstrated in five adult–child age-switching fantasies released between 1987 and 1989 (*Big* [1988] being the most popular), and was sustained as a theme in films of the '90s that featured problem parents (as in *House Arrest*, 1996), where the rebellious teens of the last generation have become the reluctantly responsible parents of the current generation.[2] The age-switching fantasy would again emerge as a theme in three popular teen films of the '00s: *Freaky Friday* (2003), *13 Going on 30* (2004), and *17 Again* (2009). Being bad has often felt good for a long lineage of youth.

DELINQUENT STYLES

As with all other youth film subgenres, a definite amount of overlap exists in the classification of the youth delinquency film and other subgenres. Chapter 2 looked at the image of the delinquent within the school setting, although most delinquency in youth films occurs outside of school. Where the strange teen behaviors in the horror subgenre could be labeled delinquent, not to mention the unleashed carnality of sexually curious teens, the delinquency film is largely concerned with the act of delinquency as defiance and empowerment within a relatively broad cultural context, a concern that these other subgenres generally eschew. Some delinquency films do offer the fanciful wish fulfillment of these other subgenres, but most are deliberate confrontations with troubling (and hence provocative) youth issues.

There is a huge range of delinquent styles that I cannot possibly cover within the scope of this book, so I will summarize them before focusing on particular delinquency themes. The fact that we can evaluate any individual form of delinquency *as* a style, one among many that youth may choose in order to adopt a specific attitude, and one that can then form a subculture, as Dick Hebdige famously argued with punk, reveals the certain actions youth utilize and follow in order to rebel.[3] Most youth do not gravitate toward actual criminal violence in pursuing rebellion, yet rather merely employ unorthodox forms of dress, speech, or music to achieve individuality, even if that often paradoxically involves conformity with a group, which in recent years has been more easily promoted through the communicative reach of the Internet, whereby youth share their stories and styles of misbehavior. There is thus a spectrum of deviance within juvenile delinquency, from subtle and often unintended acts of idiosyncrasy to more deliberate statements of defiance to outright determined acts of abuse and hatred.[4]

On the least deviant end of the spectrum are "harmless mischief" films, in which youth rebellion is represented by wild parties, escaping parental control, and skipping school. Such films deal humorously with the more serious social and moral issues that are addressed in many other youth delinquency films—here the emphasis is on fun derived from ultimately

House Party *(1990) famously depicted African American youth enjoying some level of deviance without the criminality common to many other films of the time. (Autographed image of Chris "Kid" Reid, author's collection.)*

safe teenage transgressions. Among numerous samples, those featuring boys were most popular in the '80 and '90s: *The Hollywood Knights* (1980), *The Wild Life* (1984), *Ferris Bueller's Day Off* (1986), *House Party* (1990), *Tom and Huck* (1995), *Good Burger* (1997), and *Detroit Rock City* (1999). Girls won their rights to mischief more often in the '00s: *Big Fat Liar* (2002), *The Lizzie McGuire Movie* (2003), *New York Minute* (2004), and *Sleepover* (2004).[5] Intimating that the level of mischief needed to satisfy contemporary youth has gone beyond harmless, when the boys and girls in *Project X* (2012) have the "ultimate" high school party, the results are house destruction and multiple criminal charges.

While I do explicate the "deviant dancing" film, there is another category of youth delinquency that hinges on the representative rebellion of speed, achieved through fast cars, biking, skating, or skateboarding; respective varieties include low-budget fare such as *License to Drive* (1988), *Rad* (1986), *Airborne* (1993), and *Gleaming the Cube* (1989). In the '00s studios employed more expensive productions and familiar stories in *Biker Boyz* (2003), *Lords of Dogtown* (2005), *The Fast and the Furious: Tokyo Drift* (2006), and *Speed Racer* (2008). These films support the common independence of teens mastering their "hot wheels," although the delinquency committed by youth with such vehicles is normally less problematic than that represented by fighting or guns, and the accent in these films is on the sense of accomplishment and adventure resulting from proficient use of the wheels featured.[6]

I also examine films that highlight the encounters of delinquents with animals and nature, but have here jettisoned the rather extinct "fun in the sun" category, which also has a counterpart in the "snow and ski" movie. Beach movies were a veritable staple of youth cinema in the '60s, gathering frolicking teens for sexual sublimation in the surf, but the few '80s films that took up the tradition—such as *Beach House* (1982), *Surf II* (1984), and *Private Resort* (1985)—were not very distinct from other teen sex comedies of the time, nor were their snowbound counterparts, such as *Hot Dog . . . The Movie* (1984) and *Snowballing* (1985). Less lascivious and little-seen outings such as *Aloha Summer* (1988), *An American Summer* (1991), *Phat Beach* (1996), *Psycho Beach Party* (2000), and *Surf School* (2006) further confirmed the erosion of teen beach movies. The animal and nature films, by contrast, deal with more compelling and revealing "primal" issues.

Delinquency is often addressed within a gendered context as a masculine phenomenon, and unquestionably far more boys than girls are featured committing crimes or disturbing the peace. Yet girls can be found disturbing the perception that they are obedient and deferential to male expectations in a certain category of characters I study under the label "tough girls," roles that have emerged in the wake of more assertive feminism after the '70s. Films about tough girls are not exploitation movies catering to male fantasies of women being punished, but are rather demonstrative challenges to dominant norms, previously established in childhood, with young women taking authority and demanding respect through often angry acts.

At the moral midpoint of the youth delinquency subgenre is a range of rather disconnected films that deal with teens' social struggles, in which the setting and style of the movies appear generically arbitrary and the narratives' depiction of youth confronting social oppression becomes the focus of the films. This category would include stories about groups of kids dealing with financial and racial politics in *Suburbia* (1984), *War Party* (1989), *Black and White* (2000), *ATL* (2006), and *Yelling to the Sky* (2011), as well as loners confronting their communal responsibilities in *Amazing Grace and Chuck* (1987), *American Heart* (1993), *American History X* (1998), *The Battle of Shaker Heights* (2003), and *Paranoid Park* (2007). These films raise particular and undeniable issues about the nature of youth rebellion through a wide range of plots, each of which is thematically dissimilar from other styles of youth delinquency. Such a categorical designation points to the methodological difficulty in defining coherent and consistent classifications within a subgenre, for these films clearly have common interests yet few distinctive generic traits.

More films locate the roots of youth delinquency in specific causes, and construct their narratives accordingly. Thus we also have other categories of movies about:

- Problem parents: *Ordinary People* (1980), *At Close Range* (1986), *The Day My Parents Ran Away* (1993), *American Beauty* (1999), *White Oleander* (2002), *The Squid and the Whale* (2005), *A Better Life* (2011);
- Running away: *I Am the Cheese* (1983), *Fire with Fire* (1986), *Where the Day Takes You* (1992), *Niagara, Niagara* (1998), *Catch Me If You Can* (2002), *The Secret Life of Bees* (2008), *Dirty Girl* (2010);
- Fighting and gangs: *Bad Boys* (1983), *China Girl* (1987), *Gladiator* (1992), *Tiger Heart* (1996), *Six Ways to Sunday* (1999), *Havoc* (2005), *The Invisible* (2007), *Dragonball: Evolution* (2009);[7]
- Drug abuse: *Foxes* (1980), *Less Than Zero* (1987), *Twin Peaks: Fire Walk with Me* (1992), *The Doom Generation* (1996), *Go* (1999), *Traffic* (2000), *Thirteen* (2003), *Charlie Bartlett* (2007), *The Wackness* (2008), *Twelve* (2010).[8]

As in the "social struggle" category, these depictions are quite revealing but each can be unfortunately incoherent as a study group. For instance, runaways have such diverse reasons for their flights and pursue them through such a wide range of means that they have little in common, and in films addressing youth gangs, there are not only an extensive array of crimes committed, but the juvenile offenders are alternately vindictive, repentant, gullible, and/or dangerous. All films involving teen crimes show the practice to be ostensibly repellent, of course, but as I will demonstrate in my concluding focus on crime films before and after 1999, when the Columbine massacre radically altered the perception of juvenile delinquency, some of these films provide a latent stimulation with their moral lessons.

DEVIANT DANCING

There has long been a connection between youthful expressions of energetic passion and dance, particularly dance inspired by certain musical trends. With the emergence of rock and roll music in the 1950s, American youth began dancing more forcefully and, to the chagrin of moral custodians of the time, with more sexualized movements. (The term "rock and roll" itself was a euphemism for intercourse.) Various dance trends appeared, such as the Twist and the Shag, and an assortment of musical styles—calypso, tango, cha-cha—were borrowed to encourage new dances. Youth used dance not only as a release, but to distinguish their culture from that of their parents; with its increasingly controversial nature (rock music celebrated sexuality but also implicitly challenged the status quo by promoting kinetic outbursts by teens, crossing race, class, and gender lines), youth saw that their styles of dance represented forms of rebellion.

The intersections of youthful sexuality and rebellion in dance made the medium appealing to young movie audiences, as witnessed by the dozens of dance-and-music-inspired films after WWII—including *Rock Around the Clock* (1956), most Elvis Presley movies in the '50s and '60s, the rise of the rock concert documentary, and the advent of disco in *Saturday Night Fever* (1977), which was still detectable in *Fame* (1980). Similar dance films remained popular in the '80s, through rap and hip-hop music and break dancing, Latin-influenced couples dancing, and more conventional rock and roll. Yet after the last deliberate attempt by the film industry to introduce to youth a "new" form of Latin dance, the lambada, virtually no other youth dance films appeared. *Lambada* and *The Forbidden Dance* (both 1990) were box office bombs, and the dance itself did not catch on. Hollywood thereafter dodged the potentially lingering allure of dance in youth films, despite the continued popularity of various musical styles within youth cultures. Perhaps the emphasis on particular dance styles has waned, yet given the relative safeness of dancing as a form of sexual and creative expression, one can only wonder why the movie industry has not found more ways to capitalize on recent dance-and-music trends.

Break dancing became popular in the mid-'80s, even though its origins date back to the beginning of the century, if not earlier. A number of break dancing films appeared with the trend, most of which featured performers in their early twenties, while the dance was reaching widespread practice among teens and pre-teens, especially urban African Americans. Movies featuring primarily adults such as *Breakin'* (1984), *Breakin' 2: Electric Boogaloo* (1985), *Body Rock* (1984), *Breakin' Through* (1984), and *Krush Groove* (1985) appeared alongside films featuring teenagers break dancing like *Wild Style* (1983), *Beat Street* (1984), *Delivery Boys* (1984), and *Fast Forward* (1985). Then by 1986, no further teen break dancing films appeared, and the trend, at least in movies, was over. All of these films used break dancing in what were otherwise rather traditional musical narratives—dancers need to put on a show to raise community funds and spirits, and young people hope to achieve fame through their dance skills. Anne Billson rather cynically called these films "bopsicals," about "hip-hoppers [who] bopped their way out of the ghetto on their heads and elbows, pausing in mid-bop to wrestle with their consciences and pick up a chick or two," although the films were recognizably intended to highlight the distinctive qualities of breaking as a dance form and rap and hip-hop as musical forms.[9]

Beat Street proved to be a popular archetype with its story of Kenny (Guy Davis), a black Bronx teenager who is an aspiring mix disc jockey. Along with his friends Chollie (Leon Grant) and Ramon (Jon Chardiet), a Latino graffiti artist, the three go to parties and discos where they watch music/dance exhibitions, including those of Kenny's inventive younger brother Lee (Robert Taylor). The film makes clear that these contests have become safer alternatives to the street violence that marked youth competitions years before, which led to the murder of Kenny and Lee's older brother. Yet the dancing does not prevent other teen problems, such as Ramon's resistance to getting a job and to marrying his girlfriend after he fathers her child. Ramon's story becomes the most compelling in the film, as he eventually decides to take a grocery store job and move into a meager apartment with his girlfriend and child, which his buddies help him set up. Yet soon thereafter he encounters a rival graffitist destroying his latest work and chases him down a subway tunnel, where both are accidentally killed. Kenny, who has at last been hired as a DJ at a club, dedicates his debut to Ramon, turning the closing number into a multimedia tribute to youthful creativity.

Beat Street, in addition to featuring youth who fulfill their modest dreams of musical and dance excellence, also features one of the more thoroughly positive young women of color in '80s youth cinema, Kenny's girlfriend Tracy (Rae Dawn Chong). She does serve as a love interest to the protagonist, but she also attends college and encourages Kenny and Lee's artistic development. Kenny is himself a rather undeveloped character, which may be due to the film's concentration on its many production numbers. What the film achieves in using these numbers to showcase the talents of its energetic youth is a vision of racial integration and a channeling of their ideas and impulses into slightly radical but nonthreatening expressions such as break dancing, rap, and graffiti painting. J. Hoberman observed that the film presents hip-hop culture as "a utopian community, an explicit black–Latin synthesis that, as the film progresses, reveals the capacity to encompass all races, sexes, and classes."[10] Ramon's untimely death is thus made all the more striking, with its harsh senselessness poignantly disrupting the film's otherwise cool harmony. Unlike white youth in other films who use dance to simply rebel against their parents and gain notoriety, non-white youth are connected to dance as a means of survival, not only in *Beat Street* but also in *Rooftops*, *Lambada*, and *The Forbidden Dance*. This equation of dance with survival would not be sustained in further films about urban youth in the '90s, a decade in which dance trends were all but absent from teen movies altogether. Teens were still shown dancing at parties and proms, yet the cycle of films about teen dancing was over, not to appear again until the mid-'00s.

The destined demise of break dancing movies may be detectable in the 1984 comedy *Making the Grade*. When the white urban protagonist attempts to show off his break moves to his preppy cohorts, the scene becomes an unwitting demonstration of how little the dance style was catching on with white youth: despite his finesse (carried out by a body double), the other characters consider his dancing strange, or perhaps more accurately, too difficult to emulate. With the dominance of white teen images in American cinema of the '80s, the primarily black culture of break dancing and rap was restricted in its exposure.

Footloose (1984), one of the two most successful youth dance films of the '80s, provides an easy demonstration of the dance–rebel motif and the whitewashing of the youth dance musical. Ren (Kevin Bacon) is new to his religiously rigid midwestern town, fresh from Chicago where he loved to dance and compete in gymnastics, but now stifled by the town's ordinance against dancing. He's filled with frustration over his father deserting both him and his mother, and his pent-up emotions come pouring out in solitary clandestine dance fits. The local preacher's daughter, Ariel

(Lori Singer), witnesses one of these outbursts, and becomes attracted to Ren's handsome vitality, more so after he beats her boyfriend in a game of chicken using farm tractors. Ren shows Ariel the joy of dancing (although she is already so involved in defying her father by more dangerous means that she needs little encouragement), and he further teaches his clumsy friend Willard (Christopher Penn) how to dance. Ren gradually aligns his high school senior class in proposing a prom to the town council, but they remain resistant. Finally, after moving the prom to a granary just outside of town, Ren pulls off the event, much to the delight of the senior class, and manages to win glancing approval from Ariel's parents.

Here dance is most explicitly labeled as bothersome by the town's parents, who are admittedly drawn as such puritans that they burn school books, and who all seem to be of one voice, regardless of how many of them have children teeming with rebellious impulses. Ren brings dance to the town like a religion itself, a message that the town's hungry youth have never heard. In a challenging gesture, Ariel gives Ren a list of biblical citations to read to the town council, mentioning the many references to dancing as a form of religious celebration: "Ecclesiastes assures us . . . that there is a time for every purpose under heaven. A time to laugh . . . and a time to weep. A time to mourn . . . and there is a time to dance." Ren does not present the prom as a specifically religious event, leaving that as his implication: dance will make these young people free, and will focus their rebelliousness on a much safer activity than the drinking and dope smoking they do behind their parents' backs. On the night of the prom, Ren and Willard are brought to use their fighting *and* dance moves in fending off a set of local bullies, and after they do, the parentless prom provides further proof of just how liberating dancing can be.

From a generic angle, as Donald Greig points out, "*Footloose* is a combination of two proven formulae so obviously made for each other that their marriage seems to have been unaccountably delayed: the recent musical tradition of *Fame*, *Flashdance*, and *Saturday Night Fever* and the '50s melodrama of rebellious youth and families in crisis (principally *Rebel Without a Cause*)."[11] Yet even with the box office profits of this "marriage," the films it spawned did not persist for long. Two would soon try the formula from a female perspective, the first of which was ignored (*Girls Just Want to Have Fun* in 1985), and the second of which created a sensation.

That second film was *Dirty Dancing* (1987), the most popular youth dance film of the '80s.[12] The film makes no concessions to disguise the relationship between dancing and sexual expression, and becomes another teen polemic on dance as a method of ultimately acceptable deviance.[13] The story takes

Baby (Jennifer Grey) moves across the floor to kiss her partner Johnny (Patrick Swayze) in Dirty Dancing *(1987), fully aware of the decorum she is violating on so many levels.*

place in 1963, which is not insignificant, since this time marked an era of change in American social dancing, away from the controlled formality of prewar dances that kept partners rigid or separated and toward dance styles with unrestrained, suggestive gyrations, which is what many of the youth dance films in the late '50s and early '60s promoted. Such cultural changes parallel the protagonist's development. Frances (Jennifer Grey), known as "Baby," goes on a summer vacation to a resort hotel in the Catskills with her staid upper-class family just after she graduates from high school. There she finds herself fascinated by the "underground" culture of workers at the hotel, who let loose in vibrant, sensual dances during the evenings, away from the guests who view them as little more than nameless servants. Baby soon falls in love with a worker named Johnny (Patrick Swayze), who's also a dashing dance instructor, and his supposedly bad reputation not only fuels her desire but raises further her conservative father's ire, especially after she volunteers to replace a dancer in the resort's grand show.

Unlike the religious conflicts of *Footloose*, here the resistance is about class and social image, as Baby seeks a sense of self away from the privilege of her family, and seeks a sense of abandon in the apparently primal nature of real working people who not only earn their free time but turn it into such dynamically carnal revelries. However, Roger Ebert (and other critics) pointed out a more subtle conflict, because Baby's family is Jewish and obviously has "opposition to a Gentile boyfriend of low social status," even though this is never explicitly expressed in the film.[14] Such an ethnic tension, which many dance trends and dance films seek to transcend, introduces another level on which Baby is trying to find individuality through dancing. Thus her eventual mastery of dance techniques through Johnny's training becomes her ascension to sexualized womanhood, literally and figuratively: after learning both dance and lovemaking from Johnny, and standing against her father's wishes, Baby makes her debut at the hotel's show, where she proves to her family that her own hard work has paid off and, as Johnny dances while looking up at her on stage, she achieves the visible heights of adoration and confidence that her previous lifestyle could have never allowed. As in *Footloose* yet more formally so, the transformed dancer and her transforming male leader are given temporary approval for their efforts, and convince a community that dance — even the more mildly erotic choreography she and Johnny perform at the show — unites people across class lines, backgrounds, and ethnicities.

In the wake of *Dirty Dancing* followed no less than seven youth dance films over the next three years. *Rooftops* (1989) found director Robert Wise trying to cash in on the lingering fame of his *West Side Story* from some twenty-eight years earlier, but his new approach went largely unnoticed in this dark story of urban teens using dance as a form of fighting and expression (the *capoeira* style later featured in *Only the Strong* in 1993). *Rooftops* failed by overemphasizing the violence of dance rather than the romance, a mistake not made by subsequent dance films, although *Sing* (1989) also tried to connect young urban street styles with modern dance and was also passed over by audiences. Three dance-themed films that found better reviews, if only slightly bigger audiences, were each celebratory period stories, and two of them were directed in loving spoof style by John Waters: *Hairspray* (1988) points to race and gender tensions around dance in its story of teens competing on a '60s TV dance show, and *Cry-Baby* (1990) parodies '50s rock movies with its story of a young rebel who incites local tensions through his melodramatic relationship with a "good girl." *Shag* (1989) is also a nostalgia piece, about four girlfriends spending a wild weekend together at the peak of the Shag dance craze in that significant dance year of 1963.

These films were enjoyable efforts to keep the youth dance film on its toes, until the two lambada films that appeared in the spring of 1990 — *The Forbidden Dance* and *Lambada*—effectively became the last steps of the decade. The fact that two different studios were willing to take such a calculated gamble on an unknown dance signaled the confidence the industry still had in youth dance films, but after their unmistakable failure to win audiences and start an expected revival, studios must have realized that any further gambles would not pay off. Curiously, both lambada films were unusually political, exposing North American audiences not only to the South American dance but also to issues of Latino struggles against white American arrogance. *The Forbidden Dance* addresses the deforestation of the Amazonian rain forest and the exploitation of Latin peoples by American capitalists, and features one of the few interracial *and* class-crossing romances in teen cinema. A displaced tribal princess comes to the United States to save her culture, which is best represented by the lambada, a dance so arousing in its bump-and-grind moves that it was banned in Brazil, but which she has no trouble teaching to a wealthy white boy whom she is thus able to convert to her cause. The dilemma with the film's handling of the protagonists' relationship and their plea to save the rain forests is that both are built around the recurring gratuitous display of the lambada, which forces attention on the exotic foreign sensuality of the dance and away from the film's two dominant conflicts (environmentalism and racism), exposing these plot points as mere contrivances. In many ways, the film's biggest flaw is its idealism, suggesting that dance in itself could induce spoiled rich kids to become passionate about addressing the world's needs.

Lambada took a more believable consciousness-raising approach, one more directly related to domestic race issues. A math teacher at a wealthy white high school breaks out as a lambada dancer by night, and in the process guides local barrio kids to study for their General Equivalency Diplomas; his Mexican heritage supposedly gives him the motivation to educate the Latino students while aspiring to the privilege of his white students. This implicit conflict finds formal manifestation in a climactic math contest between the two student groups, with the teacher guiding both at the fulcrum of apparent racial tension. After the barrio team wins and eases that tension, the entire student population joins in a mass lambada outside, with dance once again unifying diverse cultures. While *Lambada* can be characterized just as much (if not more) as a school movie, the film is sold on its use of the title dance, and in that way, very much like *Stand and Deliver* before it, the film preaches a message about the capacity of underprivileged Latino youth, even if its gimmick of exotic dancing and feigned cultural intrigue somewhat dilutes that nonetheless clear lesson.

The lambada films of 1990 alas suffered the same fate as other post-*Dirty* dance films, and with these last gasps, the youth dance film, deviant or not, exhausted itself for over another decade.[15] A few odd examples did continue to appear, such as the anachronistic orphan musical *Newsies* (1992), which wasn't really about dancing *per se*, and the stirring pre-WWII story *Swing Kids* (1993), in which a group of German teens find themselves electrified by big band music and dance, a force that gives them the energy and inspiration to resist the rising tide of Nazism. With such heavily dramatic historical plots, these films seemed doomed from the start, at least in trying to appeal to young audiences, who may have been more receptive to *Swing Kids* during the late-'90s revival of swing. Irrespective of that revival, and the emergence of rave culture in urban centers, not to mention the continuing popularity of dancing for teenagers as a social activity, movie studios still tended to avoid youth dance movies throughout the decade, and stumbled with their efforts to re-introduce them.

Center Stage (2000) was a cautious attempt, choosing ballet as its dance style and mixing late-teen characters with early twentysomethings, but this strategy of trying to gain a wider audience and exploiting a realm of dance not based on current trends was unsuccessful at the box office. *Mad About Mambo* (2000) was still less popular, as a movie and as an effort to inspire a new craze. Consider that the prolific dance films of the '80s, with the exception of *Footloose* and *Dirty Dancing* and the specialized draw of the breaking films, also did not provide teens with images of dancing that made them want to join in, a liability that was a cause of the continuing dearth of popular dance films.

In the new century, teen cinema began to reconsider this burden, offering youth more exciting recent dances that they could duplicate, and as the most profitable '80s dance films revealed, the narratives needed to provide the dancing within a challenging romantic context. This explained the unexpected success of *Save the Last Dance* (2001), directed by Thomas Carter of *Swing Kids*, who revised his previous narrative formula by changing Nazi resistance to a more timely interracial romance between two dancing teens (even though interracial dating is more common, and less problematic, among real teens than Hollywood has acknowledged). By replacing big band swing with contemporary urban music and dance styles familiar to young audiences, the film was received with much enthusiasm, although its successful approach would languish for years before leading to a revival of the youth dance movie. In fact, while fresh dancing would maintain its connection to traditional deviance for teens, the resulting breakdown of racial and cultural divisions with their shared moves would remain at least a superficial theme.

Youth dance movies of the later '00s carried this theme forward. The release of *Camp* in 2003—with a diverse cast of kids at a musical theater camp coping with their various personal crises—was apparently planned as a revival of the style, yet three years later an unassuming television movie truly rejuvenated the teen dancing phenomenon. *High School Musical* debuted on the Disney Channel in 2006, bringing together another diverse cast of kids in a scenario inspired by *Romeo and Juliet*: a sophomore basketball player is attracted to a smart girl in his class, and through various maneuvers the opposites end up in their school's annual musical, solidifying a romance in the process. In the context of this study, the film is notable for featuring a male athlete who becomes a musical actor and a smart girl who is not typically nerdy. Also worth pointing out is that the film was directed by Kenny Ortega, choreographer of *Dirty Dancing* and *Newsies*, who struck pay dirt when the film, and especially its soundtrack, became immediate pop sensations, leading to three foreign remakes, an ice show, and a concert tour with most of the original movie performers.

Given Ortega's direction of the first film and its two sequels, they maintain an unexpected emphasis on breakout scenes with songs focused on the plot rather than on dance acts. This was likely because the sublimation of sexual impulses inherent to dance was not as relevant to fifteen-year-olds as with older teens in other musicals (the main couple does not even kiss until the end of the second film), and the Disney pedigree would not have supported the dry-humping styles of contemporary couples' dancing. *High School Musical 2* appeared on television the next year and maintained the original's musical approach, as well as its primary plot, yet *High School Musical 3: Senior Year* (2008), given the budget to facilitate a theatrical release, did open the production to bigger numbers with more dancing. This advance did not threaten its G-rated agenda, further preserving the early teen audience the films were designed to please, and further sustaining the style that had made it such a moneymaking series.

Just as the *High School Musical* films were gaining visibility, films appeared about primarily Latin or African American characters who danced in orchestrated group numbers in public exhibitions, often implicitly meant to displace previous gang fighting. The style saw its prototype in *You Got Served* (2004), which combined more customary break dancing moves with the foot- and arm-pounding rhythms that would define step dancing, as it came to be known in *Stomp the Yard* (2007) and *How She Move* (2007), where teens use their dancing en route to declaring their personal identities. Films followed with similar ambitions of creating a rage, such as *Feel the Noise* (2007) and *Make It Happen* (2008), and *Stomp the Yard* was sequelized in 2010, yet the film and sequels with the greatest impact began with white characters back in 2006: *Step Up*.

The film is another basic teen tale of opposites attracting, only in this case through the unlikely medium of ballet. Tyler (Channing Tatum) is a teenager living with foster parents in a poor Baltimore neighborhood who enjoys showing off his moves at clubs with primarily black clientele. After he gets in trouble for vandalizing a local art school for kicks, he is sentenced to community service at the school, doing janitorial tasks. Tyler soon becomes curious about the dance students, particularly Nora (Jenna Dewan), who by coincidence loses her partner while in rehearsals for her fall showcase, on which rides her prospect of taking a position with a company. She then approaches the unemployed Tyler after watching him strut his stuff in the parking lot, and makes a deal with the school to transfer his service hours to helping her train; lacking any career direction himself, he slowly sees this is a long-term opportunity that could gain him admittance to the school. He makes plain to the school principal that he does not fully understand what he is facing: "You guys talk about dancing like it's rocket science or something."

The story proceeds through numerous dance montages as Tyler and Nora practice, with each coming to appreciate the other's style, even with his arrogant posturing. What gives their dancing a sense of deviance is not the typical sexual transgression (although Nora clearly falls in love with Tyler despite having a boyfriend), but their violation of parental and communal expectations. Nora's mother urges her to apply to prestigious colleges rather than pursue the risky dance profession, and Tyler is chided by his lone black friend to give up his dancing ambitions to pursue an easier life on the streets—the racial and class politics of the film nonetheless remain tacit throughout. Dancing for the two of them is not just a potential livelihood, but also a way to escape the unsatisfying destinies that everyone around them otherwise expects. After a series of rifts and arguments, Tyler and Nora unite for the climactic show and predictably achieve their goals. The problem with the film is that this outcome, and the entire plot, are so predictable that the stakes are never high enough for us to become concerned about the characters' plights, most incongruously Nora, whose option of a supposedly compromised life at an Ivy League school is not exactly a ruinous alternative. *Step Up* does integrate Nora's ballet with

Tyler's street style in a convincing manner, yet the integration of these two characters in a romance remains unconvincing, and their deliverance through dance is simply too facile.

The first sequel in 2008, *Step Up 2: The Streets*, retained much of the story, almost none of the cast, and all of the setting from the original, with a wayward girl abandoning her street dancing crew to attend the art school. The film was eager to capitalize on the step dancing films of the previous year, but again the characters' racial and class tensions are marginalized. *Step Up 3D* (2010) obviously promoted its capitalization on the 3D format that had become famous in recent years, and was similarly hackneyed in moving the setting to New York City so that more street dancing gangs could be featured. The college-aged students in this sequel are thus given a more complex set of dances to contest, while the central white couple continues to be the core of the multiracial cast, a pattern that persisted in the next sequel, *Step Up Revolution* (2012), which shifted sites to Miami with again older characters.

Dance remained a form of kinetic expression and rebellious liberation throughout youth films of the later '00s, and the blockbuster draw of *High School Musical* and the first two *Step Up* films indicated that young audiences continued to appreciate the energetic outlets of sound and motion that so many teen movies have celebrated since the 1950s. That would also be discernable in the success of the remade *Hairspray* (2007), which was actually an adaptation of the stage musical that had been adapted from the 1988 film. At the same time, the feeble grosses of a trio of retreads — *Dirty Dancing: Havana Nights* (2004), *Fame* (2009), and *Footloose* (2011) — and the scant attention granted to more interesting teen dance films ranging from *Take the Lead* (2006) to *Spork* (2010), as well as the inevitably merciless parodying of these films in *Dance Flick* (2009), are stinging evidence that the latest wave of teen dance movies did not remain viable into the '10s. Dance will always be an outlet for youth and often an outrage to their parents, and movie studios are wise to continue testing further forms of this minor delinquency until they again find a formula that entices the contemporary desires of teen movements.

NATURAL ENCOUNTERS

Films about youth engaging with nature have been relatively popular for generations, growing out of a long literary tradition and offering images of often misguided teens who discover direction, peace, and/or maturity through their encounters. Such films fall into two varieties: those depicting children's interaction with animals, and those which place their young characters in a more adventurous narrative built around surviving the challenge of the wilderness, desert, or ocean.

Animal movies tend to focus on pre-teens, but animals obviously have an inherent allure to youth of all ages: their playfulness and cuteness are endearing, their usual smallness gives young people a sense of dominance over another creature such as they perceive adults have over them, and in terms of wild animals, their struggle for survival and the mysteries of their lifestyles—particularly how they may communicate or express emotion— are intriguing. What all animal youth films portray is a sense of personal connection between the animals and their protagonists, a connection that most adults in the films fail to understand, and which the youth usually use in defense of the animals' worth because a humane relationship between them has been achieved. The effect of this becomes youths' defiance against unsympathetic, and apparently unperceptive, adults, in which the animals are aligned with fighting for senses of purpose and freedom that the youth are just beginning to discover for themselves.

Animal films became more prominent in the '90s compared to the '80s, although there had been many popular examples in the past, such as the numerous *Lassie* and *Benji* films. One little-seen equine tale, *Sylvester* (1985), was about a troubled girl gaining wisdom through her care for a show horse, which borrowed its common plot from the many previous child-loves-horse films, such as *My Friend Flicka* (1943, and remade in 2006 as *Flicka*), *National Velvet* (1944), its sequel *International Velvet* (1978), *The Red Stallion* (1947), *The Red Pony* (1949), *Misty* (1961), *The Black Stallion* (1979), and its sequel *The Black Stallion Returns* (1983). This same plot was used again in the '90s, first in *Dark Horse* (1992), in which a tormented girl, rapidly becoming a delinquent, stumbles on a new direction in life after being ordered to care for a horse. Less youth-oriented takes on the horse story include *Black Beauty* (1994), a British adaptation of the classic stallion story that has been brought to the screen at least five times, and *The Horse Whisperer* (1998), in which a teenage girl's mother hires the title character to "heal" her daughter and horse after a traumatic accident. And, in a less horse-oriented approach, *Wild Hearts Can't Be Broken* (1991) tells the true story of a runaway girl who becomes a carnival attraction by riding a diving horse into a tank of water, until she is blinded in an accident and finds the courage to rebuild her life.

Other '90s animal films employed a wide phylum of animals, many from the wild. *White Fang* (1991) and its sequel *White Fang 2: Myth of the*

White Wolf (1994) are adapted from one of Jack London's novels of the same name, about a youth and his supercanine who in both films help themselves and others through the Alaskan gold rush. *Far from Home: The Adventures of Yellow Dog* (1995) is another common tale of a teenage boy who is comforted by his loyal dog after they are stranded on an island. An inevitable aquatic animal movie was *Flipper* (1996), which in many ways replays the popular *Free Willy* plot on a small scale, with an irritable teenager befriending the titular dolphin, who helps in battling a toxic waste calamity.[16] A more unusual animal is the gorilla in *Born to Be Wild* (1995), where again the politically correct aspect of animal rights is combined with the story of a boy who learns to stand up to adult misunderstanding. *Wild America* (1997) featured the widest range of animals yet, in its true story of teenage animal documentarians who discover their talents for capturing the enthralling behaviors of wildlife on film. And still another version of the perennial canine favorite *Lassie* was produced in 1994, about the caring collie who in this incarnation teaches a teenage boy the importance of family values, with the dog "trying to tell us something" through her special animal perception. Youth learning to appreciate animals' special perspectives, and learning to appreciate who they are themselves—especially in the wake of familial strife—are the main features of all these animal movies. This would be borne out again in the *Air Bud* trilogy (1997–2000), in which an athletic golden retriever facilitates the "training" of an adolescent boy in basketball, football, and soccer.

By far the most successful animal film of the '90s was *Free Willy* (1993), the whale saga that became a trilogy by 1997.[17] (A quite similar but much less popular film was made before in 1976, *A Whale of a Tale*, about a boy training a killer whale for a marine show.) *Free Willy* is the story of Jesse (Jason James Richter), a twelve-year-old who has become hardened by a life spent partially on the street in the years after his mother left him. Jesse has been in and out of foster homes, and his latest new parents look as if they won't be able to tame him either. Yet after a night of vandalizing a local amusement park, Jesse is assigned to work there, where he quickly becomes fascinated by Willy, the park's disappointing animal attraction. The narrative makes a bold parallel between Jesse and Willy: both are rebellious adolescents and both long for their real family, and over the course of the story both give each other affection and teach each other how to behave. In Jesse's case, that means being responsible to a job, and for Willy, that means performing tricks that he's been reluctant to do. The stronger theme of the film remains its statement on building and sustaining family relations, as demonstrated by Willy and Jesse, leading Hal Hinson to claim, "What's great about this uncommon movie relationship is the emphasis it places on the fact that families are made and not born, that they are the products of hard work and compromise and trust that has to be earned."[18] And through each other, the adolescent boy and whale find the trust that leads them back to their respective species families.

As in other animal films, protagonist and animal openly communicate with each other in a way no one else understands. After Jesse trains Willy for a big show, Willy rebels by not performing for the audience, and Jesse can tell that he's scared, and even implies that he feels exploited. The park owners' decision to have the whale killed for an insurance settlement leads Jesse to try to save him by enlisting the assistance of sympathetic adults, including his foster parents, who have grown to respect Jesse's devotion to his new pet. The film concludes with a spectacular race to the ocean so that Willy can be returned to his family in their natural habitat, after which Jesse returns to his new home with his foster parents, with whom he has earned a mutual love. The film suggests that Jesse merely needed to find a nonthreatening channel for his emotional longings, and that by setting Willy free, he has ascended to a more mature stage of experiencing love on a selfless, familial level.

Free Willy 2: The Adventure Home (1995) is less interesting as an animal movie but revealing of certain differences in Hollywood conventions between portraying pre-teens and early teens. Like the first film, the sequel centers on a quest for familial belonging, but also introduces a shift toward romantic fulfillment for Jesse, who is now entering puberty and encountering the hormonal changes that come with it, as he develops a crush on a teenage whale-watcher who eventually helps him to again save Willy from a disaster. This plot point proclaims a normalizing heterosexuality for its main character, whose love for his whale may have otherwise begun to appear abnormal now that he's a teenager, even though the film's *raison d'être* is the connection between the boy and the whale. (A similar character device is used in *Born to Be Wild*, where a girl serves to displace the pubescent protagonist's potentially perverted affection for a female gorilla.) The third film in the trilogy, *Free Willy 3: The Rescue*, was released in 1997, and here Jesse befriends a ten-year-old boy whose father is secretly hunting whales, leading to another family confrontation that is resolved through saving Willy.

The stylish 1984 Vietnam war story *Birdy* is built around a teenager whose obsession with birds has driven him to the brink of insanity, yet setting an even higher standard of both aesthetics and scale of avian involvement is the 1996 film *Fly Away Home*, one of the few '90s animal films with a girl protagonist. Amy (Anna Paquin) is devastated when her mother dies in a car accident that she herself survives, and must then move to Canada with her formerly estranged father, Tom (Jeff Daniels). The thirteen-year-old spends her days alone and distraught, until she discovers some goose eggs among the wreckage of a nearby construction site and incubates them in her father's barn. The geese hatch and become more than pets, since they "imprint" Amy as their new mother goose, but local animal authorities remind Amy that domesticated birds cause quandaries if they are allowed to fly. The narrative thus sets up a traditional environmental conflict (also established through the destruction of local woodlands), and as Amy discovers a sense of purpose and belonging with the goslings, her strained relationship with her father becomes more caring. Tom, who is an inventor, convinces Amy that they need to teach the birds to fly south for the winter, and suggests that they build small planes to do so. Through the aid of friends, they train each other and train the birds, leading to a dramatic flight from southern Ontario to North Carolina. Along the way, national media get news of their flight, and another environmental fight ensues after Amy plans to land the geese at a wetlands preserve that is being razed for a housing project. The developers eventually relent, and Amy lands triumphantly with the whole world watching, showing the geese their winter home. The next spring, a closing caption tells us, all of the geese flew back to Amy's house.

What makes *Fly Away Home* particularly special is the sense of liberating flight that the extensive aerial shots induce, as well as the image of a teenage girl leading her surrogate children to safety via her commanding mastery of an aircraft. Where other animal films concentrate more on a communicative relationship between youth and animals, *Fly Away Home* leaves the connection between Amy and her geese on a symbolic, if still emotional, level. This actually renders Amy a somewhat less developed character than the pent-up protagonists of other animal films, because her drive to raise, train, and preserve the birds is meant as a tacit statement on her own survival without a mother, as well as the harmony she has long desired with her father. When Tom's plane crashes just before they reach their final destination, he tells Amy that she can go on without him, knowing that she has the determination and spirit of her mother, a gesture that verifies her independence and the maternal inspiration she has been unable to come to terms with. By completing the mission (and later reuniting with her dad), Amy becomes the rare teen girl heroine who fulfills a motherly fantasy in a typically masculine mechanical endeavor, and a closing shot of the jubilant geese indicates that she has indeed been successful on both counts.

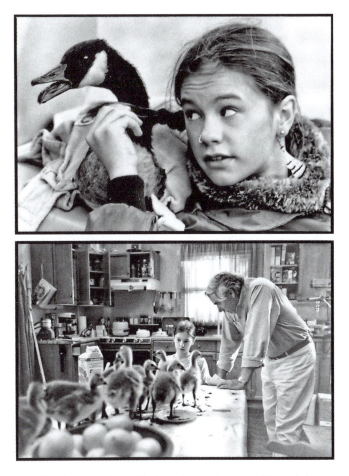

Anna Paquin stars as Amy in Fly Away Home *(1996), working with director Carroll Ballard and a gaggle of geese to learn new meaning in life.*

Bearing in mind the success and acclaim of youth films with animals, they became unusually dormant for another decade, withering in obscurity like the giant turtle tale *Mel* (1998) and patently reviled *Funky Monkey* (2004). During this time animals were still featured in films about preteens, such as *Shiloh* (1997), *Running Free* (1999), and *Dreamer: Inspired by a True Story* (2005), yet for whatever reasons, animal movies involving adolescents did not regain prominence until a plethora of productions in the late 2000s, including *For the Love of a Dog* (2008), *Lost Stallions: The Journey Home* (2008), *All Roads Lead Home* (2008), *Hotel for Dogs* (2009), and *Shannon's Rainbow* (2009). This revival subsided, yet earnest efforts continued with

The Greening of Whitney Brown (2011) and *Smitty* (2012), while the widely honored *Life of Pi* (2012), about a teenage boy stranded on a lifeboat with a tiger, achieved so much success that it may again renew interest in stories about youth and animals.

Among the many late '00s examples, at least a half-dozen had equestrian themes. *The Derby Stallion* and *Racing Stripes* (both 2005), and *Moondance Alexander* (2007), respectively tell stories about a boy training to race a horse in a steeplechase, a girl training a zebra to compete in a horse race, and a girl training a wild pony for show jumping. *Duma* (2005), directed by Carroll Ballard who made *The Black Stallion* and *Fly Away Home*, was more accomplished but unfortunately poorly marketed; it is the true story of a South African boy who befriends a cheetah as a cub only to have the wild cat grow up with him. *Eye of the Dolphin* in 2006 returned to an aquatic theme, borrowing elements from past films in its story of an expelled high schooler tormented by her mother's recent death who comes to live with her researcher father, and in the process discovers that she has a special ability to communicate with the dolphins he studies.

Another 2006 film, about a girl and her horse, enjoyed the best marketing and largest audience of these movies at this time, de-emphasizing the training aspect common to other plots and presenting the bond between human and animal more ambiguously. *Flicka*, adapted from the 1941 novel *My Friend Flicka* that was made into a film in 1943, tells the story of Katy (Alison Lohman), a distracted boarding school student on the verge of failing her junior year, who returns to her family ranch in Wyoming for the summer. Katy enjoys helping her father graze the quarter horses he breeds for sale, but she soon discovers a feral mustang that becomes her preoccupation. After learning that the term "flicka" refers to a beautiful young girl, she gives the horse that name, and endeavors to bring it to the ranch, against her father's protests. Gradually Katy calms the horse and sets out to make it her pet, not noticing that the same wild spirit that makes the horse so endearing to her is exactly what she is trying to tame.

Katy is one of the rare children in an animal movie with an intact nuclear family, albeit one with the threat of dissolution hanging over their lives. Katy's older brother does not want to become a rancher as his father would prefer, but would rather go off to college; Katy conversely prefers the ranch life to her stuffy prep school. The children's mother also has a central presence, as a voice of reason to the demanding father, who sells Flicka to a rodeo dealer even as he knows that Katy's connection to the horse is genuine. That understanding is tested when Katy and her brother enter a bucking contest at the rodeo in an attempt to regain Flicka, whereupon the girl absconds with the horse. As Flicka instinctually takes Katy back to the ranch, a puma attacks the horse, leaving both of them in parallel conditions of peril as Katy struggles to overcome a fever and Flicka is left close to death.

The weakest aspect of the film is the emotion Katy feels for Flicka, because few scenes feature the two characters actually bonding, and Katy's motivation for loving the horse is simply explained by her "free" nature, which is meant to be manifested in a history class essay that remains trite. Despite the dramatic fight for life they both endure at the end, Katy's impassioned unity with the horse—referring to herself and Flicka as one—is explained only by her willful disobedience of her father, which is itself assuaged at the end when Flicka survives and becomes Katy's very own. The story gives Katy no human love interest, and no greater goal than being with Flicka, unlike most of the adolescent activists in other animal films. Perhaps in that way *Flicka* is more legitimate as a youth movie, for all the girl really does need is her horse, not a greater cause to validate her volitions.

All of these films affirm a compassionate relationship between youth and animals, employing not only children's abilities to understand animals in a way that adults do not, but the very closeness in innocence and wonder that animals are personified to share with youth. These films portray potentially delinquent youth in their early or mid-teens, before they've grown hopelessly cynical, who discover senses of loyalty, concern, and humanity through their devotion to animals. Within the context of other youth films since the '80s about the demise of family harmony, which almost all of the animal films address, the story of youth learning to love and become caring through humanizing animals points to ongoing concerns about contemporary childhood development. These films reveal that their characters' abilities to align with animals turn them back to their natural familial impulses, a notion that is problematized by the relationships of youth with nature depicted in adventure films.

The adventure film is in many ways similar to the animal film but refers to larger social and political conditions (if less so to environmental concerns). These films are not about the potential joys of "getting back to nature" but about the inner natural qualities of youth when they are forced to fend for themselves outside of their usual familial and cultural structure. In that way, the adventure film offers a clear parallel to the challenge of surviving the rigors of school and society for youth, who must confront their inner fears and ambitions against the arduous demands of the outdoors, and in some cases, must confront the primal nature of their friends.

The inspiration for many of these films is an examination of the human condition, although the '90s films take a certain departure from the themes of the '80s films. Up to 1990, youth adventure films generally suggested that humans are more barbaric and ignoble than we, through our refined social relationships, would admit to being. The adventure films after 1990, on the other hand, depict youth as gritty and driven, casting a customarily reassuring light on their capacity to adapt, and to do so in "civilized" ways. While notions of civility are particularly arguable, the change in these films' perspectives reveals an increasingly optimistic image of current teens. By using youth to tell such stories, the films attempt to demonstrate that supposedly basic human traits are instinctual and fundamental, and the films can further capitalize on the pre-adult state of youth as being particularly volatile and impressionable. Ultimately, these films suggest that codes of socialization are necessary, that youth have a choice between barbarism and humanity, and that if they are to choose humanity, a healthy respect for nature is required in order to survive.

There have been a number of these films since the '80s, yet most gained little attention, however much studios tried to mix adventure tales with other subgenres, as in the sexual dramas of *Out of Control* (1985), the family conflicts of *The Mosquito Coast* (1986), and the political messages of *Survival Quest* (1988). Even casting popular stars such as Kevin Bacon and Sean Astin brought few audiences to *White Water Summer* (1987), and the *Cry in the Wild/White Wolves* franchise—which produced four films from 1990 to 1998—was prolific and well received but only marginally successful on video. Many adventure films were in fact met with positive reviews, and studios continued to experiment with the style, as in the promising high-seas journey *White Squall* (1996), which also failed to attract much box office despite star casting and a dynamic true story. Youth may actually resist seeing these films given the plots' blatant celebrations of the liberatory potential of nature, which is difficult to appreciate within the confines of a movie theater, not to mention from the perspective of a comfortable suburban milieu. This may explain why youth adventure films have faded away in recent years, as young people find themselves ever more ensconced in the domesticated bliss of electronic culture. Consider that perhaps the most successful film using this approach, *Stand by Me* (1986), is set in the '50s before television and computers took over children's lives, and that regardless of its intrigue around four twelve-year-old friends who set off into the woods in search of a missing boy's body, it owes its appeal to a minimizing of the their actual wilderness encounters by focusing instead on their interpersonal issues.

The apparent paradigm for many of these films is William Golding's 1954 novel *Lord of the Flies*, in which British schoolboys find themselves marooned on an island and, failing to organize themselves into certain roles, resort to animalistic brute impulses. The book was originally made into a film in Britain in 1963, and was again adapted by Hollywood in 1990. Its lucid examination of human social psychology and its youth-versus-youth plot factor in many of the adventure films.

The 1990 version is relatively faithful to the novel, with its group of military schoolboys whose plane crashes into the ocean. They must then swim to a tropical island, where they systematically resort to savagery. Initially, Ralph (Balthazar Getty) is casually elected leader of the group due to his uppermost rank, but another boy who is slightly older, Jack (Chris Furrh), develops a group of followers as well. The boys first concern themselves with gathering water and food, until Ralph pushes them to spend more time trying to be rescued. Jack begins to resent Ralph's orders, as well as his friendship with an overweight boy nicknamed Piggy (Danuel Pipoly), and he takes his band of "hunters" away to the woods. The narrative sets up two distinct communities: Ralph and Piggy, who live on the shore and whom everyone turns against, and Jack and the hunters, who carry spears, wear face paint, and kill animals for food. The hunters become afraid that a monster is living in a cave on the island, which another boy later learns is only the dying crazed pilot from the plane; when the boy runs to tell the group, who are dancing around a fire with spears, they fear he is the monster and kill him. Ralph tries to appeal to their sense of reason to no avail: his patience and tolerance are of no interest to the hunters, who next kill Piggy as he is trying to tell them that they must stop acting like children. The hunters then turn to Ralph as a target, setting the woods on fire and chasing him to the shore, where they are unexpectedly met by marines who have come to save them.

The story is a rich political allegory: as more boys shift alliances from the rational Ralph to the aggressive Jack, a statement is made about the perception of strength through violence, a statement that is broadly applicable. Gary Giddins argued that "the biggest disappointment is the film's refusal to acknowledge the implications raised by the theme applied to 1990 America."[19] Save a passing reference to Rambo, and Piggy's expressed fear that Russians could find them, the film's updating of the story does not bring with it much commentary on current political issues, which would have been relevant in its Cold War context. Another flaw in the film is its failure to illuminate Ralph's insight, because Jack's powers of persuasion are so strong. After all, Jack holds out the possibility of gathering more and better food, which are higher immediate priorities to the boys' survival than Ralph's suggestion that they maintain a fire so that adult authorities can find them. What becomes clear is that Jack and many of the boys do not want to be found, that they actually enjoy the freedom from adults and social demands. What rises in the place of those oppressions is the children's impulse to follow other hierarchical structures. Military rank, for instance, is quickly revealed as irrelevant within their setting. Jack is the meanest and toughest of the group—as signified by his increasing swearing, shoving, and use of weapons—and his rank as the most militant savage demotes Ralph's assumed leadership role. The boys who then follow Jack are, as Ralph later tells them, analogous to the willing slaves of dictators.

Within their jungle surroundings, this message is particularly political, yielding a critique of colonization that was perhaps more apropos to the novel's British schoolboys. These colonizers are not "taming" the land but branding it with their own style of primitive brutality, plundering its resources and losing their respect for human life and humane principles. This makes the film's final scene all the more ironic, when the boys are saved from themselves by the American military's fiercest division, who have presumably achieved such controlled discipline that they would not resort to the boys' savagery under the same circumstances (a symbolism that may challenge the above claim about the film's lack of current commentary). Thus the film can also be viewed as a parable on puberty, with Jack representing the most unruly element who, through his anarchy and rebellion from established civility, only creates a more oppressive order, and with Ralph representing the individual resisting conformity and upholding mature ethics.

Gold Diggers: The Secret of Bear Mountain (1995), like the tough girl films of the mid-'90s described below, represents a new image of hearty female adolescents. The story takes place in 1980 for no apparent reason (thus becoming one of the first period teen films about the '80s), and begins with young teen Beth (Christina Ricci) moving to a small Washington State town with her mother after being raised in Los Angeles. Beth is restless for something to do, and the only local excitement appears to be a rough-and-tumble tomboy named Jody (Anna Chlumsky), who tells Beth, "No one knows the woods like I do." Other girls tell Beth that Jody is trouble: she lies and steals and her mother's an alcoholic. But Beth befriends Jody all the same, finding in her an appreciating ally, because Jody relates to the recent death of Beth's father and Beth feels that she understands Jody's deviant behavior.

The adventure begins when Jody convinces Beth to explore a legendary mountain cave with her, which is reportedly filled with gold. Jody tells Beth the story of a pioneer woman named Molly Morgan, who posed as a man to escape a life of female servitude and become a miner. After a mine collapse, Molly was never found, and neither was the stash of gold rumored to still be on the mountain. Such a legend illuminates the film's promotion of young female independence and intrigue, and Jody is clearly determined to follow Molly's lead. Beth is reluctant to join her, but when Jody tells her that she killed her mother's abusive boyfriend Ray (David Keith) the night before and is running away, Beth promises her fidelity. Unfortunately, Beth cannot control the boat that they've used to get to the mountain, and she becomes trapped under rocks, prompting Jody to brave treacherous terrain on foot as she goes for help. Jody saves Beth's life, yet no one other than Beth believes Jody's stories of abuse. As it turns out, Jody didn't kill Ray after all, but Beth finds Jody's mother beaten by Ray, and realizes that he's kidnapped Jody to go find the gold. Beth sets off with her own mother and the local sheriff to find Jody, revealing that she has inherited Jody's strength and determination. She leads the sheriff to the cave and later finds Jody herself, with a strange woman saving them both from Ray. At the end of the film, the anonymous woman—who both girls know is the long-lost Molly Morgan—gives them each a bag of gold, the symbolic rewards for their preservation of her rugged spirit.

Gold Diggers is noteworthy for a number of reasons. It's one of the few adventure movies about girls, who are inspired by a legend, built from a feminist mythology, that is revealed to be true; the main characters' ability to survive in the wilderness is based not on their slight outdoors aptitude but on their sheer will. The scene of Beth valiantly braving the rising waters of the cave while waiting for Jody to bring help is evidence of this last point, as is Beth's sisterly devotion to Jody, which compels her to return to the cave to find her friend. The girls are portrayed as insightful—they know each other's true feelings, and take them seriously—as well as resourceful—each saves the other under particularly arduous circumstances. Their closeness is thus largely conveyed through their actions, given the relatively few dialogue scenes between them. This is in keeping with buddy action film conventions, but it also demonstrates that teenage girls can be developed as screen characters in terms of their sense of adventure, a narrative trait that has been granted to boys in films since the start of cinema, and long before in literature, as in the Tom Sawyer and Huck Finn stories that *Gold Diggers* has revised.

Subsequent adventure films continued to be produced on both ends of the studio scale, from the relatively high-budget *A Far Off Place* (1993) to the more modest *Alaska* (1996) to the no-budget *Castle Rock* (2000). Such films maintained an emphasis on becoming balanced with nature and learning to adapt under scary circumstances, and like the animal films, their narratives were founded on fears of family disintegration. Those fears fill *Holes* (2003), based on the critically lauded young adult novel from 1998. Essentially a fairy tale, the story follows Stanley (Shia LaBeouf), who is sentenced to a children's desert detention camp after being mistakenly charged with a misdemeanor. Stanley joins his fellow inmates in digging holes of the same shape and size every day, presumably as their punishment, while flashbacks reveal the Sisyphean fate of his ancestors who failed to complete a futile series of odd tasks, resulting in a generational curse that has been passed down to Stanley. This same futility is foisted on the boys, who endure their hard labor in the stinging sun, not knowing that their adventure lay in finding a buried treasure hidden years earlier by Stanley's family, whom he has learned was not so cursed after all.

The film's fanciful style resists realism, yet like so many films about youth in nature, its fable demonstrates that perseverance in the face of adversity is necessary to survival. The fact that Stanley's family is absent from his present life while he suffers their supposed legacy is indicative of the youthful torment of familial breakdown that youth adventure films tend to explore; the same applies in the revelation that the camp's director has ordered the digging of the holes after she was forced to do the same as a child by her greedy grandfather. Even after the treasure is discovered at the end and Stanley returns to his family, he shares his fortune with an inmate friend so that he can reconnect with his mother. Through his struggles Stanley has come to appreciate the universal value of a dynasty beyond himself.

Almost all natural encounter films operate on a threat to the disruption of typically safe familial surroundings. The protagonists' families tend to be dead or disrupted, and the youth must re-establish a sense of familial belonging through an animal or must learn to survive on their own, at least temporarily, in an otherwise dangerous environment that is analogous to the adolescents' ascent to adulthood. This pattern has prevailed through even the contemporary era of supposed electronic dependence for teens, as seen in *The Kings of Summer* (2013). By finding community with animals and security in the wilderness, the youth in these films verify that they can be responsible to a family and endure adulthood, and they provide an image of the literally wayward youth who navigates unsafe terrain and ultimately thrives through channeling delinquent impulses into primal "survival" skills.

TOUGH GIRLS

A distinct and interesting category of the youth delinquent subgenre is the tough girl film, in which one or more girls stake out their identity through rebellious acts. Because most youth delinquency films dwell on male delinquency, films about females usually take on a motivated activist aspect. In some cases, the protagonists are reacting directly to mistreatment by men, but in all cases these characters appear to knowingly question and defy patriarchy, through a wide range of means.

As the tough girl persona slowly evolved in '80s teen films, she was primarily a victimized survivor, and then by the mid-'90s many stronger girls appeared, becoming more enterprising and dynamic. Yet not all films featuring contumacious young women (such as *Election* or *Flicka*) could be fully included within this category: the tough girl is not merely conscious of her challenge to gender norms, be they enforced by men or women, but she often employs a confident aggression in expressing herself; and on a generic level, films about tough girls focus on the exhilaration of their toughness via delinquency, rather than the sensitive negotiation of power that still bothers most teen girls in other films. To be sure, the roles of many girls in recent American movies have begun to reflect a potent image of young femininity, yet these demonstrably delinquent roles have provided a particularly crucial and often questionable empowerment for girl characters, as this quite conspicuous empowerment remains aligned with deviance and criminality. Mary Celeste Kearney astutely argued that many '90s films moved "beyond the depiction of girls' heterosexual awakenings in order to explore their homosocial experiences," and thus they "significantly challenge the conventional female coming-of-age narrative upon which previous films about adolescent girlhood were based."[20] Despite their often feminist possibilities, tough girl films can unfortunately be easy devices for exploitation, as with sadistic prison films like *Reform School Girls* and *Bad Girls Dormitory* (both 1986) and other "women's" genres over the years. While perhaps the most notorious tough girl character of the '80s, Angel from the *Angel* trilogy (1984–1988), showed a certain autonomy through being an honor student by day and street-smart hooker by night, and did reform over the course of the trilogy, the films also capitalized on their lead actresses' sexuality, and were marketed accordingly. When the mid-'90s saw a visible increase in the number of tough girl films, their themes changed as well; after all, girls were at least upholding their buying power in the marketplace, and the swell of girl-oriented magazines and TV shows were supporting young feminist ambitions. By 1996, Peggy Orenstein wrote in her article "The Movies Discover the Teen-Age Girl" that the recent films about girls featured characters "in charge of their own fates, active rather than reactive," in stories "about girls' relationships to one another rather than to boys, that tackle the big themes of teen-age life, like alienation and displacement."[21] Orenstein's examples are not limited to the delinquency subgenre, but include school comedies such as *Clueless* (1995), and romances such as *The Incredibly True Adventure of Two Girls in Love* (1995), and imports such as *The Professional* (France, 1994), while the most noticeable evidence of the shift in young female representation remains within delinquency films.

The common past practice of depicting girls as the spectators to or victims of male rebellion definitely changed in the mid-'90s, and girls found themselves not only able to band together and seek unity through their own rebellion, but often in the same predicaments as their male cohorts because of it. The consequences of crimes, drug use, and sexual irresponsibility (which rarely weighs as heavily on boys) became problems for the tough girls, who also juggled confusing aspects of their gendered existence such as choosing careers, being attracted to boys (or girls), wanting to have children, and wanting to get married. Yet Orenstein adds, "The ground for exploration in these films becomes not the stuff of day-to-day life but the wreckage that occurs when the boundaries of feminine behavior are crossed."[22] Tough girl films often become examinations of the tensions around young women declaring their independence from men and conservative gender roles, as well as their seeking of a new cultural identity based on feminine ideals that have not been engendered by patriarchy.

Depictions of tough girls in American films before the 1980s were often diffuse and degrading. As Thomas Doherty points out, a cycle of "dangerous teenager" films began to appear in the 1950s such as *Reform School Girl*, *Teenage Doll* (both 1957), and *Teenage Bad Girl* (1959), movies in which girls were often shown to be just as corrupted by postwar excesses as boys were.[23] In that way, these films addressed the patriarchal fear of teenagers *and* women: in virtually all cases the transgressors in these movies were either killed or brought back under the authority of (adult male) law. Girls still provoked discord in the '60s, paying for their deviance by being stalked (*I Saw What You Did*, 1965), prostituted (*Run Swinger Run!* 1967), or lured into stripping (*Night of Evil*, 1962; *Girl in Trouble*, 1963; *The Grasshopper*, 1969), exploitation plots that could hardly be called progressive. Perhaps the roles of young female survivors of trauma, as in *The Exorcist* (1973) and *I Never Promised You a Rose Garden* (1977), could arguably be called the first signs of a stronger, stoical portrayal of young women, even though the narratives of these films hinged on their protagonists being abused.

Yet the best sign that the tough girl was becoming a recognizable teen role arrived in '80s films that featured groups of girls helping one another through good and, more often, bad times. The first was the notably disreputable *Foxes* in 1980, in which four girlfriends struggle through their teen years with scant adult guidance, partying hard along the way until one of them dies from a drug overdose. A short slew of less seen yet timely exemplars were about girls forming renegade punk rock bands: *Times Square* (1980), *Ladies and Gentlemen, The Fabulous Stains* (1982), and *Desperate Teenage Lovedolls* (1984). Eleven years after *The Exorcist*, Linda Blair starred in *Savage Streets* (1984), leading a gang of high school girls against a much meaner street gang who raped her deaf sister; the rape scene is excessively violent and prolonged, pointing to the film's calculating aims, and vitiating the vengeance carried out by the end of the film. As these "girl gang" movies began to appear, depictions of lone tough girls were emerging as well, such as *Scarred* (1983), which bears comparison to the relatively popular *Angel* released the following year: the story is of a single teenage mother who becomes a prostitute to keep her baby.

Angel may have had similar aspirations to portray the Madonna/whore role in its teenage protagonist. Molly (Donna Wilkes) is a straight-A student who cruises Hollywood Boulevard as Angel, a child prostitute. The fifteen-year-old is surrounded and supported by a street family of curious characters—a homeless former Western star called Kit Carson (Rory Calhoun), a benevolent transvestite named Mae (Dick Shawn), and a sturdy lesbian landlady. Stanley Crouch interprets this cast arrangement as the film's parallel to *The Wizard of Oz*, and adds, "It is perhaps a comment on our era that the tin man, the scarecrow, and the cowardly lion have been replaced for our young heroine by old movie cowboys, transvestites, prostitutes, and a butched-up lady who would herself be a lady killer."[24] These figures represent Angel's orchestrated attempt to replace her own parents, both of whom left her years before, so she walks the streets to raise money for living expenses, and her hardened job persona fuels the confidence and drive she has at school (of course, where she finds time to do homework is hazy). Angel is the teen female in charge of all aspects of her life, and while she still longs for the return of her parents, she is raising herself rather well.

The plot revolves around a psychopath who is killing hookers on the strip, and after Angel finds one of her own friends murdered in a motel room, she turns to a detective for protection, who later discovers her secret life. A group of lecherous athletes from school also discovers her secret, but she dispatches them by brandishing a gun. Now that everyone knows the truth, Angel goes after the killer, who first kills Mae. The scenes of Angel chasing the killer through the streets with a gun bigger than her forearm are charged with a palpable energy, yet alas she doesn't kill the killer—the detective shows up to save Angel, and quick shot Kit Carson fills the killer full of lead. This ending thereby feels like a compromise of the determination and strength Angel has developed through the course of the story, especially when she cowers under the detective, but the film as a whole preserves a very autonomous image for its title character. The irony is that her financial, sexual, familial, and social autonomy all arise from her selling of her pubescent body to despicable men, and given that by the end of the film Angel has not vowed to give up hooking, this deplorable condition remains a statement on the power imbalance between young men and women. Just as she's about to be gang-raped by her jock classmates, Angel escapes only by wielding a phallus more dangerous than theirs, reminding us that the very authority she has taken in her life has been through the operations of patriarchy. (On another level, the film is easily readable as a black comedy, in view of some of its stranger touches, and thus its ironies may be intended as a critique of past child hooker roles in films like *Pretty Baby* and *Taxi Driver*.)

The two sequels to *Angel* follow the character later in life: in *Avenging Angel* (1985) she has become a law student, and now takes to the streets to retaliate for the murder of the detective who, we learn, turned her away from prostitution after all. With *Angel 3: The Final Chapter* (1988) the story returned to prostitution, only now Angel is trying to save her long-estranged sister from the life she previously led. Both of these films continue to feature the main character in powerful positions, but by moving her into a more successful and less immoral lifestyle, the films expose their exploitative motive, the contrast between "good girl with a purpose" and "bad girl on a mission."

Another important '80s film spoke to the developing mythology of the tough girl role through its name alone, *The Legend of Billie Jean* (1985). Helen Slater plays the title character and Christian Slater (no relation) plays her younger brother Binx, two poor Texas teenagers. After Binx accidentally shoots a lecherous local who tried to rape his sister, the siblings and two female friends go on the run, drawing media attention and hoards of young followers, more so after they manage to air Billie Jean's plea for justice on television. As their notoriety continues to grow, more youth rise up in allegiance with the outlaws, protesting their abuse by adults, with girls emulating Billie Jean's appearance and helping the "Billie Jean Gang" evade arrest. The heroine eventually arranges a surrender that becomes its own media spectacle when she confronts the man Binx shot and stages a revolt against his burglary of her body, which was first enacted by his sexual assault, and more prominently by his selling of merchandise emblazoned with her image. Her speech becomes a rally, and the crowd joins in by burning their Billie Jean memorabilia, resulting in a fire that engulfs a large effigy of her as well.

Billie Jean becomes such an automatic authority figure in the film not only through her uprising but also thanks to the typical absence of the children's parents; all of these kids have such a commitment to defiance since they have been left to raise themselves. In terms of Billie Jean's use of the media, she shows her deft understanding of visual persuasion through adopting the image of Joan of Arc, self-consciously making herself look like a martyr for the cause by simply cutting off her long blonde hair and tearing off her shirt sleeves—a symbolism driven home when her effigy "burns at the stake." She then uses the media's interest in youth rebellion to generate awareness of their protest—exploiting the exploiters—squarely placing the responsibility for their oppression on the adults who otherwise run the media: "You think you can do anything you want and then lie about it and we just have to take it, because of what we are? Just a bunch of kids. Well, not this time. From now on we're doin' this our way. No lyin', no cheatin', fair is fair."

Some question can be raised if the narrative is offering this message as critique or irony, as David Edelstein points out: "*The Legend of Billie Jean* . . . has nothing to do with civil disobedience or self-reliance or feminism. Like a lot of our myths these days, it's about the thrill of overnight celebrity. . . . And what these girls [in the film] really love is not her deeds but her stardom: they want to look like her and act like her and someday be as famous as her."[25]

Yet the film is indeed promoting at least a *vision* of young fortitude, for if its characters are inspired to act like Billie Jean through being manipulated by the media, they are still being encouraged to rebel, a postmodern paradox to be sure. When a small army of girls emerges looking like Billie Jean and promoting her continued flight, the potential of organized youth rebellion is demonstrated, and is made more remarkable for its feminist social aspirations, which would not again be so substantial in American teen films for nearly a decade.

Less popular films, however, did continue to introduce various incarnations of the tough girl. *My Little Girl* (1987) embodies the style in a more subtle way, with its story of a headstrong rich girl who turns away from her preoccupied parents and takes a job at a home for delinquent women. A film that utilizes the image of erstwhile delinquent girls within a rock music setting is *Satisfaction* (1988), which presents a rare organized girl "gang" of the '80s, whose loyalty to their band is their means of avoiding delinquency, as their only hope for self-improvement appears to be in staying together. The film's ending, with two of the girls rejecting romantic options, is an endorsement of female self-determination, yet the film was attacked by critics and failed at the box office. Not until the mid-'90s would another film about teen female unity be praised or popular.

Cemetery High (1989) could have made a statement on previous rape-revenge scenarios about teens (*The Last House on the Left*, 1972; *Lipstick*, 1976; *Savage Streets*) but overreached into comedy with its tale of high school girls avenging their abuse, and *Far from Home* (1989) could have provided a boost both for tough girl roles and its star Drew Barrymore (in her first teen role), but failed to do either. Barrymore plays a self-assured and rebellious teenager on vacation with her father when she becomes the unwitting target of a killer, and the film was so poorly received that its faint release has rendered it obscure. *No Secrets* (1991) is slightly less obscure and more bizarre, the strange tale of three high school girls who take in a deceptively handsome male drifter while staying at a cabin in the woods. The girls are really too dissimilar to be friends, and thus the film implicitly argues that all girls long for a liberating sense of adventure through competing against other girls for the attention of an alluring, even dangerous man. Unfortunately, the girls lose interest in one another, like the story loses interest in the girls, for the sake of extolling masculine mythology.

Another problematic depiction of tough girls appeared in *Brutal Fury* (1992), which presented the first organized girl gang of the '90s: a secret high school sisterhood sets out to eradicate the drug dealers and date rapists that have sullied their school, yet their efforts at justice eventually corrupt and destroy them. As the decade continued, more of these vengeful and sometimes violent portraits of girls appeared, although the characters tended to become more purposeful and understanding. For instance, in 1994, two films about girl delinquents were released which not only staked out new terrain in the depiction of tough young women on screen, but brought up previously unspoken issues about the influences of race, class, and sexual preference on their protagonists. The less visible (though no less haunting) of the two was *Fun*, in which two girls meet one afternoon and, after sharing stories of their childhood abuses and going on a cross-neighborhood prank spree, end up murdering an elderly woman in a cathartic rampage of unleashed aggression. Their lack of motive for the crime and their passionately nonsexual devotion to each other baffle the authorities who question them: for these effectively parentless children, the path from conversation to confession to stealing to games to jokes to murder is a logical progression, and the film leaves open the unsettling possibility that many young women are simply waiting for the right partner with whom to follow a similar epiphanic trajectory. In the end, after being imprisoned, one of the girls kills herself when she learns that the two of them will be separated, which becomes her twisted attempt to immortalize their uniquely understanding relationship. The film wisely concludes that the diffuse yet damaging oppressions of girls may lead to all manner of inexplicable adolescent outbursts and reactions.

Mi Vida Loca (*My Crazy Life*) depicts young barrio women in Los Angeles, all Latinas, who have formed the Echo Park Home Girl gang. Two members of the gang, Sad Girl (Angel Aviles) and Mousie (Seidy Lopez), had been friends, but after both having children with the same kindhearted drug dealer, Ernesto (Jacob Vargas), they meet for a fight. At that same time Ernesto is killed over a broken deal, and Ernesto's gang vows revenge against his killer, who they believe is a rival named El Duran (Jessie Borrego). Sad Girl and Mousie make up, and are concerned for their homegirl Whisper (Nelida Lopez), who was shot in the incident; the women decide to sell Ernesto's customized truck to pay Whisper's hospital bills and support his babies. In a related subplot, Sad Girl's sister Alicia (Magali Alvarado), who has not joined the gang and goes to school, is crushed when her ex-convict pen pal stops writing, only to discover that he is El Duran, when at that moment Ernesto's gang kills him. In retaliation, El Duran's girlfriend tries to kill one of Ernesto's friends, but inadvertently shoots a young girl, leading to a somber closing scene where the homegirls gather at her funeral.

Mi Vida Loca testifies to the deplorable chain that is gang warfare through the struggles of its strong female characters who long to break it. These girls do not enjoy the thrill of violence, yet have become defensive of their home turf and friends due to the treacherous conditions of their surroundings, which are made treacherous primarily by the activities of men. They clearly enjoy the vibrant energy that otherwise runs through their neighborhood—fancy cars, children playing, decorated buildings—only they have tried to bond with one another to create an insularity that can protect them. This protection is not merely from other gangs (who make their presence known by specialized hand signals), but from the deterioration of their local identities; their ability to preserve their group is integral to the preservation of their individuality.

Despite the success of the male-focused African American crime films of the early '90s, no similar films about African American girl gangs have been made (with the arguable exception of *Set It Off* in 1996, about a group of four black women in their twenties who take to robbing banks for various personal and political reasons). One way *Mi Vida Loca* distinguishes its Latina gang members from their black male counterparts is by letting us hear their childhood memories through voice-over (Ernesto narrates as well), imbuing them with a sense of innocence that would threaten the virility of most male gangsta characters. White filmmaker Alison Anders was nonetheless criticized for her handling of the characters in *Mi Vida Loca* by writers such as Kevin Thomas, who claimed that regardless of her good intentions, "Anders has ended up confirming a decidedly negative stereotype of young Latinos as aimless, dangerous, and incapable of thinking for themselves, not to mention welfare-dependent . . . (none seem to be employed)."[26] Yet Anders also provides points of contrast to the gang girls, such as Giggles (Marlo Marron), a former member herself, now out of prison and looking for a computer job to support her daughter, and Alicia, whose tender appreciation of El Duran—at least before she knows who he is—speaks to the romantic resolve that sustains many "women reared on cheap romance and the religion of the gun," as Leslie Felperin saw the characters.[27]

What *Mi Vida Loca* may best demonstrate about the image of young tough Latinas is the tension they bear in wanting better lives for themselves despite the fact that they have few concrete ideas about how to achieve them, which is the essence of most delinquent depictions. These young women suffer the indignities of the men around them, all the while hoping—or gambling—that the men they pick as partners will help them survive. The film paints this hope as futile, with single motherhood an inevitability. In that way the film is fatalistic, but it shows that these women's enduring identities are synergistically dependent on one another, and because Anders cast many actual Latina gang members in the film, it further offers a tentative verisimilitude based on a feminine constancy and reliability that films about male gang members seem determined to break down.

As previously stated, the mid-'90s saw a boom in the output of tough girl films, which was met with varying degrees of success. Lesser-known films such as *Spitfire* (1994), *True Crime* (1995), *Freeway*, and *Ripe* (both 1996) offered increasingly complex interpretations of the hardened teen female—specifically the latter two, which were, respectively, a postmodern updating of "Little Red Riding Hood" in which the cast-off heroine escapes from prison to kill a murderous psychopath (read: wolf), and a true-life account of fraternal twin sisters who wind up on a military base where they discover different aspects of their emerging sexuality, leading one to kill the other's lover.

Foxfire (1996) offers a more coherent image of young female "outlaws," four high school seniors who are joined by a runaway girl of the same age and begin a latent feminist movement on campus while trying to cope with their own personal issues. First they retaliate against a sexually harassing teacher, and then begin hanging out in an abandoned house, casually drinking whiskey, smoking dope, and dancing, but unfortunately revealing little more about themselves. The runaway girl is the group's catalyst, only she is a necessary cipher, for the film suggests that these girls have been longing to break free and simply needed a shove to do so. In the end, the runaway continues on her run, and a final shot of one of the remaining girls ascending to the top of a bridge tower illustrates that she has gained similar independence and strength. Working against the transparent messages of the movie, which is based on a Joyce Carol Oates novel, the characters are kept remarkably distant. Like *Ripe* and the utterly impudent *Freeway*, the film plays as a parable, and given the realism of its setting, this makes the narrative's force a bit weaker, denying these strong, growing characters more complete identities. The film is not subtle in message—it is loudly telling girls to unite and stand up for themselves—yet its characters are too subtly drawn.

Girls Town (1996) offers more developed characters and presents them in a more informed way. The story begins with four New Jersey high school friends about to graduate: Patti (Lili Taylor), a single Latina mother who's grown into her early twenties as she's had to put school aside; Emma (Anna Grace), a white girl contemplating college; Angela (Bruklin Harris), a middle-class black girl also planning on college; and Nikki (Aunjanue Ellis), a black writer who has already been accepted to Princeton. The four meet to exchange the daily frustrations of their lives—Patti and Emma come from impoverished backgrounds, Angela rebels against her working mother—while Nikki is hiding her gnawing self-contempt, which the other three do not realize until Nikki suddenly kills herself. Reading through Nikki's diary, they learn that she was raped by a man at work, leading them to begin confronting one another about the tribulations that they do not discuss.

The narrative proceeds with each of the three remaining friends accounting for their anger at both men and women. Emma, who'd been raped by a school football star, vandalizes his car with Patti and Angela, writing "RAPIST" on the hood, "an act that not only outs this boy as violent toward females," Mary Celeste Kearney noted, "but equates the damage of a teenage boy's most prized possession (his car) with that of a girl (her body)."[28] After Emma's confused boyfriend hears of the incident, she becomes impatient with his lack of understanding and tells him to go away. Patti enlists the other two in stealing items from her abusive ex-boyfriend to pawn so they can buy food and clothes for her baby. Angela, who has kept a stolid composure, cuts loose on a smaller girl when she brings up Nikki's death in a disparaging way. Their acts are all motivated by a realization of their inner anger and a resolve to stop tolerating their teenage plights, especially those imposed by men—a more distinctly political agenda than the tough girls of past films. The girls become "feminist in praxis rather than ideology," Emanuel Levy noted.[29] Yet their implicit ideological agenda emerges after they begin a list of sexually abusive students and teachers on a bathroom stall at school, and other girls come forth to add to the list, quietly augmenting their rebellion. Slowly they realize that their sole strength is through one another, and "institutions like church, school, police, and family are uncaring, absent, or ineffective," as Phil Riley observed.[30] The girls' harmonious diversity of race, class, and interests further testifies to the similar problems shared by a wide range of women, as well as the solidarity they must rely on to overcome those problems. (Queen Latifah's closing song "U.N.I.T.Y." makes this message adamant.)

Director Jim McKay worked through improvisation with his performers, who developed each of the character's stories and identities collaboratively. This lends the film a certain realistic cohesion of vision, as each of the girls becomes more fully cognizant of changes she wants to make in her life; in that way, Levy claims, the story "conveys effectively the sheer joy and catharsis in the girls' reluctance to quietly accept their place in society."[31] Their climactic collective step in that direction is when they pay a visit on Nikki's rapist and beat him in the street, not to the point of serious injury, but enough to make their virulent rage known. The film concludes on a bittersweet note, as the girls realize that their summer will pass quickly and they will then be separated, yet they have given one another a sense of confidence and control they never had before.

After these portraits of girl groups in the mid-'90s, the film industry returned to more solo depictions of tough girls, such as *The Opposite of Sex* (1998), which is perhaps most indicative of late-'90s tough girl roles, even if the heroine is somewhat sinister. Christina Ricci plays Dedee, a disenchanted teen who moves in with her upwardly mobile gay half-brother and proceeds to seduce his boyfriend. She later finds that she's pregnant and goes on the run, eventually deciding to have the baby so that it can be raised by her more caring brother. Dedee is the tough girl as confident to the point of being self-centered, and thus she doesn't stand up for a cause like previous protagonists, although she does reveal by the end her sense of frustration with the world, and she does come to realize her limitations without succumbing to them. Such a character thereby retains her sense of humanity while remaining dedicated to finding her own direction in life.

In many ways the tough girl films are still seeking an identity for their attitude and style, just as the characters are within the films, because this remains relatively new terrain in youth cinema. The tough girl films before the mid-'90s never found a specific identity, let alone a niche in the movie market. By the turn of the century, as Bernard Weinraub pointed out, teenage girls had gained potency at the box office as well as on screen.[32] Many films about tough girls established themselves within the juvenile delinquency genre, with their ethos more successfully crossing over to other genres such as horror in *The Craft* (1996), *The Rage: Carrie 2* (1999), and *Tamara* (2005); dark dramas like *Wicked* (1998), *Crime + Punishment in Suburbia* (2000), and *Pretty Persuasion* (2005); thrillers like *Wild Things* (1998), *The Mod Squad* (1999), and *The Quiet* (2005); and comedies such as *That Darn Cat* (1997), *10 Things I Hate About You* (1999), and *Saved!* (2004). Even period films like *Whatever* (1998), *A Soldier's Daughter Never Cries* (1998), and *Dick* (1999) presented revisions of the tough girl image through their protagonists, suggesting that the impetus for young female authority began manifesting itself long before the current generation.

Tough teenage girls continue to thrive in American cinema as the twenty-first century goes on, having emerged as more aware of their past mistreatment and misrepresentation and more in control of their destiny, both politically and sexually. Most of them continue as primarily lone figures, as in *Girlfight* (2000), *Real Women Have Curves* (2002), *On the Outs* (2004), *Hard Candy* (2005), *Nancy Drew* (2007), and *According to Greta* (2009), while groups of girls have become less antagonistic, if no less supportive of one another, as in *The Sisterhood of the Traveling Pants* (2005) and its 2008 sequel. Further attempts to reintroduce the girl rock band as a force of female unity with odd productions such as *Josie and the Pussycats* (2001), *Bandslam* (2009), and *The Runaways* (2010) were faint indictments of the negative masculine dominance in popular music that did little to actually gain more authority for girls. This condition may signal the film industry's ongoing diffusion of the synergy girls find in groups, yet the solo tough girls in recent years have been strikingly dynamic. *Girlfight* is especially demonstrative in this regard, as its Latina heroine trains to become a boxer in the heavily male-dominated sport, while she also confronts struggles at home with her abusive father, and must ultimately fight her new boyfriend in the ring, all the while maintaining her integrity and drive for a better life.

Of equal interest is another film about a tough Latina, *Real Women Have Curves*, with a protagonist quite unlike the gang girls in *Mi Vida Loca*. The film begins in Los Angeles on the day that Ana (America Ferrera) is finishing high school, and though she has the intelligence, she has decided to not apply for college, thinking it would be too expensive and too disruptive for her symbiotic Mexican American family. Rather, she becomes resigned to working for her older sister at a dressmaking factory, where her mother gives her daily grief "to lose weight in order to perform femininity more effectively, to make herself attractive to men, marry, and have children," as Yvonne Tasker argued.[33] Ana is nonetheless proud of her body and her image, and smoothly takes on an adoring white boyfriend, pursuing sex with him while anticipating that they may not have a long relationship. When she convinces her coworkers to strip down to their underwear for an impromptu contest of body fat, her mother is appalled, but Ana and the other women take on a resilience, flaunting their sizable yet real bodies against the thin, headless dummies on which they work. This release is soon followed by a dubious contrivance in which Ana is accepted with a full scholarship to a prestigious college at the end of the summer, and with her father's approbation overtaking her mother's mortification, she moves to another big city, on a new path of her own.

The film's admiration of Ana's spirited East LA neighborhood through numerous scenes of daily life emphasizes the comfort she feels in living there, and portrays the Latin community as familiar and common, in no way a threat to her like the urban surroundings of so many other movie youths. The greatest threats to Ana are her mother's constant reproach and ongoing insistence that she follow a more traditional feminine ideal; the rhetoric of the film is persuasive in depicting the gravity she feels under such pressure. In contrast to more vicious and tormented tough girls, the dangerous behavior that Ana engages in to achieve her goals is simple deviance from her mother and from deference, and that deviance is serious indeed for a young woman expected to remain in a mold that does not fit her. Ana must steel herself against stifling family expectations, cultural customs, and gender assumptions, ultimately revealing that sheer self-determination is perhaps the most potent weapon any contemporary girl can have.

In terms of specific sexual power, no girl in American cinema history has ever wielded a more brutal tool than Dawn (Jess Weixler) in *Teeth* (2007). She seems to be an ordinary Christian teenager, devoted to staying virginal until marriage, to the point that she promotes a commitment to

"YOU HAVE NEVER, EVER, **EVER** SEEN ANYTHING LIKE THIS BEFORE...
FANTASTIC & COMPLETELY **UNFORGETTABLE**"
ROBBIE COLLIN - NEWS OF THE WORLD

IT'S WHAT'S INSIDE THAT COUNTS

The tough girl character in this poster for Teeth *(2007) is minimized to the right, yet the engorged image vividly represents her internal power.*

chastity at high school rallies. She begins dating her classmate Tobey (Hale Appleman), who seems to share in her sexual abstinence, until one day when he makes assaultive advances on her. At first Dawn physically resists, but after Tobey starts to actually rape her, she suddenly uses her vagina to bite off his penis. Dawn is horrified by her own mysterious actions, and after learning of a mythological curse known as the *vagina dentata*, she seeks advice from a gynecologist. Alas, the doctor is too rough with his exam, inserting his fingers into Dawn's tight orifice and causing her excruciating discomfort, whereupon a struggle ensues as her vulva clamps down and its submerged cogs chew off half his hand. Now convinced that she herself is cursed, and feeling guilt from the resulting death of Tobey, she turns to her friend Ryan (Ashley Springer) for solace, who also has designs on seducing her, only his attentive and gentle approach results in satisfying intercourse for Dawn without dismembering his manhood. Dawn temporarily believes that Ryan is the fabled hero who has relieved her of the curse, so now in control of her genitals, she assertively mounts him to have sex again, yet when he reveals that he bet a friend she would be submissive, she retaliates in anger by literally fucking his dick off.

The sheer amount of graphic emasculation in the film is astonishing to be sure, yet aside from her cursory religious beliefs, the narrative does not provide Dawn with enough emotional complexity to exploit her effusive puissance until the end. After chomping off Ryan's bit, she next comes on to her hated stepbrother, who has always harbored perverted lust for her, and showing that she's gained some fulsome finesse with her technique, she uses her flange to detach his shaft, then holds it with her labia until she drops it on the floor in front of his ornery pit bull, who promptly munches on the glans herself. Dawn thereafter runs away from home with no particular plan, and is later picked up hitchhiking by a dirty old man who will apparently be her next victim; she thus begins a new day, suggested by her name, as a revolutionary feminist heroine for teen movie girls, avenging abuse like a vagilante.[34] The film's flat form of levity is effective for such an extreme cautionary tale, since Dawn is able to slay men in their most virile and vulnerable area when they enter her. As Steve Biodrowski points out, Dawn has "become a full-blown *femme fatale*, confident—and even eager—in her ability to level the playing field that so long favored men."[35] Because she is further able to command the jaws inside her masticating pudendum, she becomes impregnable in the truest sense, able to enjoy sexual pleasure for herself and permanently punish the men who cause her sexual pain. Perhaps the visceral reaction to the visual result of Dawn's abilities is enough to convey the numerous messages of the film that are otherwise left implicit.

The '10s continued to feature the lone tough girl character as alternately comical (the proud virgin in *Easy A*, 2010), conflicted (the guilt-ridden *Margaret*, 2011), and creative (the self-designed Latina of *Girl in Progress*, 2012). The flourishing of these character types continued in *Kick-Ass* (2010) with its depiction of a pre-teen crime-fighting superhero girl; *Hick* (2011), about a thirteen-year-old Nebraskan who embarks on a westward odyssey and survives trying ordeals in her exodus; and *God Bless America* (2011), an audacious tale of a teenage girl joining a middle-aged man motivated by pop culture outrage to kill despicable people.

Certain proof that the tough girl role has become solidified in contemporary American movies is the successful roles of Jennifer Lawrence in two popular films, *Winter's Bone* (2010) and *The Hunger Games* (2012), the latter being the first of a franchise scheduled to run until 2015. In *Winter's Bone*, Lawrence plays Ree, a seventeen-year-old Missouri girl who lives in abject poverty with her younger brother and sister surrounded by a dilapidated landscape of distressed shacks. Her mother has gone catatonic from crystal meth abuse, and the drug has become the scourge of Ree's family and essentially their entire region, with the locals all seemingly involved in cooking it or doing doses. The story opens with a visit from the county sheriff who is looking for Ree's missing father, a cooker due for a court appearance who posted his bail bond against the house Ree lives in; if her father does not show up for court the next week, the house will be forfeited. Thus ensues what Ree thinks will be a simple journey to find her father by asking area residents—all of whom seem to be related to one another—for any information that will point her in the right direction, yet she soon comes to realize that everyone is under some omertà: no one will mention his chicanery that has left them so irate.

In the course of her search, Ree is severely beaten by some local women she questions, and her very resilience in persisting against the concealment of her father's whereabouts, as well as the brutality she suffers from the cruelest in her community, attests to her physical strength and emotional resolve. Her status as a teenage matriarch, with the burden of a severely disabled mother and two siblings too young to care for themselves, is remarkable as well, as the strain of saving her house and her household is placed squarely on her young shoulders. Ree is indefatigable, working with minimal resources and trusting in unreliable sources as she continues on her quest, which ends with the same women who beat her offering to show her where her father's been buried. The revelation of his death comes as little surprise to Ree because it had become apparent, yet she needs proof of his death in order to void the bond duty, so she reluctantly accompanies the women to a distant pond where she's told his body lay underwater. As if she has not endured enough torture from her father's legacy, she suffers one last indignity when she must pull his hands from the water and use a chainsaw to cut them off for evidence of his demise.

Ree represents the contemporary tough girl in a distinctly primitive environment, without the literal means of power to help her survive. She must live off the land, eating squirrels and relying on occasional food from neighbors to feed her family. She has no money whatsoever, and even considers joining the army for the financial bonus, but learns that she needs parental permission to enlist, which is impossible. After her father's death is verified and she is thereby able to secure the house, she then comes into money as part of the reimbursement, yet makes no suggestion she will abandon the home she has now earned, telling her siblings, "I'd be lost without the weight of you two on my back. I ain't goin' anywhere." Ree does not enjoy the attention of friends who can be advocates of her determination; rather, she must take on her obligation alone and against hope, against parents and an entire society that has forsaken her. In that way, she is the teenage girl as id, focused on sheer survival, overcoming every obstacle thrown at her with whatever force she can muster from inside.

The character of Ree provides the perfect foundation for Katniss Everdeen, the heroine of *The Hunger Games*, who has been directly transposed to a similar environment of poverty with a needy younger sibling, a withdrawn mother and deceased father, and a meager lifestyle of hunting and gathering. The crucial difference is that Katniss lives in a dystopian world where twelve different labor districts of the population are ruled by a central government whose people enjoy exceptional wealth and gaudy attire, and once a year they engage in a televised ritual to watch a random boy and girl from each district gather in a wild but contained area to fight one another to the death until only one child remains.[36] This contrast of urbanity with barbarism is visually abundant; what is lacking are more details of how the game will be played. Despite the seventy-four years in which the ceremony has been enacted, the teenagers randomly chosen to participate know very little about it. The onerous effort of the script to convey what the admired literary trilogy presented with such aplomb makes the film an awkward mash of sci-fi adventure, melodramatic character study, and conventional teen combat that translates well for viewers raised on video games.[37]

The narrative proceeds with Katniss volunteering to be the girl representing her district after her younger sister is initially selected, and she is paired with Peeta (Josh Hutcherson), a boy with whom she's only had a fleeting encounter. The duo is aided by an odd assortment of advisers in preparation for the game, yet just two of these characters, and almost none of the other youth in the game, are given enough personality to confirm the competence of their skills or elicit concern about their fates. Once the game commences, the action takes over and Katniss is left to forage the wilderness for food and safety with a sparse few items, none of which has the lethality of most other competitors' tools, which include knives and swords. Katniss does eventually procure the weapon she is most proficient at using, a bow and arrow, and in the process of defending herself against an alliance of teens including Peeta, she comes upon the much younger Rue (Amandla Stenberg). She saves Katniss after deadly wasps sting her, yet Katniss cannot save Rue when another contestant descends on them.

At this moment in the film, Katniss bares the deeper sensitivity that inhabits her character, pausing from the fight to give Rue a compassionate funeral. Yet such depth is rarely shown throughout the rest of the film due to its flashy emphasis on the game, even with Lawrence's compelling thespian efforts. While the masses watch the game play out on their enormous televisions, a mutiny begins in Rue's district that must be quelled, and the game leader announces rule changes to encourage Katniss and Peeta to ally, resulting in a romance that she entertains only on the surface. One predictable outcome for both characters is that they never kill any of the other players, making them moral in their survival, although in the end Katniss must shoot the penultimate survivor in the hand with one of her arrows so that he falls to a pack of dogs and she and Peeta are left alone. Facing this result, he tells her to kill him, revealing his love is true, yet she defies the rules by suddenly plotting their simultaneous suicide, whereupon the game is immediately halted and they are declared dual victors.

Katniss does not articulate any sense of accomplishment after this, but instead faces the scolding of an adviser who claims that she has disrupted the government's ideals by making herself a trailblazer who may foment further rebellion within the districts. Katniss scarcely seems inspired by this potential, and so the film, with its necessary sequel already planned, necessarily ends in suspended ambiguity about her fate.[38] This condition of the production notwithstanding, Katniss could have been a much more physically active and intellectually sophisticated heroine for the masses inside the film and in front of the screen. Her fortitude is displaced onto her resolve to not play the game according to the government's demands, granting her a mighty authority indeed, only one which is not realized until the conclusion, and which she never set out to achieve. The result is that her supremacy is all but coincidental, and while saving the boy and surpassing the hazards of the other youth are noble acts, they are not the result of any determined agenda on her part.

Tough girl characters continue to proliferate in American youth cinema in a refreshing array of roles. While they do not all achieve the blockbuster success of *The Hunger Games*, the fact that such a film will become a trilogy is a promising sign that conservative cultural attitudes about young female power have been changing. This is even more amply evident in the huge success of both the *Underworld* (2003–2012) and *Resident Evil* (2002–2012) franchises, despite some of their lingering sexist aspects. The recent representations of tough girls display a cautious effort by the film industry to provide increasingly active images of young women, most of whom remain conflicted about their new senses of power. These films and their characters will continue to discover the range of their authoritative attributes as they alleviate their internal conflicts, and as all young women in cinema continue to achieve greater authority without "delinquent" actions.

CRIME UNTIL 1999

Juvenile delinquency finds its moral and practical extreme in stories about youth committing actual crimes such as robbery, rape, and murder. These actions, which do gain attention for their perpetrators, are born from origins more desperate than the need to rebel against norms or stand up to oppression, and tend to find their root causes in poverty, parental misguidance (or absence), abuse by elders, and on occasion, mental illness. These are backgrounds given to young characters who are then often placed in treacherous situations such as urban blight and corrupt social circles, and the results are sensational movies that have had an enduring appeal since the tales of wayward slum boys during the Depression-era 1930s.

Criminal activity changes with the laws that forbid it, from age restrictions on alcohol consumption to banning of controlled substances, as well as limiting access to "tools" that can facilitate deviance such as guns, cars, or now the Internet. Thus, cybercrimes were not a possible threat in the pre-net age the way they became with *WarGames* (1983), *Hackers* (1995), *Swimfan* (2002), and *@urFRENZ* (2010), which curiously displayed a decreasing reach for the transgressions of their protagonists who, respectively, accidentally provoke the risk of war, upend companies' confidential data, stalk their love interests, and become suicidally obsessed. As the following study shows, that decreasing potential of youth crime to yield cinematic drama led to a deliberate erasure at the end of the decade, since the real-life rate of youth criminality began to decline after the mid-'90s, just as the output of African American crime films had passed their peak. During that same time, however, heavily publicized shootings by students at schools across the country quickly made the topic of juvenile delinquency a newly immediate concern, and with the brutal massacre at Columbine High School in Colorado in 1999, Hollywood studios largely withdrew from the topic altogether, leaving independent filmmakers to address what was otherwise a prevalent, if passive, national crisis.

The independent market began relying on JD dramas in the 1950s, after major studios promoted the likes of Marlon Brando (*The Wild One*, 1954) and James Dean (*Rebel Without a Cause*, 1955) to embody the young tough guy who would become a stock character in profuse exploitation fare thereafter: *Crime in the Streets* (1956), *Four Boys and a Gun* (1957), *Juvenile Jungle* (1958), and many more. These films were all reacting to the swell of teenagers in the population as a result of the postwar baby boom, teenagers who were breaking with past customs of conformity to norms. Most '50s

delinquents found their motivations in troubled childhoods and social expectations, until later '60s films found youth rebelling against the establishment, often under the influence of drugs, as in *Wild in the Streets* (1968), *The
Hooked Generation* (1968), *Free Grass* (1969), and *Beyond the Valley of the Dolls*
(1970). While on-screen delinquency faded during the overall decline of
youth cinema in the '70s, two notable films of the early '80s indicated that
nostalgia for the previous era of JD films was still fertile.

The *Outsiders* and *Rumble Fish* were both released in 1983 and both based
on S. E. Hinton novels and directed by Francis Ford Coppola, joining in
the increasing legitimacy of the youth film genre during that decade.[39]
The first is set in 1960 with a group of friends who have formed a ragtag
gang of working-class dudes that fights over disputed territory against a
clique of upper-crust kids. Where the first film is rather traditional in its
styling with a cinematic form common to high-quality studio productions
of the '60s, the latter is altogether different in appearance yet similar in featuring familiar characters with rough lives who have been driven to crime.
Through black-and-white images shot in expressionistic modes to convey
imbalance, the story follows the reluctant leader of a street gang who must
face the return of his edgy brother; the era and location of the story are
vaguely 1950s Midwest, and this opacity provides the rebel characters with
a timeless omnipresence that effectively deflates the raw aggression of their
delinquency through diluting the characters' place and purpose. Critics and
audiences consequentially dismissed the film, even though as a pair both
films are stimulating celebrations of the pathos that imbues JD roles across
generations.

Youth in further '80s films were involved in crimes within contemporary settings, always promoting the message that the only two outcomes
of such a lifestyle are prison or death, as in *Bad Boys* (1983), *Tuff Turf* (1985),
At Close Range (1986), and *China Girl* (1987). In the case of the most critically discussed teen crime film of the '80s, *River's Edge* (1987), death has
already befallen one of the characters, after John (Daniel Roebuck) casually
strangles his girlfriend alongside a river. John brings his friends to see the
body, and they agree to keep it a secret until Matt (Keanu Reeves) is finally
struck by his conscience and goes to the police. John is later killed by a local
sociopath who strangely understands that John will never feel as good as he
did when he killed the girl. The somber conclusion finds the young friends
again gathering at the river's edge to look at John's body, where Matt confronts his younger brother, who had planned to kill him over his betrayal
of John, and the two reconcile through a vague fraternal connection.

Perhaps more than any other youth film of the '80s, *River's Edge* ironically screams out the apathy that many disenchanted youth have felt. As one boy explains to the group, the murder is not an issue of morality but of unifying privacy, and loyalty to a cause that does not exist, invoking as he does the fictional ethos of *Starsky and Hutch*. Richard Combs thus points out that *"River's Edge* sees life's lack of values as somehow connected with popular culture's overwhelmingly artificial values."[40] When the murder of John is intercut with Matt having sex with his girlfriend for the first time, a clear link between death and sex is made, which becomes a statement on the lack of emotion all of these characters feel toward two such extreme experiences. The fact that Matt's younger brother—who adores John's disregard for the world—despises Matt for his moral awakening, only further speaks to the narrative's suggestion that all levels of affectation are suspect.

Attention must also be paid to the teenage character who is at once over- and underdetermined here, the innocent dead girl. A veritable matrix of '80s youth film representations runs through the image of her naked, stiff body next to the river. She is the end result of all the abuse inflicted on prematurely sexualized young women in the exploitative sex romps from earlier in the decade. She is the victim of ultimate teen anomie without an identity. And she is the spectacle of a male sadistic fantasy in which youth fail to comprehend the significance of their actions. In the (disem)body of this girl, which the film employs as its index to adolescent nihilism and depravity, the most comprehensively articulate image of youth delinquency in the '80s is achieved.

Youth crime films in the early '90s took on an urgency more intense than the category had experienced since the 1950s. Few youth films to that time had chronicled the lives of African American youth, or else had integrated them as characters within the generally Caucasian confines of most teen settings.[41] In the early '90s, a distinct trend developed in which African American youth were shown in films fighting for their lives, under the hegemony of a racist legal and political system, under difficult family and class conditions, and under the sway of the media that were rapidly codifying the image of young black "gangstas" through certain rap music acts.[42] This presented a set of tricky issues to these films, for many wanted to reveal the long-suppressed conditions of their characters' real-life equivalents, but many also appealed to a notion of criminality as a way of life, in the face of all of these films' explicit messages that crime does not pay. Critics often attacked the films as beholden to the expectations of routinely white audiences, or as glorifying the image of violent young black men who mistreat women and fail to achieve their ambitions.

This argument may help explain the gradual demise of the African

American youth crime film by 1995. More diverse and less ghettoized representations of African Americans began reaching the screen by the mid-'90s, and the repetitive themes—and problematics—of the youth crime film had become apparent. The youth film market had also become saturated with these films, and further, less violent portraits of African American youth began appearing by the mid-'90s on numerous television programs, as well as in the popular documentary *Hoop Dreams* (1994), and in spoofs of the "hood" films (*Friday* [1995], *High School High* [1996], and the well-titled *Don't Be a Menace to South Central While Drinking Your Juice in the Hood* [1996]).[43]

As significant as these films were in exposing audiences to (male) African American youth culture and questioning the current state of race relations in the nation, from a generic perspective these films were instrumental in reviving critical and financial legitimacy for all youth films, which had been declining throughout the late '80s. The African American youth film was the dominant variety within the genre from 1991 until 1995, when a wider range of youth films began to again appear. Further, for as much as these films addressed violence among youth, they always condemned it within their narratives, and seemed to spur a cross-generic incentive to raise critical issues about youth conditions in other films as well. Whether the African American youth crime drama of the early '90s was a mere industry fad is moot. I argue that the more unsettling and direct representations of youth conditions presented in these films have had and will continue to have a lasting impact on the cinematic depiction of youth, if only in terms of questioning their cultural context, specifically issues of race, class, and morality.

Many chronicles of the '90s African American youth crime film would begin with John Singleton's massively contributory *Boyz N the Hood* in 1991, although two low-budget precursors by independent filmmakers should be cited for directly or implicitly raising the same issues as the films that followed. *Up Against the Wall* (1991) is about a drug runner who vocally questions race and class obstructions in the black community, and further criticizes his father, from whom he'd been estranged since birth, for not caring more about him and his mother. *Straight Out of Brooklyn* (1991), one of the rare feature films written and directed by a teenager, draws a sensitive portrait of an overwrought youth with the misguided notion that his felonies will give him the money to save his family and move away to a better place. With these two early texts, connections between race, family, and crime were ascertained as the foci of subsequent narrative conflicts in these films.

Boyz N the Hood opens with young Tre (Cuba Gooding Jr.), the son of a strong-willed mother, in his rebellious years as a pre-teen, and then moves on to his teen years spent living with his equally strong-willed father, Furious (Larry Fishburne). Director John Singleton, as Jack Mathews claimed, "deals with a lot of issues here: the permanence of psychological damage on children living with unchecked violence; the degrading attitude of many black males toward women; the economic opportunism of people from outside the neighborhood; and the frustration of many blacks toward black cops in their community. But the point he drives home hardest is the need for more African American men to take responsibility for raising their sons, to give them direction and make them accountable for their lives."[44]

This message of paternal responsibility is made clearest through Furious's straightforward lectures to his son about standing up to oppression and overcoming adversity, and by the time Tre is a teen, he has become one of the most respected kids in his community. He stands out among his group of friends, particularly the heavy drinker and dope dealer Doughboy (Ice Cube), who went to juvenile prison for killing an older youth and has now returned home, uninterested in finding a job or going back to school. Tre and his pals have the same interests as other guys their age—cars, parties, and girls—and for much of the film these are their sole pursuits. Tre has a girlfriend in Brandi (Nia Long), who has been resisting his requests for sex because she doesn't think it is worth the risks involved, and Tre reluctantly respects her. Brandi wants to go to college after high school and would like Tre to come with her, so Tre must decide between his hanging-out lifestyle in South Central Los Angeles and the prospect of college in Georgia with Brandi.

This decision becomes secondary to a more central conflict in which Tre and his friends find themselves the target of a small black gang, who eventually murder Doughboy's brother. This prompts Tre and Doughboy into retaliatory action, until Tre becomes racked by his conscience and backs out before going through with the climactic gunning down of the rival gang, which is carried out by Doughboy. The film ends with the forlorn Tre realizing that he needs to leave his hardened neighborhood as Doughboy wonders of the likelihood of his own death by other killers, and an end title tells us that Tre did indeed go on to college with Brandi, and Doughboy was murdered just weeks later. Despite this sobering ending, the climax can still be seen as a rationalization of vengeance, and the film's depiction of Tre as wiser than such behavior is effectively undermined by Doughboy's tough hero status and off-screen demise.

Yet *Boyz* is not about moral retribution as much as it is about the struggle for righteous survival; an opening title alerts us of the statistic that one in twenty-one black men is murdered, and it sets the tone for the film's examination of the sad and senseless violence that is part of the lives of certain urban African Americans. This is what made the film so provocative and prominent at its time of release, and from a generic perspective, such a story was already well suited to drama. *Boyz* helped to establish an altogether new image of youth in American cinema, the young black warrior–survivor, and while none of the films that featured this new role achieved the same success, the image would be pervasive and profound in many other films over the next four years. Paula Massood argues that *Boyz* "lays the groundwork and maps the route for the narrative and signifying systems" that the subsequent *Menace II Society* (1993) would "then use in a shorthand manner."[45] I would expand this point to include essentially all of the African American youth crime films that followed *Boyz* in the '90s.

Although only a few similar films had appeared before *Juice* was released in 1992, many critics called it part of a formula.[46] The story of four black youths who pull off a botched robbery was not as well received as *Menace II Society* the next year, about a drug dealer who denies various opportunities to escape his criminal practice. As in most of these films, the story does not dourly simplify the social disorder it presents, which David Denby pointed out: "[*Menace*] doesn't lay off the problems on somebody else; it doesn't say that whitey is to blame for everything, or that there's no way out. There are ways out; the tragedy is that people aren't always ready or able to take them."[47]

Two more films in this cycle appeared in 1994: *Above the Rim*, bringing sports drama to its story of a high school basketball player lured into drug dealing, and the extraordinary *Fresh*, focusing on a preternaturally confident yet pint-sized twelve-year-old criminal who is still young enough to change his direction in life.[48] Then, with *New Jersey Drive* and *Clockers* in 1995, the African American youth crime drama came to an end. By then the moral lessons of these films had become worn, and the characters stale, excepting that both films remain stylish and well made. *Drive* focuses on a car thief who runs afoul of the law, which is the same crisis faced by the drug dealer in *Clockers*.

Strike (Mekhi Phifer) is a teenage "clocker," a hustler of crack, who has both the Brooklyn cops and the community against him. His supplier is an unassuming gangster named Rodney (Delroy Lindo) who, as a test of Strike's reliability, asks him to murder a local troublemaker. The twist in this story is that Strike's older brother Victor (Isaiah Washington) turns himself in for the murder, even though he has no criminal connections and is a respectable family man. The cops don't believe Victor and continue to

Sean Nelson plays the title character in Fresh *(1994), who survives tragedy and uses his intelligence to confront the criminal elements of his surroundings.*

pressure Strike, whose mounting stomachaches are a sign that the stress of his lifestyle is getting to him. Like all the other drug-running black youth in these films, Strike never ingests what he deals, and he warns his fatherless pre-teen protégé Tyrone (Pee Wee Love) against ever taking the drugs, as he's forthrightly molding him into a pusher. After the police arrest Rodney under suspicion of murder, he orders a hit on Strike, only the hit man is gunned down by Tyrone with Strike's gun. In another twist, Strike and Victor's mother comes forth to confess that Victor is indeed the killer, and one of the nicer cops who's been following Strike takes him to a train so that he can get out of the city and get on with a new life.

Strike's centrality to the story is fixed, yet the plot spends much time on the white investigating detectives (Harvey Keitel and John Turturro), most likely due to the actors' star presence, and also to shift attention away from Strike's culpability in his gangster lifestyle. Strike is like all of the other hardened heroes of these films: he owns his decisions and can't blame them on the system. However, he actually shows evidence that he can't handle the gangster lifestyle, and unlike many other similar protagonists, he gets out of town in the end, evading his past transgressions. This indicates a certain optimism on the part of director Spike Lee that may have ironically signaled the further resolution of tensions within African American crime films, which thus made them lose interest for audiences. James Berardinelli commented on this change in the story's resolution compared to other films of this variety: "Productions like *Boyz 'N the Hood* and *Menace II Society* deliver their final blow through bloodshed. While Lee doesn't shy away from violence, his methods are less straightforward. Like 1994's *Fresh*, *Clockers* uses unexpected narrative turns to accentuate the themes of lost innocence and uncultivated potential, and affirms that tragic melodrama is not a prerequisite for emotional impact."[49]

The tragic melodrama of the film actually arises from its unusual imaging of family relations. For all of Strike's sense of independence (he lives alone on money from his dealing), he has a nefarious, if generically inevitable, surrogate father in Rodney, and yet he looks toward Tyrone as a surrogate son. This hints at not only Strike's longing for familial unity—which is further strained after his brother goes to jail—but his capacity to accept parental responsibility. Of course, his moral standards are still very much in question: no sooner does he share his love of toy trains with Tyrone than he's teaching him about running drugs. Then, after Tyrone saves his own surrogate father's life, Strike must face his lack of parental presence as Tyrone is taken away to jail, feeling a sense of failure as a father where previous protagonists felt their failures as sons.

Otherwise, *Clockers* provides still more of the same understandable messages as the past films, and continues the trend in alleviating the moral indiscretions of its protagonist by displacing the most violent acts onto another character. The rules to be learned from the African American youth crime films were plainly clear by this point: that broken families cannot be unified by crime; that crime is not lucrative, at least not for long; that crimes perpetrated against other blacks merely reinforce the racist social system; and that youth do not have the moral grasp to appreciate the repercussions of their crimes, even though they may gain it if they stay criminal long enough. Those who stay in the hood (as in *Straight Out of Brooklyn*, *Juice*, and *Fresh*) do so in the face of tragedy, with their own futures in great doubt. This cycle of films did not discourage young black men from finding alternatives to crime, despite their action–violence, nor did they deny race as a factor in the difficulties their young characters face. Rather, these films all suggested that the greatest menace is the city itself, where crime, racism, and death are pervasive and constant. Those who survive must find a way out of the hood, which is their best way out of strife.

The youth crime films of the late '90s, like those of any subgeneric category after a significant wave of productivity, were insignificant in relation to those that had just preceded them, excluding *American History X* (1998).

While only partially about a teen, the film was intriguing in its examination of racism as an element of youth crime, taking the perspective of bigots who cultivate and exacerbate hatred. Two other films were cogent in their examination of vulnerable families, *Before and After* (1996) and *Fear* (1996), and others resorted to customary arenas like school (*187*, 1997) and the city (*Hurricane Streets*, 1997). The 1999 film *Pups* debuted on April 18, featuring two teens with a gun taking hostages in a bank; two days later, two teens with numerous firearms took over Columbine High School in Colorado and shot thirty-four people, killing thirteen of them, and radically changing the perception of youth crime as movie entertainment.

CRIME AFTER COLUMBINE

Columbine soon affected the making and marketing of youth crime films, particularly *O*, an adaptation of Shakespeare's *Othello* that was made in early 1999 and then had its release postponed because its distributor feared backlash for its story's climactic multiple killing at a private school; the film was not released until late 2001.[50] *O* was initially owned by Miramax, a branch of the family-friendly Walt Disney Company, so the corporation's sensitivity to social response was not unexpected. Other major studios ordinarily stayed away from the topic of teen violence in movies for the rest of the decade, and to this day have not opened another film featuring youth crime at the level seen on screen in the early 1990s.[51]

Nevertheless, youth films focusing on school shootings were unusually plentiful in the 'oos among independent film companies, not unlike the wave of exploitation fare that arose in the subgenre during the late '50s. The first of these, *Home Room* (2002), dramatized the aftermath of a high school shooting as experienced by the survivors, and was virtually withheld from theaters. The next such film appeared just two months later, *Bang Bang You're Dead*, in which the specter of bloodshed hangs over a school after a bullied student pulls off a fake bomb threat and aggression escalates between opposing factions of teens. As a straight-to-DVD title, it too reached only a small audience. *Heart of America*, made in 2002 but not released until early the next year, was a Canadian production that nonetheless knowingly intended to capitalize on Columbine and was met with general contempt by critics.

The school shooting plot took on much greater prominence and acclaim in 2003 when *Elephant* premiered at the Cannes Film Festival that spring and won the Palme d'Or. The narrative, somewhat based on the Columbine events, casually follows a number of students at a nondescript high school while building curiosity about two boys who are gathering weapons for a planned assault. The film is deliberately vapid in its character development as well as its repetitive action, listlessly suggesting that the mundane lives of these kids ensues at every school in every town, and that the motives of the killers, while obliquely tied to some flaccid misanthropy, are essentially inexplicable. (Before the attack, the two boys shower together to provide some hint of homosexual angst, but like the rest of the action, this event is ostentatiously unsubstantiated.)[52] As the shootings commence, the victims are supposedly chosen at random, and the film concludes with the obvious and glib message that the vile cowards who killed so many children their own age were the product of a disaffected culture where mass murder has become the existential result of individual ennui. This approach, Jennifer Rich argues, "sheds a disturbing spotlight on the real 'elephant in the room': apathy, alienation, and dislocation."[53] The film continued to be met with critical praise as it went on to theaters, yet audiences were slight. Given the overwhelming cultural attention to the topic of teen violence, the film's banal presentation of youth crime is strikingly unemotional and arguably irresponsible, since its dilution of cause and blame for the carnage at its core renders such events impassive and, worse yet, inexorable.

Zero Day (2003) opened a few months after the debut of *Elephant*, approaching the topic in a recurring style of the time, the video diary: two teenage boys record themselves preparing to shoot up their school, and secure the tapes to be discovered after the murders and their suicides. This time, the killers themselves declare that there is no reason for their actions, continuing the mystique manufactured by other films, although a later film that year, *Detention*, insinuated that the entire allure of these stories had devolved into cheap thrills. In this case, a teacher assigned to the titular ritual defends his charges against terrorists who invade their school, resulting in much ballistic mayhem. As usual, these films were low-budget products of independent studios and were buried at the box office before going to DVD.

The barrage of these movies in the early '00s ebbed, but the theme reappeared in *The Life Before Her Eyes* (2007), about a woman reflecting on a mass shooting at her high school fifteen years earlier, and in *Mad World* (2010), which more directly added the up-to-date subject of bullying to its story of four distraught boys who decide to retaliate against the tyrants of their school.[54] Another recent film to enlist the school shooting story was the bizarre British production *We Need to Talk About Kevin* (2011), which follows a similar strategy of portraying its killer teen as a mysteriously evil American child with a typically privileged upbringing, who improbably carries out his evil slaughter within a locked school gymnasium using a bow and arrows. As with so many of the school shooting films following Columbine, the concluding indifference of the killer is intended to provoke exasperation at the inanity of youth crimes within the context of otherwise contented families and communities. Ultimately, the preoccupation with the entropy of these offenses has often made the films about them duly mediocre. Those few films that at least endeavored to explore the emotions of the criminals and their victims, and to show them confronting incidents arising from manifest influences, had more in common with other films about youth crime that were not distracted by the senseless school shooting story.

Other youth crime movies perused certain themes throughout the 'oos while usually examining more of the motives and effects of violence for perpetrators and victims. Bullying, and vengeance for it, remained a recurring plot in films like *Bully* (2001), *Mean Creek* (2004), *The Final* (2010), and *American Bully* (2009), which oddly uses the latent anger from the attacks of 9/11 and the consequent video broadcasts of terrorists killing Americans to show how such violence can lead misguided youth to murder and suicide. A more comprehensive study of bullying addressing generational and cultural factors is the superb *Gran Torino* (2008), which was the first big studio production to address youth crime in many years because it was directed by star Clint Eastwood, who plays Walt, a retired autoworker and widower quietly living out his twilight years in the suburbs of Detroit. His Polish background aside, Walt hypocritically laments the influx of immigrants in his neighborhood during recent years, and his Korean War service has left him particularly prejudiced against Asians. His contempt for the local Hmong causes him to stand down a youth gang that harasses his timid teenage neighbor Thao (Bee Vang), who has been refusing the lure of his cousin Spider (Doua Moua) to join his criminal circle. In the face of his own irritability, Walt warms to Thao's family, including his sister Sue (Ahney Her), after they lavish him with special foods in thanks for saving Thao.

To be sure, Thao seems to have no desire to join Spider in his thuggery, even when he reluctantly agrees to steal Walt's prized Gran Torino as an initiation ritual, but the boy's slight build and lack of a forceful father figure are meant to explain his easy intimidation. After Thao's family orders him to work for Walt for a week in penance for his attempted car

In Gran Torino *(2008),* Thao *(Bee Vang, left) is taunted and beaten because he resists a local Hmong gang that wants him to join in their lawless activities.*

theft, the elder takes the opportunity to teach the boy how to "man up" to American gender customs, which includes learning to curse and talk to girls. In a more enduring gesture, Walt arranges a construction job for Thao, only Spider perceives this as an intrusion on his efforts to recruit the boy, and further confrontations escalate until Spider and his gang rape and beat Sue. This leaves Thao and Walt hell-bent on revenge, but in a great twist, Walt does not attack the gang, instead sacrificing himself to their attack on him, with his voluntary suicide resulting in the hoodlums being taken away by police. Walt thus achieves a lasting peace for Thao and his family—his martyrdom made conspicuous by extensive Christian symbolism throughout the film—and Thao accepts Walt's car after the bittersweet reading of his will.

Thao may be vulnerable to Spider's bullying at first, but Walt provides for him the missing paternal guidance and work skills that will help him rise above his anticipated criminal destiny. In many youth crime films, the protagonist is not allowed such a caring (if cantankerous) mentor to halt his ascension to the criminal lifestyle, to avert the negative effects of friends, drugs, and/or local bosses that could divert him away from a righteous life. Bullying is of course the province of those insecure enough to derive authority from the less powerful, usually through empty threats, although many teen movies are made to provide the exhilaration of retaliation against the offenders. *Gran Torino* is a rare film thoughtful enough to pose its response to bullying in passive but highly effective terms that save the victim from submitting to the same brutality as his nemesis.

Youth crime continued to remain the domain of independent productions throughout the rest of the decade with the exception of *Murder by Numbers* (2002), about two detectives investigating two suspected teen killers. Other dualities were addressed in lower-budget productions such as those between counselors and patients at a psychiatric detention center in *Manic* (2001), between upstanding Asian American students and those turned on by deviance in *Better Luck Tomorrow* (2002), and between penologists and the incarcerated boy in *The United States of Leland* (2003). Beyond these examples, youth crime sagas continued with little continuity into the next decade, except that none gained much attention: the lighthearted heist caper *Catch That Kid* (2004), the flashback murder mystery *The Lost* (2006), and even the timely teenage gambling parable *The Odds* (2011). *The Bling Ring* (2013), with its adoring condemnation of teens robbing young celebrities' homes, had widespread hype yet a blasé audience.

Naturally, the popularity of a film often reveals nothing of its quality, as was the case with the wildly inventive *Brick* (2005), which at least had the fortune of finding a cult following later in the decade. Joseph Gordon-Levitt, who had begun turning in impressive teen performances starting with *Manic*, stars as Brendan, a high schooler who finds himself mixed up in a web of intrigue with a bevy of nervy characters culled from film noir types in the '50s. The cinematic form is hard-boiled as well, shot with canted angles and jarring edits that propel the time-shifting mystery of how Brendan's girlfriend was found dead after a botched drug deal—the distinction here is that almost all the players are teenagers themselves, living in a world of ruthless, shrewd youth embittered beyond their years. Michael Atkinson adroitly observed, "The cynicism of noir is deployed as a near-tears metaphor for pre-adult isolation, insecurity, and self-destruction, and it's such simple fusion between potent American cultural ideas it feels sui generis."[55] That unique attribute is bolstered when Brendan's gumshoe interrogation of leads takes him to the underworld kingpin controlling the local heroin trade, who turns out to be a disabled young man living with his mother. Brendan finally comes to understand that his girlfriend was murdered in a multifarious exchange of addictions, deceptions, theft, and jealousy, and gracelessly explains these cumbersome machinations in an amalgamated coda with a surviving dame. Pardoning this tactic, the film remains the kind of dynamic and engaging story that is true of only the best in this sub-genre: morally responsible without being didactic, exciting without being fantastic, and stylistically radical while staying accessible.

CONCLUSION

The complex and varied images of youth presented in these delinquency films evince the spectrum of character concerns, behaviors, and types that the film industry has employed in examining the way young people express their most tormented anxieties and enjoy their most libera-tory outlets. Unlike the school film, myriad character types are visible in the delinquency subgenre—at least one for every type of delinquency—and then within each type the motivations and actions of teen characters often cover a wide range.

The increasing articulation of anger by youth from the '80s into the '90s decreased in recent years, revealing how the intensity of and sensitivity toward juvenile delinquency changes with cultural conditions. At times, youth films have attempted to connect delinquency to so many sources of unrest—parents, school, law, race, class, gender, drugs, television, music, communication, capitalism—that the examinations of these potent forces have become diluted. The open evaluation of youth rebellion that has been a hallmark of juvenile delinquency films for generations has moved toward more implicit arguments, embodying greater ambivalence, unable to offer either clear critiques or celebratory assurances. Delinquency films in the twenty-first century have often seemed unable to understand why youth rebel, although most of them still determine that such rebellion is an in-evitable necessity, for the teens who wreak it as they confront adulthood and the adults who endure it as they try to comprehend constantly evolving youth.

Four THE YOUTH HORROR FILM

Slashers and the Supernatural

Grown-ups think it's funny to be scared.
DISPOSABLE TEENAGER TO LITTLE GIRL IN *JASON
LIVES: FRIDAY THE 13TH PART VI* (1986)

*Have you ever heard of invoking the spirit? It's when you call
him. . . . It's like . . . it's like you take him into you. It's like he
fills you. He takes everything that's gone wrong in your life and
makes it all better again.*
NANCY (FAIRUZA BALK) EXPLAINING HER WITCHY
PRACTICE IN *THE CRAFT* (1996)

*We're all here because we did some stupid things. We expressed
ourselves with drugs, alcohol, self-mutilation, sex, and with
suicide. And our lives, our minds, our selves are gone because of
our bad decisions. We took the road less traveled. And we died.
And we never will recover from that. But that's part of the whole
plan.*
SILVER (CELESTE MARIE DAVIS) REFLECTING ON HER
LIFE IN *PURGATORY HOUSE* (2004)

Of all the subgenres in this study, youth horror has been—
perhaps appropriately—the most enigmatic. It enjoyed massive financial
success and public popularity in the late '70s and early '80s: in 1981, *Variety*
claimed that "slasher" films (many of which featured teens) accounted for
60 percent of all U.S. releases that year, and twenty-five of the fifty top-
grossing films of that year were slashers as well.[1] Given this voluminous and
lucrative output of horror films at the time, and considering how many
of them were about teenagers, certain popular beliefs and assumptions

emerged: the youth horror film was excessively violent and gory; the vast majority of its violence was perpetrated against female characters; characters engaging in sexual activities paid for their indiscretions by being killed. Like all clichés, these perceptions were partially based in fact, because a number of youth horror films seemed to follow predictable formulas and motifs.

Nonetheless, many teen horror films since 1980 have deliberately challenged the structure and consistency of the subgenre, and the subgenre itself has gone through varying cycles of popularity, style, and content. The true consistency in virtually all the teen horror films of the past generation has been their concentration on youthful fears of being different, becoming sexual, and confronting adult responsibilities, fears that the horror film is ideally suited to examine (at least on a metaphorical level), and which themselves may not have changed much in the past few generations. These fears take on a strikingly wide array of manifestations—there are more types of horror movie dangers than types of teen characters themselves—and are thus confronted in a number of ways, making the youth horror film far more complex and significant in its representations of young people than popular belief would generally allow.

CONTEXTS AND TRENDS
IN THE SUBGENRE

Perhaps the most peculiar feature of the 1980s teen horror film was its excess of sex and violence, at least compared to its predecessors. There had been few horror films about youth before the '80s, although each had indeed been pushing the boundaries of acceptable excess: the violence of *I Was a Teenage Werewolf* in 1957 and *The Blob* in 1958 may have been shocking then, but was relatively tame compared to *Teenage Strangler* in 1964, which was far less gory than *Carrie* in 1976, a film that became a literal bloodbath and essentially came to represent the starting point of contemporary youth horror films. In the wider horror genre, Alfred Hitchcock's *Psycho* (1960) had crossed a clear threshold of bloody brutality, and the gore fests of Herschell Gordon Lewis (*Two Thousand Maniacs!* 1964) and zombie feasts of George Romero (*Night of the Living Dead*, 1968) began gaining mild attention in an era of otherwise declining cinematic attendance in the United States. Then the overwhelming popularity of *The Exorcist* in 1973 further demonstrated two phenomena of the genre that would

Sissy Spacek received an Oscar nomination for her performance as the title character of Carrie *(1976), a girl who is subjected to so much abuse—such as being doused in pig's blood at the prom—that she uses her telekinetic powers to enact a terrifying revenge.*

be fundamental to its greater success in the late '70s: audience acceptance of and fascination with morbid gore, and the use of a young character as the victim of (and in this case also the perpetrator of) inexplicable terror.

Carrie capitalized on these two phenomena with a teenaged protagonist facing adulthood, as evidenced most dramatically by the onset of her first menstrual period. *Carrie* was thus able to explore classic youth fears of adult transformation, plus its title character had the further "dilemmas" of super-natural telekinetic powers and a zealously religious mother. In the film's remarkable climax, Carrie uses her powers to unleash years of pent-up aggression at her high school tormentors—who have seen no end of humiliating the shy girl and decide to dump a bucket of pig's blood on her at the prom—and at her mother, whom she "crucifies" with knives.[2] *Carrie*, based on a Stephen King novel, set a high standard in the teen horror subgenre for character development as well as overall violence. Films that followed in the violent mode tended to minimize character development, as films that pursued character development tended to minimize violence.

A notoriously nervy 1974 horror film called *The Texas Chainsaw Massacre* began to have an apparent influence on various filmmakers over the rest of the decade. The film featured a family of psychos whose two sons stalk and murder four young victims, while a fifth barely manages to escape the carnage. As Carol Clover notes in her perceptive study *Men, Women, and Chainsaws: Gender in the Modern Horror Film* (1992), the film was instrumental in codifying what would become the classical practice of slasher films in the late '70s: a seemingly indestructible killer tracks down and cruelly kills a number of helpless young victims, sparing the last one, who is (according to Clover) always female, a character type she dubs the "Final Girl."[3] Coupled with the sensations of *Carrie* and *The Exorcist*, *The Texas Chainsaw Massacre* heralded a new era in Hollywood, not only for the graphic depiction of youths being brutally murdered by mysterious forces—hence the "slasher" moniker—but for low-budget films that became so successful they provided an industrial antidote to the blockbusters emerging at the time (e.g., *Jaws* [1975], *Star Wars* and *Saturday Night Fever* [both 1977], *Superman* and *Grease* [both 1978]—all of which were largely aimed at a young audience).[4]

The film that confirmed the new era of youth-oriented horror was John Carpenter's *Halloween* in 1978. The film earned at least seventy-five times its production costs, a massive profit ratio for an independent "exploitation" film.[5] With *Halloween* the teen die was cast: a shadowy figure stalks and kills four teens, all of whom are sexually active, while a fifth escapes with her life, ostensibly since she is a virgin. *Halloween* thus added an explicit sexual dimension to the formula (*Texas Chainsaw Massacre* and plenty of previous horror films offered copious, yet often implicit, sexual issues), and further evacuated the expansive subgenre of the character development seen in *Carrie*. Much time in *Halloween* was spent on lengthy creepy silences and suspenseful pauses in action that did not provide much background on the featured characters other than their ages, their senses of hedonism or puritanism (the four who are murdered have or are planning to have sex, and the survivor is dutifully babysitting), and their ignorance to the danger at hand (the babysitter continually tells her charges that they're only imagining the "boogeyman" they see outside). What the film did provide was a rousing time for its audience, as well as a paradigm for the image of most youth in the horror films of the next few years.

Thus ensued the onslaught: *Halloween* was followed in 1980 by two Canadian films that featured the now-typecast Jamie Lee Curtis (the babysitter in *Halloween*), *Prom Night* and *Terror Train*, in which a killer systematically eliminates high school and college students, respectively, and *Friday the 13th*, in which teenagers at a summer camp are stalked and killed by a dead boy's mother. The killers in all three films were avenging previous abuses or neglect inflicted by past teens, a familiar motive that would characterize many future villains; the youth in all of these films also remained rather firmly divided between the sinners and the sinless, with death coming to those of lesser moral stature. In this way, the teen horror subgenre that would thrive in the '80s relied on classical notions of misfortune falling on transgressors of purity, only now such "transgressions" as premarital sex and youthful hedonism weren't resulting in punishment by social institutions like parents, teachers, or the law, but in death at the hands of a greater evil.

By 1981, a cycle of slasher films was firmly established in the American cinema, and at least six such films that year concentrated on teenage characters (many more were about older characters). Proof of the slasher as an emergent category of the teen horror subgenre also came that year in the form of *Halloween* and *Friday the 13th* beginning their franchises with sequels, and a parody called *Student Bodies* that easily referenced the many slasher films of the previous few years.[6] The image of contemporary youth presented by these 1981 horror films was facile and incomplete at best, but it was undoubtedly a prominent image compared to other subgenres (I locate just over a dozen other youth films that year not in the horror subgenre, most of which are obscure), and it forms a strong starting point for the current study.

Slasher films, particularly those about teens, were already showing signs of lost prominence by 1982, and by 1983 only a few youth films featured the slasher formula of past years. Then in 1984 the teen horror subgenre found new momentum with the release of *A Nightmare on Elm Street*, a successful and somewhat refreshing take on the slasher scenario. The number of teen horror films released in 1985 doubled over the previous year, as a new industrial routine was emerging: the release of low-budget horror films straight to the video rental market, where youth who were otherwise barred from seeing the R-rated films alone in theaters were now able to watch the frightfests at home. The majority of teen horror films released from 1986 to 1990 all had scant, if any, theatrical releases, but many gained their profits in the growing video trade. In fact, there were more teen horror films released in these five years than in the more-discussed 1977–1981 span.

Consider that in the Reagan era (1981–1989), a new notion of American conservatism was sweeping the country, and horror films about wild youth were replaced by less metaphorical narratives about youth actually enjoying the pleasures of rebellion and sensuality; thus the teen sex film flourished in the early '80s (as detailed in the next chapter). Later, with public awareness of AIDS growing by the late '80s and a marked shift in the teen sex film from promiscuity to romance, the youth horror film again seemed to capitalize on otherwise classic youth fears of sexuality and adulthood. Perhaps the relative drought of slasher films by the early '90s was only indicative of the general decline in all teen film output at the time; perhaps the overdone violence of so many slasher films brought an entertaining glamour to more diverse terrors of the supernatural; perhaps the subgenre simply lost financial support from studios, given the theatrical failure of virtually all youth horror films from the late '80s to the mid-'90s (slasher films did not have a significantly profitable release between *A Nightmare on Elm Street 4: The Dream Master* [1988] and *Scream*, eight years later).[7]

The slasher scenario itself remained a dominant style of the subgenre into the late '80s, but a wider category of youth horror had been appearing: supernatural stories, some with occult themes, vampires, zombies, or other monsters, and some focused on lighter depictions of mystical people and places.[8] These films often offered less violence and more intellectual tussling with youth concerns, built on mythical solutions to their very real problems, such as proving proficiency (*The Last Starfighter*, 1984), preserving family (*Casper*, 1995), gaining acceptance (*The Craft*, 1996), and finding romance (*Twilight*, 2008). By the '90s, the subgenre had taken more interest in supernatural stories with a wider audience appeal, which was cemented in the '00s with the development of multiple series in this category, such as *Harry Potter* (2001–2011) and *The Chronicles of Narnia* (2005–2010). Sequels that were not planned as series had already become standard practice within the subgenre for any film that gained attention—the three most enduring franchises being *Halloween*, *Friday the 13th*, and *Nightmare* with at least seven versions of each by 2012, and lesser franchises emerging after *Slumber Party Massacre* (1982; a trilogy by 1990), *Sleepaway Camp* (1983; a trilogy by 1989), *Children of the Corn* (1984; eight versions by 2011), *Return of the Living Dead* (1985; five versions by 2005), and the Canadian *Prom Night* (1980; five versions by 2008).

After the industry's run of youth horror films on the video market in the late '80s, conditions of the subgenre and the industry again changed: very few teen slasher movies were released after 1990, and even fewer had more than one sequel. The plots of many films shifted focus notably toward more critical narratives dealing with social issues (e.g., *The People Under the Stairs* [1991], *Ticks* [1993], *Tales from the Hood* [1995]), and the overall output of youth horror films declined precipitously (the combined releases of 1993–1996 were fewer than the twenty-four youth horror films released in 1988 alone). However, the unexpected success of the revisionist *Scream* in 1996, along with *Scream* screenwriter Kevin Williamson's similar film *I Know What You Did Last Summer* (1997) and then the sequels to these films, revitalized the genre in the late '90s. By 2000, films like *Scary Movie* and the impressively mordant *Cherry Falls*—which features the twist of a psycho killer targeting teenage virgins—were both exploiting and satirizing the subgenre's most visible elements.

As in other youth subgenres, the question of generic cycles and evolution is germane to understanding the changing representations of youth within the teen horror subgenre. If the sheer industrial exploitation of the video market in the late '80s can explain the uprising of youth horror films at the time, what explains its popularity in the late '70s before video and its decline in the early '90s when video was still thriving? Perhaps the novelty and extremity of violence in the late '70s films help explain their success, as special effects artists were making reputations for themselves by developing ever more gruesome gore and the MPAA was allowing more gratuitous graphic violence to pass for an R rating, fulfilling audiences' fascination with excess. The late '70s were also characterized as an era of greater consumption by Americans, and with the expansion of malls and multiplex theaters within them, studios must have seen the advantage of tapping into social tensions of the time, with the literal consumption of people by eerie entities becoming a metaphor for the excess consumption of goods by the new yuppie generation. For youth, moral lessons about consumption were becoming ever more conspicuous in horror films about them—those who indulged in sex and drugs paid the price—a message that sublimating adults in the disco era must have felt compelled to drive home.

After the conservative attitudes of the '80s gave way to more liberal thinking in the '90s and a relative rise in personal wealth across the country, supernatural and fantasy films gradually became more successful, and by the '00s literary adaptations of young adult novels brought a fresh abundance of such tales to the screen. Studios were still invested in pushing the MPAA ratings boundaries, but now for PG-13 films that would not restrict youth attendance at theaters and would be met with more approval by parents monitoring movies at home. Meanwhile, the straight-to-video market converted from VHS to DVD, which allowed higher definition televisions to depict deeper details of fantastic worlds than had ever been seen before, and the media market enjoyed the recharged integration of written texts (including comic books) and screen stories (including video games) with technology. The plots about merciless killing of youth that had been so common in the subgenre during the '80s reformed by the '00s as more miraculous achievements of youth through mystical powers and space-time manipulation.

The roles of youth in this subgenre are an indicator of their development within films that initially afforded them a minimal sense of identity and now offer them extraordinary identities. Indeed, the slasher film may have also declined because it relied on less intelligent, less sophisticated young characters, an image of themselves that youth began rejecting in recent years (case in point the welcome reception of movies like *Scream* and *Twilight*, wherein the heroines are smart, tough teens). Youth in most horror films have evolved beyond the survival of violence to the conquering of fear.

HORROR STORIES

While other youth film subgenres have been occasionally taken up by previous scholars, the horror film has generated much literature over the years, and Carol Clover's *Men, Women, and Chainsaws* is integral to this study, even though little of the book addresses issues about youth. Clover's thesis is that horror films since the 1970s have problematized certain received notions about gender identification in cinema, if only because these films reveal "the possibility that male viewers are quite prepared to identify not just with screen females, but with screen females in the horror-film world, screen females in fear and pain."[9] I argue that the teens in many of these films are presented in images that are superficial and accessible enough for a dual-gendered appreciation of their plight, especially as men and women are almost equally likely to be victims (other research on this follows), and even though more attention has been paid to female survivors, a role that Clover calls the "female victim–hero" in her coining of the phrase "Final Girl."

Clover's articulation of the Final Girl role in recent horror films sheds some light on the use of teens in the horror film system. As previously mentioned, Clover identifies the Final Girl character emerging in the 1974 film *Texas Chainsaw Massacre* and traces her role through horror films of the next fifteen years, describing her as such: "She is the one who encounters the mutilated bodies of her friends and perceives the full extent of the preceding horror and of her own peril; who is chased, cornered, wounded; who we see scream, stagger, fall, rise, and scream again. She is abject terror personified."[10] She is thus the sole survivor of the terror wreaked in the film, and usually she is identified as the most morally "pure" of the group in which she travels, often as a virgin. While Clover is wrong in her claim that since 1974 the survivor figure in slasher films has always been female, a point that calls attention to the skewed direction of her argument, she traces an important change in the image of the Final Girl after *Halloween* in 1978: the Final Girl begins to fight back, often killing the killer on her own. Another interesting characteristic of the Final Girl in the post-*Halloween* films is that she becomes less "feminine": "Just as the killer is not fully masculine, she is not fully feminine—not, in any case, feminine in the ways of her friends. Her smartness, gravity, competence in mechanical and other practical matters, and sexual reluctance set her apart from the other girls and ally her, ironically, with the very boys she fears or rejects, not to speak of the killer himself. Lest we miss the point, it is spelled out in her name: Stevie, Marti, Terry, Laurie, Stretch, Will, Joey, Max."[11]

As I describe in the analysis of these films that follows, the identification of the Final Girl, as well as the identification of other victims, killers, and parents, is indicative of a struggle with various notions not only of feminine empowerment but also of youth empowerment and difference. Clover's observation of this character type is heavily focused to accommodate her central argument on gender identification, yet I use her term and its application throughout my analysis, and further develop the changing image of this role, specifically in regard to the changing nature of the teen horror subgenre itself.

Another study of contemporary horror films worth mentioning but also having little to say about youth is Vera Dika's *Games of Terror: "Halloween," "Friday the 13th," and the Films of the Stalker Cycle* (1990), in which she explicates various generic characteristics of nine slasher films from 1978 to 1981 yet is otherwise so concerned with the theoretical establishment of a generic methodology (particularly in comparison to the Western) that she avoids discussing the role of youth in these films except in terms of their use as plot elements.[12] Then in the short section in which Dika discusses characters of the stalker cycle, she amplifies Clover's assertions about the Final Girl type, noting that "the heroine of these films is usually presented as a strong, practical character with a variety of well-developed skills," whose "ability to see and to use violence gives her the status of a valuable character."[13] She goes on to say that "in contrast with the killer's deformed and destructive qualities, the heroine and her friends are attractive, healthy, and lively."[14]

The most valuable observation that Dika makes about these young characters is that they form "an easily identifiable series of binary oppositions," which she goes on to label "valued/devalued," "strong/weak," and in terms of the youth community, "in-group/out-group," labels that have clear applications within the films' narratives.[15] Dika also describes three oppositions that are more conceptual, if not subjective: "normal/abnormal," "life/death," and "controlled/uncontrolled."[16] What these oppositions foreground is both the very dialectical tension of horror film narratives — how will the conflicts set up by these oppositions of right and wrong be resolved (or will they)? — and the subsequently conflicting images of the young people within the films, who, as I will argue, tend to be firmly ensconced on the sides of good (in Dika's terminology, the valued, strong, in, normal, lively, and controlled), or else they face terror for their transgressions. These "sides" parallel natural adolescent identity crises, which is another reason why horror films can be such rich, if obvious, texts for studying images of youth.

Adam Rockoff expanded on the work of Clover and Dika while minimizing their theorizing in *Going to Pieces: The Rise and Fall of the Slasher Film, 1978–1986* (2002).[17] Rockoff admittedly fawns over most films in the category, writing as he is for fans, and not limiting his scope to American cinema. Even with his encyclopedic knowledge, he admits that defining the slasher film is difficult, because, "it is tough, problematic, and fiercely individualistic," yet common elements prevail, such as a killer whose point of view is depicted as he utilizes sharp weapons to slay his victims.[18] The majority of his study concerns the first three slasher series examined hereafter, with limited attention to youth representation, although he goes on to consider the work of Kevin Williamson during the resurgence of the style in the late '90s.

A more recent study of the slasher/stalker film is *Blood Money: A History of the First Teen Slasher Cycle* (2011), by Richard Nowell, which offers a detailed account of production and distribution conditions around these films in the late '70s and early '80s.[19] Challenging many long-standing assumptions and misperceptions about this category of the subgenre, Nowell "demonstrates that filmmakers and marketers actually went to extraordinary lengths to make early teen slashers attractive to female youth, to minimize displays of violence, gore, and suffering, and to invite comparison to a wide range of post-classical Hollywood's biggest hits, including *Love Story* (1970), *Saturday Night Fever* (1977), *Grease* and *Animal House* (both 1978)."[20] Advancing through a classification lineage that includes "pioneer productions" like the Canadian *Black Christmas* (1974), Nowell brings together theories of gendered viewing with the production activities within American independent cinema that resulted in so much interest for the slasher film by the early '80s.

Robin Wood's work on horror films, while applied primarily to adult roles, is also integral to the imaging of youth. Wood describes a Freudian "return of the repressed" in his "Introduction to the American Horror Film" (1979), using rather arguable psychoanalytic theory to advance a nonetheless compelling taxonomy of horror movie repressions.[21] Wood points out four social repressions of sexuality in American culture—sexual energy, bisexuality, female sexuality, and the sexuality of children—the last of which Wood notes is a repression in the form of oppression, "from the denial of the infant's nature as sexual being to the veto on the expression of sexuality before marriage."[22] This is an important insight into the future operation of teen horror films: repressed or displaced sexual energy and anxiety are almost always the central sources of conflict in the films' narratives, and transgressions by premarital youth into carnal praxis are met by the oppressive terror of pathological, supernatural, or simply parental forces.[23]

Wood goes on to describe another important horror concept, that of "the Other" which must either be annihilated by society or assimilated within it, listing such recognized others as women, the proletariat, ethnic groups, and finally children, about whom he says, "When we have worked our way through all the other liberation movements, we may discover that children are the most oppressed section of the population (unfortunately, we cannot expect to liberate our children until we have successfully liberated ourselves). Most clearly of all, the 'otherness' of children (see Freudian theories of infantile sexuality) is that which is repressed within ourselves, its expression therefore hated in others: what the previous generation repressed in us, and what we, in turn, repress in our children, seeking to mold them into replicas of ourselves, perpetuators of a discredited tradition."[24]

This observation about children can be applied to the imaging of youth in films overall, and certainly in the horror genre: the burgeoning preadult population that threatens to express the repressed, in the form of sexuality, crime, hedonism, and basic resistance to social norms, must be contained and controlled. When parents fail to do so and institutions such as schools and the law cannot make up for the parents' shortcomings, "higher" natural and supernatural resources are brought down on the youthful others. In teen horror films, figures such as monsters and inde-structible killers become parental surrogates demanding that youth con-form to more repressive ways or else be destroyed, and since those who are already repressed tend to be the only teens who survive, the teen horror film formulation of "natural selection" hinges on the social elimination of undesirables and the preservation of the obedient.

Another review of youth in horror films is Jonathan Bernstein's chapter "Dead Teenagers" in *Pretty in Pink* (1997). Bernstein makes a few relevant observations ignored by other studies, such as the idea that teens relate to horror films because they sense a familiarity with the monstrous (every teen is "morbid and miserable, paranoid and tragic, sick and scared").[25] Bernstein goes on to claim that slasher movies of the '80s were more likely supported by young male aficionados of gore than by teens at large; the general decline of the slasher film may have come from teens' realiza-tion that "when an enemy cannot be killed, the victory of the last man or woman standing is an empty one."[26] Bernstein does promote the sex and death connection typical of many studies, making the point that the vir-ginal survivors of '80s slasher films represented the "real revenge of the nerds," but that "the amount of sadism and cynicism that went into these movies increased apace, swiftly sucking the fun out of them."[27] Bernstein says little else about the roles of teens in horror films and proceeds with lengthy plot synopses, missing many opportunities to explore critical issues about youth representation.[28]

What I borrow from Wood and Bernstein, and have subsequently ex-panded on, is the further division of the horror subgenre into categories relevant to the types of terror involved. As in other youth subgenres, cer-tain generic conventions of the youth horror film are often intrinsically linked to certain depictions of teens, connecting the actual image of the teen or teens being depicted more to the film's style than to its attempted messages about youth. Thus, I consider the subgenre of teen horror ac-cording to the films' already established thematic categories: the slasher/stalker story that focuses on youth being tracked and killed by psycho-pathic freaks, and the supernatural story in which mysterious forces haunt youth, which contains the fantasy variety of less violent yet often scary creatures and places that persist beyond the bounds of reality. There could be further refinement to these categories, such as subdividing the super-natural stories into tales of the occult or myths about monsters: the former variety would thus include demons, ghosts, and witches, while the latter would include vampires, werewolves, and zombies.[29] However, I do not formally pursue particular varieties, since so many of these films address overlapping and similar youth issues about fears of the unknown, torments of transformation, and longings to be superior.

As in other youth subgenres, the image of teens as both social types and historical references is complex and evolutionary in horror films of recent generations. This subgenre offers a surprisingly thoughtful notion of the most excessive of teen fears through its exploitation of the more realistic displaced fears of all teens: difference, alienation, rejection, sexual and bodily transformations, aging, authority, and the unknown, especially the future in which adulthood may appear more terrifying than the most malevolent beast.

THE SLASHER/STALKER FILM

The youth horror film featuring a maniacal killer on the loose stalking victims one at a time was the dominant mode of the subgenre throughout the 1980s and much of the '90s before giving way to more supernatural films in the '00s, predominantly those with fantasy plots. While Vera Dika appropriately referred to the early output of these films as being part of a "stalker cycle," the more common appellation for such films has been "slashers." Such films were a dominant category of the subgenre in the '80s, consistently earning the highest profits compared to other varieties. The first three series of these films, not one of which was a planned franchise (as would become common by the '00s), emerged by 1984, becoming some of the most recognizable of all teen horror titles — *Halloween*, *Friday the 13th*, and *A Nightmare on Elm Street*. Other series would not gain the visibility of these first three, although many continued the custom of capitalizing on mild hits, principally through the video and DVD market.

Many of the slasher narratives are built on a revenge scenario, usually realized at the end of the film after the killer has been captured or killed (typically the killer eventually escapes, even from death); a main character stumbles on the motive behind the killer's actions, which usually involve avenging the past irresponsibilities of youth (and/or their parents) so that now further youth will be killed to accommodate the killer's anger.[30] Such revelations are almost always brought out only in the last instance, after the ambiguous killer has stalked and murdered a number of victims for what seem like arbitrary intentions. David Edelstein has commented on the generic ironies of the slasher film in relation to this sense of oblique identification: "Slasher movies are teen sex comedies; the only difference is the presence of an outsider, someone who watches the fun — like a moviegoer—and, presumably, becomes enraged by it. I say presumably because, while we frequently observe the action from the killer's point of view, no anger is verbally expressed—most of the psychos in these movies say nothing and wear blank masks. They slash away in anonymity, partly, I think, because they are anonymous."[31]

The lack of audience empathy toward characters in these films—victims or killers—is striking, if only for the reason that the stories are meant to shock but inevitably allow us to too easily enjoy the "pleasure of terror" against their defenseless characters. The use of teens seems uniquely effective in this regard: they embody a wanton exuberance for experimentation with sex and drugs, which is continually met with virtually instant death, although little suffering. Teens in these films are often murdered for their forays into adult morality, providing a skewed justification for punishing them, and more so enforcing a safe distance for their teen viewers, in the notion that since sex and drugs do not *really* lead to death in the ways depicted in these fantasies, the reality of sex and drugs must pose less sinister consequences. As Edelstein implies, teens can enjoy their depictions within these films as comical extremes, and the box office success of these films over more realistically moralizing tales—such as the African American crime films of the early '90s—can be explained accordingly.

Slasher films also critique many cultural conditions beyond youth, as Pat Gill astutely argued: "These films seem to mock white flight to gated communities and parental attempts to shield their children from the dangerous outside influences represented by the city: widespread crime, easy access to drugs, unsupervised friendships. The danger is within, the films seem to say; the horror derives from the family and from the troubling ordeal of being a late twentieth-century teenager."[32]

As in all forms of horror, youth are endangered not only by their own innocence and ignorance, but also by the authorities that should be protecting and educating them. Time and again, parents, police, and teachers are either feeble or simply prey to the same evil as their young charges, which grants the killers in so many of these films a more powerful authority that subsequently becomes acutely appealing to teens rebelling against norms.

The First Three Series

Halloween established a variety of slasher modes in 1978, foregrounding the killer's motives with an opening sequence in which young Michael Myers witnesses his teen sister's sexual congress with a boy and then hacks her to death with a butcher knife. Michael is sent to an insane asylum and escapes at the age of twenty-one to go back to his neighborhood on Halloween, where he locates other sexually active teenagers and kills them. Tension in the plot is then built on Michael's slow discovery and murder of these teens as a doctor desperately attempts to find Michael and stop his killing. The film's virginal and dutiful protagonist, Laurie Strode (Jamie Lee Curtis), became the model of the Final Girl.

Four sequels to *Halloween* were made over the '80s, one of which, *Halloween III: Season of the Witch* (1983), had generally nothing to do with the story line established by the first two. At the time of *Halloween II* in 1981, the slasher style was enjoying its peak of profitability, and, while the film was indeed a true sequel to the original story (revealing that Laurie and Michael are siblings), it went farther afield of the original's psychological tension and relied more on what had quickly become slasher stocks-in-trade: the killer who won't die, the car that won't start, gratuitous sex met with gratuitous violence. About the only interesting element of this film is how it points to the mounting disposability of teens and adults in slasher films; lest one lose count, at the end we are told that ten characters have been killed, which does not include a teenage boy who was killed by a cop because he was wearing a Halloween mask that looked like Michael's. Perhaps the "accidental murder" of this teen is the most important contribution of *Halloween II* to the subgenre, in that anonymous death by association is carried out even by the criminal justice system, which is already incapable of controlling child killers.

Halloween 4: The Return of Michael Myers (1988) clearly signaled to audiences that the killer was back, and now his target is his nine-year-old niece; en route to her, Michael hacks his way through a group of teenagers until he is again "killed" by police, leaving his niece somehow possessed by his spirit, yielding a virginal Final Girl who is a new menace. This film's attempt to connect with its sequel, *Halloween 5: The Revenge of Michael Myers* (1989), relied simply on featuring the niece traumatized while Michael returns to kill more teens, yet the end of the decade, and the end of the film, did not deliver closure to the series, since the story was left open enough for *Halloween: The Curse of Michael Myers* (1995). Its lack of a number in the title was likely motivated by hopes that audiences would rediscover the series anew, which is further evident by the fact that college students are now Michael's prey, based more on timely occult mystique than the sheer bloody mayhem of the past. As with the later films in the *Friday the 13th* and *Nightmare on Elm Street* series, this installment ages its protagonists to their twenties, supporting my theory that the filmic image of youth was itself aging with attitudes about the elongation of adolescence within the Generation X demographic.

Each teen slasher series at various times has promised to deliver a concluding chapter, which is never certain in a market built on recycling previously successful stories, as well as a market that can supply a new audience every five years or so. *Halloween H₂O: 20 Years Later* (1998) seemed to hold that promise, with Jamie Lee Curtis returning to play Laurie Strode, now a middle-aged private school headmaster fearing that Michael will return. Of course a few teens at the school become Michael's victims, but to the film's credit much of the predictable formulation between sex and death is discarded, and Laurie—the Final Mother—does at last provide an absolute destruction of Michael.[33] Alas, the revenue from this film ensured a sequel with Curtis again returning as Laurie in *Halloween: Resurrection* (2002), another update employing an Internet storyline to engage the Millennial audience seeking similar, if unfamiliar, thrills from Michael's enduring rampage.

The series as it started some twenty-four years earlier essentially ended with this last installment, only to be reborn again as an altogether new franchise in 2007 with *Halloween* and its hackneyed sequel *Halloween II* (2009). These films have thus far provided more developed backgrounds for their characters, particularly Michael, although they were criticized for also providing superfluous gore and nudity; Ryan Lizardi further argued that horror remakes of the time "show remarkable ideological continuity" with the originals because they "not only adopt the return to hegemonic normalcy and misogynistic torture, but they also expand and emphasize these socially destructive themes."[34] This remake's sequel obviously sets up another, with Laurie assuming Michael's role at the end, yet to this time, the trilogy is incomplete. As many critics have said, teen horror franchises themselves seem to be as indestructible as the killers they celebrate.

The original *Friday the 13th* in 1980 launched the most prolific, if least creative, of the slasher series. The film plodded through the murders of various teens at Camp Crystal Lake, where years earlier a boy named Jason Voorhees drowned while his counselors were off having sex.[35] Years later, the currently murdered teen counselors are revealed to be the victims of Jason's avenging mother, whose head is eventually lopped off by a final surviving teen girl. While the mother, unlike most other slasher killers, actually dies accordingly, her undead son returns at the start of *Friday the 13th Part 2* (1981), five years later in diegetic time, for another season of killing counselors. The sequel provides at least twice as many teens to become potential victims, as Jason kills the counselors while they are in an assortment of sexual situations. *Friday the 13th Part 3* (1982) quickly establishes its interest in its 3D effects with various objects pointing at the screen, a welcome distraction from the stereotypical teens who get together for a weekend at Crystal Lake and are killed by the waiting Jason, who here first sports his now trademark hockey mask. Alas, Jason would be back for more, in the optimistically titled *Friday the 13th: The Final Chapter* (1984), in which the killer maims his way through six rambunctious teens on a vacation at Crystal Lake, only to find himself brought down by a pre-teen named Tommy (Corey Feldman), who's been studying his "case" and, after violently killing the killer, seems to usurp Jason's deadly impulses. His older sister remains the Final Girl, but Tommy becomes an outlet for the preservation of malice, reminding us that Jason was the product of trauma, and foreshadowing yet another return of the killer.[36]

That return is *Friday the 13th Part V: A New Beginning* (1985), in which Tommy (John Shepherd) has become a teenager, with the twist that Jason is *not* really the killer after all, but actually the father of a murdered teen, whose psychosis has led to him killing more teens: the admonitions about the dangers of teen sexuality had thus shifted to a greater threat against the preservation of family. This concern for the family is carried over in the somewhat comical *Jason Lives: Friday the 13th Part VI* (1986), its title foregrounding the return of the "real" Jason. Now Tommy (Thom Mathews) accidentally brings Jason back to life, who then goes on yet another killing spree that includes more sexually active teens at Camp Crystal Lake. Tommy and his new girlfriend appear to eventually drown Jason in the lake, their unconsummated relationship thereby granting them the title of Final Couple. Only those who honor Jason's terror and avoid sex can survive, revealing Jason as the ultimate oppressive, abusive parental authority figure, a teenager's true nightmare.

That notion is manifest even more explicitly in *Friday the 13th Part VII: The New Blood* (1988), which focuses on a psychokinetic teenager (shades of *Carrie*) who also accidently brings Jason back to life, just in time for him to kill a number of her sexually active friends, until she and her boyfriend drown him yet again. *Friday the 13th Part VIII: Jason Takes Manhattan* (1989) brought the killer to the title city to terrorize more teenagers, until a Final Couple survives to drown him, this time in toxic waste (it *is* Manhattan). *Part VIII* would be the last *Friday* for four years until the dreadful *Jason Goes to Hell: The Final Friday* in 1993. With another optimistic title, this supposedly conclusive chapter in the series focused more on post-teens, emblematic of the "twentysomething teenager" in many '90s films. Of course, the series did not end with this second "final" film, because Jason returned for

The Final Girl of A Nightmare on Elm Street *(1984), Nancy (Heather Langenkamp), uses her ingenuity and determination to confront and conquer the psychic stalker Freddy Krueger (Robert Englund).*

a tenth excursion, appropriately entitled *Jason X* (2001), which relocated the story to a spaceship far in the future. The cryogenic Jason is reanimated while two teenagers have sex, but otherwise the story, like its predecessor, moves away from the past emphasis on sexual activity. *Freddy vs. Jason* (2003) finally delivered on the promise of the ninth film's ending a decade earlier, pitting the slayer from the *Nightmare on Elm Street* films against the *Friday* slayer, further minimizing sex as a plot point, and once more ending with a Final Couple of teenagers who only *seem* to kill the anti-heroes.

In similar fashion to *Halloween*, the series was restarted for the Millennial generation with *Friday the 13th* in 2009, which manages to be both a remake and a sequel, referencing the original murders at Camp Crystal Lake and bringing to it a group of sexually active young people who will be systematically slaughtered by the returning Jason. This film has yet to be sequelized, but given the tendencies of the industry, that seems inevitable, especially since the next installment would be the *thirteenth* of the franchise.

The third major slasher series began in 1984, when established horror director Wes Craven introduced the last enduring monster of the '80s, a deformed killer with razor blades mounted to his hand. *A Nightmare on Elm Street* utilized many of the then-typical motifs in teen horror films—

a seemingly indestructible killer stalks and pitilessly slaughters teenagers, primarily those who have or want to have sex, avenging past violence against him—yet now the killer was not only more developed within the narrative, his very existence was predicated on the fears and dreams of his teenage victims. The *Nightmare* series entertained the idea that teenagers had themselves brought Freddy Krueger, a notorious child murderer played by Robert Englund in all the films, back to "life" through their frightful nightmares, allowing the otherwise dead killer to cross over to a reality in which he could actually harm and kill more youth.

From the first film onward, the teen victims of Freddy had to learn how to control their own mental processes, particularly their fears and fantasies, in order to conquer and defeat the killer. Although as the series progressed, a mixture of social issues became intricately connected to the killer and his victims: Freddy himself became an abused child after being the result of a sadistic rape (reminding us that evil adults breed monstrosities as children), and his young victims had to overcome their given problems (e.g., drug use, parental neglect, sexual aggression or confusion) on their own, lest they endure his wrath, a wrath that was essentially wrought by the victims' own weaknesses. Judith Williamson added, "In social terms it is possible to read Krueger as the unsavory working classes suppressed and fought off by the aspiring, middle-American parents who are presented as at best inadequate—alcoholic mothers and dictatorial fathers abound. Freddy is their victim even as their children, in a vicious cycle of effects, are his."[37]

This cyclical contest of power for teen characters was considerably different from the *Halloween* and *Friday the 13th* series, where the protagonists spent more time eluding the alien killer than confronting their own familiar fears. In the *Nightmare* series, the true danger comes from within, and the classic teen achievement of higher self-esteem and confidence becomes the most imperative weapon in avoiding destruction. These films tell teens that they must grow up smart and tough or else perish. Craven himself called horror films a "boot camp for the psyche" and said that teens like horror films since they "put them under terrifying conditions and show that you can survive. You come out feeling better and stronger."[38] Craven also realized that only certain characters survive, and that their actions embody particularly admirable human qualities such as integrity, purity, intelligence, and loyalty—a veritable pledge for teen horror heroines and heroes.

The first *Nightmare on Elm Street* was perhaps the most typical of past slasher films, with its connection of sex and death, gradual stalking of teens who are savagely killed, and its revelation of the killer avenging his past.

On otherwise quiet Elm Street in Springwood, Ohio, a group of teens including Nancy (Heather Langenkamp) and Glen (Johnny Depp) each have
a nightmare about a man in a boiler factory who has a burned face and fingers with razors. After a girl in the group has wild sex with her boyfriend,
a mysterious force abhorrently lacerates her, causing Nancy to have more
visions from her nightmares while her cop father ineffectively works on
the murder case. Her mother, rapidly becoming an alcoholic, tells Nancy
that the man is Freddy Krueger, a local child killer who was unjustly freed
years before, and so she and other parents had set him on fire in a boiler
factory. When the mother tells her, "He's dead because Mommy killed
him," the connection of parental revenge and child victimization is unmistakable: Nancy and her friends have been suffering the attacks of Freddy
through their dreams due to their parents' repressed anger and guilt from
killing Freddy. Or, as David Edelstein saw it, "the children are vulnerable
to their nightmares because their drunken, divorced, and inattentive moms
and dads have failed them. That's a reactionary message, but it's still the
source of children's most powerful nightmares."[39] Douglas Rathgeb proposes that the teens are more culpable: "Although the sins of the parents
are clearly being visited upon the children, the children's sexual offenses
provide more than enough horrific justification in the film's moral scheme
for their own victimization. Their mores have become somehow identified with Krueger's own sexual offense."[40] This is an issue that will later be
challenged in the sequels, as the teens' "sexual offenses" become morally
ambiguous if not altogether displaced.

After many failed attempts, Nancy sets up one last trap to "catch" Freddy,
trying to bring him out of her dream state into reality where he can again
be destroyed; meanwhile, Freddy calls on her disconnected phone and tells
her, "I'm your boyfriend now," with a grotesque set of lips and a tongue
forming on the mouthpiece and kissing her. This slimy sexual assault is
contrasted with Glen's obscure but bloody death at midnight, he having
fallen asleep instead of helping Nancy to capture Freddy. The irresponsible Glen thereby pays for his lack of dedication, while Nancy's growing
strength is met with her subconscious fears of sexual violation. Having
rigged her house with various booby traps and going to sleep to bring
Freddy back, she tells him that she knows he's only a dream, and stands
him down with demands to return her missing mother and friends. Such
a show of conscious authority causes the monster to disappear, until the
final scene, where Nancy has returned to a serene morning on which her
mother sends her off to school with her friends, and they suddenly become
trapped in the car as Freddy appears to grab her mother again.[41] Despite this

typical unresolved coda, *A Nightmare on Elm Street* offers perhaps the most commanding and resolute of female horror heroines in the subgenre: Final Girl Nancy insulates herself against the death traps of the killer and the disbelief of her parents to successfully eliminate Freddy single-handedly, which she does not by force but by sheer will. This revision of the Final Girl led Kyle Christensen to challenge Clover's enduring treatise, arguing that Nancy is a "stronger model of feminism" than previously recognized, due to her "refusal to abide by the arbitrary, female-belittling restrictions of true womanhood."[42]

The second film in the series, *A Nightmare on Elm Street Part 2: Freddy's Revenge* (1985), switched the gender of the protagonist and concentrated less on the hero's ultimate comprehension of the killer, addressing more his latent homosexuality and his "use" of Freddy to confront it.[43] Here Jesse (Mark Patton) fears Freddy has taken over his body, and his girlfriend works to convince him of her love, which ultimately allows him to free himself from his intimate union with Freddy; it is also a restoration of heterosexual order in the form of a Final Couple that finally returns Jesse to "normal" even though Freddy—as Jesse's previously confused sexuality—has killed so many other normal teens. Perhaps Freddy's real revenge was simply to use Jesse as such a pawn, exploiting his sexual fears to carry out his more nefarious task of killing children about to become sexual. *A Nightmare on Elm Street 3: Dream Warriors* (1987) took a less individualistic approach about sexuality by focusing on a group of institutionalized and virtually asexual teens, all terrorized by Freddy in their dreams, who learn that he was the offspring of a nun raped hundreds of times by asylum inmates, "the bastard son of a hundred maniacs," thus explaining Freddy's pathology as the creation of ultimate perverse sexuality. The teens create various hypnotic fantasies to empower themselves, and in the end three Final Teens survive, having conquered their deepest fears after Freddy is supposedly eliminated once and for all.

A Nightmare on Elm Street 4: The Dream Master (1988) kills off the surviving teens of the previous film early on, leaving only one of their friends, Alice (Lisa Wilcox). By this point in the series, the teens who are killed are less morally suspect than their predecessors, with no greater transgressions than intelligence and confidence, so perhaps these qualities are meant to be the very essence of what a child killer like Freddy seeks to snuff out. The film ends with Alice harnessing her positive dream capability and dressing up in a teen-styled samurai outfit to fight Freddy, who releases his victims from his body as spirits sent to the heavens. Once again the series offered a puissant image of the Final Girl, who would return in *A Nightmare on Elm*

Street 5: The Dream Child (1989), as Alice (Lisa Wilcox) confronts Freddy's mother in her dreams, who wants to take her son back to his pre-birth, pre-evil state. Alice, who's been impregnated by her slain boyfriend, realizes that Freddy plans to pose as a fetus growing inside her, but rather than abort the baby, thereby killing the possibility of spawning another monster, she adamantly declares her choice to keep it. In a less fanciful film this could be read as an ironic pro-life stance, but here Alice uses her capacity to give birth as her maternal defense against Freddy's patriarchal power. In a convoluted showdown, Alice violently pulls the diseased Freddy fetus out of her body, an image of monstrous birth *and* abortion, and this mutant then enters Freddy's mother, where he is finally re-contained in her womb. Alice retains her original "good" baby, and thus the result of her having sex is both death and life; the film's irony is that this teenager is faced with the challenge of raising a child alone, perhaps a more realistic nightmare for teen girls than any offered by Freddy.

Freddy's Dead: The Final Nightmare (1991) retains this focus on parental responsibilities after a group of abused teen mental patients are killed by Freddy, and their therapist realizes that he is her father: she had repressed her memories of him killing her mother after she found his torture chamber where he killed children. This therapist becomes the rare non-teen Final Girl after she kills Freddy, having learned that he was abused by his own father and took to slicing himself in the stomach to displace the pain (joining other films of the time in commenting on teen self-mutilation). The film actually raises sympathy for Freddy in its condemnation of all parental abuses and further removes the weight of responsibility from children themselves: the teens, their therapist, and Freddy are all by this point merely reacting to the acts of their authoritative parents in a sad attempt at self-preservation. As L. J. DeGraffenreid points out, "In the *Nightmare on Elm Street* films, authority figures either dismiss teenage pleas for assistance or pose direct physical threats. . . . The slasher, then, can be seen as underage society's revenge-seeking doppelganger, its desire for rebellion made manifest in the murderous tendencies of powerful, sadistic Freddy."[44] Springwood becomes a final symbol of irresponsible authority, a childless town where the parents must forever bear the horror of losing their children because they did not raise them right, an appealing image to the teenage sense of vengeance and anger at one's family for not being appreciated enough.

The next film in the series, *New Nightmare* (1994), a self-reflexive study of Craven's own frustrations with the *Nightmare* franchise, is endlessly interesting but alas of little value to this study since it does not prominently feature teenagers. The film is decisively the seventh and last of the series that started a decade earlier; still, the fabled killer would return in the *Freddy vs. Jason* outing, and then in the same fashion (and order) as the first two series, the first film was remade in 2010. *A Nightmare on Elm Street* once again follows a group of young friends who dream about the razor-fingered Freddy, providing merely slight variations on the original story line, such as leaving a Final Couple to confront the monster at the end.

The fact that all three of these major slasher series have been reincarnated in the twenty-first century is not only indicative of the industry's reliance on recycling known stories, it offers enduring proof that youth continue to long for mysterious torments as reassuring entertainment: in reality none of the sex, drugs, music, or crimes they take on have remotely similar costs as those put on teenagers in slasher films. Even as the films moved away from the puritanical punishments for premarital intercourse that permeated '80s films, youth remained relieved to see that there were forces far more vile and oppressive than their parents and the law.

Slashers After the Series

Considering how many teen slasher films were released between 1980 and 2012—I count at least seventy-five—the number that were *not* part of series is strikingly small, less than half. Of that number, the majority are obscure and largely not worth analyzing in depth, although a chronology of teen slasher films since the '80s, highlighting some pertinent examples as well as some further series, is warranted by their ongoing presence as part of the subgenre.

The year 1981 was the banner one for the teen slasher film, with the first sequels to the *Halloween* and *Friday the 13th* films being released as well as the parody *Student Bodies* and three lesser-known films, *The Burning, Eyes of a Stranger,* and *Graduation Day,* all featuring a maniacal killer stalking and murdering teens. Two lesser-known series emerged soon thereafter, *Slumber Party Massacre* starting in 1982, and *Sleepaway Camp* in 1983. The former became a unique slasher trilogy written and directed exclusively by women, nonetheless featuring rather standard slasher plots, gratuitous female nudity, and the depraved killing of teenagers. The killer in the first film is distinguished by his choice of weapon, a huge construction drill (phallic symbolism being obvious), and the Final Girl lops off his long bit with a machete—the castrating virgin—yet lest the killer become the "star" as he did in the major slasher series, the killer actually dies. Regardless of the film's faint notoriety, *Slumber Party Massacre II* (1987) followed with a leather-jacketed musician using a spiked electric guitar as a weapon, and *Slumber Party Massacre III* (1990) became the least intriguing of the bunch, whose killer is a traumatized college guy.[45]

Sleepaway Camp was distinctive in terms of gender as well, offering a Final Girl who turns out in the last scene to be a Final Boy, one of the more satisfying (and undetectable) twists in the subgenre. The two initial sequels, also made in the late '80s when the industry was turning out dozens of teen horror movies destined for home video, did feature the protagonist "sexually reassigned" to be a girl, but carried little interest otherwise. A fourth video product was released based on outtake footage from a planned sequel in 2002, which was repackaged and released again as a portmanteau picture in 2012 titled *Sleepaway Camp IV: The Survivor*, although a different, unnumbered sequel, *Return to Sleepaway Camp*, had been made in 2008, marking the return of the original killer.

Desperate efforts by the industry to capitalize on previous and similar slasher films have obviously remained epidemic, just fluctuating in output, such as the decline of the original cycle by the mid-'80s, which yielded sparse creations like *Fatal Games* in 1984 and *The Mutilator* in 1985. By 1986 the slasher cycle was finding renewed momentum, and the next few years became prolific again; that year saw the release of *Girls School Screamers* and another college rendering of *Slumber Party Massacre* called *Sorority House Massacre*, plus the mildly popular *The Hitcher*. One more 1986 slasher film was *Slaughter High*, in which an erstwhile nerd, now a mental patient due to the abuses he suffered from teen tormentors in high school, dreams of exacting his revenge against them—a film that is in many ways the literal "revenge of the nerd" that Jonathan Bernstein claimed as the motivation behind so many teen slasher films.

The year 1987 produced a slew of minor slasher films such as *Blood Lake*, *Hide and Go Shriek*, *The Last Slumber Party* (another film inspired by *Slumber Party Massacre*), *The Majorettes*, and *Night Screams*, and then 1988 saw the release of four sequels in slasher series as well as the notoriously titled *Bloody Pom Poms*: many of these films had been attempting to combine the fading formulas of the teen sex romp with the slasher film. After 1988 the slasher film continued to be produced mostly in series with the exception of obscure films like *Offerings* (1989), *The Invisible Maniac* (1990), and *Lunatic* (1991), and for five years after 1991 there were no teen slasher films outside of established series, such as the incongruous and failed remake *Return of the Texas Chainsaw Massacre* (1994).

Then in late 1996 Wes Craven released *Scream*, a genre-revising semi-satirical slasher film met by great critical and financial success.[46] The scenario may initially seem familiar but the film is full of vital shifts in the slasher method. First, teenage Casey (Drew Barrymore) is terrorized on the phone by a voice that quizzes her with questions about her knowledge of teen horror films, and after she gives a wrong answer, the faceless killer eviscerates her boyfriend and then her. The film thereby immediately signals its intent to dissect the generic traditions of teen horror, and continues to do so through its introduction of classic characters. Sidney (Neve Campbell, with a Final Girl's masculine character name) is a virginal high school student recovering from the brutal rape and murder of her mother a year before and delicately warding off the sexual advances of her boyfriend Billy (Skeet Ulrich, looking much like Johnny Depp from Craven's first *Nightmare* film). Now Sidney's school and town have become gripped by the fear of a psycho killer on the loose, and her friends crudely exacerbate the tension: Stuart (Matthew Lillard) is obnoxious enough to joke about Casey's death even though he'd dated her, and Randy (Jamie Kennedy) is a conspiracy theorist convinced that the killer is following "the rules" of slasher films. Only Sidney's friend Tatum (Rose McGowan) is sympathetic to the tensions she feels, especially once she begins to suspect that her mother's killer, Cotton Weary (Liev Schreiber), has escaped.

Sidney is next to be attacked by the killer, but she shows her mettle in fighting him off, and her suspicions point to Billy. Stuart soon holds a party at his house attended by a large group of students (who could care less that two of their classmates have just been murdered by an uncaught killer) during which Tatum is crushed in a garage door. While this is unbeknownst to Sidney, she decides to go against her better judgment and have sex with Billy to get over her "sexual anorexia," feeling that she can now lose her virginity since "this isn't a movie." Afterward, Sidney finally realizes that there are two killers, Billy and Stuart, who reveal that they framed Cotton Weary and killed Sidney's mother because she was sleeping with Billy's dad, a heavily contrived motive that nonetheless speaks to Billy's dual oedipal fixation in killing the woman who broke up his family and then sleeping with the daughter of his father's lover (whom he also raped), as well as Stuart's domestic misogyny in killing his former girlfriend Casey and current girlfriend Tatum. Sidney then fights Billy in the same costume he'd been using to kill everyone else, temporarily taking on the identity and the power of the killer herself, and later kills Stuart by smashing his head with a (symbolic) television. Surviving virgin Randy warns Sidney that the killer always comes back to life in slasher films, and when Billy makes one final lunge, Sidney shoots him in the head, saying, "Not in my movie." This final statement offers an additional sense of potency to Final

Girl Sidney, who has not only survived the loss of her virginity and killed the killer, but who essentially lays claim to the entire film, taking no risk that the killer could become deified, unlike her female counterparts in so many earlier films.

Scream is significant for a range of reasons, not the least of which is bringing so much depth and attention to what had appeared to be a dead subgenre. The fact that Scream yielded a sequel within a year after the original and became a trilogy in 2000 is testament to the film's appeal as well as its vivification of the slasher style, although the characters in the film, including the killers, mark a patent departure from their initial inspirations. Billy and Stuart are actually teenagers killing other teenagers as well as parental authority figures, and despite their murder mania they are otherwise portrayed as rational, nonpsychotic (and thus ultimately vulnerable) human beings. Sidney is not killed for having sex, surpassing an even greater transgression by actually sleeping with the killer—the killer and rapist of her infidel mother—and she is left standing as a strong survivor of the terror with the one virgin left in the film, Randy, who is redeemed only by his knowledge of horror films (the rare Final Guy who's not romantically involved with the Final Girl).[47] Craven remains rather indebted to his own postmodern notions of self-reflexivity (at one point Tatum tries to comfort Sidney by telling her she's not in a "Wes Carpenter" movie), and ends the last scene with a reporter, who also survived the bloodbath, doing a live shot from the site of the tragedy, signaling that the television media have become the purveyors of real horror in the years since the slasher film lost prominence.[48]

Scream 2 (1997) is even more reflexive in its critique, right down to an early scene featuring college film students discussing the "best" movie sequels. The story again focuses on Sidney, yet the killer is Billy's distraught mother, out for revenge, a hokey revelation that, like the sequel's statements on the subgenre, had grown obvious and tired. Scream 3 (2000) is weaker still, with all of the characters well past their teen years, and the killer a son that Nancy's mother gave up for adoption—and thus the whole trilogy, like Craven's Nightmare series, is founded on the deeper sins of parents, the consequences of which children must endure. Alas, the director was not yet done capitalizing on his own recycled ideas, and made Scream 4 in 2011 with much of the original cast and a new slew of teenagers to be victims.

Another popular slasher film appeared in 1997 with a less reflexive approach, I Know What You Did Last Summer, which was soon sequelized the following year as I Still Know What You Did Last Summer. In the first film, two graduating high school couples cover up their accidental killing of a pedestrian, and the next year someone begins taunting them with notes alluding to their crime. As they make various inaccurate assumptions about the identity of the note writer, the characters become the targets of increasingly disturbing pranks, and before long two of them are murdered. The stalker turns out to be the pedestrian himself, who survived the accident and is now out for revenge, yet a surviving Final Couple are able to elude his wrath and supposedly drown him in the ocean. The heroine, Julie (Jennifer Love Hewitt), at last returns to college, until a clichéd studio ending suggests that the killer is still alive, which obviously provides the foundation for the sequel in which Julie and some new friends are inevitably stalked by the same psychopath. The relative success of these two films suggested that the slasher style was still thriving at the end of the decade, while their lack of generic revision—placing a strong heroine within yet another sadistic scare fest—reveals how little slasher conventions had changed in the past generation, even if the moral issue of the stories had shifted to criminal guilt rather than sexual guilt.

Common slasher conventions thus continued in *Campfire Tales* (1997), *If I Die Before I Wake*, *Strangeland* (both 1998), *Sleepy Hollow High* (2000), and *Dead Above Ground* (2002), none of which would have the renown of more generalized teen horror films emerging in the new century, and certainly not compared to the renewed fascination with youth fantasy stories after the *Harry Potter* franchise debuted in 2001. Occasional endeavors did persist, offering different gimmicks in hope of rejuvenating the waning visibility of slashers: *Serial Killing 4 Dummys* (2004) borrows its title from the popular how-to series with a teenager trying to learn the slasher's craft; *Chaos* (2005) partakes in the escalating wave of extreme cinema violence known as torture porn; *Cry_Wolf* (2005) utilizes Internet rumors to develop its killer; *Five Across the Eyes* (2006) effectively stages the terrorizing of girls completely within a single vehicle; and *When a Stranger Calls* (2006) remade a 1979 film in a surprisingly profitable effort that was not immune to the contagious decline of recent teen slasher films. *Disturbia* (2007) was also essentially a remake, in this case of Hitchcock's *Rear Window* (1954), yet was improbably venerated given its formulaic reversal of the stalker role, with teens spying on a suspected serial killer. Yet even Wes Craven's latest attempt to refurbish his own forte, *My Soul to Take* (2010), which borrows from his *Nightmare* concept by depicting teens in a small town stalked by a psychopath, did not bring the slasher film back to prominence, leading Marc Savlov to comment, "This utterly mediocre forget-me-now could've been crafted by any faceless serial director at all."[49]

Current youth may simply be preoccupied by the ongoing output of literary adaptations from safer make-believe stories, as detailed hereafter, and the fact that such films have been less violent attests to the declining interest youth have had in seeing themselves survive brutality. Or, from another perspective, the indifference current youth show toward slashers reveals how pampered they have become, since they cannot endure the wrath of mysterious killers teaching them lessons about immorality with even greater immorality. After all, sex is not nearly as scary in a culture that encourages youth to become sexualized at increasingly younger ages, and the calamitous consequences of deviance that previously threatened children may seem unconvincing when delivered by progressively insatiable killers. Perhaps the access youth have to images of violence in the Internet age has simply diluted the disgust and fear previously reserved for the acts of sadomasochism so rampant in slasher films. In any case, the industry has yet to discover the next form of teen terror that is truly as proficient in conveying the satisfying experiences of torment and redemption that these films provided for their viewers more than thirty years ago.

SUPERNATURAL MOVIES

A tradition of movies related to the supernatural goes back to the earliest days of cinema, although rarely did these films address teenagers (such examples as *The Ghost of Dragstrip Hollow* [1959] and *The Ghost in the Invisible Bikini* [1966] were few, even in the exploitation circuit). In fact, stories of the supernatural and fantastic did not become particularly popular in teen films until after the wane of the early '80s slasher/stalker trend, and even then their narratives were wildly divergent. The box office smash *Poltergeist* in 1982 featured a family terrorized by unsettled spirits in their house, yet the role of its lone teen character was rather undeveloped. Two years later the even more successful *Gremlins* featured a young man saddled with the terrifying invasion of little monsters launched from the mishandling of supposedly harmless teddy-bear creatures. The contrast between these two films would presage the generic division between supernatural youth films of a more dreadful sort and those that, while often scary, were based on the enchantment of mysterious characters and places. The goblins in *Poltergeist* were nothing but unleashed shock to their traumatized victims; the title trolls in *Gremlins* offered an amusing challenge, and could even be "contained" in a state as adorable pets.

After the bombardment of maniacal slashers in early '80s youth films, the next few years became a nascent period for supernatural stories, including those intended to terrify and those more comfortably entertaining. Few were very profitable, yet studios continued releasing further fabrications over the next decade, apparently searching for a blockbuster to finance a franchise, resulting in a relatively consistent output of supernatural teen films thereafter. Young viewers were endeared to these films, if not at theaters then on home video, because their teen characters tended to be smarter and less passive in their possession or captivation than the numerous cowering casualties in slasher/stalker films. Further, the stories offered youth a form of escape that they could potentially manage, and daunting yet remotely possible capacities to, for instance, explore life after death, communicate with spirits, overcome evil with virtue, and (most similar to slasher films) defeat monsters with their own power.

These films offer a wide range of explanations for their ethereal machinations, tending to hinge on relatively straightforward characterizations of teens. Youth either confront phantoms or deities in gaining deliverance from their adolescent plights, find themselves in strange new worlds that they must survive to prove their bravery, or discover latent superpowers that endow them with the ability to surmount their personal problems. Nerdy characters can thus turn tough and cool; disregarded teens become valuable saviors; unpopular pariahs gain appreciable recognition. Likewise, families can be sustained or reunited by their children, teenage ambitions can be validated, and civilization can be liberated from blights that only youth can conquer. Pat Gill commented specifically on familial horror, in which "family structures gone horribly awry" are composed of "not merely deep-rooted dissatisfactions and unbearable repression, but also of simulated or makeshift family units engaged in repugnant, gruesome behavior, of obsessed father–creators and refractory son–monsters, of appalling mothers and endangered or psychotic sons and daughters, of creatures in savage search of or in rebellion from deficient parents, and parents in hideous hunt for or in ghastly revenge of lost children."[50] Similarly precarious structures surround youth in all of their relationships, and in the end, the teens usually realize that they must face bewildering forces greater than they are, and most teens successfully utilize such forces; yet if they are greedy, careless, or disrespectful, then they perish accordingly. Most often, abuses of authority are met with castigation, while mastery of mystery is rewarded.

The inclusion of fantasy films within a subgenre labeled "horror" may seem a taxonomic error, because stories about mystical creatures do not generally entail the same degree of danger as those about mutant monsters and psychopathic slashers. However, almost all fantasy stories directed at adolescents—and certainly those about adolescents—contain a clear level of fear: the perils posed by "bad" creatures, the possibility of failing at a mission, or the simple suspense that strange changes in life may actually become harmful. The entertainment of fear is something that adolescents can begin to enjoy beyond younger children, after learning to distinguish between the real and the imaginary with the confidence of knowing that the latter is controllable and, usually, more exciting. The vast majority of fantasy films about youth thus participate in some aspects of horror in their conveyance of doubt, dismay, or delusion, and the fact that so many of these films appeal to adult viewers expresses the enlightening pleasures many people experience from otherwise frightening circumstances.

Supernatural Dread

The variety of supernatural films that deals with the dread accompanying lethal enigmas follows a long tradition of mythologies based in primitive fears of the unknown. Darkness, wilderness, oceans, outer space, and of course death have all been origins of such myths, from which have sprung monsters, plagues, demons, and aliens, all of which have compelled humans to defend themselves against impending doom with solutions as mundane as knowledge or as exotic as the occult.

Waves of popularity for youth films about supernatural dread have not been as reliant on franchises as those in the slasher/stalker category, even though they have often featured recurring types of characters—particularly vampires and zombies—across different films. This variety has tended to rely on creatures with human qualities in form or conscience, as in the one early franchise that has persisted throughout the decades, the *Children of the Corn* films (1984–2011), an endless string of xenophobic reveries in which Amish kids rise up from the countryside to terrorize interlopers. Scary teenagers had already appeared in *The Watcher in the Woods* (1980), *The Funhouse* (1981), *The Beast Within* (1982), *Full Moon High* (1982), and *Sweet 16* (1983), but they were also the targets of improbably destructive entities like cars in *Christine* (1983) and *The Wraith* (1986), which examine how teenagers are affected by automotive apparitions. The latter film follows an automotive spirit avenging the death of a teenager killed by nefarious street punks and was not widely seen, whereas the former film was a mild hit and provided an important foundation in characterizations from which other supernatural youth films would grow.

Christine was adapted from Steven King's novel about a fiendish 1958

Plymouth Fury and was directed by John Carpenter of *Halloween* fame. The film is set in 1978 California and features a Faustian tale of a high school nerd, Arnie (Keith Gordon), paying too much money for the junky old car, spending an excessive amount of time bringing it back to its original form, and then seemingly falling under its spell. Arnie and his friend Dennis (John Stockwell) are just starting their senior years of high school, and Dennis teases Arnie that this should be the year he gets laid, preferably with a girl. The irony of his statement is that since Arnie is unable to find "normal" sex, he has to buy it in the form of the car, which he lovingly refers to as "Christine" as he spends much time literally laboring over her body. Arnie gradually transforms from meek and accommodating—his first sign of rebellion is arguing with his overbearing parents that he's been a dutiful son and should be allowed to keep the car—to acting tough and uninterested in anything but the car. Apparently as a result of his transformation, he gains a highly coveted human girlfriend as well, the virginal Leigh (Alexandra Paul), who's such a contrast and a threat to Christine that the car tries to kill her, forcing Arnie to declare his devotion to the car over Leigh.

The film's imaging of Arnie and Dennis is rather unusual: Dennis is a popular jock at school who defends Arnie from auto shop thugs, and he does not envy Arnie for winning Leigh as much as he becomes concerned that Arnie is acting self-destructively, an unexpected portrait of a high school jock who's not only emotionally invested in a friend but a nerd friend moreover. Arnie's change is signaled by his upturned collars, doffing of his large glasses, and newly aggressive manner with his parents (as if the car has regressed him from '70s nerd to '50s rebel), and further by his dismissal of Dennis, who in an emotional scene actually cries over how Christine has affected Arnie. Referring to Wood's classic horror film argument, Sheila Johnston describes Arnie's metamorphosis as "the 'return of the repressed' which surfaces through the supernatural aspect of Christine, the disturbing side of masculinity normally glossed over in 'growing up' movies," the opposite of which—a reassuring side of masculinity—can be said of Dennis.[51] The horrific parts of the film come when Christine chases down and kills Arnie's high school antagonists, who had also earlier broken into his garage and viciously destroyed the car, going so far as shitting on the dashboard, whereupon the car seemed to "heal" herself. The vile "gang rape" of the car is thus the motivation for Arnie's revenge scenario, with Christine's connection to demonic dynamics (the car has been killing passengers since it was first assembled) the force that simultaneously restores her and keeps Arnie pathologically attached. In the climactic showdown, Dennis and Leigh unite to crush the car with a bulldozer after it kills Arnie, although the film ends with a typical shot forewarning that the car may still be "alive." (Fortunately, there were no sequels.)

Christine offers a troubling notion of how far an outcast teen may go to gain respect and attention, even with Arnie's culpability supposedly alleviated through his "possession" by the feminine auto, as if a nerd could only gain such respect and attention via supernatural influences. The narrative offers little explanation for why this one car is so wicked, but in its examination of the relationship among the three main teenagers, the film's message becomes one about the pitfalls of artificial rebellion, if not more so about the dangers of neurotic devotion, which in this case is the result of Arnie's displaced sexual frustration. Before Christine kills him, Arnie tells Dennis that love has a voracious appetite that consumes everything around it unless you "feed it right," and Arnie says he has such a love for Christine. This pathetic and demented perspective on love as destruction is one high school nerd's rationalized attempt to explain his difference from his peers, a degenerate product of adolescent social frustration at its worst.

Other supernatural monsters could be found in later '80s teen horror films such as *Fright Night* (1985), *Night of the Demons* (1987), *976-EVIL* (1988), and the short-lived phenomenon of "rock and horror" films at the end of the decade (e.g., *Trick or Treat* [1986], *The Gate* [1987], *Slumber Party Massacre II* [1987], *Black Roses* [1988], and *Rockula* [1990]). *Fright Night* offers a self-conscious critique of the vampire apologue with a sexually frustrated boy who is tormented by a suave bisexual vampire that moves in next door. *Night of the Demons*, while not theatrically or critically successful, nonetheless generated two sequels by 1997 and a remake in 2009, and all four films revolve around the haunted goings-on at an abandoned funeral parlor, where high school girls become "sexually possessed" and go on an erotic-homicidal rampage, maintaining the series' theme on the latent tribulations of female sexual domination. *976-EVIL* features a teenage boy who tries to transform from a wimpy nerd to a hip demon through an occult phone service, and like so many youth who attempt to use supernatural sources to improve their personal life, the protagonist perishes accordingly. Not unlike *Christine*, this is a nerd transformation scenario gone bad, warning that if wimps do not accept the minimal appeal of their sensitivity and insight then they will be damned in denying it for any greater power, which will definitely destroy them.

The Lost Boys (1987) would be quite popular in this era due to its careful casting of young stars as a coterie of vampires who lure a new kid in town to join their gang. Michael (Jason Patric) not only wants to be accepted, but he's attracted to the inamorata of gang leader David (Kiefer Sutherland), who gets him drunk on blood and turns him into one of them. Michael may be susceptible to the peer pressure of "drinking" but he refuses to attack other teens with his new biker brothers, which does not stop him from seducing David's girl, an act that diverts his bloodlust into sexual satisfaction. Michael's ability to resist the vampiric drive by displacing it with his lascivious human nature shows his ultimate strength in renouncing compliance with the gang, a theme that is revisited in variations through many supernatural youth films, which continually teach the lesson that sex and love triumph over pain and evil, and that authority by independence is a higher attainment than acceptance by conformity.

The 1988 remake of *The Blob* combined teenage social tensions with extraterrestrial fears and government conspiracy theories. In this rare supernatural plot where the teen protagonists have no role in initiating the terror, juvenile delinquent Brian (Kevin Dillon) finds himself teamed up with previously snobby cheerleader Meg (Shawnee Smith) in fighting the oleaginous monster, the residue from a "meteorite" which is really a government experiment in chemical warfare that has mysteriously failed.[52] After the blob begins consuming various people, the prim Meg actually defies her parents and seeks out Brian to ask for help, revealing her respect for his toughness and showing him that she means business by saying the word "shit." Brian and Meg eventually run into the clutches of a corrupt government biological team that is trying to control the blob and that views its victims as expendable test subjects.

Brian rushes to the rescue on his mighty motorcycle, while Meg realizes that the blob must be stopped by being frozen, and so engages the locals to train gas fire extinguishers on it. Brian then hijacks a snowmaking truck and drives it into the blob, only Meg becomes the hero when she loads the truck with a bomb, causing it to explode into ice crystals, thereby saving Brian and the entire town. The film's development of its teen characters is inconsistent—a stereotypical high school lothario becomes one of the first victims when he tries to take advantage of his blob-infested girlfriend— yet Meg's image as an indefatigable savior, rescuing her new boyfriend and everyone else, is worth emphasizing, not only for the rarity of being a teen female action hero, but for her swift dismissal of her clean cheerleader image to become the intrepid avenger of the town's destruction. Meg and Brian make no pretentions to take on the government or the professionals who set the blob on its rampage, nor is their allegiance to each other excessively romantic or joyful. In their determination to simply destroy the blob and protect themselves, Meg and Brian become two of the most resourceful, smart, and ironically realistic teens in the entire horror subgenre.

Less-intriguing supernatural youth films ensued over the next few years, somehow becoming even more prolific: *The Kiss* was released in 1988, followed by *Clownhouse, Teen Witch, Girlfriend from Hell,* and *Society* in 1989, the latter of which is one of the few accomplished entries in this horde, a spectacular examination of teenage alienation in relation to class and family rendered with arguably the most splendidly repulsive and mentally disturbing special effects in the whole subgenre. The pattern of familiar products continued in the '90s with *The People Under the Stairs* (1991), *Teenage Exorcist* (1993), *Shrunken Heads* (1994), and *Black Circle Boys* (1997), although *Tales from the Hood* (1995) was unusual in addressing supernatural torments within the highly charged racial discourse of the decade's African American crime films.

One of the best of this variety was the fascinating *Mirror Mirror* in 1990, which features unusually complex teen characters in Megan (Rainbow Harvest) and Nikki (Kristin Dattilo), who form a friendship after the recently relocated Megan enrolls in Nikki's cliquish private high school. Megan is an outcast from the start, wearing conspicuously gothic fashions, and when the established students tease her, the well-adjusted Nikki comes to her defense. Megan soon realizes that an old mirror left in her new house has a flair for granting distorted wishes: she longs for her dead father, who returns and then decomposes in front of her, and a rival at school develops a massive nose bleed as the mirror seems to bleed as well. What Megan wants most is not for the mirror to grant her wishes but to achieve them on her own, which is the very sense of power and confidence that she fails to muster. At one point Megan lures a boy to her through the mirror, but when he seems to reject her, she orders the mirror to take him away. She later conjures up the mirror's energy to kill two more students, mistakenly believing this will impress Nikki, and Megan finally realizes that the mirror has grown out of her control as it leads her to kill her mother and Nikki's boyfriend, and eventually kills Megan herself. In a narrative twist, Nikki inadvertently wishes everything would return "to the way it was," and finds herself back in 1939, when the mirror first witnessed a woman killing her sister, who now turns out to be Nikki killing Megan, thereby continuing the cycle of murder that possessed the mirror in the first place.

Mirror Mirror, like *976-EVIL* and other supernatural teen films, demonstrates the consequences of using mysterious forces to gain social acceptance. Megan initially believes that she can learn to control the mirror's sway—a particularly potent scene shows her caressing the blood-dripping mirror as if it were a lover, pointing to the masturbatory narcissism that has arisen from her need to feel desired—but eventually the dark phantoms of the mirror, generated as they were by a generational hatred between sisters, pervert her wishes. Megan's lack of faith in herself leads her to exploit the deceptive authority the mirror temporarily grants, and Nikki's distrust of Megan fuels the tragic tension between the two. Nikki tries to save Megan from the mirror's clutches only to find herself damned by her own desires for restoration, as if the mirror represents the lost sororal connection enacted by the original murder between the two 1939 sisters, a system of revenge in which the "good sister" destroys her less attractive counterpart. *Mirror Mirror* portrays the tyranny of teen popularity in its image of Megan oppressed by both benevolent and malicious social operators, and ultimately posits that one's self-image is shaped less by true reflection than by social construction, as distorted as that image may be.[53]

Body Snatchers, a 1993 remake of the 1956 classic *Invasion of the Body Snatchers* (which had already been remade in 1978), uses a teen as its moral and rational conscience, as she tries to evade the jackleg platoons of army agents infiltrated by aliens that are harboring pods to erase all humans' identities and make them into the same type of automatons. John Powers observed that the film's "real subject is adolescent angst, the terror that the adult world will turn one's youthful uniqueness into a dull, quiescent middle-aged conformity," a viable reading that still requires a more complete historical perspective.[54] The 1950s story was read as a metaphor of McCarthy-era communist mania; after *The Blob* in 1988 and the disarming *Return of the Living Dead* trilogy (1985–1993), this *Body Snatchers* further summoned the paranoia of military–industrial conspiracies, so that the role of the lead teen is, if somewhat weakly, connected to distrust of organized authority. Perhaps the film's most insightful point about its protagonist is her inability to fake the unemotional manner of the aliens—she is a genuinely sincere soul in a sea of poseurs. *Body Snatchers* is a fable of individuality in the face of overwhelming conformity, which in this context seems more a critique of the political status quo than a message to youth seeking their true selves.

Three films exploring girls' identities through witchcraft appeared in 1996, the most famous being *The Crucible*, Arthur Miller's allegory about blacklisting. Perhaps the low-budget *Little Witches* and better-financed *The Craft* were meant to capitalize on the anticipated success of *The Crucible*, but its seventeenth-century setting limited its commentary on contemporary youth.[55] In *The Craft*, Sarah (Robin Tunney) is a new teen in town, trying to make friends and recover from a suicide attempt. She meets Chris (Skeet Ulrich) at her Catholic prep school and warms to him, and he warns her about three girls who are looking for a fourth to join their mini-coven, a conceit that Roger Ebert wryly questioned "since they have messy hair, slather on black lipstick, wear leather dog collars, smoke a lot, have rings piercing many of the penetrable parts of their bodies, sneer constantly, and, in short, look like normal, popular teenagers."[56] The nonetheless marginalized girls, who are led by Nancy (Fairuza Balk), befriend Sarah and tell her about their worship of a spirit who gives them their witchy clout. Sarah is initially reluctant to join despite her own obvious mystical talents, but she unites with the group after Chris spreads lies that she had sex with him, thereby establishing a galvanizing revenge scenario. As the story proceeds, each girl in the group is further revealed to have a certain private hindrance: Nancy lives in squalor with her floozy mother and abusive stepfather, Bonnie (Neve Campbell) has burns covering much of her upper body that make her feel ugly, and Rochelle (Rachel True) is taunted by a popular girl at school who makes racist remarks about her. These dilemmas are meant to motivate the girls' turn to witchcraft, but as they systematically use the occult to eliminate these problems, their desire for more power corrupts them. Only Sarah, who does not need the "craft" to correct her personal misfortune, tries to maintain a safe distance: she commands a spell on Chris that makes him irrationally devoted to her and shows the other girls how they can levitate and, in a more cosmetic abuse of their obscure gifts, change their appearance.

What seems like female bonding with the girls' adopting goth styles and exchanging intimate stories becomes suspect as their occult encounters yield more dramatic results: Rochelle's racist agitator loses her hair, Bonnie's scars heal, and Nancy's mean stepfather dies, leaving her and her mother a small fortune in life insurance. These changes fulfill what these characters have desired all along, but in true Faustian fashion, they do not guarantee happiness. Sarah is attacked by Chris after his irrational devotion turns him into a brutish rapist, and Nancy becomes hysterical in her jealousy toward Sarah because she wanted Chris herself. In a scene that confirms the dual tensions of good/evil and virgin/whore that the film sets up, Nancy tries to seduce Chris at a party in the form of Sarah: Chris desires the virginal Sarah, but Nancy cannot lure him to her aggressive carnality, resulting in Nancy "casting" him out of a window to his death. Dismissing this moral portent about Nancy's inability to fully accept her true nature, Sarah appeals to further occult dominions as a way of leaving the group, "binding" Nancy from doing harm and invoking the spirit of her dead mother, who she realizes was a witch herself. This doesn't stop Nancy from enlisting Bonnie and Rochelle in a climactic assault on Sarah, in which Bonnie appears to be given back her scars, Rochelle loses her hair, and Nancy fights Sarah with violent spells and incantations. In the end, Bonnie and Rochelle are relieved of their capabilities and Nancy is confined to a mental hospital, leaving just Sarah with a sense of the craft, which seems more richly evidenced by her rejection of Bonnie and Rochelle's friendship than by her mental felling of a tree limb with a lightning bolt.

Pagan critic Peg Aloi wrote in 2007, "*The Craft* has undeniably been the single greatest influence on the growth of teenage Witchcraft in America," and yet it is as much a critique of perfidy in school cliques as it is an appraisal of witchcraft.[57] Sarah simply wants friends, and at first the small group seems supportive and congenial, yet her role in showing the other girls how they can manipulate themselves to get what they want makes her responsible for the dangerous drives they harness. The girls lose sight of their own weaknesses and need for improvement when they see that they can "cure" their crises through superficial means—Bonnie, for instance, becomes a salacious tease as soon as her scars are gone—and in that way they lose their true identities in the fantasy roles they play. Nancy, with the most serious frustrations, suffers the most serious results, and only Sarah, who had previously come to better terms with her burdens after her suicide attempt, is able to thwart the temptation of abusing the occult for selfish purposes. In this way *The Craft* undercuts its image of young female empowerment by its concentration on self-acceptance, and its promotion of witchcraft, which Aloi describes in further detail, succeeds despite its trite tactics. Further, as in almost all supernatural teen stories, the occult offers an alternative explanation for the mysteries of the universe that is no less codified, rule-bound, and unreliable than the conventional forms of worship that the teens are resisting.

The theme of girls retaliating for their mistreatment through troublesome measures remains a chronic theme in supernatural youth films, going back to *Carrie* (1976) and evinced quite prominently by the well-received (if distant) *Carrie* sequel, *The Rage: Carrie 2* (1999), which again took up the story of a downtrodden teenage girl using her psychokinetic talents to avenge her mistreatment by villainous classmates.[58] One important revision this film offers over its original is making the title character more wise and cynical about the behavior that is cast on her, so that her vulnerability to the clique's scorn is less threatening, and her ultimate revenge against them is, consequently, less satisfying. *Tamara* (2005) would pursue a similar route some years later, with its dejected title character returning from the dead by using witchcraft to, first, transform into a wanton hottie, and then exact punishment on the schoolmates who killed her.

In contrast to the end of the '80s, the later '90s showed less interest in supernatural films. Mutant malformations still arose to torment teens, albeit in fewer examples, such as the militaristic machines in *Small Soldiers* (1998) and the title body parts of *Idle Hands* (1999). A popular film of this variety was *The Faculty* (1998), another revision of the *Body Snatchers* scenario, this time with a group of unlikely teens banding together to resist the alien invaders who imitate their teachers and then their classmates. The film diligently applies the five school character types and yet there are six teens: as it turns out, one of them is an alien, and the other youth must rely on their idiosyncratic qualities in order to survive. Thus, the nerd provides necessary information, the popular girl supplies inspiring attitude, and in the narrative's oddest element, a smart delinquent develops the amphetamine that determines just who is an alien and who is human, so that doing drugs for these teens is their only means of showing just how "in" they are. Again, the fear for these youth is conformity, and they find themselves proudly upholding their senses of identity as they battle their way through the emotionless invaders until the nerd emerges as hero and destroys the mother monster, saving them all. Yet afterward, each of the characters find themselves on the verge of an unexpected transformation—the nerd has become a desired celebrity, the rebel girl has given up her "fake" lesbian identity to take up with the jock—and while this seems another homage to *The Breakfast Club*, it points to an interesting irony, since the teens' conquering of expansive malevolence has actually freed them from their previously restrictive roles, or conversely, through making them so acceptable, has rendered them even more conformist.

Aliens posing as humans makes for compelling stories about the nature of truth, but a more metaphysical monster would become relatively common in the '00s: the zombie, a corpse raised from the dead that slowly feeds on living humans. The undead had recurring roles in the three *Return of the Living Dead* films from 1985 to 1993, the third of which becomes a cutting critique of teenage self-mutilation as its heroine punctures her body multiple times in an effort to displace her lust to consume human brains. After a wave of successful zombie films in the early '00s directed at adult audiences, the industry resurrected this series twelve years later in 2005, spawning two sequels in quick order, both with the *Return of the Living Dead* title: *Necropolis* and *Rave to the Grave*. The former more closely replicates the original story about a shady corporation developing toxic chemicals that turn people into zombies, which a group of teenagers then endeavor to destroy, and the latter takes on a timelier moral about drugs with college students synthesizing the zombie chemicals into party drugs with predictably disastrous results.[59]

These and other teenage zombie movies over the next few years were not exactly illustrious, regardless of their quantity: *Die and Let Live* (2006) overcomes its zero budget with a sardonic story of a school party interrupted by zombies; *Pathogen* (2006) follows a girl who gathers kids to combat zombies propagated by the local drinking water; *Automaton Transfusion* (2006) features teens defending themselves against a zombie outbreak; and *Dance of the Dead* (2008) fuses many elements of past zombie stories with conventional high school characters who band together when zombies jeopardize their prom. *Make-Out with Violence* (2008) earned scattered acclaim with its creatively amalgamated story of adolescent love and abstruse existence as a boy falls in love with a girl after her animated carcass returns from the dead, questioning the downright insalubrious nature of necrophilia. Coincidentally, a similar story line was addressed through more specifically sexualized terms in the beguiling *Deadgirl* that same year. Despite the overall oblivion of these earlier zombies, two 2009 films did gain some attention. *Jennifer's Body*, written by Oscar-winning *Juno* scribe Diablo Cody, tells the story of a girl who becomes a succubus after being sacrificed in a ritual for her supposed virginity, which now causes her to feed on young men. The cleverly comical *Zombieland* was even more profitable with its cast of popular actors, including Oscar nominee Abigail Breslin as a twelve-year-old on a cross-country trip with her older sister, cautiously forming an ersatz family of human renegades in the wake of an apocalypse that has turned the population into zombies.[60] Overall, zombie movies have not yet reached the profusion of other supernatural tales, a condition continued by the faint release of *Detention of the Dead* in 2012, although the modest hit *Warm Bodies* (2013) did suggest the further potential of youthful horror romance.

The enthralling impermanence of death presented in zombie stories was also the haunting topic of two series that persisted throughout the 'oos sans zombies, *Final Destination* and *The Brotherhood*. The latter was a low-budget collection of made-for-DVD films by David DeCoteau, the inexhaustible schlock director and B-grade John Hughes of sexy teen horror. *The Brotherhood* began in 2001 with college characters seeking eternal life, then moved to a high school setting in the first sequel later that same year; *The Brotherhood 2: Young Warlocks* depicts a new student luring his buddies into the occult. Naturally, all of the films are thinly veiled in their homoerotic agenda to peruse often half-naked boys in peril, which would continue in *The Brotherhood III: Young Demons* (2003), prompting Jared Roberts to muse, "Were the random, scarcely-diegetic beefcake particularly attractive, this might make the film enjoyable for studwatchers. However, they're not quite as aesthetically pleasing as they ought to be."[61] The fourth film in 2005 returned the young beefcake—and the story line—to college, and the settings alternated between high school and college in the fifth and sixth films (both made in 2009), maintaining the theme so often seen in supernatural youth films, that of using black magic to conquer life and death and, more immediately, be accepted by peers, banally resulting in failure all around.

Final Destination (2000) began a far more popular series about youth trying to navigate the ontological boundaries of being, in which a high schooler foresees his plane crashing before a trip and convinces his friends to disembark, which turns out to be prescient after the plane actually does explode after takeoff. The student cannot explain his premonition, and the mystery deepens soon thereafter when his friends start dying through strange means, leading him to theorize that they had all been predestined to die on the plane and now their previously ordained deaths are being enacted. There is no indomitable creature or sinister sylph to explain the teens' situation, just the teens' growing sense that their inclusion in this club of the deceased is inevitable—a club to which, unlike other supernatural youth films, no one wants to belong. Alas, the tentative ending is inevitable as well, with the boy suddenly killed and his girlfriend institutionalized, thus leaving the character to return in the 2003 sequel with the same premise, now initiated with a massive car crash. The third film in 2006 transposes that disaster to a roller coaster collapse, and the fourth film in 2009—which abandoned any sequel number in its title—moved on to post-teen characters, as did *Final Destination 5* (2011).

The resurgence of the supernatural youth film thrived in the '00s alongside the growing output of youth fantasy in general, bolstered by booming literary sales in the *Harry Potter*, *Twilight*, and *Hunger Games* series. Some stories blurred genre boundaries by aligning with science fiction, further exploring the separation—or convergence—between life and death in films such as *The Invisible* (2007), with a teenager who is killed yet struggles in a nether state to return to his living body. More recent films continue to exploit sci-fi themes with tales of youth battling byzantine government conspiracies in *Push* (2009) and *Super 8* (2011), and battling corruptive subterranean energies in *Chronicle* (2012). While these films are loaded with expensive special effects and the latter two were hugely profitable hits, none of them could approach the hype engendered by Stephenie Meyer's four-book *Twilight* series, which yielded one movie each year from 2008 to 2012, earning well over $1.4 billion at the U.S. box office alone.[62]

The series begins with the subdued opening of *Twilight* (2008), in which high school junior Bella Swan (Kristen Stewart) moves to a sleepy town in Washington State to live with her divorced father. Like most new kids, she cautiously attempts to fit in at school, surprised at how welcoming some classmates are, and quickly frustrated with one initially repelled by her: the handsome, pale, cold, and uprightly coiffed Edward (Robert Pattinson), who limits his socializing to a small group of supposed teens in his adoptive family. Like so many girls, Bella is engrossed by the inaccessible marvel, especially after he shields her from a car accident by demonstrating super-human strength. Ignoring the warnings of her fast friends to avoid him, Bella pursues Edward, implicitly relating to his sense of estrangement, even after being told by a sympathetic Native American friend, Jacob (Taylor Lautner), that Edward's family is rumored to have descended from a lineage that harbors a shocking secret.

Such a rumor is just further enticement to Bella, who dismisses the affection Jacob shows for her so she can effectively nourish her attraction to the unreadable Edward, even more so after he explains how her impenetrable nature is reciprocally irresistible to him. "Bella must decipher Edward's ineffable weirdness," Cynthia Fuchs points out, yet "no matter how appealing his infinite pain and pretty grimacing . . . he brings considerable baggage."[63] Indeed, after reading up on some of the local native folktales, Bella becomes convinced that Edward is a vampire, and he not only verifies this "baggage," he vindicates his initial surliness to her because her blood is so uniquely arousing to him. All the same, he is adamant that his family is unusual in that they have learned to resist the prodding temptation for human blood, and instead feed on animals, which explains their distinction from a trio of visiting vampires haunting the community at the same time. Thus a climactic contest is set up with Edward battling one of the rogue vampires and saving Bella from death by extracting the attacker's venom from her, denying his own longing to consume her blood himself. The denouement finds the couple at their junior prom, with Bella declaring her endless love for Edward and offering him her neck in recompense for his devotion, which he declines by asking her to simply spend her human life with him.

This first entry sets up many of the themes and conflicts that imbue the following films, most particularly Bella's choice between life as a human or a vampire, Edward's willpower in not ravishing Bella, and the preservation of family—and later, romantic monogamy—that is so common to youth stories. While ostensibly too young to make such a lifelong commitment as becoming a vampire, Bella's comfort with Edward is intended to justify her pure knowledge of being, as she says, "unconditionally and irrevocably in love with him," a classic teenage fallacy of eternal romance. She dismisses his difference, and his difficulties: her love is so certain, with the narrative itself offering little explanation of her innate sense of oneness with him, as she scarcely comments on his looks, his charisma, or his apparent wealth. Later, when Edward lingers over Bella's wrist and neck with his lips near her skin, smelling her erotic redolence and heaving with the feral craving to just suck her sanguine essence, a physical parallel is made to the confusing carnal desire that so many teens feel. "Edward's love for her has become his religion and his sin," as Richard Corliss asserts, which is even more evident after the vampire invokes a parallel to another teenage turmoil when he says her blood tempts him like a drug.[64]

Religion and sin are very operative terms of desire for the protagonists. For the ravenous fever they project, their chastity becomes fanatical, as in the lone scene to feature particularly sensual contact between the two, when Edward first kisses Bella and she advances for heavier petting, then he recoils with a patently moralistic repression of his urges to go further. He employs this withdrawal method in order to safeguard her humanness *and* her virginity, so when he tells Bella, "I am wanting you so badly I still don't know if I can control myself," he becomes only more alluring. Much of that repression is inherited from his foster parents, who have three other adopted teenage children, and who are protective of their family's secret customs, which have limited their love to other vampires. Bella knows that she is privileged to be allowed into their world, and to experience Edward's special powers—which include rapid speed and mind reading as well as momentous muscle—and the family's hesitant acceptance of her resembles that of any young outsider learning about a lover's family. In this case, of course, the stakes of survival for the outsider are life-threatening and the social alienation of the family is more extreme than that of "normal" strangers in small towns.

The tension over Bella's impending deflowering is practically suspended in the completely pedestrian *New Moon* (2009), with the narrative dutifully driven by the purpose of advancing the plot for the next episodes. Jacob plays a much more central role in this story, after Edward and his family leave since they have stayed in the area for too long, a device that conveniently allows Bella, now an "adult" of eighteen, to become attracted to the local boy who has liked her all along. Yet a substantial part of her attraction is based on Edward's conditional request that Bella not try anything "reckless" after he departs, because once "her vampire has gone guardian angel on her," Manohla Dargis observes, "Bella, like a classic crazy ex, begins throwing herself into ever more dangerous situations to summon him."[65] Once she experiences the thrilling rush of knowing that Edward watches over her, she is more motivated to throw herself at the bulging and bare tawny torso of the slightly younger Jacob. He may thus be her temporary

The typically topless Jacob (Taylor Lautner) lingers over Bella (Kristen Stewart) in New Moon *(2009), the second film in* The Twilight Saga. *Here he races to her rescue, once again trying to save her from the self-destructive impulses she flaunts throughout the series.*

drug of choice to overcome the pain of Edward's distance, but she rebuffs his furtive pressure to make their relationship more tantalizing.

As it turns out, Jacob and his constantly shirtless friends — not family, but other young Native American men, who are bonded by generational tribal history rather than some judicial fraternal treaty like Edward's family — are actually werewolves, and particularly large ones at that. Notwithstanding the escalating diffidence Bella has for her love of Jacob, and his clan's antipathy for vampires, the climactic contest in this entry takes her to Italy to prevent Edward from sacrificing himself to the draconian Volturi, an imperial council of vampires that regulates his family's activities. As if this lumbering contrivance was not enough of a formality to advance the story, Bella makes a deal with the Volturi to become a vampire herself, and upon returning to town she tells Edward she wants him to "do it" to her, reintroducing the all-but-forgotten erotic ascension that saturated the first film. In a last gesture to keep her (and her virginity) safe from Jacob and to solemnify her imminent conversion to a vampire, Edward simply says, "Marry me, Bella," and the film abruptly ends. This indeterminate coda is indicative of the plain presentation of Bella throughout the series until the final film, which is further emphasized by Kristen Stewart's detached acting, rendering her so "casual and mystifyingly average," that Bella is "thus a perfect surrogate for the audience's romantic projections," as Mick LaSalle claimed—a surrogate that undeniably captivated many viewers in the lucrative youth demographic.[66]

The imminence of both Bella's marriage and conversion are then suspended in *Eclipse* (2010) as Edward soon learns that the surviving vampire of the rogue gang in the first film is now building a small army of new vampires to kill his family in revenge. Bella meanwhile renews her friendship with Jacob and finds her fidelity to Edward no deterrent to cultivating Jacob's ongoing affections, alternating as she does between taunting Jacob with her attentions and prodding Edward with her indifference to his envy. Jacob grows frustrated to the point of kissing Bella forcefully, prompting Edward to become hostile, and she feigns surprise at both of their actions. The tensions of the trio are nonetheless disrupted when the "new blood" army moves in for battle, and risking his fealty to his own clan, Jacob volunteers the wolf pack to help Edward's family fight the invasion, if only because he wants to convince Bella of his superiority. The romantic intrigue of the film's first half then gives way to violent action in the second half, as the impending contest between the vampires parallels the virile conquest Edward and Jacob seek in Bella.

The plot temporarily returns to the question of sexual culmination established in the first film, with Bella rather listlessly attempting to seduce Edward, yet he abruptly declares his abstinence until marriage, since he originally grew up over a century earlier in a more conservative era. (Nowhere in the series does Edward mention having another love during his numerous years.) This declaration betrays the agenda of the story to divert youth from premarital intercourse, markedly so when Edward suddenly performs a standard proposal to Bella immediately thereafter. The presumed value of Bella's virginity is thus equated with Edward's dedication to courtliness, although her tepid reaction continues to suggest her reservation about loving Edward in the first place. When Jacob later learns of their engagement and walks away in disgust, Bella follows with an unleashed fervor, asking him to kiss her, presumably to keep him from abandoning the upcoming vampire fight, but more so to confirm her love for him. She does tell Edward that she loves him *more* than Jacob, as if that is any consolation. In this regard, the film accomplishes the common girls' fantasy of being coveted by competing boys, and Bella exploits her fortune by expanding and enjoying the conflict.

This middle film of the pentalogy works well as a fulcrum between the beginning and end of the series, posing Bella directly between the polarities of Edward (regal, frigid, mortality) and Jacob (primal, warm, vitality). Further divisions become clear: Edward is refined and upper class to Jacob's raw modest means; Edward holds out eternal life fraught with bloodlust while Jacob promises natural life supported by labor; Edward is rationalized superego, Jacob is emotional id. Even her friend who gives the school graduation speech implies these disparities: Bella has a choice between Edward's rule-bound tradition and Jacob's exciting experimentation. With Bella wavering, she seems to merely favor Edward, appreciating as she does how much Jacob adores her, yet "of course she chooses the rich, sophisticated, cosmopolitan vampire over the poor half-clothed wolfboy who has spent his entire life on the reservation," as Kelly Oliver so bluntly articulated Edward's confirmed commodity value over Jacob's fleeting potential passion.[67]

The final *Twilight* novel, *Breaking Dawn*, was one volume, but the likely profits to be made by expanding the story must have impelled the studio to break it into two movies (which, after all, was the strategy with the final *Harry Potter* installment the previous year). As it were, *Breaking Dawn—Part 1* (2011) was actually made by the same crew and shot at the same time as its "sequel," giving the final two films in the series a stylistic coherence that the first three films did not share. The film opens with Jacob once again doffing his shirt, angered after receiving Bella and Edward's wedding invitation—and thereby providing Bella's predictable resolution of her connubial options, so thereafter the film takes on a considerably orthodox trajectory, as the long-awaited ceremony ensues. While dancing with Jacob outside the reception, Bella callously implies that she will lose her virginity before becoming a vampire, manipulating him to express his worry that sex with Edward could be deadly. Bella—still just eighteen—has been eager to marry Edward, yet her hesitation about the conversion has been evident, mounting to an edgy apex on their honeymoon when she wants more "human time" before the consummation of their relationship. After three movies filled with mild foreplay, the lovemaking between the two is remarkably tame, until Edward's excessive strength emerges and he partially demolishes the bedroom with his hands, which is not staged as comical yet rather embarrassing. Todd McCarthy elaborated on this belated and belabored moment of sexual discharge: "We never see anything . . . no moment of surrender, which is what the series has been building to all along. Where one legitimately hopes to register what Bella feels upon finally giving herself over to what she has so long desired but resisted, all we get are languid and lax interludes of what still seems like puppy love."[68]

The disappointing embarrassment of the night before turns to shame the morning after when Edward realizes he bruised Bella during the act, portending the damage he will inflict on her forever after. With the same masochistic abandon she brought to the marriage, Bella dismisses this sign of spousal violence just as she had dodged the fear of pain in her de-flowering, yet cannot be so impassive when she becomes visibly pregnant a mere two weeks later.

Even more than the partisan topic of premarital sex in the previous film, the ideologies of pregnancy and abortion quickly become the central con-cerns of this episode, raising further questions about the ambiguities be-tween life and death. Edward's sisters split into pro-choice and pro-life stances on Bella's uniquely hybrid pregnancy, given that the pregnancy is endangering her life but the baby must be protected. Edward relents so far as asking Jacob for assistance in persuading Bella to avoid going full-term with her potentially lethal gravidity, and since Jacob knows his wolf pack wants to kill any new vampire born in the community, he abandons the clan. Kelly Oliver views the conflict in a political context, because "Bella's insistence that it is her choice to have the baby echoes recent Hollywood pregnancy films that shun abortion and endorse family values."[69] And no sooner than this choice is made, Bella's gestation rapidly advances to labor, and in scenes outrageously graphic for the PG-13 series, Edward carefully performs a caesarian section by gnawing open her abdomen to remove the baby while Jacob holds her hand, whereupon Bella dies despite their heroic efforts to save her.[70] As a fight commences between the werewolves and vampires, Jacob plans to kill the mutant baby, only to startlingly—and in-voluntarily—"imprint" on the girl, binding him in his love with the child, and sending away his pack in defense of her. Edward, who resorted to re-peatedly biting Bella and injecting his venom in order to resuscitate her, accepts her death with peculiar composure, while intercut special effects shots reveal how his venom is working within her blood to bring her back to life. (Conversely, the earlier injection of his semen is what later brought her to death.) When she at last opens her eyes, their color is even more in-tense than that of her vampire daughter.

Ironies abound with life bringing death and death yielding life, as the series has prominently moved away from its past focus on adolescent occu-pations to more metaphysical matters about existence and morality, which is maintained in all films about youth and the supernatural. Curiously, the series relies on a connection between sex and death that is not altogether different from that in slasher/stalker films. Whereas youth in those horror movies are often killed without warning for their transgressions by psychotic strangers, here the advance admonitions about sex have been trumpeted by virtually every character, and the sex act itself is not only bruising, its aftermath is a botched pregnancy *and* brutal death, all at the hands of the ex-virgin's lover. Granted, that same lover provides the fluid to generate life *and* to restore it, an aspect that adds a further duality to the complications of the pregnancy. As we learn in *Breaking Dawn—Part 2* (2012), Bella's daughter, now named Renesmee, is a half-breed of human and vampire, and her lack of a "pure" heritage threatens both the vampire lineage in which she will be an aberration and her human community which is itself the prey of vampires.[71] Bella's maiden decision to have sex with Edward while still a human results in successfully converting her to a vampire, giving her the assets of super-speed and -strength as well as making her a more dominant presence, yet also introduces the problematic liability of the miscegenation that Jacob warned her against.

Jacob continues to factor into this final film of the series, which does not pursue so much the interracial (or interspecies) issue of Bella and Edward's progeny as it surveys the pervasive global reach of the vampire realm. Renesmee promptly grows from infant to child, and in the process irks the ire of the Volturi back in Italy, who plan to halt her development to adulthood since they believe such a creature would kill without restraint and expose their practices to the human world. Jacob, having imprinted on the girl and thus being committed to her safety, appeals to his pack to join in defending his future love from harm, and aligns with Edward's family as they gather a dramatically multicultural accumulation of international allies. While at first the various vampires of multiple talents are called to simply avouch that Renesmee is not a menace, they soon become trainers for the upcoming battle between Edward's family and the Volturi, and their participation in the fight becomes inevitable, revealing a sharp political divide between the diverse international coalition of working vampires and the exclusive elite formation of the royal cloister, many of whom even wear hoods to hide their faces.

Keeping with the previous films, the second half takes on another focus with the onset of combat, as Edward's family and their allies are vastly outnumbered by the Volturi and their minions. What then develops as a lengthy scene of carnage between the two sides resulting in the deaths of several major characters turns out to be a vision of the future supplied by Edward's sister, who not only illustrates the mutually assured destruction

that will result from this conflict, but provides the series' conclusive statement on the union of Bella and Edward that produced Renesmee.[72] She
introduces a crossbreed native from Brazil, half vampire and half human,
who can live on food or blood, and who can thus survive without killing.
The Volturi are at least provisionally satisfied that Renesmee may continue
to grow as such a harmless creature, and thereafter depart, with two rogue
members of the new alliance chasing after them, denoting the eternal conflict among vampire factions. A contrasting anticipation of harmony appears when Edward's sister foresees that Renesmee will mature to a young
woman with Jacob still loving her, and the film concludes with the original
fantasy concept that has so preoccupied Bella throughout, when she and
Edward return to the meadow where they often meet, and she confirms
in her visions that they will live not only happily ever after, but forever.
The perfect teenage dream of channeling the supernatural, in this case for
romance, is complete: love is found, fought for, and formalized, its preservation ensured through marriage, expanded through offspring, and endowed with faith in mystical higher powers.[73]

For all of the attention cast on the *Twilight* films, audiences were largely
unaware of perhaps the best youth vampire film ever made, based on a
Swedish novel and film from 2008. *Let Me In* (2010) places its protagonist on
the younger side of the scale, twelve-year-old Owen (Kodi Smit-McPhee),
a scrawny seventh-grader who endures bullying by a group of classmates
and lives quietly with his mother. He notices when a girl moves in to the
apartment next door with an older man, and he slowly discovers their
oddly nocturnal behavior, which begins to coincide with murders in the
local area. Abby (Chloë Grace Moretz) haltingly befriends Owen after an
awkward start, and tries to explain to him that she is unusual, even telling
him she is not a girl as he develops a crush on her, but his naïveté prevents
him from deducing what we already know: she is a vampire and the older
man kills people to provide her blood. The story is deliberately coy in developing Owen's knowledge about Abby, for he is simply grateful to have
a friend, one who communicates with him by tapping Morse code on their
adjoining bedroom wall, and moreover inspires him to stand down the
bullies at school. As Abby reveals more of her secrets to Owen, including
how she bleeds profusely if she enters a house uninvited, he is accepting,
and in the film's most tender scene, he asks her to "go steady" while disre-
garding that she is naked in bed next to him. Yet Owen is disarmed when
he realizes the older man has now gone, having killed himself, and that decades earlier this man had been her young love, doomed to age while she
stayed "twelve."

Unlike many other youth films that utilize the vampire theme, *Let Me In* moves beyond the aspect of eternal life to consider endless adolescence as a conflict. The age certainly does not suit Owen, who is easily ignored by his mother and abused by peers, yet unlike *Twilight* and films about older teen vampires, sexual tension and romantic destiny are not plot elements. Owen and Abby simply connect over their common problems as tweens who are distinctly different from their cohort and disabled by their conditions. Amy Biancolli expands on this: "Theirs is the story of any young outcasts who bond over shared pain and social ostracism. The true horror in Owen's life isn't the ghoul next door but the kids in gym who torture him with wedgies."[74]

Abby tells Owen to fight back against the bully who taunts him with homophobic insults about being a girl, and he achieves a boost of virile confidence by whacking the kid with a pole. This gratification gives Owen a boost of affection for Abby as well, making him selfless enough to accept that she must leave before being linked to the local murders; he does not feel a greater sense of cosmic fate binding them together. Yet when the bullies retaliate by trying to drown Owen, Abby emerges to violently slaughter his tormentors, a scene made magnificent by being rendered translucent from underwater. In the end, Owen leaves town on a train with a large trunk in tow, from within which Abby taps out their discreet Morse code. He will forever be her provider, she will forever be his protector.

Let Me In is not only a superb paradigm of the subgenre due to its suspenseful form, it excels at representing the adolescent experience of the supernatural in the same curious, eager, and fragile terms as a twelve-year-old might feel. Owen is initially dumbfounded by Abby like he is by all kids his age, yet her strange nature—and her shared enjoyment of puzzles—draws him to her. Abby is herself a puzzle, and when he later learns that her interest in him is based on needing a "servant" to find her blood, he is initially disappointed, but soon finds that her need for his help gives him a meaning he has not known before. Even when Owen makes his most genteel suggestion that they go steady, Abby agrees just because nothing will change, and thus Owen can feel secure in her approval and she can continue to trust him without complication. The symbiosis of their relationship is ideal for barely pubescent kids, with their pre-sexual needs fulfilled through means parallel to the traditional vampire's quasi-sexual needs, on the boundaries but not let in.

Teens are stalked by spirits from alternate realities in an ongoing number of supernatural stories, which have tended to remain rather consistent in output, ranging from low-budget fare such as *Wishcraft* (2002), *Hangman's*

Curse (2003), and *Resurrection Mary* (2007), to mid-level projects like *An American Haunting* (2005) and *The Covenant* (2006), to opportune hits like *The Grudge 2* (2006). Interest in tales of the macabre challenging youth continue to be appreciated, if not always successful, as manifest by the recently cast-off production of *Bad Kids Go to Hell* (2012), which, more faithfully and fruitfully than *Detention of the Dead*, proffers a straight-up send-up of *The Breakfast Club* with its library setting and small group of disparate students who goad one another's fears as an amorphous phantasm haunts their detention hall. These bearers of gruesome death and dread will persist in youth movies for as long as young people are concerned about their own loss of youth to adulthood, and fascinated by the mysteries of mortality that they discover in adolescence. (Further proof of this is *The Mortal Instruments* [2013], which as of this writing is poised to become a new franchise.) Understanding mystery is, in fact, the guiding compulsion behind the more fanciful variety of supernatural youth movies that have become ever more common over past generations.

Supernatural Fantasy

Fantasy youth films in the supernatural category were not as plentiful as the more dreadful variety throughout the end of the last century, but many well-regarded examples appeared in those two decades, and the approach would become radically invigorated in the '00s. Virtually no examples of youth fantasy appeared in the early '80s outside of animation, until the mid-'80s brought on a new tradition of films largely built on current scientific and technological curiosities. *Explorers* (1985) followed two boys who develop computer programs allowing them to travel through time, and then *Flight of the Navigator* (1986) took a more psychological approach to time travel with a boy who goes missing at the age of twelve and returns eight years later without having aged.

Neither of these films would have the same reach as a time-travel trilogy that began in 1985, *Back to the Future*. The film is undoubtedly a Hollywood product designed to appeal to a wide age range, offering a visible cross-generational charm in its story of 1980s teen Marty (Michael J. Fox) being sent back to the 1950s. After fumbling with bizarre equipment alongside a scientist friend, Marty not only discovers he has been relocated to his hometown many years earlier, but that he travels in the same social circle as his future mother and father, whom he must force together to ensure his own destiny. As he plays matchmaker with his awkward parents, he endures the nightmare of a culture that has not evolved to his experience of

'80s excess, and finds himself relieved when he returns to his present time to realize that his parents have become shallow yuppies. *Back to the Future* earned ten times its production costs and led to two sequels in 1989 and 1990.

In addition to exploiting space and time exploration, *The Last Starfighter* (1984) tapped into the decade's fascination with arcade games.[75] The story opens in a California trailer park community, where working-class Alex (Lance Guest) is hoping to qualify for a student loan and, as he says, "do something with my life other than going to City College and getting drunk on weekends with my high school friends." The class tensions among these characters are different from many teen films, if only because they do not have nearby middle- or upper-class peers reminding them of their plight, and because Alex's recognition of his class position is meant to explain his displaced attention to a video game at a local convenience store. He does not stand out at school or in society, but he becomes so proficient at the game that one night the entire community comes out to see him break the high score, a feat he completes in a fit of frustration after being notified that he's been denied for his college loan.

The film's connection of working-class dreams with such otherwise impractical skills as playing video games is then amplified by Alex's sudden recruitment by space aliens who take him to their planet to defend their population against an enemy rebellion. The aliens, it turns out, had been using the Earth-based video game (actually called *Starfighter* and manufactured by Atari) to seek out the best fighters, and their confidence in Alex's skills provides an esteem he did not enjoy back home. After a battle in which all of the other planet's ships are destroyed by the enemy, Alex is left as the "last starfighter," and with the help of another alien, Alex uses his knowledge of the video game system to pilot his ship into enemy territory and destroy their entire fleet, working his way up through "levels of difficulty" that climax in a game-winning defeat of the main enemy base. Despite his victory, and a global celebration in his honor, Alex must then pursue the enemy leader, who escaped during the attack. Nonetheless, he makes a quick stop at Earth, where he tells his mom he's okay, and picks up his initially reluctant girlfriend, who realizes that a life in space fighting enemy aliens is more exciting than living in a trailer park. *The Last Starfighter* aims for a moral message that clearly attempts to connect game playing to a higher purpose, indicating that these games are not only effective fantasy outlets for teens, but may possibly serve a more profound or even professional purpose. After all, a number of billionaires in the computer industry of the '90s were teen video game players in the '70s and '80s, and their skills in comprehending those systems obviously served them well, a fantasy for many young men.

Other metaphorical stories about changing time remained common during the fading days of the Cold War era, which often connected to post-apocalyptic near futures in which civilization has run amok, such as *Night of the Comet* (1984), *Radioactive Dreams* (1985), *Wired to Kill* (1986), and *Prayer of the Rollerboys* (1991). Lighthearted takes on typical supernatural monsters were also swelling at this time: *My Best Friend Is a Vampire* (1987), *The Monster Squad* (1987), *Teen Vamp* (1988), and *My Mom's a Werewolf* (1989). Far more popular in this period were bigger-budget productions about youth encountering strange new worlds, as in *The Goonies* (1985), with seven kids seeking treasure in a spooky cavern; *Labyrinth* (1986), about a girl trying to save her little brother through traversing the imaginary title maze; and *Edward Scissorhands* (1990), a fairy tale set in quasi-America with its pre-goth title creation trying to navigate suburban youth culture.[76]

Youth fantasy in the '90s continued to reflect a mixed interest in contemporary and classical stories about youth, and a range of tones from comical to creepy. Kids still sought help through mystical means such as the magical talking skateboard in *The Skateboard Kid* (1993), the title character in *My Uncle: The Alien* (1996), and the alien space suit in *Star Kid* (1997), while warping the space-time continuum remained fun for those inspired by the Salem witch trials in *Hocus Pocus* (1993), the Arthurian legend in *A Kid in King Arthur's Court* (1995), the mythical figures of American folklore in *Tall Tale* (1995), and gauche Taoist ideals in *Warriors of Virtue* (1997). Studios remained adept at adapting current youth consumption to the screen, as with the production of *Double Dragon* (1994), about two brothers using their martial arts skills in the future to fight ancient Chinese evil, which was based on a popular series of video games. *Mighty Morphin Power Rangers: The Movie* (1995) was an even bigger coup, based as it was on an existing television series and toy line, featuring six teenagers who transform into dynamic superheroes with the sole purpose of battling a long line of trite villains. Box office for *The Movie* more than doubled the production costs, but a more renowned youth fantasy in 1995 would be one of the biggest hits of the entire year: *Casper*.

The title character was a boyish "friendly ghost" in cartoons and comic books for five decades starting in the 1940s, so he was familiar to both parents and children. Christina Ricci plays Kat, the teenage daughter of a deceased mother, with a father who has become a dubious "ghost psychologist" hired to exorcize the mischievous ghosts in a decaying mansion. Casper happens to live there, dealing with the annoying presence of his

Kat (Christina Ricci) is the object of affection for the title ghost in Casper *(1995), yet she encounters an often disturbing array of spooky dangers as the young couple copes with their childhood issues.*

three antagonizing uncles, and he quickly develops a romantic crush on Kat, until she tries to explain to him that she needs a human boyfriend—who can apparently do things a ghost cannot.[77] Kat and Casper are both frustrated with their liminal states: she longs for a human touch because she is becoming a woman, while he is mired in a childhood without memories. Both conditions—the onset of romantic and sexual desire, and the need to grow beyond youth—illustrate these characters' dual adolescent goals of confronting life after death (since Casper is already dead and Kat is trying to move on after the death of her mother) and becoming romantically "real" (since they each want a human partner). How the film fulfills these goals is strange indeed.

After talking about their situations, Casper lies with Kat in her bed, kissing her on the cheek and curling up at her feet after she falls asleep. This faintly necrophilic moment then gives way to further bonding between the two, as Kat discovers Casper's literal toys in the attic and helps him to recall his death as a child. As it turns out, years earlier Casper's inventor father had spent the end of his life trying to revive his son with a special resurrection machine, but before they have time to test it, Kat's father accidentally dies after getting drunk with Casper's uncles and falling into a ditch. When her father returns as a ghost, Kat brings him back to life by using the machine with Casper's help. Speaking to the film's dual fantasies, Caryn James points out that "Casper proves he is Kat's truest friend, and in a turn that is part *Cinderella* and part *Pinocchio*, he temporarily gets his fondest wish."[78] That wish arrives from a spiritual medium, as Kat's mother appears and gives him the ability to be a boy for the next few hours, which leads to the film's eerie resolution in which the now-human Casper dances with Kat and they float off the floor together. Their parting kiss is an ideal consummation for two kids who, after all, were not looking for a lover as much as the validation a lover represents. Casper, having experienced humanness again as well as the feeling of a girl's body, can then return to the ghost world to finish the business of reclaiming his childhood (and, of course, to make sequels).[79] Kat's validation is achieved through kissing a boy as well as through her mother's brief return, which provides her father with the closure he needed to move on in life. When the mother reminds the father, "Our daughter is . . . a teenager," the label essentially identifies Kat as a new person, one who can now find healthy relationships with real boys and a healed father.

Fantasy films about youth continued within the three integrated arenas established by films like *The Last Starfighter* and *Casper*: the mystical, the heroic, and the otherworldly. Curiously, after the abundant output of these varieties into the mid-'90s, they were relatively defunct until the early '00s, with scant ventures like *Deal of a Lifetime* (1999) dealing with the possibility of a teenager selling his soul. Other mystical stories were often more exceptional, such as the family that lives forever in *Tuck Everlasting* (2002), creating quite a mortal conflict for the teenager who falls in love with one of them, and *Purgatory House* (2004), a low-budget spectacle written by and starring a fourteen-year-old girl whose character has committed suicide and now exists in some sweet hell struggling to accept the consequences of her actions.[80] Less notable stories of mystique would include girlish *Harry Potter* imitation *Sarah London and the Paranormal Hour* (2007) and the story of a boy deformed by his inner hatred, *Beastly* (2011). These different stories covered the decade, yet had an altogether fractional importance compared to the eight *Harry Potter* films from 2001 to 2011.

British author J. K. Rowling started the seven-book series in 1997 and the beginning entries were such a success that the first volume, *Harry Potter and the Philosopher's Stone*, was adapted into a movie long before she finished the final publication in 2007. The films were essentially British productions about British youth simply funded by American studios, nevertheless with such an impact on American youth that some inclusion of them is warranted here. Hollywood manipulation, for instance, was evident from the start with the altered title of the first film, *Harry Potter and the Sorcerer's Stone* (2001), although the Warner Bros. studio was only following the lead of the books' publisher, Scholastic, which had made dozens of changes from Rowling's "English" text to that distributed for American readers.[81] The new name actually added to the story's themes of dark magic for its title character, an eleven-year-old boy who goes off to a school that teaches wizardry, themes that led certain critics to complain that the book was promoting an unhealthy uncovering of sinful stimuli among children. Such criticism aside, the stories promoted aspects of self-determination, loyalty to causes and to friends, respect for elders, and excitement for education.

Harry (Daniel Radcliffe) begins his schooling in the first film, meeting most of the teachers and friends he will follow throughout the series. The two key children who join him in the traditional trio of supernatural allies are Ron (Rupert Grint) and Hermione (Emma Watson), who return to witchcraft and wizardry school with *Harry Potter and the Chamber of Secrets* (2002). The third film, *Harry Potter and the Prisoner of Azkaban* (2004), considers more of the thirteen-year-old's troubled family life outside of school, and the teens' blooming sensual feelings for each other are amply palpable by the time of *Harry Potter and the Goblet of Fire* (2005). The children continue to learn their defenses against "dark arts" in *Harry Potter and the Order of the Phoenix* (2007), and the series continues the progression of the students through school years as they enter their sixth in *Harry Potter and the Half-Blood Prince* (2009). By this point the literary series had been finished and the vast global following of the stories had been confirmed, so Warner Bros. understandably divided the final book, *Harry Potter and the Deathly Hollows*, into two films that built to a carefully explained climax. The trio of teens align with their cohort against the corrupt forces that have taken over their school in *Part 1* (2010) and unleash the ultimate barrage of magical munitions to conquer their nemeses in *Part 2* (2011), with this last film closing on a day some two decades hence when the three adults now send their children off to their alma mater.

To date, *Harry Potter* is the most lucrative youth franchise of all time, even if precise figures on the combined income of its extensive merchandise are impossible to determine due to sheer exponentiation, although the revenue is well in excess of $20 billion. That level of earnings and influence has led to an unprecedented level of interest by media markets seeking profits, and an even more immeasurable interest by audiences that have been enchanted with a boy aging through the entire scope of his adolescence, within stories glorifying numerous fantasies about youth.

Casting a central hero like Harry Potter in a fight against mercurial and merciless pests is perhaps the most common device of all fantasy plots, especially for young audiences seeking role models who overcome adversity such as adolescents feel. Fantasy films focusing on heroic characters provide consistently conflicted youth facing the potency of their special abilities and their responsibilities to use them, and allow movie studios to recycle these heroes over time while merchandizing their products to ongoing generations of children. *Spider-Man* (2002) is a primary example, based on a comic book hero invented in the '60s who was a teenaged orphan, and like so many of these films, showcasing the hero's name in the title. After no less than seven television series also bearing the name, the film took up the well-documented story with Tobey Maguire in the title role, a nerdy high school photographer named Peter Parker who is bitten by a spider that endows him with superpowers overnight. Peter lives modestly with his aunt and uncle, and has a long-standing crush on a classmate, which motivates him to take on his initial Spider-Man role as a wrestler so he can raise cash. He does not become a crime fighter until his uncle is killed, and he immediately avenges his death, thereafter helping his city put down further evil, such as that of his first archenemy, whom he defeats by the end.

A new villain emerges in the sequel, *Spider-Man 2* (2004), by which point Peter is in college and his Spider-Man role is not enough to guard him from adult troubles such as losing his job and paying his aunt's mortgage. Inner turmoil becomes a greater obstacle in *Spider-Man 3* (2007), which closed this trilogy for the '00s, yet it was reborn in 2012 with *The Amazing Spider-Man* (2012), taking a new Peter (Andrew Garfield) back to high school within a plot similar to the 2002 film. As of this writing, the first sequel of this new trilogy is set for release in 2014, with the goal of following once again the superhero from his adolescence into adulthood, preserving the fantasy that an awkward poor orphan can save the day and win the girl.

By comparison, throughout the '00s, many heroic figures appeared in youth fantasies with no established background and little anticipation of being reborn in sequels or remakes, such as *Like Mike* (2002), which entertains the possibility that magic sneakers can elevate a short teen to a professional basketball team. Taking a core idea from the *Harry Potter* series, *Sky High* (2005) and *Zoom* (2006) both feature teenagers in schools for superheroes, and *The Adventures of Food Boy* (2008) places its unique protagonist in a normal high school. Two films at the end of the decade drew attention to the increasing absurdity and commercialization of films in this variety, one intentionally as a parody, *Superhero Movie* (2008), and the other unintentionally as the pinnacle moment for a television character begun in 2006, *Hannah Montana: The Movie* (2009). Hannah (Miley Cyrus) was a Disney creation that almost immediately launched a massive line of merchandise related to the fantasy of an average teenager by day becoming a superstar by night—not heroic thanks to supremacy, but infinitely popular thanks to being a media commodity. The protagonist may have been intended to represent the capacity of a young woman to achieve success, and with generally empowering songs for girls, yet her luxurious aspirations and her progressively sexualized image—which the actress embraced in her later teens—questioned to what extent the character functioned beyond patriarchal norms.[82] Alas, no complaints could halt the boundless attention she garnered until the show ended in 2011, having also generated a theatrical concert film, a video game, more than two dozen novels, hundreds of products, and profits that her multinational conglomerate cannot even estimate.

Agent Cody Banks (2003), about a teenage spy for the CIA, made enough money to generate one sequel in 2004, but another spy story became a franchise during the '00s. *Spy Kids* began in 2001 as the project of director Robert Rodriguez, who wanted to create a family-friendly adventure film, and cast pre-teens in the first of what became four episodes. In the debut, a sister and brother join forces to save their secret agent parents from peril, and in the first sequel, *Spy Kids 2: Island of Lost Dreams* (2002), the kids have joined the profession themselves. By the time of *Spy Kids 3-D: Game Over* (2003), both children are young adolescents, continuing their spy work not with superhuman powers *per se*, but with an array of gadgets and intelligence that grant them the capacity to defeat various villains. The films were a smash with young audiences, and Rodriguez notably infused the stories with themes of familial primacy; he was also credited for working in the relatively new technology of high-definition digital video on the latter two films, and the series easily lent itself to a video game in 2004. After three movies in as many years, the series was suspended as a trilogy until a fourth film, *Spy Kids: All the Time in the World in 4D* appeared in 2011, with a nearly new cast, and a gimmick that likely detracted from its draw, an "Aroma-Scope" scratch-and-sniff card to accompany prompted scenes.

After these many films featuring disparate heroes, an unexpected film came along that rather literally exploded the various mythologies and ironies of the youth fantasy figure, and in this case the nebbish title character, *Kick-Ass* (2010), does not so much transform into a superhero as he becomes one by way of association. Dave (Aaron Johnson) is a nerdy New

York City high schooler who hangs out with his two buddies at a comic book shop and daydreams about having some of the strengths they so avidly read about, until one day he decides to don a gaudy green costume and the name Kick-Ass as he confronts two local thugs. The resulting confrontation lands him in the hospital, but when Dave returns to school his friends are amazed that so much of the surgery from his attack has rendered him impervious to pain. Better yet, the ordeal has secured the attention of his crush, and after he is recorded warding off some ruffians, Kick-Ass becomes a media sensation. Feeling emboldened by his situation, Dave takes on an even larger set of hoodlums and is about to be killed when he is miraculously saved by Hit Girl (Chloë Grace Moretz), who has been working with her father, Big Daddy (Nicolas Cage), as superheroes out to destroy a local drug lord. The killing skills and proficiency of Hit Girl are astonishing, particularly in this "scene of bug-fuck gore set to the kiddie theme from *The Banana Splits*," as Peter Travers observed.[83] Compared to protagonist Dave, she's a few years younger, about half his size, and arguably the most extreme of any tough girl to ever hit the screen.

Realizing he has but minimal abilities to be an actual superhero, Dave confesses to his crush that he is Kick-Ass, achieving his fantasies of getting the girl and, through his rising fame, becoming a comic book character himself. As it turns out though, the drug lord's teenage son decides to take on his own superhero identity as Red Mist (Christopher Mintz-Plasse), and eventually helps his father's henchmen to trap and torture Kick-Ass and Big Daddy, until Hit Girl shows up to kill more hoodlums, yet alas too late to save her father. Again the scenes of Hit Girl's prowess are breathtaking, for never has such a young character brandished so much homicidal efficiency and balletic violence, with knives and swords as well as guns.[84] These aspects are only amplified at the climax when Hit Girl joins with Kick-Ass to avenge her father's death and, after scenes of bodily combat between the drug lord and the child, Kick-Ass at last blows up the gangster with a bazooka. In a closing shot clearly designed to continue the story, Red Mist remains free to avenge his own father's death, and the 2013 sequel appeared after this book went to press.

Kick-Ass is a rich text full of commentary on the motives of superheroes. Those of manic yet noble Hit Girl and her father are to avenge the death of her mother, while those of Dave are simply to have a higher sense of privilege, and accordingly the latter ambition is shown to be selfish. Hit Girl may need Kick-Ass to help ultimately rid her city of the criminals' scourge, but Big Daddy's planning (training and stockpiling massive weaponry) and her dynamic actions are what accomplish the primary objective. This film would have likely received a much more resistant reception if it had been released too soon after the Columbine killings, or the 2012 Newtown, Connecticut, massacre that left so many young children dead, because the film's violence against youth, and its fantasy of an invincible child superhero who can defend against so many threats, is indeed merely that: a fantasy. In the end, Dave simply wants to return to life with his crush as a new girlfriend, and Hit Girl, really named Mindy, is happy to enroll in high school as just another kid, albeit one who can strongly protect herself. The two have learned that vengeance is destructive, and even when achieved it remains virulent. Further, being a superhero is not only unrealistic but also unappealing.

The heroic protagonist is sometimes diminished by his or her surroundings, which become more significant to the fantasy than the characters themselves. In these cases, the otherworldly location is the primary subject of the story, often made prominent by its name in the title, as with *The Chronicles of Narnia* series, based on seven books by C. S. Lewis published in the 1950s. While made as films before, the latest franchise began in 2005 with *The Lion, the Witch, and the Wardrobe*, which begins the story of four British children who discover the secret world of Narnia, and like the *Harry Potter* series, the films are primarily British productions. (Two films have since followed, with the rest in development.) Youth fantasies set in other worlds — and other times — have been common throughout the subgenre, and in recent years have included the product-placing *Transformers* (2007), the environmental fable *City of Ember* (2008), and the Greek-updating *Percy Jackson & the Olympians: The Lightning Thief* (2010), which is set to become a trilogy by 2015. Three more respected examples were the remake of *Alice in Wonderland* (2010), with the heroine now a teenager; the tale of two twelve-year-olds in a pretend Paris of the 1930s, *Hugo* (2011); and the post-apocalyptic *Hunger Games* trilogy that started in 2012.

Fantasy films for youth tackle many unsettling concerns of young people: missing parents, broken families, the need for friends, finding love, and gaining respect. In their conclusions, these stories strongly tell their young viewers that even after enduring childhood troubles and adolescent adjustments, there are nonetheless more challenges ahead as life brings further changes such as new homes, new schools, and new relationships. Such films may not often overtly confront serious issues like crime or sex, but through confrontations with life and death, they often give young people a dose of encouraging empowerment within their otherwise unreal stories and highly commercial contexts.

CONCLUSION

Jessica Robinson's *Life Lessons from Slasher Films* (2012) operates from their familiarity and uniformity, and she elaborates on six key
messages such as "the past will catch up with you," "listen to your elders,"
and "never feel sympathy for the killer."[85] Her citations cover the period
from 1960 (*Psycho*) to 2010 (*A Nightmare on Elm Street*) and in those fifty
years countless collective elements had been repeated and recycled, yet
studios and audiences remained eager for more. Robinson elucidates the
recurring incidents of slasher films that have provided so many asinine sequels and remakes, and she concludes that they have "shattered the illusion
of a conservative, ideal past full of nuclear families and teens who didn't
question authority."[86] In many ways, that shattering is the essence of their
appeal, since youth are able to break through the facades of life with far
more extreme dramas than they will ever endure in reality.

Because teen films in general have become so persistent, they have
gained enough maturity to be parodied, as has been accomplished in *Wet
Hot American Summer* (2001), *Pretty Cool* (2006), and *Hamlet 2* (2008). Yet the
extremes of the teen horror subgenre have made it even more susceptible
to satire, first in the 1981 spoof *Student Bodies*, and then, as Richard Nowell
points out, these satires became their own cycle with *Class Reunion*, *Pan-
demonium*, and *Wacko* all being released in 1982. More predictably goofy
productions followed, such as *Revenge of the Teenage Vixens from Outer Space*
(1986), *Return to Horror High* (1987), *Cutting Class* (1989), and *There's Nothing
Out There* (1990).

The lapse in teen horror parodies thereafter signified the culturally dormant period of the subgenre when such parodies would have been met
with scant enthusiasm (and would have had few recognizable films to
mine for their humor), but after its revival in the late '90s, the subgenre
spawned more sendups such as *Psycho Beach Party* (2000) and *Shriek If You
Know What I Did Last Friday the 13th* (2000). The incredibly successful *Scary
Movie* (2000)—which lifted the original title for *Scream*—made a happy
mockery out of youth horror *and* sex film trends, and brought in recent
films outside of the teen genre, such as *The Blair Witch Project* (1999) and *The
Sixth Sense* (1999). And like many lesser horror hits, the film mutated into
sequels, first in 2001 and then 2003, until the fourth film in 2006 largely
moved away from teen characters.

To be true, jokes and stereotypes about teen horror have been predominantly focused on the slasher/stalker varieties of the subgenre, for supernatural films have been made with rather broad themes and dissimilar plots

resulting in a lack of cohesion that has made aping them more difficult. Further, the legendary and literary pedigrees of many supernatural stories have granted them legitimacy beyond the flat brutality of contemporary killer tales. At the same time, the increasing popularity of the supernatural category over the slasher/stalker films has ensured that parodies would eventually emerge, as they did in two examples released after the *Twilight* series began, *Vampires Suck* (2010) and *My Sucky Teen Romance* (2011), the latter of which was written and directed by eighteen-year-old Emily Hagins and received widespread acclaim.

There's Nothing Out There (1990) was also made by a very young auteur, Rolfe Kanefsky, who had devoted his early college years to studying and challenging the practices of the entire horror genre. The film tells the story of teens spending spring break at a remote cabin who are systematically killed by a lubricious supernatural entity. In fact, main character Mike (Craig Peck), with his constant reminders to his friends of how teens like themselves are killed in similar situations in horror movies, seems to have been the direct inspiration for the Randy character in *Scream* six years later; he at least represents the parodic potential Wes Craven exploited in his film by having Randy mimic Mike from this little-seen low-budget prototype.

This film provides an appropriate closing point to reflect on the subgenre, in which teens have been sadistically assaulted and have yet been expected to enjoy such a negative representation of themselves with noxious frivolity. Kanefsky himself was barely twenty when he wrote and directed *There's Nothing Out There*, trying to "take back" the genre that he felt had so misrepresented youth that the only effective response was to implode the genre's conventions.[87] Perhaps Kanefsky saw himself as the Mike character in his own film, warning his cohort against ignorance and gullibility, trying to make the experience of terror as informed and pleasurable as it could be for a population that had been asked to quiver and die so much at the hands of older filmmakers who told them that they would like the pain. The "driller killer" in *Slumber Party Massacre* expresses this duplicity when he tells his final female victims, "All of you are very pretty. I love you. Takes a lot of love for a person to do this. You know you want it. You'll love it."

For all of the lessons, entertainment, and provocation that the teen horror subgenre has brought to at least its core audience, most of its films have not managed to combine the emotional intensity of fear with the fragile mysteries of entering adulthood while *also* gaining respect or credibility with the public at large, despite the valuable, if extreme, portraits of teenagers that the subgenre presents.

Five

YOUTH ROMANCE

Falling in Love and the Fallout of Sex

I gave her my heart and she gave me a pen.
LLOYD DOBLER (JOHN CUSACK) AFTER BEING
DUMPED BY DIANE COURT IN *SAY ANYTHING . . .*
(1989)

Cheers make girls do stupid cartwheels. Orgasms make them feel good.
GRAHAM (CLEA DUVALL) OFFERING A REJOINDER
IN *BUT I'M A CHEERLEADER* (1999)

I know these will all be stories someday . . . but right now these moments are not stories. This is happening, I am here, and I am looking at her. And she is so beautiful. I can see it. This one moment when you know you're not a sad story. You are alive, and you stand up and see the lights on the buildings and everything that makes you wonder. . . . And in this moment, I swear, we are infinite.
CHARLIE (LOGAN LERMAN) IN *THE PERKS OF BEING A WALLFLOWER* (2012)

Romantic longing and sexual curiosity take on heightened intensity and profundity for youth in the adolescent years. A large part of working through puberty to adulthood is the struggle to recognize and cope with the emotional and physiological changes that arrive with the onset of secondary sexual characteristics: young people get crushes and question their sexual impulses as they witness their bodies changing, members of the opposite (and/or same) sex becoming more attractive, and their friends becoming more occupied with the processes of dating. Because adolescent sexuality is so confusing for those who experience it and is still difficult to understand for those who have endured it, the topic provides ripe tension and drama for films about youth. Further, because adolescent sexuality is a socially taboo topic—the threats of pregnancy and sexually transmitted diseases, tensions about pedophilia, and the general moral concern over how sex could "corrupt" youth, among other reasons—the subject becomes both a way of stimulating supposed prurient interests while also addressing the very oppression and repression of teen sexuality. One attitude would allow youth no flavor for their fare and the other would have teens on a straight pepper diet. These approaches could offer certain liberations for the natural development of youth sexuality that is so often stunted by social codes, or they could exploit and further suppress the natural exploration and healthy acceptance of youth sexuality.

CONTEXTS AND TRENDS
IN THE SUBGENRE

Youth films that have depicted teens pursuing love and sex have offered a wide spectrum of perspectives for and about their subjects, in an erosphere of experiences.[1] Encountering sexual feelings and practices for the first time, young viewers are told, can be exciting and terrifying, fun and tragic. More often than not, the emphasis in youth films since 1980 has been on positive aspects of young love and negative aspects of young lust, often depending on the time period of the story. The major wave of teen sex romps in the early '80s was inaugurated by the Canadian film *Porky's* in 1982, which was about young men's pursuit of sexual hijinks in the '50s and aspired to be a simply more graphic updating of the nostalgic *American Graffiti* (1973) and, to a lesser extent, *Grease* (1978). All of these films were huge box office hits, and all of them pointed to their adult directors' sentimental attachments to their own discoveries of sex (and love), which were apparently playful, humorous, and ultimately safe. If these films had concentrated on potentially negative aspects of teenage sexuality as later contemporary films would do, they would have likely failed to draw young audiences, who would have likely perceived them as preachy message movies: such failure was and remains the fate of many films that do depict negative aspects of teen sexuality, such as *Class* (1983), *"For Keeps"* (1988), *Fear* (1996), *Lolita* (1998), *The Quiet* (2005), and *Hooking Up* (2009).

That teenage sexuality has often been depicted as tormented by Hollywood is not surprising, especially given its implicitly negative depictions in the horror subgenre, and the "need" for teens' anxieties about sex to be addressed (or occasionally alleviated) by the entertainment media, a need that translates into industry profits. Also not surprisingly, studies have shown that the "types of information teens may be acquiring about sex from the media show that the group is not receiving the proper educational information needed to make educated decisions," and thus youth films in the romance subgenre since 1980 have undoubtedly moved through particular trends that are not always consistent *or* progressive.² After the sexual revolution of the '60s gave rise to the late-'70s disco era in which adults were encouraged to revel in a number of excesses, youth seemed to be pushed toward the same moral loosening. The year 1980 saw the taboo-breaking success of *The Blue Lagoon*, a sexual awakening story (which was itself a remake of a tamer 1949 British film) whose Edenic myth symbolized the fanciful discoveries of youth sexuality in subsequent '80s films. Two less successful 1980 films, *Foxes* and *Little Darlings*—the latter featuring two teen girls racing to lose their virginity—also raised the stakes of sexualized youth depictions. These films seemed to indicate that audiences were ready, if not eager, for more explicit portraits of youth sexuality, and over the next few years, large and small studios flooded the market with depictions of teens' rowdy and occasionally educational forays into sexual practice, even if many of them failed to profit from their slyly suggestive titles, such as *Private Lessons* (1981), *Goin' All the Way!* (1982), *Getting It On* (1983), and *Snowballing* (1984). What was less prominent in the early '80s were depictions of youth dealing with the more romantic aspects of their burgeoning sexuality. Yet films that did just that by the mid-'80s became quite successful, and the relatively explicit youth sex trend waned with the appearance of more sensitive narratives, specifically those written and/or directed by John Hughes, such as *Sixteen Candles* (1984), *Pretty in Pink* (1986), and *Some Kind of Wonderful* (1987), and non-Hughes productions like *Seven Minutes in Heaven* (1985), *Lucas* (1986), *Can't Buy Me Love*, *Square Dance* (both 1987), and *Mystic Pizza* (1988).³ By the late '80s, when social discourses around AIDS had made youth sexuality an even greater concern and teenage pregnancies were on the rise (the number of unmarried pregnant teens increased by over 10 percent between 1985 and 1990, to one out of every ten girls), American youth films made a visible move away from the sexualized images of youth that had dominated the screen in the early '80s and concentrated further on romantic pre-sexual relationships among teens.⁴ Period films harking back to more "innocent" eras for youth became increasingly popular—*Peggy Sue Got Married* (1986), *La Bamba* (1987), *A Night in the Life of Jimmy Reardon* (1988), *Dead Poets Society*

(1989), *Mermaids* (1990) — and in the case of the biggest youth film of the late '80s, *Dirty Dancing* (1987), seemed to sublimate teenage sexual energy into safer, if nonetheless still erotic, outlets. A few films began to explore the more serious consequences of teenage sexual activity (*Hairspray*, *"For Keeps"* [both 1988], and *Immediate Family* [1989] featured pregnant teens), although again such films tended to draw relatively smaller audiences.

In the early '90s the film industry largely continued to avoid or displace depictions of teenage sexuality (the brief lambada craze in early 1990 was an example of such deliberate displacement), and the technique of using period settings to do so became more prominent (in 1991, six period youth romance films were released compared to four set in contemporary times). However, as the mid-'90s approached, some low-budget independent films began taking more direct and often serious approaches to teen sexuality (e.g., *Gas, Food Lodging* [1992], *Just Another Girl on the I.R.T.* [1993], *Spanking the Monkey* [1994], *Art for Teachers of Children* [1995], *Carried Away* [1996]), while nonconfrontational period romances remained safer for studios (e.g., *Calendar Girl* [1993], *The Inkwell* [1994], *Little Women* [1994], *That Thing You Do!* [1996], *Titanic* [1997]). The depiction of adolescent love and sex on the whole had clearly become problematic in many '90s films, with a host of "dangerous deviants" appearing in films such as *The Crush* (1993), *Fun* (1994), *To Die For* (1995), *Ripe* (1996), *Wild Things* (1998), *The Opposite of Sex* (1998), *Cruel Intentions* (1999), and even a teen deviant trilogy, *Poison Ivy*, from 1992 to 1997. As more American films in the mid-'90s made specific statements about youth love and sex than in the early '90s, their messages became rather pessimistic and cynical. This cynicism may have been emblematic of revived anxieties about youth sexuality in society at large, may have been the effort of the industry to appeal to teens' curious but serious concerns and fears about sexuality, may have been indicative of teens' own confusions about the increasingly sexualized culture in which they live, or most likely a combination of all these factors. As the '90s closed, films featuring young love spoke to a revived notion of romantic destiny — *Drive Me Crazy*, *She's All That*, *10 Things I Hate About You* (all 1999) — and many films featuring youth sexuality continued to be rather dark — *American Beauty*, *Boys Don't Cry*, *Cruel Intentions*, *Election*, *Never Been Kissed* (all 1999). In both cases, films about love *or* sex retained definite cautionary messages.

This reproving atmosphere remained prominent in depictions of young love as the '00s began: the tragic topics of *Crime + Punishment in Suburbia*, *Here on Earth*, and *The Virgin Suicides* (all 2000), and the ongoing torments for teens in *Hedwig and the Angry Inch*, *Igby Goes Down*, and *Save the Last Dance* (all 2001) openly indicated that the new millennium did not bring with it any delusional amorous fantasies. In fact, the overall attitude about young love and sex at the time was strikingly negative as the movies tackled romance in the context of such difficult topics as teenage parenting (*Riding in Cars with Boys*, *Sugar and Spice* [both 2001], *How to Deal* [2003]), mental illness (*Crazy/Beautiful*, *Donnie Darko* [both 2001], *Swimfan* [2002]), and even death (*My First Mister*, *O* [both 2001], *A Walk to Remember* [2002]). By the middle of the decade, the industry lightened the tone somewhat with the promotion of new young stars in happier scenarios—*A Cinderella Story* (2004), *The Sisterhood of the Traveling Pants* (2005), and *Step Up* (2006)—yet the prevailing sense of despair about youth love remained unmistakable in *Dandelion*, *Stateside* (both 2004), *One Last Thing . . .* (2005), *The Babysitters*, and *Towelhead* (both 2007).

Beyond expressing any mere pessimism about teen sex for the commencing century, the romance subgenre took a decidedly darker turn in the second half of the '00s with films featuring an unprecedented lineup of perversions and problems. The sexual intrigue of children in *Me and You and Everyone We Know* (2005) may have been considered perturbing, but numerous other films more aggressively depicted issues of youth sexuality in terms of drugs (*Thirteen* [2003], *Brick* [2005], *Remember the Daze* [2007]), rape (*Speak* [2004], *Bad Reputation* [2005], *Hounddog* [2007]), incest (*The Quiet* [2005], *Georgia Rule* [2007], *Precious* [2009]), and pedophilic abduction (*Hard Candy* [2005], *Trade* [2007], *Gardens of the Night* [2008], *The Lovely Bones* [2009]). The most problematic depiction, a true story of abhorrent group molestation in *An American Crime* (2007), was deplorably fictionalized in *The Girl Next Door* that same year, then followed by multiple acts of necrophilia in *Deadgirl* and *Make-Out with Violence* (both 2008).

The prevailing output of so many dramatically dismal films in the subgenre has not stifled the industry's interest in promoting more encouraging, though pained, experiences of romance in the past decade. Films such as *All the Real Girls* (2003), *Whirlygirl* (2006), *Keith* (2008), and *Restless* (2011) told heartfelt stories of teens fumbling toward love and with sex, even if the subgenre declined by the '10s in visibility and productivity, especially since its peak of popularity in the '80s. Rather than focusing on adolescents' quests to lose their virginity or find loving relationships, many recent films have located these pursuits within other subgeneric categories such as deviant dancing (2006–2011), nerd transformations (2009–2012), and of course supernatural fantasies such as the *Twilight* series (2008–2012). In any case, cyclical idiosyncrasies will continue to affect the characters of youth romance films over time, but the persistence of the subgenre itself is reliably assured by the perpetual evolutionary process of life.

FROM ADOLESCENT ARDOR
TO JUGGLING GENDER

One generic pattern of these films that became clear after the
teen sex romps of the early '80s is the division between narratives in which
the pursuit of intercourse is the focus and narratives in which the attainment of love is more prominent. While some characters in youth films after
1980 seem to pursue both love and sex, the vast majority are preoccupied
with one goal or the other, and not both. In fact, in most stories about
young love, sex is either not an issue or is experienced as a natural result of
romantic achievement, whereas in most youth sex quests, love is either not
an issue or is experienced as a natural result of sexual achievement.

This division does not consistently provide reliable categorical distinctions within the subgenre, however. Just as delinquent youth are identifiable by their outward forms of deviance, romantic youth are identifiable
by their internal conflicts, which provide their characters with experien-
tial variables over time, such as how they respond to disappointment or
celebrate consummation. Thus, teens longing for love struggle to confirm
their amorous feelings and secure a union in the face of an oppressive obstacle that must be overcome for the couple to either live happily ever after
or realize that their union was not meant to be. Variables in the love story
arise from the different obstacles that prevent the teens from realizing their
romance, most commonly codes of family expectations, which I examine
here. Social barriers, once quite often a source of romantic rifts, began declining in impact after the '90s. Racial and ethnic differences that had en-
cumbered young love in *China Girl* (1987), *Gas, Food Lodging* (1992), *Bleeding
Hearts* (1995), and *Save the Last Dance* (2001) became all but extinct thereafter. Class status, which had impeded relationships in *Valley Girl* (1983),
Reckless (1984), *Can't Buy Me Love* (1987), and all the John Hughes teen films
of the mid-'80s, became notably scarce thereafter, with only scant examples
such as *Titanic* (1997), *What a Girl Wants* (2003), and *Material Girls* (2006).

Variables in stories dealing with teen sex arise from the different obstacles that young people encounter in their transition from adolescence to
adulthood, such as developing a sexual identity, becoming sexually active,
and accepting the consequences of those processes. Many narratives place
emphasis on the simple quest to lose virginity, although characters also find
themselves confused over their sexual attraction to an adult or a member of
the same sex, or they are left to deal with pregnancy or, in remarkably few
cases, a sexually transmitted disease. I examine each of these topics except
adult/teen pairings, which have become less common in recent years, and

Given the widespread appeal and historical scope of Titanic *(1997), many critics have disregarded the teenage romance at the heart of its plot. Here Jack (Leonardo DiCaprio) shares his sketches with Rose (Kate Winslet).*

have always worked on tensions about sexual responsibility yet tend to be adamantly diffident in placing "fault" on both characters for their illicit desires; such diffidence can be seen in *My Tutor* (1983), *Blame It on Rio* (1984), *Smooth Talk* (1985), *In the Mood* (1987), *The Crush* (1993), *To Die For* (1995), *Tadpole* (2000), *Down in the Valley* (2005), *Shanghai Kiss* (2007), and *Hello I Must Be Going* (2012).

Unlike the universal frustrations of sexual curiosity and ardent longing that all adolescents experience, American youth quite often endure a rite of passage in high school that has become so entrenched in teenage experience that it represents a category of romantic experience unto itself: the prom. A strikingly high percentage of youth films have depicted the "big dance" as either a crucial event or a driving force in their stories, and these assemblies of students—at or toward the end of their high school experience—are imbued with a gravity for most participants far greater than their actual graduations, if only because the stakes of passionate fulfillment and social culmination are so high. After early films featuring proms such as *Vivacious Lady* (1938) and *Margie* (1948), many more presented this supposedly stupendous experience of young romance in the '80s, building to the climactic year of 1999 when the industry offered no less than eight examples as diverse as *Trippin'* and *The Rage: Carrie 2*. Proms have continued to show consistent appeal ever since, with further productions like *Not Another Teen Movie* (2001), *The Girl Next Door* (2004), *Bart Got a Room* (2008), and *Prom* (2011).

The images of youth across romantic and sexual narratives of the past generation are actually quite diverse, yet as in the school subgenre, a certain hierarchy of competence is established and enforced according to character types. Nerds usually have the most difficulty attaining love or sex, and popular teens most often struggle with a surplus of suitors and sexual opportunities that come their way. Caring and copulatory competence may have little relation to social stature in reality, but in youth films the characters' level of acceptance is integrally linked to their attractiveness, which is often (mis)taken as an index of sexual and loving "skills." Some films challenge this notion, especially love stories, which often reveal that the most popular teens are self-centered or ignorant lovers and the less popular (because poorer, rebellious, unattractive, or different) teens are more affectionate, or at least more appreciative of affection.

An interesting discourse on youth politics is also presented in youth romance films. Less popular teens sometimes achieve self-respect and acceptance through their romantic and sexual pursuits, and the sheer "possession" of a girlfriend or boyfriend is a calculated social statement among youth, signifying success and competence. Girls, ever the object of boys' desires, realize the power they can gain through carefully regulating boys' access to them, yet they are accordingly displayed for the voyeuristic pleasure of boys far more than the opposite. While films in the 'oos were less sexist in their portrayals of women's exploitation by young men than those of the previous generation, the subgenre has nonetheless maintained a retrograde tendency to focus on girls' experiences with love and boys' experiences with sex. A positive turn has been the increasing number of refreshingly assertive perspectives on young female sexuality, giving girls more volume in expressions of pleasure and disapproval, with boys depicted as more willing to admit their confusions. And regardless of romantic politics, movies provide young viewers with persuasive images of and ideals for their first intimate relationships.

FAMILY MATTERS

The classical romantic drama of "boy meets girl, boy loses girl, boy gets girl back" operates (with genders sometimes switched) in the youth film, although the reasons why the relationship is threatened are always motivated by factors external to the characters. Rarely does a screen teen in love wrestle with personal notions of self-fulfillment or readiness to be in a relationship; rather, teens know their love is sure and true and simply have to overcome whatever pressures prevent them from expressing it and achieving reciprocity. These conflicts may be motivated by adults' doubts of and prohibitions against the success of young love, and they may demonstrate to youth the fallibility of emotional security, but like virtually all romances, virtually all youth love films allow their characters at least the temporary fulfillment of their amorous ambitions.

From simple love advice to pre-arranged marriages, youth have witnessed their parents shaping, or often controlling, their romantic endeavors. Youth are often conditioned to evaluate potential lovers according to scales of attraction dictated by their families, ranging from financial and social status to appearance and manners. While many youth are inevitably influenced by these familial codes, many also rebel against them, deliberately falling in love with and even marrying partners who clearly violate their family's hopes and expectations.

The family is also an index to larger social structures for youth. In loving outside the family code, youth can assert an individuality that would otherwise be compromised by the generally conformist practices of heterosexual dating and the pursuit of marriage. In youth love films, the characters still want to find love and (usually) marriage, but they want to find it in their own ways and on their own terms, and going outside an established "acceptable" range is a way to verify that independence. In finding a devoted partner who is unacceptable to one's family, a young person achieves a level of social rebellion and personal fulfillment.

Youth films since 1980 that have employed the family as the oppressive mechanism to teen love have been fairly consistent in demonstrating that parents do *not* know best when it comes to young romance. Parents' often good intentions—to see their child married to a "proper person"—become a barrier to their children's more sincere insight that love is not based on propriety but rather on feelings. Sometimes parents ultimately capitulate to their children's desires, often remembering their own youthful ambitions for true love; some of these films feature teens trying to restore just such a perspective in parents who have grown cynical after being divorced or widowed. Parents who do not ultimately honor their children's romantic wishes always face losing their children altogether. Despite the importance of the family, these films make it plain that young love outside the family is stronger, or at least more dedicated, than love for the family itself.

When *Endless Love* appeared in 1981, its blunt discussion of young sexuality was on the cusp of the new wave in teen sexual representation. As David Considine points out, after the controversial British film *Friends* in 1972 "encouraged the franker depiction of sexuality in American motion pictures" about youth, Hollywood products such as *Jeremy* (1973), *The Little Girl Who Lived Down the Lane* (1977), and *Manhattan* (1979) portrayed increasingly sexually sophisticated teens, while *Taxi Driver* (1976) and *Pretty Baby* (1977) codified images of teenage prostitutes.[5] By the time of *Rich Kids* in 1979, the feigned marital harmony between two twelve-year-olds — whose relationship is a rebellion against their self-absorbed divorced parents — demonstrated a rather involved level of sexuality for adolescents, particularly when their contact fills the void of emotional intimacy left by their parents, and appears to represent a more mature psychological and sexual experience than their parents can sustain.

Unlike the sex-centric films of the early '80s, *Endless Love* combined the classic *Romeo and Juliet* story of forbidden young love and the growing presence of teen sexual activity to yield an image of young romance so potent that few other youth films took the issue seriously for the next five years. Most early '80s youth love stories after *Endless Love* were comedies — exceptions included *Reckless* (1984), *Nickel Mountain* (1984), and *Tuff Turf* (1985) — and while this may not demonstrate a causal effect within the subgenre, the critical drubbing that *Endless Love* received, and the fact that *Reckless*, *Nickel Mountain*, and *Tuff Turf* all failed to profit, must have influenced the industry. Only after the notable success of John Hughes's teen comedies and dramas from 1984 to 1987 did the industry start to release a few more serious teen love stories such as *Lucas* (1986), *Square Dance* (1987), and *China Girl* (1987).

Endless Love is something of an updating and revision of *Splendor in the Grass* (1961) with the genders and circumstances switched. In *Splendor*, a teen girl ends up institutionalized, apparently due to parental restrictions against her having sex; her sexual repression seems to literally drive her crazy. In *Endless Love* a seventeen-year-old, David (Martin Hewitt), ends up institutionalized after having an apparently excessive sexual relationship with his fifteen-year-old girlfriend Jade (Brooke Shields), whose parents eventually prohibit her from seeing him. The family difference between these two is made pellucid from the start: David's wealthy parents are conservatively introverted, while Jade's parents are middle-class bohemians who are passionately active with their children.[6] Jade's previously permissive father realizes the extent of his daughter's intimacy with David and forbids her from having him over — he doesn't quash her having sex, he's just angry that she gets so little sleep. This quickly depresses David, and in a pathetic attempt at heroism he lights a small fire on Jade's porch, planning to rescue her and her family and thus demonstrate his worth, but the whole house burns down and the family barely escapes. David is then sent to a mental hospital, where his love for Jade borders on mania for the next two years. The family conflict is made more dramatic when David learns that both his and Jade's parents have split up after lengthy marriages—the teenage couple's love having led to the literal dissolution of their families—thereby showing, as Sheila Benson wrote, "the purity and strength of the kids' love versus the failure (corruption, abrogation of duty) of the parents'."[7] *Endless Love* further presents the parents as thoroughly culpable in the corruption of their children's romantic morals: David's parents simply don't understand him and can't help him, and Jade's parents' liberalism is revealed to be rather immoral itself when her mother tries to seduce David and her father finds his own younger girlfriend. Further, Jade's sexual confusion is only amplified by her father's sudden and serious possessiveness of her.

The film uses a strained contrivance to enact a final moral dilemma for the protagonists: after David is freed from the asylum and sets to finding Jade, her father is run over while chasing him. With her father's restrictions thus gone, Jade reluctantly goes to David and gives in to his aggressive plea for the renewal of their relationship, but her brother "rescues" her and turns David over to the police for his role in their father's death. The security of family remains tentatively in place, until the last scene of the film shows Jade going to visit David in jail after her mother tells her to find the love she "deserves." This ending questions whether David's devious love for Jade is indeed what she gets for not recognizing how problematic their relationship is. Jade ultimately makes the decision to return to David after his enactment of two tragedies that figuratively and literally destroyed her family, and given how little Jade has articulated any real passion for David throughout the film, *Endless Love* shows this young woman returning to her vexatious lover for the same ambiguous reasons that attracted her to him in the first place. The mythology of inexplicable love, beyond the codes of family and society, is thus preserved.

That mythology is conveyed with less serious consequences in many youth love films, especially comedies like *Secret Admirer* (1985), which is built on a wild goose chase over a love letter written by a teenage girl that affects both her circle of friends and her parents, and *Nice Girls Don't Explode* (1987), a comic fable about a girl whose "pyrotechnic sexuality" is revealed to be a ploy by her mother to stop her daughter's natural urges. The film treats the cliché image of the overbearing mother with obvious humor and levity, although this theme had been more often conveyed with devastating effects in youth dramas such as *Rebel Without a Cause* (1955), *The Restless Years* (1958), *Home from the Hill* (1960), *Five Finger Exercise* (1962), and *Carrie* (1976). In fact, while many youth love films after 1980 feature overbearing fathers, only *Nice Girls Don't Explode* and few others—the black comedies *Trust* (1991) and *Welcome to the Dollhouse* (1996) among them—feature the excessively protective mother that intimidated youth in previous generations, a sign that perhaps mothers are no longer perceived to have such power over their children. This may be most evidenced by the mother in *Gas, Food Lodging* (1992), who attempts to keep her lascivious older daughter in line by threatening to kick her out of the house, only to have the child leave on her own terms when she becomes pregnant.[8]

Dirty Dancing (1987) and *She's Out of Control* (1989) also feature prohibitive fathers, yet an apparently more caring and ultimately more devious father is featured in *Say Anything . . .* (1989). One of the best-received youth films of the decade, *Say Anything . . .* is the story of new graduate Lloyd Dobler (John Cusack), who rather impulsively decides to ask out Diane Court (Ione Skye), the pretty class valedictorian (a non-nerd intellectual), whom every other student has regarded as unattainable. Lloyd is quirky yet dependable, which is why he's the designated "keymaster" on his first date with the otherwise reclusive Diane at the school graduation party (ensuring his peers don't drive home drunk), and why Diane finds him so appealing. Roger Ebert, who was effusive in his praise of the film, explains its careful chemistry: "The romance between Diane and Lloyd is intelligent and filled with that special curiosity that happens when two young people find each other not only attractive but interesting—when they sense they might actually be able to learn something useful from the other person. Lloyd has no career plans, no educational plans, no plans except to become a championship kickboxer, and then, after he meets Diane, to support her because she is worthy of his dedication."[9]

However, her divorced and protective father, who appears to have been Diane's sole "friend" until Lloyd, soon grows concerned about her deepening affection for him, more so after Diane wins an illustrious fellowship to study in England. Lloyd doesn't pose any direct hindrance to Diane's ambitions—he just does not want to "sell anything, buy anything, or process anything as a career"—and still her father, who definitely doesn't understand their level of intimacy, tells her to end their relationship before she leaves on her trip, and she complies, sinking Lloyd into a somber depression. The image of Lloyd outside Diane's window, holding his boom box over his head after their breakup and playing the song they heard when they lost their virginity to each other, has become an icon of teen romantic longing.

The film is one of the few youth love stories to feature the protagonists successfully negotiating their own differences: the fact that Diane is clearly smarter and from more wealth than Lloyd, and Lloyd is more gregarious and humble, are not problems to them, just to Diane's dad. Diane's dad, however, is revealed to be embezzling funds from the nursing home that he operates, supposedly to support her future, and after she learns of her father's crime she turns on him, whereupon Lloyd thankfully takes her back. Jonathan Bernstein explains the moral that many youth may have derived from this, since the father's "stated crime was bilking the aged, but his implicit and far more heinous felonies were smothering his daughter with love and interfering in her romance with a cool dude."[10] The pretense of this plot twist notwithstanding, the film's climax becomes a compelling emotional showdown between Lloyd and Diane's father, who ends up in jail and insists that Diane not go to England with her loyal boyfriend. Diane's devotion to her father is nonetheless completely shaken, and she invites Lloyd to go on the trip with her.

The final scene of *Say Anything . . .* is one of the rare moments in youth love films where the teen characters are happily united and facing a promising future together: on the plane waiting to leave for England, Lloyd holds the nervous Diane's hand and reassures her that they will be safe. Yet this ending also leaves open an ambiguity and tension about their destiny (critics have pointed to its similarity to *The Graduate* [1967]). The film is then not merely a parable about the morality of devotion—Lloyd's is righteous while Diane's father's is selfish—but about the risks and rewards of romantic patience and loyalty. Despite Lloyd's pain at first being dumped by Diane, and his friends' advice that he should find another girlfriend, Lloyd recognizes in Diane a special quality founded not on her looks or popularity but on an emotional fulfillment rarely afforded to teens in films. The sophistication and maturity of their relationship are rare as well, and justify the film's hopeful ending.

Youth love stories, as previously mentioned, took a decidedly different turn over the early '90s: fewer young romances reached the screen, and many of those that did began to reveal an increasing wariness about the topic (as in *The Man in the Moon* [1991], *Gas, Food Lodging* [1992], *Guncrazy* [1993]), or else they softened the narrative concentration on the couple's success by introducing other dominant dramas (both lambada movies in 1990 did this, as did *Alan & Naomi* [1992], *What's Eating Gilbert Grape* [1993], and *Foreign Student* [1994]). However, the role of the family in youth love films of the '90s was no less prohibitive than in the '80s. While some '90s romances featured more supportive families, such as the period fantasy *Edward Scissorhands* (1990), the general attitude of parents toward their children's lovelorn ways was one of suspicion and occasionally scorn. Even in the absurd *Coneheads* (1993), two parents from another planet grapple with strangely familiar worries about their teenage daughter dating. *Clueless* in 1995 tried to make such attitudes ever more ironically humorous (not unlike *She's Out of Control*), but more films at the time depicted the family in stern, sometimes violent modes, with their children facing serious fallouts, as in *Mad Love* (1995), *Fear* (1996), *Romeo + Juliet* (1996), and *Titanic* (1997).

Two comedies that balanced both irony and parental contempt were Hal Hartley's independent productions *The Unbelievable Truth* (1990) and *Trust* (1991). In the first film, Adrienne Shelly plays Audrey, an atypical high school senior who dumps her steady boyfriend and develops an interest in a thirtyish ex-convict she believes is a kindred spirit, leading to much family strife and a series of tense but often humorous confrontations. The fact that Audrey is *not* attracted to him for wealth and rescue from her low-income background is, as in many other youth films that present class as a barrier to romance, only realized after she becomes involved with a wealthier man and attempts to assimilate into a higher-class lifestyle. *The Unbelievable Truth*, like Hartley's next film, demonstrates that not only are ambitions for wealth corruptive, but that his young characters' relationships are necessarily founded on non-financial, mutually honest—albeit eccentric—goals for leaving the confines of corruptive families.

Hartley's thesis on relationships continues in the richly textured *Trust*, so much so that he again cast Adrienne Shelly as a suburban high school senior looking to get away from her strange family. Shelley plays Maria, whose brash manner is so assaultive to her father that he keels over from a heart attack after she tells him she's pregnant with her boyfriend's baby, prompting her mother, Jean (Merritt Nelson), to tell Maria that she'll need to devote her life to providing for her. Maria descends into a cowering depression that carries her far away from her previously consumerist and carefree style: she feels the contempt of her football-focused boyfriend who blames her for getting pregnant, the guilt of "killing" her father, and the condemnation of her vengeful mother. Into her life walks Matthew (Martin Donovan), an even more depressive twentysomething whose obsessive-compulsive working-class father hounds him constantly. Matthew has grown so disgusted with the world of capitalist technocracy that he quits his computer repair job, and against his claims to love no one, he becomes instantly concerned with Maria's well-being after finding her drunk and despondent. These are more-kindred spirits than the couple in *Unbelievable Truth*: what then becomes Maria's sudden change to dutiful daughter in pragmatic penance for her wanton past intertwines with Matthew's resolution to live his cynical life without upsetting his abusive father, and together they seem to reluctantly agree that life is founded on dour survival. J. Hoberman responded to the characters' plight: "The emphasis on shame pushes *Trust* well beyond the discomfort zone of early John Hughes, but where *Trust* seems most adolescently heartfelt is in its vision of a nightmarish older generation. *Trust* is a kind of allegory about growing up in which children and the absence of children each produce its own form of misery."[11]

Maria and Matthew's destiny is pulled in the two directions that offer them either the preservation of their stoic suffering for the sake of familial calm or the opportunity to fulfill more ambiguous yet beneficial goals. Matthew proposes to move in with and get married to Maria to help her to raise the child, only soon their laborious and tedious days—they both take menial jobs and begin to argue—quickly aggravate the young couple's originally placid personalities. The possessive Jean, who has felt competitive with Matthew from the start, tries to exploit the couple's troubles and break them up, whereupon Maria, after much melancholy over the decision, has an abortion and tells Matthew that she doesn't want to marry him. What costs this couple their capacity to stay together then is not their lack of affection for each other but their attempt to conform to the familial standard that has been handed down by their parents. At one point Matthew expresses the code by which essentially all familial romantic dramas operate: "A family is like a gun—you point it in the wrong direction and it could kill someone." Maria's decision to have the abortion and not start a family with Matthew (a topic further discussed in a later section) is her liberation from the stark low-income ennui she sees ahead, and which she's already seen her divorced older sister endure. However Matthew, on the wrong end of these family triangles and feeling completely dejected after learning of Maria's decision, finally decides to kill himself with the hand grenade he has morbidly carried throughout the film.

Trust, which is full of symbolic touches such as Maria wearing Matthew's dead mother's dress in recognition of his regressive desire to find a new family, ends with a wistful and obliquely optimistic denouement after Maria finds Matthew sitting with his unexploded grenade, which doesn't go off until she throws it away. While lying with Matthew after the explosion and with the police coming to take him away, Maria expresses the arbitrary nature of their relationship by telling Matthew that she cares for him just because he "happened to be there." Matthew then never takes his eyes off of Maria as he's carried off to jail, and the film ends with a shot of Maria gazing back at him, framed by two green traffic lights. Philip Strick observed the film's excursion as such: "Logically, Maria kills her father at the start of the film and her unborn child at the end, leaving her free to put her glasses on in conscious assumption of scholarship while traffic lights suspended behind her indicate a clear road ahead."[12] For all of their intellectual wrestling with purpose and destiny—Maria and Matthew have many talks about the meaning of life and love, or the lack thereof—the young couple find themselves at a literal intersection in their lives that promises greater wisdom, if less certainty, than the bounded lifestyles of marriage and children that they leave behind. Whatever decisions they make together or individually will be better than what their families had wrought in the small town of their youths.

Such sobering messages are present in other '90s youth love stories that followed, although two—*Cool as Ice* (1991) and *My Father the Hero* (1994)—used familial tensions about romance as mere plot devices for respectively younger and older star vehicles, in the former film for poseur rapper Vanilla Ice, and in the latter for French star Gérard Depardieu. Serious approaches to familial influence on young love were more common, even though *Clueless* (1995) did comically employ the device of the protective father, who is nonetheless so absorbed in his work that he doesn't notice or care about the growing attraction between his daughter and stepson. *Clueless* thereby offers an ironic critique of familial love, since Cher (Alicia Silverstone) finds her long-sought boyfriend right at home, a resolution that I have argued elsewhere infers "that the world of sexuality has become so difficult for teens to navigate that Cher's choice of her stepbrother for a boyfriend is completely rational despite its dilemmas."[13]

A most explicit and tense depiction of family relations affecting teen desires can be found in *Fear* (1996), which is something of an adolescent *Fatal Attraction*. Where other films have shown even irrational young love to be a sanctuary from despair, *Fear* offers up an antagonist who is himself crazy, and who uses his pathological devotion to terrorize the object of his affection. Nicole (Reese Witherspoon) is that object, a virginal high school student just beginning to explore the more deviant sides of youth culture—drinking, drugs, raves—much to the consternation of her father, Steve (William Petersen), who lives with a relatively compassionate second wife. Nicole is only tamely rebellious, understandably growing angry about her father's contradictory attempts to promote family activities and remain devoted to his work. When Nicole meets David (Mark Wahlberg) at a rave,

In Fear *(1996), concerned father Steve (William Petersen) gently tells bad boy David (Mark Wahlberg) to stay away from his daughter: "If you don't disappear from my family's life, I'm gonna rip your balls off and shove 'em so far up your ass they'll come out your fuckin' mouth!"*

he is the essence of tough-guy sweetness, rescuing her from a riot and respecting her resistance to anything more than kissing. David turns on still more charm when he meets Nicole's dad and stepmother, with Steve immediately sensing something sinister; "David is without affect," as Mick LaSalle points out, "an emotionally naked psychopath who anticipates no long-term problems for his and Nicole's relationship were he to shoot her father in the head, for example."[14] That suspicion inevitably leads Nicole to further covet David, and thus the film sets up its central conflict between paternal overprotection and quixotic danger.

Immediately after Nicole consummates her relationship with David—in a scene that shows her as especially passive and unsure—he detonates his furtive lunacy, violently beating Nicole's friend Gary (Todd Caldecott) when he sees him hugging her, and smacking Nicole in the process. At first Nicole abandons David, ignoring his attempts at apology, but once her father suspects that David hit her and blames her for being irresponsible (a scolding that is made paradoxical with his discovery of a condom wrapper), she soon hears David's apology and takes him back. The scales of resistance are proportional: the more her father threatens her, the more Nicole seeks to find comfort in David. However, as if to verify paternal authority and wisdom over all, the film shows Nicole being further duped by David as her father learns of David's criminal past and confronts him directly, telling him to stay away from her. Nicole does not realize David's truly devious nature until she sees him violently grabbing her friend Margo (Alyssa Milano) at a party, ostensibly en route to raping her. David is then further incensed by Nicole's resistance to him, killing Gary and beating Margo in response. Steve finally boils over with rage and smashes up the house where David lives with four churlish cronies, prompting the young gang to launch an all-out assault on Nicole and her family.

The conclusion of *Fear* makes the film's message about extrafamilial dangers dramatically graphic: Nicole and her family are temporarily safe from David's friends' rampage because architect Steve built the house to resist such as assault, only the safety of home is broken after Steve goes outside to confront David himself and winds up as a hostage to the hoodlums. While most of David's friends are dispatched by the fighting family, David himself kills his last surviving friend to be alone with Nicole, and then as he prepares to kill her father, she stabs him in the back, giving Steve the chance to throw David out a window. The family, along with the traumatized Margo, is reunited after the harrowing ordeal, with the monstrous threat to family unity dead outside the house. *Fear* unfortunately carries out this preservative message through excessive violence against its young female cast, particularly Margo, and posits that teenage girls will endure great abuse by young men in the service of attaining romantic ideals. *Fear* is ultimately reactionary in regard to its handling of Nicole's otherwise typical discovery of first love, for in the face of its pertinent warnings about deceptively attractive young men, it exploits female fears of masculine aggression, obsession, and devotion. The film's one concession to less menacing masculinity, Gary, is killed, and given that "father knows best," Nicole is ultimately empowered only by his paternal authority, and remains a victim of the very love and affection she was seeking from men in the first place.[15]

In 1996 the schlock studio Troma released its rarely seen *Romeo and Juliet* story *Tromeo and Juliet*, a very '90s updating of the classic original tale of teen love rent asunder by family difference and oppression, this time incorporating copious doses of sex and violence. Another updating that was less prurient but almost as excessive was *Romeo + Juliet* later that year, a postmodern adaptation of the sixteenth-century play that is a quickly paced flashy commentary on contemporary media, capitalism, and law, still keeping the original drama's concerns with family relations that doom the star-crossed lovers.[16] Leonardo DiCaprio plays Romeo and Claire Danes is Juliet, both actors delivering their Shakespearean lines against the backdrop of Verona Beach, an apparent Floridian setting wherein cultural clashes among whites, blacks, and Latinos parallel the class rivalry between the protagonists' families, the Montagues and Capulets. The young men of the rival families now battle with guns instead of swords, and an early fight scene staged at a gas station conjures up current urban crises of gang warfare.

But the story centers on the title characters, who meet at a lavish masquerade party where Juliet's parents are trying to interest her in the handsome Paris (Paul Rudd), a wealthy young businessman. Instead, the angelic Juliet becomes immediately entranced by Romeo, dressed as a literal knight in shining armor. The teens are filled with the rush of attraction, yet realize that their opposing families—here made foes by corporate competition—will not allow their union. They quickly agree to a secret wedding, and after further fighting erupts between the Montague and Capulet youth, Romeo kills Juliet's cousin Tybalt, forcing him to leave town. He nonetheless finds his way back to Juliet and they consummate their relationship, only to learn that Juliet's father has planned a hasty wedding for her and Paris. The suicidal Juliet plans to fake her death so that afterward she can be reunited with Romeo. The news of this ruse fails to reach Romeo, and after a rousing race in which he fights his way to Juliet's unconscious body, believing she is dead, he takes poison to kill himself, prompting the arising Juliet to shoot herself in the head. The moral of the story is then pronounced by the presiding police officer, who chastises the families for allowing their mutual contempt to destroy their innocent children.

What was already an enthralling play about the consequences of social hatred is here brought to the screen with an energetic illustration of loosed romantic longing overcoming familial and cultural differences, only to fail in its attempt to escape those conflicts. The contemporary updating suggests that the Romeo and Juliet of the 1500s are little different from teenagers today kept apart by intolerance and prejudice, which was partially addressed in the gendered critique of another Shakespeare adaptation in 1999, *10 Things I Hate About You*. The family remains the foremost site of youthful romantic obstacles, and the appearance of *Romeo + Juliet* in the mid-'90s signals the film industry's understanding of that dilemma—and its continuing appeal—to young audiences. The somber message of the movie is nonetheless the most pessimistic of any youth romance film, and is perhaps only so due to its historic source; vilifying family in contemporary terms is easily permissible when the inspiration is four centuries old. Yet other period films such as *Titanic*, *The Ice Storm* (both 1997), *The Adventures of Sebastian Cole*, *Slums of Beverly Hills* (both 1998), *Outside Providence* (1999), and *The Virgin Suicides* (2000), and contemporary-set films such as *American Beauty, Anywhere But Here* (both 1999), *Crime + Punishment in Suburbia,* and *Girlfight* (both 2000) further portrayed the family as a destructive force in teens' romantic–sexual development.

The desperate tone of other youth love stories in the later '90s closed the decade in stark contrast to the many '80s comedies, including *Welcome to the Dollhouse, Boys* (both 1996), *Trojan War* (1997), *Eden* (1998), *Niagara, Niagara* (1998), *Cruel Intentions,* and *She's All That* (both 1999). The lighter moods of many youth romances in the 'oos nonetheless betrayed heavy topics such as death and politics, which pervade most of the decade's films about family and love. In some cases, the familial gravity was not so great as to sour the film's promotion of its protagonists' love, as in *Tuck Everlasting* (2002), *What a Girl Wants* (2003), and the two odd 2004 films about teenage daughters of presidents, *Chasing Liberty* and *First Daughter.* At other times, spirited fare like *A Walk to Remember* (2002) could not avert its ultimately fateful message, using its dominant "opposites attract" formula in featuring not only parental obstacles to young love but, most unusually, religious beliefs. Landon (Shane West) is a popular senior responsible for a dangerous prank who is assigned the unlikely punishment of helping with his school's play.[17] Just as everyone knows, Jamie (Mandy Moore) is the plain but confident daughter of a local minister, so Shane is uninterested in working with her on the play, and joins his peers in dismissing her as a zealous Christian kid with little to offer. The film does not amplify Jamie's beliefs to the point of doctrinaire details, leaving assumptions to be made that she is an unfashionable virgin and does not party like many teens in town, and in fact her specific religious identity is all but erased under such contemptuous perceptions.

Of course, the *raison d'être* for *A Walk to Remember* is watching Landon come to realize that the depth of Jamie's religious faith somehow gives her faith in him as well, and the fact that she is actually a knockout once she dresses up and sings for the play helps him appreciate her even more. Landon subsequently softens his cool attitude and slowly defends his growing affections for Jamie to his suspicious friends. Jamie's father, however, knows kids like Landon are trouble, and quite directly imposes his presence to keep the blooming couple from getting any closer than collaborators, yet rather than rebel against this patriarchal impediment, Jamie's evident reason for liking Landon is the latent possibility of making him a better man. The dad has an altogether different reason to be worried, however, which is revealed to Landon only after he is quite smitten: Jamie is terminally ill and dying soon.[18] After this revelation, the narrative rushes through the remaining romance in which Jamie teaches Landon the beauty of life and, to fulfill her dying wish, the couple suddenly gets married. Rather than allowing them another few scenes of precious moments and the implicitly suspended consummation of their relationship, the epilogue arrives immediately thereafter to tell us that Jamie died after the wedding and, four years later, Landon visits her father with news that he intends to go on to medical school, a "miracle" that she had always hoped to witness. What had been a story filled with such emotional and moral stakes for the characters is not only cut short by Jamie's death, but essentially denied the opportunity to explore so many profound issues for youth about love, sex, and family conflict, and more so, fundamental beliefs in humanity and beyond. Both Landon and Jamie have dramatic paternal conflicts (his estranged father agrees to pay for Jamie's care before she dies), and issues of parental authority and familial structure are also germane to how the children learn to love, yet are left undeveloped with so many other poignant aspects of the story.

Family intervention in young love became a less customary topic in the later '00s, as traditional teen romance was marginalized as well. Queer youth relationships and the foreboding atmosphere in so many depictions of heterosexual love dominated the handful of struggling romantic comedies that appeared at the time, such as *The Good Student* (2006), *Sydney White* (2007), *Nick and Nora's Infinite Playlist* (2008), and *I Love You, Beth Cooper* (2009). The few family conflicts concerning couples could not garner much attention with prominent actors, as in *Down in the Valley* (2005), *Snow Angels* (2007), and *The Ballad of Jack and Rose* (2005), which portrayed a distraught father whose excessively doting daughter deviates from their borderline incestuous union when she loses her virginity to a local chump. Even the well-regarded *Flipped* (2010), with its shared observations between a teenage girl and boy pondering their attractive differences under their parents' watchful eyes, was underappreciated by audiences.

One exception to the recent trend has been *Moonrise Kingdom* (2012), bolstered by the closed form of auteur Wes Anderson's visual style: its troubled family scenario contains stolid characters composed within balanced sets in juxtaposition to their inner upheavals. This is especially so for twelve-year-old Sam (Jared Gilman) and Suzy (Kara Hayward), who begin their relationship through a series of letters in 1965. Sam is a troublesome orphan whose overburdened foster parents send him away to a scout camp on a nondescript New England island, where subtly fuming Suzy lives with her strange parents and little brothers. As early adolescent children can do so well, the two gain an affection that is based less on any sexual or

romantic impulses and primarily on grief with their failed authority figures, which in Sam's case includes not only his foster parents but his fumbling scoutmaster. Jeffrey Anderson argues, "It's the grownups who have
imposed their sadness, disappointments and insecurities on the children.
Anderson illustrates the gap between child and adult with costume choices,
continually drawing attention to the children's eyes with eyeglasses, eye-
liner and binoculars, while the grownups wear funny pants."[19] After many
epistolary exchanges, Sam and Suzy plot an escape together, not knowing
that a massive storm is about to hit the island within a few days.

Anderson's style and laconic wit keep the story from rising to any emotional pitch that would allow the young renegades to vent much deep
angst, but they clearly long to share intimacies with each other—Suzy's
love for fantasy novels, Sam's ambitions for exploration—and they enact an
alternative familial structure by setting up a tent, building a fire, hanging
laundry, and lounging about barely clothed. They do dance and cuddle,
verging on more carnal contact but not pursuing it. "Not yet able to feel
or express passion," Todd McCarthy explained, "they rotely go through
the motions of what they know they're supposed to do—briefly French
kissing and touching certain key spots—and acknowledge that they love
each other."[20] Theirs is a temporarily utopian and ingenuous existence, sullied only by the searching scouts from Sam's camp, whom they drive back
with Suzy's mild violence, which continues to shame her. Alas, not long
after this incident, Suzy's parents arrive with Sam's scoutmaster to finally
destroy their homestead, and the two are immediately disjoined. Suzy's
parents do little to understand why their daughter chose to run away in
such dramatic fashion, although Sam does gain the sympathy of a local
policeman, and the difference in their fates is manifest: Suzy may have a familial structure yet it remains stifling and cold, whereas Sam has no family
and yet the freedom to escape. This parallel is drawn out one last time when
Sam's scouts stage a rescue of him and Suzy, reuniting the couple and going
so far as providing a fake wedding ceremony, and when her parents and
his scout leader attempt to return them again, the imposing storm diverts
them to a church where, miraculously, the two are saved from suicide by
the policeman, who has agreed to adopt Sam as his own.

Such a dramatic climax and optimistic conclusion is unexpected in this
case, and quite rare in most others, where the family intervention normally
leads to some level of permanent harm for one or both of the children involved. The pre-sexual nature of Sam and Suzy dismisses concerns about
them forming a *real* family on their own, which is so often the threat in
other scenarios, and their demonstrated behavioral problems actually legit-

imize their desire to be with each other, a desire that is too easily slighted for older youth whose romance may be perceived as too necessarily sexual. Lacking family, in Sam's case, and being so detached from family, in Suzy's case, are mutual crises that the couple find the means to alleviate, yet the strictures of family organization are reinstated on them in the end. Young love is once again invalidated by the expectations of adult authority, and even outside the context of typical teenagers, *Moonrise Kingdom* demonstrates how persistent the family remains as a force that prohibits, or at least inhibits, adolescents' relationships. While the number of such films has declined in recent years, similar stories will flourish as long as elders struggle to accept their children's love and overcome the apprehension it poses, just as they endeavored to do in *Romeo and Juliet* more than four hundred years ago.

PROMS

Most American high schools hold a vaunted ritual that few of their students manage to escape, most attend with strained amusement, and some even manage to enjoy for its intended purpose: the senior prom. Traditions differ between states and school districts as to which grades are actually invited to the event and when it is held. Many allow both juniors and seniors to attend, some invite all students in the school, and some limit it to just seniors; most schools hold the event in the final month of the school year, some in the final days before graduation, whereas others hold the event up to a few months before the end of the last term. In all cases, the focal point is a large dance attended in formal attire, usually by couples (who are not necessarily dating), at a venue big enough to accommodate the crowd (such as the school gym or a local hall), and often in conjunction with an evening meal. Activities after the prom are often more significant than the sponsored event itself, as students wander off to parties and tend to partake in further amorous pursuits.

Because these events became so entrenched in the secondary school experience during the twentieth century, and because they occur toward the end of required schooling for youth, extensive cultural expectations have grown around them, not the least of which involve the shared romantic possibilities that proms offer. Research on these rituals, however, has been surprisingly meager given their place in adolescent history. Published guides on staging proms date to 1936, but not until the turn of the century did serious book-length analyses of proms emerge, beginning with *Prom*

Night: Youth, Schools, and Popular Culture by Amy Best (2000), which locates the earliest movie about proms in 1976, *Carrie*.[21] At least ten other films prior to that landmark had also featured high school senior dances, one of the earliest being *Harold Teen* (1934), although likely the first film to use the term "prom"—*Vivacious Lady* (1938)—applied it to a college senior dance. *Margie* (1946) was the first film to feature a high school prom in the capacity it came to represent by the time of *Carrie* some thirty years later, as the ultimate event of the story for the title character, in which social pressure is high and romantic resolution is essentially assured.

Some sweet drama almost always ensues when proms have been held in teen films, if only since students express deeply held desires for each other, or feel liberated to act on such desires. As Richard Calo has detailed in his collections of prom experiences, an articulated set of delicate decisions are enacted for proms, such as the selection of a potential date (and the myriad emotions intertwined with that choice), means of invitation, style of clothing purchased or rented, mode of transportation, negotiation with parents for time of return, and range of intimacy with date during and after the dance.[22] These decisions are denied triviality by the imposed pageantry of the prom, and thus become suitable fodder for narrative climaxes across all youth film subgenres. After *Carrie* took its prom to horrific extremes with blood-soaked carnage and the most humiliating episode ever for a girl who was actually crowned queen of the ball, the Canadian *Prom Night* (1980) followed with another story capitalizing on the metaphorical terror so many teens feel when faced with the prospect of attending their prom. *Zapped!* (1982) featured its prom as part of some pseudoscientific shenanigans two boys concoct to impress girls, *Footloose* (1984) staged its prom as a teen rebellion against repression, and *Back to the Future* (1985) infamously reconsidered the proto-rock prom as set in 1955. All of these films emphasize the romantic or sexual tensions at least one set of characters feels as they proceed to the big dance, and these tensions would be most fully realized in two other hits of the time that effectively brought the prom depiction to an iconographic status within youth cinema.

The first film was *Valley Girl* (1983), built around the current San Fernando Valley (California) image of excess consumption and vapidity, even though the story offers a surprisingly thorough and often sensitive critique of the Val lifestyle and its alleged antithesis, the punk lifestyle of Hollywood.[23] Deborah Foreman plays the main Val, Julie, a high school junior who breaks up with her awfully visible but lecherous boyfriend Tommy (Michael Bowen) and soon meets the totally tubular but grubby Randy (Nicolas Cage), a punk who crashes an expensive sushi party thrown by one of her friends. Randy is immediately attracted to Julie (their names hint at the story's debt to *Romeo and Juliet*) and she senses in him the adventurousness and fun that were missing in Tommy, but her friends warn her of the risks to her reputation if she were to date a Hollywood boy. Julie nonetheless pursues her interest in the tripendicular Randy, and their relationship proceeds accordingly, with her hanging out at his downtown dives and him learning (less so) the suburban culture of Julie's world; as he simply puts their common lifestyles, "It's the way we do things that makes the difference." Julie's friends inevitably threaten to disown her though, and systematically convince her to go to the upcoming prom with Tommy, if only to preserve their clique's wealthy image.

After a temporary funk of rejection, Randy retaliates by sending Julie various messages of his lingering love for her, and then launches his greatest declaration by crashing the prom. Once again the barriers that Julie's middle class has set up to keep out people such as Randy—exclusive parties, high-priced neighborhoods, and the sacrosanct prom—are breached by the rebel. Randy gains access to the dance easily enough, egged on by his best friend who rightly anticipates that their mere presence among the trendy Val kids will generate a response, leading to a fast fight when Randy slugs Tommy and runs away with Julie. In further insolence toward prom decorum—and victory over Tommy's plan to deflower Julie as part of the evening—the dissident duo jump into Tommy's rented limo and ride off to his reserved hotel room. As they ride away, Julie tears off a bracelet that Tommy had given her, thereby jettisoning her symbolic connection to wealth so that she can renew her love for Randy. This ending remains somewhat problematic in that Julie only returns to Randy after he resorts to violence, his barbaric impulses erupting to preserve his perceived right to her prized virginity. Further, Randy's raid on the prom usurps the wealth—car, hotel, girl—he has stolen from Tommy. The prom in this case is a battleground of class conflict, yet the proletariat succeeds through overtaking bourgeois tradition with no intention of actual revision. Even though the traditional trappings of proms hold out many opportunities for desecration by mutinous teens, so often in youth cinema the event becomes a party of conformity.

Following the class issues that so often permeate prom dramas, David Ansen used a ubiquitous comparison in drolly describing *Pretty in Pink* (1986) as "a Marxist *Romeo and Juliet* in which the warring clans are the haves and have-nots of a Midwestern high school," with its class divisions conspicuously marked by the areas where the poorer students eat their lunch away from the "richie" students, and in the intraclass dating rituals of the

Teen film auteur of the '80s John Hughes (seated) poses with his young cast from Pretty in Pink *(1986): Dweezil Zappa, Molly Ringwald, Andrew McCarthy, and Jon Cryer. (Autographed image of John Hughes, author's collection.)*

school.[24] Molly Ringwald plays Andie, an attractive and smart working-class senior, whose doting friend Duckie (Jon Cryer) joins her in a certain contempt for the rich students, even if she does not share his more vehement disdain after she nurtures a crush on the wealthy and shy Blane (Andrew McCarthy). Jealous and hurt, Duckie immediately points out to Andie how different they are from Blane and his snobby friends: Andie lives in a dilapidated house with her unemployed but caring father and works part-time at a record store, while Blane lives on an estate with horses and often-absent parents. Indeed, Andie's attraction to Blane is rather weakly developed, considering how long she has lived under the constraints of class confines, as is Blane's attraction to Andie, although both characters seem determined to prove that they can successfully cross class lines for some subjectively special kind of love, and the climactic scene of that demonstration is inevitably the prom.

Yet after Andie accepts Blane's invitation to the prom, they are assailed with instant reminders of their class transgression, most dramatically by Blane's loutish friends and by Duckie's insulting of him, leading to a separation between Andie and Duckie, and to Blane moving away from her under the direct pressure of his shifty peers. Such disrespect could be enough for a character as proud and resilient as Andie to forget Blane, which she starts to do as she prepares to go to the prom alone, making her own dress and bucking up with the enthusiasm of her older coworker at the store. Nonetheless, the controverted coda of the film generates much debate to this day. Duckie shows up at the prom after Andie arrives on her own, implicitly offering to be her date, with the plan of the two defying the richies by brazenly enjoying themselves. Many critics claimed that the original ending was changed because test audiences criticized Andie's lack of romantic fulfillment, and some claimed that John Hughes's scripted ending was changed by producers who desired a more traditional *Cinderella*-style closure.[25] Whatever the reason, the fantasy wins out: Duckie and Andy walk into the dance together, only Blane shows up and makes a sincere apology to her, even claiming he loves her. After Blane walks away, Duckie pushes Andie to go after him, and the cross-class couple reunites in the parking lot while Duckie, not to be left alone, is called over by another attractive girl.

Despite how badly Blane has treated Andie due to her class status, she still returns to him after he admits that his rich friends were wrong about her and, as Duckie suggests, the moment is too precious to abandon. Proms are designed for fantasies such as this, which is unmistakable given their themes like "One More Night," "Save the Best for Last," and "A Moment Like This," all borrowed from songs contemporary to their era. Here the previous wallflower blooms from the affection of a prize suitor, dismissing the abuse she has suffered because she still thinks their love transcends class lines. David Denby questioned if the film ambiguously pointed to larger social issues about class: "Is [it] telling us that the rich always hate and fear the poor—or that in the Reagan period there's a new mean-spiritedness among the moneyed suburban kids?"[26] Like *Valley Girl*, the film abandons its critique of proms as a cultural celebration of wealth, adding a treacherous gender myth: that young women want men with money and will reject men more loyal and better suited to them to achieve that financial-romantic goal.

Molly Ringwald would attend another prom as a high school heroine in *"For Keeps"* (1989), yet she is nine months pregnant and finishing her senior year in night school, so the occasion is inherently bittersweet; her maternity dress is not the kind of prom gown girls envision. Irrespective of their hype and promise, proms would continue to present problems to teen characters throughout the next decade, as in *The Night Before* (1988), where Keanu Reeves wakes up after bizarre events at his senior prom led to a series of dangerous deeds. The title reference in *She's Out of Control* (1989) is warned by her father that she's too young to attend a prom, and is almost raped by her date in dreadful confirmation of Daddy's wisdom. *The Next Karate Kid* (1994), previously discussed, depicts its prom as teenage terrorism just short of the *Prom Night* movies. And *Pep Squad* (1998) actually exceeds that terrorism with its comically caustic story of a rejected prom queen bent on homicidal retribution.

A strange combination of *fin de siècle* sanguinity and Hollywood's longing for a new wave of prominent young actors must explain the *annus mirabilis* of 1999, when eight prom movies appeared, half gaining little attention (*Drive Me Crazy, Jawbreaker, The Rage: Carrie 2, Trippin'*) and the other half becoming certified sensations. *American Pie* and *10 Things I Hate About You* were ensemble showcases leading to memorable proms, the former resulting in sexual experiences for most of the characters, and the latter dramatizing a carnival of errors. Proms remained evident sites of drama for confrontations over acceptance in *Never Been Kissed*, where an infiltrating reporter exposes the school's harmful hierarchy, and *She's All That*, which regressed to a conformity scenario for its title reference. The brainy Laney (Rachael Leigh Cook) is cast aside by the popular and wealthier school kids for her artistic aspirations and social insecurity, until elite jock Zack (Freddie Prinze Jr.) takes on a bet that he can change even this "loser" into a desirable girl. He does this not out of any affection but to save face after his girlfriend dumps him, for his task becomes not only romancing the introvert but also turning her into a prom queen. Thus is set in motion an explicit transformation narrative, with Zack's sister taking off Laney's glasses and giving her a tight dress to miraculously make her attractive.

At first Laney shows an informed suspicion of Zack's intentions, which makes her seem confidently independent. Nonetheless, his unusual intelligence does not appear to impede his unethical manipulation of her, as he boosts his inflated ego by being the motivation for her change *and* the organizer of it as well. After Laney learns of Zack's scam she dismisses him and accepts the prom invitation of a worse lothario, not knowing he placed the bet against Zack. The prom itself is a lavish affair where the movie, "which has never really had its feet on the ground, takes leave of reality altogether and lets its senior class members break into an elaborate choreographed line dance," as Stephen Holden noticed.[27] Such absurdity allows one of Laney's friends to learn that her date plans to see through on the wager and seduce her that night, prompting Zack to chase after her; to her credit, she repels the date rapist, but against reason she still takes Zack back afterward, as both forego the rest of their prom to dance in her backyard. Just as Laney lost the prom queen title at the dance, she loses herself in her spoils from the bet, winning the prize boy. She further retains the artificial appearance that she has desired all along, and she's still unaccepted, unknown, and essentially anonymous, a condition that she can presumably ignore on prom night.

The number of movies with proms could only decline in the following years, but the '00s maintained a somewhat hardy output of the sagas, beginning with *Whatever It Takes* (2000), a teenage remake of *Cyrano de Bergerac* with two boys helping each other win dates to a prom that slavishly steals the dance scene from *It's a Wonderful Life*. Stealing for satire was the central purpose of *Not Another Teen Movie* (2001), with a bombastic prom that strings together many of the recent cinematic proms before it. Proms continued as significant events in *The Kingston High* (2002—the rare film to feature the ritual among primarily African American students), *The Girl Next Door* (2004), *Infection* (2005), *Nearing Grace* (2005), *Fat Girls* (2006), *Tammytown* (2007), and the potentially lethal conclusion of *Twilight* (2008). The ongoing popularity of movie proms—and the *Twilight* series—likely explain their suddenly profuse mockery in horror films as well: *Dance of the Dead* (2008), *Cabin Fever 2: Spring Fever* (2009), and *Vampires Suck* (2010). *Bart Got a Room* (2008) even pays homage to earlier odysseys of proms with its title character indebted to making his big night special yet needing a girl to do so.

A recent film that more completely understands the inverse gravity of proms was aptly titled simply *Prom* (2011), which "understands why the prom is less important than it seems—and also why it still looms so large," according to Owen Gleiberman.[28] Senior class president Nova (Aimee Teegarden) has been working on her school's prom for months when the decorations are destroyed in a fire three weeks before the event. All of the many students who have worked with her—including the boy she hopes will be her date—have various reasons for not being able to help with reconstruction, a contrivance that results in a more classic scheme when bad boy Jesse (Thomas McDonell) is assigned to work with Nova to rebuild the prom decor. This easily criticized clichéd setup, anticipating the opposites will attract, is nonetheless buoyed by the actual labor involved in working on the decorations, a process that predictably reveals much more about the characters than their superficial roles, such as Nova's sensitive intelligence and Jesse's skillful fortitude. When Jesse argues over the relevance of their work in making the dance happen, Nova articulates the dreamy communal objective of proms for students: "It's just all of us together in this one perfect moment. And I want to be part of that."

The story progresses through dramatizing the other students' troubles leading to the prom as well, including a nerd without a date, a girl who suspects her boyfriend is cheating on her, and an art student who has been accepted to a prestigious college far from her boyfriend. In this way, the film offers a more representative spectrum of stresses that students assume for their proms, which often go beyond the events of the night itself. Even Nova is initially disappointed that the boy she had hoped would invite her backs out, conveniently allowing her to grow affectionate toward Jesse as they continue to work on restoring and revising the prom sets. Nova's father, concerned that Jesse is a bad influence, warns the boy to avoid his daughter, setting in motion further confusion for her, adding to her frustration after toiling so diligently on a prom she will attend alone. While the other kids manage to alleviate their prom crises—including the nerd taking his kindly stepsister—Nova feels her efforts have been unfulfilling until Jesse appears and they share a dance together. With the film's sincere tone and lengthy focus on the prom, the narrative resolution of the students' longings and torments is unsurprising, yet the film remains rare as a realistic portrait of the struggles students take on for an event that is so typically arduous, and in many other films, downright unpleasant. The film may be unrealistic in the broader context of 2011—with justice prevailing for the deserving, no drugs or alcohol in sight, and teens almost never attached to an electronic device—yet in terms of the sheer amount of labor, creativity, money, and frayed emotions that are still spent on proms, it does beg the pertinent question of whether they are even worth it for the participants. *Prom* answers, like so many films about romance, that somehow surviving the torture is its own reward. The persistence of proms in the cultural lives of teenagers testifies to this as well.

LOSING VIRGINITY

The start of sexual practice for young people has been a topic of concern and captivation for centuries, both to youth, who themselves have much to learn and experience, and to adults and parents, who re-call their discoveries of sexuality with both nostalgia and alarm, thereby treating these facts of life with alternating doses of sensitivity and hyper-bole. Many people have their first sexual exchanges (intercourse or other-wise) in their adolescence, and so youth films are likely sites for the dis-cussion and dramatization of carnal knowledge. Yet while many youth films from 1980 to 2013 featured teens in a quest to have sex, the majority were decidedly negative in their portrayals, demonstrating the complica-tions of sex, as well as the aggravations, confusions, and potential dangers. Youth find themselves involved in sexual activities in one form or another, whether intercourse, foreplay, or the basic negotiation of sexual prefer-ences, and the majority of narratives in this erosphere could be character-ized as comedies, even when they tend to take seriously the stakes of sex.

Within the romance subgenre throughout the early 1980s, the loss of virginity was a common agenda in stories about teens' sex quests. First sex is a classic rite of passage for young adults, especially as adolescence induces the hormonal and physical changes that instill suddenly strong sexual im-pulses in teens. For all gender identities, sexual practice is often a signi-fier of adulthood, and with it comes a level of intimacy and responsibility beyond the experience of children; however, like children, most sexually active teens are still learning to handle their increasing senses of potency, obligation, and maturity, all of which are components of sexuality even though many teens are unprepared for how these aspects of adulthood will change them. The 1969 film *Last Summer* may be the best example of how unresolved virginal tensions can lead to unexpected moral consequences: the idyllic arrangement of two teen boys and a teen girl is disrupted when a second teen girl tries to befriend them, ultimately resulting in the three original friends raping the newcomer. Such excessive reactions would be rare in future youth films, perhaps because teens themselves would likely avoid paying to see such harsh possibilities.

Before the era of AIDS, the most serious outcomes of teen sexual prac-tice were pregnancy, venereal disease, and emotional distress. While AIDS was recognized in 1981, its capacity to be spread by heterosexual con-tact was not acknowledged until the mid-'80s, and not coincidentally, there was a dramatic decline in the number of youth films featuring the loss of virginity after 1986. In fact, with the exception of the parodic *Virgin High* in 1991, losing virginity movies were effectively nonexistent from 1986 to the mid-'90s; then when *Kids* appeared in 1995, the previously playful loss of virginity was portrayed as sinister and as reviled as any crime, although like the depiction of much youth criminality, it also retained a cachet of rebellion. Over the following few years, with social concerns about AIDS being defused in the United States, teenage sexual activity found its way back to the screen in less threatening but more mature ways. Few of the early '80s tales of losing virginity featured any of the potential medical hazards of sex, but many of them did weave emotional issues with the cravings of their characters. To most of the teens in these films, sex was a new dark continent to be explored, and most of them faced specific fears and frustrations in that exploration, and, at least until *Kids*, the vast majority prevailed with some level of happiness. Nonetheless, few of these films could be said to have capriciously promoted sex for the population they were directed to, if only since the sex act itself was so rarely portrayed in as pleasurable terms as its anticipation.

The 1980 film *Little Darlings* helped to solidify the explicit elements of this category at the start of the decade: two teenage girls at summer camp compete to see who can lose her virginity first. One girl lies about having sex with an adult counselor while the other is greatly aggrieved when she actually has sex with a teenage boy, and the film, like many others after it, reveals the anticlimax of first sex for many teens. Two years later the very successful *Porky's* further capitalized on the group pursuit of first sex from the male perspective, albeit removed to the 1950s. While less profitable, another 1982 film, *Goin' All the Way*, has a title that suggested the salacious manner in which many of the losing virginity sagas would operate; the story revolves around a high school senior who can't convince his girlfriend to have sex. After much wrangling, some of which is admittedly heartfelt, the boy convinces the girl of his love for her, and she is so thrilled that she finally "goes all the way" with him. Her systematic process of deciding to lose her virginity is a narrative paradigm common to almost all "good" girls in youth sex films: boys always want to have sex and must learn to control their urges, but moral girls are so anguished by their sexual ideas and impulses as to ensure their resistance to boys' urges, granting them a confident sense of power via the denial of potential satisfaction. Like many other youth sex films to follow, *Goin' All the Way* ends with the suspense-relieving consummation of the protagonists' relationship, wherein the loss of virginity and not the sex act provides the ultimate resolution for both teens' tensions. Meanwhile, the characters remain clearly confused and overwhelmed by sex, a condition that is typical of virtually all youth sex films.

The losing virginity plot became dominant in American youth cinema of the early '80s with the huge hit *Fast Times at Ridgemont High* in 1982. The film takes on high school life in broad terms, and thus sex is merely one aspect of the narrative's matrix, even if the sexual evolution of Stacy (Jennifer Jason Leigh) is a dominant plotline. First she decides to lose her virginity to a man in his twenties—she tells him she's nineteen when she's really fifteen—and then later has casual ten-second sex with the satyric Mike (Robert Romanus); in both cases, her enjoyment of the experience is fleeting if existent. Stacy bears the further brunt of her deflating sexual initiations when she finds herself pregnant and decides to have an abortion. Sex comes with a definite price for the spacey Stacy, who thinks nothing of contraception, although David Denby accurately notes that while "Stacy and her friends are shucking off their clothes before they've explored friendship or the pleasures of courtship or romance," this theme is "developed satirically, not as a moral judgment."[29] Such satire is carried on in the loss of virginity for Mark (Brian Backer), which is opposite to Stacy's—more arduous and less consequential. Mark, working against but confirming his nerdy image, takes Stacy out on a formal dinner date and forgets his wallet. He's even more awkward when they return to her house and she tries to seduce him. Yet Mark is the one character who, by the film's end, does not have sex and seems best off for it: Mike is despised, Stacy is dejected, and her oversexed best friend is alone as well. Stacy, having had her fill of troubling sexual experiences, agrees to proceed patiently with Mark, portending that this approach will be the best for both of them, and thus Mark's virginal status is rendered more reassuring rather than frustrating.

The title of *The Last American Virgin* (1982) is both humorous and, within the context of the film's bleak narrative, ominous. Gary (Lawrence Monoson) and his two buddies Rick (Steve Antin), a good-looking stud, and David (Joe Rubbo), a rotund jovial goof, are three teenage boys eager for their first sexual experiences. Rick is a smooth operator compared to shy Gary, which becomes a big problem for him when Rick wins the heart of Karen (Diane Franklin), for whom Gary pines away through the entire film. Gary is one of the most sympathetic and sensitive characters in any teen romance film: he has the same raging urges as other young males and still appears genuinely conflicted over his affection for Karen, yet he ultimately resists his friends' forays into quickly losing their virginity. When Rick convinces three teen girls to join him and his two friends for a little party, Gary is not only left with the "least attractive" girl but ungraciously fumbles when he tries to make out with her. After more frustration, Gary tries to lure Rick away from Karen by taking his friends to a prostitute, and he denies himself another opportunity to lose his virginity (even though all three boys get infected with crabs). What Gary wants more than sex, unlike his cohorts, is love. The film is certainly filled with plenty of bawdy sex scenes though, and plays up masculine sexual aggression, as when Rick proudly announces that he's deflowered Karen. This upsets Gary visibly, and after Rick arrogantly refuses to help Karen when she becomes pregnant, Gary becomes further infuriated with Rick, and devotes his Christmas vacation to helping her get an abortion.

The last section of the film then becomes surprisingly depressing. Gary scrambles to raise the money for Karen's abortion and hides her away during her recovery, after which he finally tells her he's been in love with her all along. Gary assumes that he's proved himself to her enough to secure their bond, but he soon finds Karen back in the arms of the lecherous Rick. The final shot of the film is Gary driving away into the night, crying, and still a virgin. For all the work the film does in portraying the virtue of Gary's patience and understanding, this conclusion declares that he's been a fool to invest so much in Karen, and on a larger scale suggests that waiting for the "right person" to lose one's virginity to is a detrimental ambition. Like so many youth romance films, the division between love and sex is thus enforced—the two rarely occur in the same relationship. *The Last American Virgin* becomes a warning to youth against the pursuit of sex, which leads to disease, pregnancy, and the loss of friends, and the pursuit of love, which is unpredictable and unrewarding.[30]

In early 1983, Tom Cruise had his first starring role in the period film *Losin' It*—whose provocative title was indicative of the increasingly direct sexual marketing of youth films at the time—as one of four boys who travel to Mexico to alleviate their virginity. Cruise would find greater visibility as a frustrated virgin later in 1983 when he starred in *Risky Business*, one of the highest-grossing youth films of the decade. The story uses the classic device of a teenager's parents going away on a trip, leaving high school senior Joel (Cruise) alone at home. First Joel does little more than dance around in his underwear and sample his dad's scotch, until his sexual insecurity boils over after his friends tease him for his lack of prowess and spontaneity. As one buddy famously advises him, "Say 'what the fuck.' If you can't say it, you can't do it." The enterprising Joel knows that he should concentrate on his school business project, but he breaks down and calls a young prostitute named Lana (Rebecca De Mornay), who promptly fulfills his carnal curiosities.

The film parallels Joel's ambitions to become a successful capitalist with his venture into the world of sexuality: after Lana steals his mother's prized crystal egg in payment for her services, Joel rescues her from her maniacal pimp Guido (Joe Pantoliano) to make a deal for the egg. Lana suggests that

Joel (Tom Cruise) initially uses the services of young prostitute Lana (Rebecca De Mornay) to alleviate his virginity, then later finds her oldest profession is necessary for his financial security.

he can get the egg back and make even more money if he were to hook up his rich friends with her prostitute colleagues, a proposal that Joel at first resists but soon finds a necessity after he crashes his father's expensive car, an "accident" that Lana appears to have caused. Joel thus learns that the exchange of sex for property is a potentially lucrative business and has no shame in taking advantage of his friends, from whom he immediately gains respect and admiration. Lana helps Joel set up his house as a one-night brothel, and then provides special accommodations for a college interviewer from Princeton, only the business goes sour the next day when Guido comes to collect for the services of his "employees." Joel madly scrambles to rectify the situation and succeeds in the nick of time, getting back the egg and furniture that Guido had stolen from him, gaining acceptance to Princeton, and cleaning the house just before his parents return. In a final scene, Joel demonstrates his newfound savvy and sophistication to Lana by teasing her that she'll now have to pay him to be his girlfriend, thereby shifting the economic power of sexual value onto himself, and more so by implying that he wants to continue his prostitution service in college, pointing to Joel's dubious perspective in which he has become a "proper pimp." David Denby further observed that when "Joel surmounts his sex and career anxieties by turning himself into a pimp," it is "presented without irony or a hint of criticism, as a triumph of free enterprise."[31]

Risky Business accommodates its losing virginity agenda within the first third of the story, following Joel through his role as virginity-ender for the young male population around him. Joel's own sexual activity is thus less relevant to the narrative than his selling of sex, and he gains his sense of acceptance and authority accordingly, such as when he coolly pitches his service to a diverse range of young men he meets. That Joel is a salesman of commodified women is obvious, as he claims to be selling "experience" to his eager clients, who see no liability or danger with having sex for money (again, early enough to not make AIDS an issue, although other diseases were still prominent) and are happy to lose their virginity with complete strangers, and moreover, with the same complete strangers to whom their friends are also losing their virginity. *Risky Business* thus pitches the morality of young men especially low, and makes Joel's sexist business an acceptable sign of his financial acumen—he earns far more money for his "project" than do his fellow aspiring classmates—even if Guido takes back his profits. Joel can be viewed as the teen baron of Reagan-era capitalist scheming, which is justified by the gratification it provides to the masses, and his image as a slick, successful dealer is an explicit inspiration for young men to continue the tradition of patriarchal economic practice. With such an endorsement being rendered so entertaining by the comic style of the film, Joel's coming-of-age is more a celebration of his daring business education than a questioning of the licentious methods by which it is achieved.

Other sexual adventures pursued the sleeper success of *Risky Business*, introducing mildly diverse variations. Products such as *Private Lessons* (1981), *Homework* (1982), *Class*, and *My Tutor* (both 1983) offered the services of older women to teenage boys seeking sexual initiation. *Private School, The First Turn On!* (both 1983), *Hollywood Hot Tubs, Joy of Sex* (both 1984), *Mischief*, and *Paradise Motel* (both 1985) enlisted groups of friends in attaining or commemorating sex, which was also the case in *Hot Moves* (1984), a film that provided the now archetypal plot of boys taking an oath to lose their virginity by a set deadline. The cycle of these films started showing some signs of change by 1985, when the third and final Canadian *Porky's* film was a bomb, and the most successful sex quest was *The Sure Thing*, about college students who show some level of maturity over their predecessors.

Further evidence of change would also come that year with *Once Bitten*, a horror comedy in which a sexually frustrated teen (played by a young Jim Carrey) is doubly relieved of his virginity, first metaphorically through the not-quite-sexual blood sucking of a lady vampire, and then literally through his girlfriend, who must finally have sex with him to save him from the virgin-hungry vampiress. The film thus fantastically makes losing virginity a matter of life and death, or on another level, insinuates that if teens wait too long to have sex they will be susceptible to monstrous consequences. Yet when the protagonists consummate their relationship in a coffin, the film tacitly hints at the increasingly morbid notions of youth sex that would prevail in the later '80s and '90s as the fear of AIDS became more prominent and did indeed make sex a matter of life and death.

A low-budget soft-porn youth film called *The Big Bet* (1986) then became not only one of the most offensive portrayals of teen sexual activity among the many of the '80s, but effectively its death knell. Chris (Lance Sloane) becomes attracted to new girl at school Beth (Kimberly Evenson), yet is so insecure that he bets a rival that he can have sex with her within ten days, a tactic apparently meant to inspire him in pursuing Beth and win him praise among the cool kids at school. The narrative uses a recurring device in which Chris fantasizes about having sex with numerous naked women, including his attractive older neighbor, and with each new fantasy he becomes progressively frustrated at his inability to bed Beth, despite his variously preposterous efforts. What then appears to be a possible sign of Chris's respect for Beth—he begins to feel guilty for wagering on her virginity—is completely compromised when he gets mad at her and becomes so distraught that he runs off and has sex with his suddenly willing neighbor. The idea that the older woman teaches Chris "how to make love" caters to a primal male fantasy, but far more depraved than this oedipal fiction is Beth's sudden forgiving of Chris after he beats up his rival at school. Beth is supposedly so turned on by Chris's show of masculine violence and so flippant about her objectification by Chris and all the other boys (who've also placed bets on her having sex) that she becomes the seductive aggressor, inviting Chris to take her on the living room floor. The story appears to end right there, with the sexual conquest thus reached, until the end credits continue the tale: we see Chris and Beth graduate and later happily have a child. The still images do not suggest how long this process takes, yet it remains an odd recuperation of an otherwise irredeemably macho scenario. This ending suggests that the inevitable pregnancy of Beth justifies Chris's reprehensible treatment of her, as if creating a family nullifies the tension over her role as a mere sex toy—he must love her if they're staying together.

The Big Bet was little seen in theaters but definitely represents the worst of its kind, an unfunny, unfeeling, and ultimately deceptive teen sexploitation movie that further maligned the image of youth. Given that these

kinds of products had become so common by the mid-'80s, teenagers may
have grown insulted at such insensitive stories, although considering how
many the film industry made in the first seven years of the '80s—at least
twenty-five—the industry's sudden cessation of these films in 1986 remains intriguing. With the more sincere sexual portrayals of teens in John
Hughes's films of the mid-'80s becoming more popular, the pornographic
quality of a teen-oriented film like *The Big Bet* may have signaled to studios
the paucity of options left in portraying teenage sexual discovery in explicit terms.[32]

Nearly a decade elapsed in which the losing virginity film appeared to
have vanished. Even though teenage characters in some youth films continued to have sex, the narrative emphasis on sexual inception was not
prominent in these films like it had been in the early to mid-'80s. Films
featuring teens in sexual experiences were often vague about the virginal
status of their protagonists, such as *River's Edge* (1987), *Satisfaction* (1988),
Heathers (1989), *Rambling Rose* (1991), and *Gaby: A True Story* (1987), which
features one of the most extraordinary lovemaking scenes between teens in
cinema history. The title character, afflicted with cerebral palsy and played
to astonishing effect by Rachel Levin, maneuvers from her wheelchair to
the floor, unable to control her arms yet with the energetic desire to make
love with her similarly disabled boyfriend. Films that did contain scenes
suggested as first sex between teens—*Boyz N the Hood* (1991), *Zebrahead*
(1992), *The Incredibly True Adventure of Two Girls in Love* (1994)—were not
built on stories in which losing virginity was the primary ambition of any
character.

Then the appearance of Larry Clark's *Kids* in 1995 presented a radical revision of the teen sex quest story, a faux documentary approach not only
to youth sexuality but general delinquency, drug use, and disease. The film
revolves around two teen boys, Telly (Leo Fitzpatrick) and Casper (Justin
Pierce), the first of whom begins the film's day-in-the-life of debauchery
by deflowering an apparently pubescent girl while the other is drinking
the first of many forty-ounce beers. Telly prides himself on being a "virgin
surgeon" who pursues particularly young girls, and on this day his goal is
to have two of them. He waxes philosophical on the commanding significance he feels in being so many girls' first sex partner: to him, the conquest
of virgins—all of whom he abandons after having sex with them—is more
than a sign of his masculine prowess, it is the very means by which he gains
identity. The few girls who are presented in the film are less developed
characters but, as an early dialogue scene shows, they are just as sexually
excitable as are the boys who pursue them. The one conspicuous excep-

tion is Jennie (Chloë Sevigny), who reveals that she only ever had sex one time, with Telly, and discovers soon thereafter that he has infected her with HIV. The film's narrative thus becomes something of a picaresque journey for Jennie as she tries to find Telly before he infects another girl by the end of the day.

Even with Jennie's presence in the story and the one dialogue scene offered between girls, *Kids* never offers a balance or reprieve from its objectified positioning of young women, and is ultimately boldly exploitative of its entire young cast. Critics made much of the fact that the script was written by Harmony Korine when he was just nineteen, and perhaps he was making a statement on the difficulty girls face in dealing with urban boys, for he appears himself as a friendly nerd who meets Jennie at a rave and, with empty consolations, forces her to take a drug that he insists will make her feel better. By the end of the film, Jennie finds Telly but doesn't bother to stop him when she sees he's having sex with yet another virgin, and she is so stoned that she becomes submissive when Casper later rapes her, a scene made all the more brutal by the sustained filming of it for over two minutes. As I have written elsewhere, "The film cheaply offers a false empowerment for its female characters, who initially appear confident in their knowledge and appropriation of sex, and who are ultimately victimized by it. The film is not merely sexist or patriarchal, it endorses an understanding of youth sexuality that is degrading for both genders."[33]

The ribald search for hedonistic pleasure that suppurates under *Kids*— all of its young characters are looking for beer, drugs, sex, and/or the next party—is based on its distinctly masculinist perspective, or as bell hooks claimed in more assertive terms, "What is being exploited is precisely and solely a spectacle of teenage sexuality that has been shaped and informed by patriarchal attitudes."[34] *Kids* does not make sexuality for youth appear effortless; however, the film's one-dimensional perspective—that is, that boys are dogs and girls are not much better—denies the psychological intricacy of the issue. The main, if singular, aftermath of sexual practice in *Kids* is the potential spread of HIV, a serious issue to be sure, but Telly's habitual practice of deflowering virgins is left on the moral surface. The main lesson of *Kids*—that sex can be deadly—is never realized on screen. The film concludes with Telly visibly infecting another girl with HIV and reciting in a voice-over, "When you're young, not much matters. . . . Sometimes when you're young, the only place to go is inside. That's just it— fucking is what I love. Take that away from me and I really got nothing." This ending may be meant as further ironic commentary on the fact that Telly is likely to die from his fucking practices, except he is never driven to confront them. As Owen Gleiberman said, "We never get to see if the little son of a bitch has a soul after all."[35]

The perspective on youth sexuality offered by *Kids* is incomplete and misogynistic, even though within the context of so many vilified images of teen sexuality in the '90s, the film can appear to be merely marking a moment in the cultural zeitgeist. Very much like *Teenage Crime Wave* (1955) and other extreme portraits of the "youth threat" in the 1950s, *Kids* attempts to inflame the otherwise serious conditions of youth sexual practice by celebrating the unbridled decadence and anomie of ignorant antiheroes like Telly and Casper, and in that way is similar to the basest of the teen sex comedies of the early '80s. Tom Doherty rightly said, "*Kids* can probably be best described as an ethnographic film on urban teen subculture for an art-house crowd ready to be appalled at what's the matter with kids today."[36] The fact that *Kids* portrays the urban working class instead of the middle or upper class, and that it directly addresses issues of AIDS (as little as it actually informs about the disease), does not nullify the film's reactionary approach of depicting youth sexuality as dangerous and deviant, beyond being devoid of any real pleasure.

Portrayals of teen sex in other '90s youth films are not quite as pessimistic or condescending, although it is usually shown to be distinctly more complicated than it was in the '80s, and instances of "first sex" are portrayed far less often because teenagers tend to be either virgins for the entire film or sexually experienced before the start of the story. The first case persisted in films such as *Clueless* (1995), *Welcome to the Dollhouse* (1996), *Trojan War* (1997), and *American Beauty* (1999), while the second case was evident in films like *Hackers* (1995), *Manny & Lo* (1996), *Wild Things*, *The Opposite of Sex* (both 1998), and *10 Things I Hate About You* (1999). Even films that did continue to feature deflowering scenes, like *Fear* (1996), *Titanic* (1997), *Can't Hardly Wait* (1998), *The Rage: Carrie 2* (1999), and *The Virgin Suicides* (2000), featured the fated moment as solemn and serious, quite a remove from the silly and lascivious nature of teen sex scenes in the more immature early '80s. And in a derisory indictment of the commercial reification that virginity has achieved in popular culture, *American Virgin* (1999) taunts its internal and external audience with a girl paid to be deflowered in an online exhibition that can be electronically simulated for viewers.[37]

Three 1999 films offered critical revisions of the losing-virginity film, one aligned with the sinister quality of *Kids*, another an almost nostalgic return to the sex romps of the '80s, and the third a fittingly feminist take on achieving a first orgasm *after* losing virginity. *Cruel Intentions* is a young updating of *Dangerous Liaisons*, in which the wealthy roué Sebastian (Ryan

Phillippe) makes a wager with his sexually alluring stepsister Kathryn (Sarah Michelle Gellar) that he will be able to bed down proud virgin Annette (Reese Witherspoon).[38] The film plays with ripe sexual tension between the step-siblings—Kathryn will allow Sebastian to "put it any-where" if he wins the bet—and the contemptible rich kids are portrayed as unbearably selfish and venal. However, Sebastian finds himself unex-pectedly falling in love with the endearing Annette, and though he does succeed in stealing her prized virginity, he ultimately becomes more con-cerned with the preservation of their relationship. The resolution of the story then speaks to the moral consequences of the characters' villainous use of sex: Sebastian is killed in a car accident and Kathryn is exposed in front of her entire school as the vindictive phony she is. These character assassinations, both literal and symbolic, arise from treating sexual con-quest in such a ruthless way.

The sexual conquests of the characters in *American Pie* are not only more lighthearted, but they are in many ways redemptive. Such a condition still did not insulate the film from pedantic criticism, such as the notional de-bate raised by academic Sharyn Pearce about whether the film and its se-quels are "actually a 'new age' effort that, via insubordinate performances of gender, contests the hegemonic field of signification that regulates the production of sex, gender and desire, or whether [they constitute] a retro-gressive hetero-conservative opus with a veneer of sexual radicalism."[39] The plot is lifted straight out of the early '80s, with four male high school seniors making a pact to lose their virginity. Jim (Jason Biggs) emerges as the main character, an inexperienced bumbler humbled by his parents' dis-covery of him masturbating with a sock, which is actually less embarrassing than his later use of a warm apple pie. He joins his friends for a party where they each anticipate some level of sexual activity, a longing that brings nothing but dejected frustration, and convinces them to pledge allegiance to having sex before the prom, a mere few weeks away.

Given this objective, the story could easily emulate the excessive con-cupiscence of the '80s films it echoes (as it certainly raises the level of gross bodily fluid gags), yet the film often handles the libidinous boys' travails in an honest, believable fashion. There are some unrealistic sexist moments, such as when Jim invites attractive exchange student Nadia (Shannon Elizabeth) to his house, with the ulterior motive of seducing her while his friends watch over an Internet feed, which would publicly verify his virility. First, Jim steps out to join his buddies in a communal orgy of voy-eurism as they watch Nadia undress in his bedroom, where she happens to find one of his porn magazines and impulsively decides to masturbate

in front of the hidden camera. This scenario then becomes even more improbable when Jim returns and Nadia invites him to fondle her, but as
if countering his "visual conquest" of her with his deeper insecurity, her
simple contact causes him to prematurely ejaculate. Such twists mark the
film's sense of balance, for the boys realize that their horny desires will take
them nowhere, and the girls they pursue want more than to be chased: they
want a level of affection and attention not accorded to teen girls in many
previous sex comedies, or as Jonathan Foreman made the comparison, "the
girls in *American Pie* are much more than life-support systems for breasts."[40]

Thus, as Kevin (Thomas Ian Nicholas) tries to convince his girlfriend
Vicky (Tara Reid) to go all the way, he realizes that he needs to make their
foreplay more pleasurable to her. He then learns to practice other sexual
techniques (including oral approaches detailed in a secret "sex bible"),
which help to both encourage Vicky's interest and convince her of his
devotion; more significantly, this further promotes the attainment of a
girl's orgasm as a plot point in teen films. The jock "Oz" (Chris Klein)
woos a girl by joining a jazz choir, risking his reputation and his place on
the lacrosse team, only to discover his talents as a singer as well as his own
sensitivity, making him all the more endearing to her. And refined dork
Finch (Eddie Kaye Thomas), who pays a female friend to spread rumors of
his potency — in an effort to "buy" a sexual identity after fearing he'll never
earn his own — resigns to give up on dating his classmates, only to find
himself seduced by a friend's randy mother.

Alas, the hapless Jim has the toughest luck of the bunch, after he ends
up with a nerdy date at the senior prom and little prospect of losing his
virginity, until she shows him the carnal carnivore she really is, resulting
in the boy being used for sex by the girl, another twist which is recu-
perated by his ensuing pride in being so used. In fact, as the boys move
toward their climactic first times, they each earn a modicum of self-esteem
by rising above their initially base impulses and learning to treat the self-
assured girls with respect, so that all of their eventual sex scenes are rendered tender and/or humorous, and further, they are all ultimately celebratory, a phenomenon that had been minimized in American youth films
for over a decade.[41] Perhaps the common acceptance of safe sex (which is
clearly practiced in the film), and the refreshing sense of confident *female*
sexual pleasure that the film promotes, signal further changes in the film
industry's attitudes toward teen sex.[42] As Owen Gleiberman noted, "It re-
flects a major shift in contemporary teen culture that the girls in *American
Pie* are as hip to sex as the boys."[43]

Coming Soon was not nearly as widely seen as *American Pie*, if only because the protagonists seeking sexual initiation are girls, and their initiation is not to intercourse—the last of the trio loses her virginity at the start of the film—but to achieving orgasm. Written and directed by women, "The film is refreshingly direct and even courageous in its confrontation of female pleasure," Amy Taubin argued, "specifically orgasms and masturbation, the staple of teen-boy comedies, but hitherto off-limits for girls."[44] Through a series of casual conversations and awkward escapades, Stream (Bonnie Root) and her two wealthy private school girlfriends realize that what they thought they knew about sex was based on misconceptions and often patriarchal misinformation. Stream actively seeks out more satisfying sexual experiences, first with a conceited boyfriend, then on her own, and finally with a guy who has her interests in mind. Meanwhile, the film offers other possible trajectories for her friends, as one realizes she is a lesbian, and the other admits her sexual perplexity despite her abundant sexual activity. Yet due to the film's extolling of young women's sexual satisfaction, it garnered an NC-17 rating in its initial release, leading to considerable distribution dilemmas. *American Pie* became a huge hit after being re-edited from its initial NC-17 rating to an R; the more sensitive *Coming Soon*, without the support of a major studio, faded to video, where few teens saw its beneficial gender inversion of the sex quest plot.

In the new century, teen sex remained comical and problematic, if not always a popular subject. *American Pie* retained its appeal for audiences as the characters moved on to college in the 2001 sequel and then gathered for Jim's nuptials in *American Wedding* (2003), curiously just a few years after Jim's one-off predacious prom date has become the love of his life. The Universal Studio maintained the raunchy spirit of the original (with no hope of retaining its profits) in four straight-to-video releases from 2005 to 2009 that featured virtually none of the first cast, although that cast was reassembled for the surprisingly successful *American Reunion* (2012), which revisited the friends on the cusp of their thirties.[45] Stories dealing with teen sexuality remained generally less visible, including *Skipped Parts* (2000), *Happy Campers* (2001), *Roger Dodger* (2002), *Virgin* (2003), *The Door in the Floor* (2004), *One Last Thing . . .* (2005), *Mini's First Time* (2006), and *Normal Adolescent Behavior* (2007), or the sex was pushed off-screen as in *The Sisterhood of the Traveling Pants* (2005). Even the beatified art house pedophile Larry Clark failed to generate satiating publicity for his latest foray into the arch deviance of teens with *ken park* (2002).

One losing-virginity saga of the mid-'00s did gather some attention, and offered a bracing revision for the category, *The Girl Next Door* (2004), a film that was marketed as a teen sex comedy but has acerbic ironies throughout.

Matthew (Emile Hirsch) is an accomplished high school senior competing for a lucrative scholarship who feels that his teen years have been rather dull. Aside from his smarts, he does not stand out at school, with just two gawky buddies as friends, until he meets Danielle (Elisha Cuthbert), an attractive young woman who happens to be housesitting next door. Danielle takes a quick liking to Matthew, and he is immediately smitten, at least until he learns from one of his pals that she is a porn actress, which so degrades his opinion of her that he takes her to a motel, thinking she will be an easy conquest. Matthew is soon ashamed when she appears to give in to his angry lust, only to expose his crass treatment of her.

In a lesser teen sex comedy, Matthew would have lost his virginity to Danielle and merely had his comeuppance after the fact, yet *The Girl Next Door* quickly reveals a surprising sensitivity as Matthew follows Danielle to a porn convention and tries to woo her away from the business, a comically brave gesture that initially seems to work. Proceeding in full homage to *Risky Business*, however, Matthew becomes indebted to Danielle's manager and a porn producer, resulting in a fast need for cash, especially after he loses his college scholarship as a result of his recent bad company. In scenes that build through humorous suspense, Matthew and Danielle enlist the producer and their friends—hers in the trade, his in the school video club—to make a porn movie during the prom. As fate would have it, Matthew is needed to perform the closing sex scene on camera, yet can't go through with it since he is in love with Danielle, so his most insecure friend gallantly volunteers. Thereafter, having pulled off this amazing scam, Danielle is so enamored of Matthew that she quietly has sex with him in their limo after the prom.

By effectively shrouding Matthew's deflowering, the film confirms that his sexual initiation is in personal growth, or in jarring parallel to the subject of his scholarship speech, "moral fiber." The alleged porn film he orchestrated turns out to be a wildly successful high school hygiene movie, granting him wealth far beyond his debts, and further respect as a purveyor of "safe sex," which is not coincidental to a story that uses the titillation of pornography to ultimately advance a mildly informed enjoyment of sexual practice. Such an outcome allows for sex to sell as it did in '80s youth cinema, while preserving a haler moral message for teens in the '00s.

Teenage sexuality in the later '00s took on a decidedly farcical tone in a number of comedies such as *Happy Endings* (2005), *Pretty Cool* (2006), *Sex Drive* (2008), *Extreme Movie* (2008), and *Fired Up!* (2009), none of which was a box office hit, yet one movie in this mode was a blockbuster, *Superbad* (2007). Like many youth comedies, events in the film are built around one big night featuring a party, for which the nerdy Evan (Michael Cera) and Seth (Jonah Hill) tell their friends they will supply alcohol. Both are attracted to girls in their class, although Seth seems to know little about the popular Jules (Emma Stone) whereas Evan at least has a tentative friendship with Becca (Martha MacIsaac). The boys have been friends for years, and now confront the possibility that they will be separated after graduation, a tension that is displaced onto their attractions to the girls, and into their friendship with an even nerdier friend, Fogell (Christopher Mintz-Plasse), who has managed to procure a fake ID under the ludicrous name McLovin. Evan and Seth are a portrait of contrasts, the former a tenderly bumbling milquetoast and the latter a horny hefty buffoon; however, both of them have equal desires to hook up with their respective targets, which both of them think will be aided by plying the girls with alcohol. As Seth boasts with no chivalrous reservations, "You know when you hear girls say, 'Ah man, I was so shit-faced last night, I shouldn't have fucked that guy'? We could be that mistake!"

While a series of wild events transpire en route to the party, including McLovin befriending two childish cops, when they finally arrive Evan is surprised to find that Becca is already intoxicated and Seth, thinking he needs to become drunk to entice Jules, is flummoxed when she says she does not want to drink. After all of his obscene gesturing and crude talk about Jules, Seth is predictably reduced to babbling about his affection and fails to recognize her modest attraction to him, ending in his passing out on her. Becca absconds with Evan to a bedroom and begins to seduce him, but he softly resists her drunken advances, ending in her throwing up on him. McLovin only had transitory thoughts about an unnamed girl, but he appears to be the most successful of the trio when he meets her at the party and later begins having sex with her, until he is cock-blocked by the cops. Thus none of the boys loses his virginity, although McLovin is given instant status when the cops fake his arrest, and in an inebriated moment, Evan and Seth declare their amicable love for each other.

Superbad garnered enormous publicity not only for its box office success but also for its candid profanity spoken by minors. Such ignominy may have sunk a pointlessly raunchy film with immoral protagonists, but as Manohla Dargis argues, "It works because no matter how unapologetically vulgar their words, no matter how single-mindedly priapic their preoccupations, these boys are good and decent and tender and true."[46] That goodness, tinged with lamentation, emerges in the ending when Evan and Seth bump into Becca and Jules at a mall the day after the party, and after some embarrassing small talk, the couples pair off. As they walk away in opposite

directions, Evan and Seth look back at each other, knowing that this beginning foray into romance with girls means the demise of their boyhood
intimacy. The fact that they have each joined a girl to go shopping is significant as well, suggesting that their destinies with these girls is domestic
consumption rather than the decadent frivolity they have enjoyed together.
And both boys are still virgins, still suspended between carnal desire and
postcoital disillusion.

The quest for sex in *Superbad* was simply a failed mission, and subsequent films about losing virginity have maintained only a slight emphasis
on the sex while still innovating portrayals of the quest. This was evident
in two 2009 films: *Wild Cherry*, where girls conspire to actually keep their
virginity, and *Youth in Revolt*, with a protagonist who cultivates a sinister
alter ego to chase his dream girl. The suave and sassy *Easy A* (2010) explores
the quest in almost theoretical terms, as its protagonist deconstructs on
camera—via her computer—the malignancy resulting from lying about
losing her virginity. The film and the character have much less to say about
having sex (which she does not do) than about social perceptions regarding
the act, and this has been common to many films about youth sexuality
since the early '00s. Even when first sex is filtered through humor, teen
cinema now rarely engages in the carefree salacious behavior of its fore-
bears, and continues to detail the complications of sex beyond traditional
parental warnings about pregnancy and disease, as in *The First Time* (2013),
with a boy and girl unprepared for their emotional mayhem. By exposing
more of the enigmas of sexual initiation and depicting its disappointments
as well as delights, youth cinema has been maturing toward an overdue appreciation of adolescent sexuality with more sincerely confused characters
having more healthy—if still sophomoric—relationships.

BEING QUEER

Any sexual practice for youth outside of normative heterosexuality in American cinema up to the 1990s was handled in often vague
if not symbolic terms, and when it was handled, the characters in question
were almost always troubled and trying to deny their nonheterosexual impulses, lest they face the consequence of ridicule, condemnation, or even
death. In *Queering Teen Culture* (2006), Jeffrey P. Dennis details the emergence of nonheterosexual youth, which was certainly cautious after WWII,
as in films where "the homoerotic bond between the boy and his buddy became increasingly overt . . . and the penalty for failing to embrace hetero-

sexual destiny increasingly brutal."[47] These penalties were more cinematically detailed in David Considine's examination of homosexual youth
depictions, wherein he discusses the ostracizing of thinly coded gay characters in '50s films such as *Rebel Without a Cause* (1955) and *Tea and Sympathy*
(1956), pointing out that European films dealt with the issue of adolescent
homosexuality more often and more confidently. By the time of *Ode to
Billy Joe* in 1976, Hollywood appeared still uneasy with the queer youth
concept, for the fleeting homosexual encounter of the title character results in his suicide. Considine cites the 1980 film *Happy Birthday, Gemini* as
"a quantum leap forward in Hollywood's treatment of adolescent homosexuality," where a father supports his twenty-year-old son's questioning of
his sexual preference.[48]

Considine goes on to list a number of adult gay and lesbian characters in
films of the '80s, but his enthusiasm for the progressive potential of *Happy
Birthday, Gemini* appears optimistic, since images of queer youth remained
rare in American cinema for some time longer. For instance, another 1980
youth film, *Fame*, featured one gay character within the relatively high
queer population of the New York High School of Performing Arts, who
is handled sympathetically through the film's implication that, as Considine himself points out, "he is doomed to a loveless life of unhappiness."[49]
Two 1982 films promoted grim images of young gay males, *Forty Deuce*,
about teen hustlers involved in heroin dealing and pedophilia, and *Night
Warning*, about a boy suspected of murder on the grounds of "homosexual
psychosis." In *The Celluloid Closet* (1987), Vito Russo provides commentary
on two other obscure and troubling films featuring gay teens: *Abuse* (1982),
the story of a gay boy who falls in love with a filmmaker who's studying
how the child is brutalized by his parents, and *The Boys Next Door* (1986),
in which a repressed teen becomes so upset over his latent homosexuality
that he becomes homicidal.[50] A rather underdeveloped gay teen appears at
the end of *Torch Song Trilogy* (1988) as the adopted son of the lead character,
and queer issues do surface for protagonists in a select few other '80s films
such as *A Nightmare on Elm Street 2: Freddy's Revenge* and *Vision Quest* (both
1985), and likely the first transgender teen film, *Willy/Milly* (1986). Perhaps
the clearest sign of tension over queer youth in American films of the '80s
was the de-emphasized practice of a teenaged male prostitute in *Less Than
Zero* (1987), who became more sexually ambiguous in his translation from
page to screen.

An argument for this absence of queer youth could be made that many
young people do not openly question their sexuality until their college
or post-teen years, and more so, that the very notion remains a threat to

the established heterosexual norm, especially for young people whose impressionability is very much a concern for conservative parents.[51] Another potential problem with the depiction of queer youth may be the already popular perception of teens as oversexed, and therefore being gay or lesbian at such a young age could appear more sexually irresponsible, a concern that may have been more acute in the early AIDS era of the '80s. This of course unfairly shifts the substance of same-sex relationships to the sexual and away from the romantic, yet many queer youth depictions by the '90s tended to deal with tensions around both sexual experience and romantic longing, or in other words, the same tensions that heterosexual teens are shown dealing with in other films. Concerns about AIDS and controversies over gay rights legislation notwithstanding, serious academic study of queer theory and measured compassion toward GLBT lifestyles progressed in the '90s, and the number of nonheterosexual characters in American films, both youth and adult, increased, sometimes in stereotypical roles, but usually in a more positive light.[52]

In 1991, gay director Gus Van Sant turned two of the '80s heterosexual heartthrobs into young hustlers in *My Own Private Idaho*, a film definitely directed at an adult audience that still provided the most complete exploration of young homosexuality in American films up to that time. River Phoenix and Keanu Reeves play narcoleptic Mike and forsaken rich stud Scott respectively; the characters become involved in a far-reaching search for Mike's mother, during which Scott takes up with a young woman and abandons his previously gay ways. The characters are at the fringe of their teen years—they are both around twenty—while a number of older and some younger gay characters populate the story, which acts as a very loose adaptation of Shakespeare's *Henry IV, Part 1*. The film is sometimes difficult to appreciate as a drama of young gay life, if only because its conspicuous stylization renders its often poignant characterizations rather esoteric. Mike's narcolepsy is analogous to his ongoing sexual crisis in which he is effectively resisting heterosexuality—when he's picked up by a rich woman and gets excited he falls asleep—where Scott's heterosexual calling comments on the influence of wealth in negotiating sexual practice, as his father's inheritance and upper-class background appear to directly carry him away from his temporarily alternative lifestyle.

A sweet if sad affection exists between Mike and Scott that conveys the humbling complications of being a young homosexual, yielding a particular sympathy for same-sex attraction among youth. Scott will have sex with men only for money, while Mike longs for a shared loved with Scott that remains unrequited accordingly. Scott appears to recognize Mike's interest but cannot manifest the level of emotion needed to actually love another man like Mike loves him, and thus the film points to a crucial difference between gayness as a sexual practice and as a way of life. Scott's inheritance from his famed father is not only money but also the very tradition that is heterosexuality, whereas Mike is left at the end of the film on his apparently perpetual search for a waking comfort that is, in the context of the film and of American culture, simply not available to many young gay men.

The ambitious gender-bender comedy *Just One of the Guys* (1985) had browsed the complications of same-sex attraction for teens, but eight years later its essential opposite, *Just One of the Girls* (1993), demonstrated a direct turn toward dealing with the homosexual tensions of its plot. The unisexually named Chris (Corey Haim) is a sixteen-year-old who dresses as a girl to avoid the taunts of local bully Kurt (Cam Bancroft), and as fate would have it, Kurt becomes attracted to this new "girl" at school. After Chris finally reveals himself as a boy in front of the entire school, Kurt's buddies tease him that he must be gay, and that he should beat up Chris to prove that he's not. In an unexpected show of tolerance and homosocial camaraderie, Chris immediately allows Kurt to hit him, knowing that he won't, and both boys shake hands. *Just One of the Girls* does not feature any homosexual characters but it does entertain many issues about homosexual attraction and gender relations among teens. Kurt's lack of being able to explain his love for the "female" Chris speaks to the common belief in young love—that it is powerful and inexplicable—while it also blurs the distinction between hetero- and homosexual attraction, because Chris looks rather the same in both forms and has the same social qualities. The fact that Kurt cannot "win" Chris in female or male form despite his own over-masculinized performance leads to his difficult recognition of his own vulnerabilities, which include desiring a masculine girl. The film's lack of restoring heterosexual normalcy—Chris is still left alone, even with his crush on Kurt's sister—is a further sign of its suggestion that youth attractions may be motivated by homo- or bisexual impulses, and that such impulses are understandable, at least under certain circumstances.[53]

A film that boldly paints its teen characters as queer regardless of circumstance is *Totally Fucked Up* (1994; the film was marketed as *Totally F***ed Up*, but its full title is spoken as a front credit by one of the main characters). The film showcases a thriving yet endangered young queer population, and remains a strikingly complete depiction of a queer teen ensemble. Directed with a nod to formal experimentation by young gay filmmaker Gregg Araki, the story follows six homosexual friends through fifteen segments, a conscious homage to the approach used by Jean-Luc Godard in his famous youth film *Masculin Féminin* (1966), which Randy Gener comments on by calling the characters "the postpunk children of MTV and HIV," since "Marx is dead and Coca-Cola is a cliché."[54] Appropriately, the film deals with a number of masculine and feminine gender issues for young people, although more so than other youth portrayals, these characters' lives revolve around their sexual activities. Steven (Gilbert Luna) and Deric (Lance May) are interracial lovers; Steven is an aspiring film student who's making a video documentary about his gay friends, including the mopey Andy (James Duval), confident Tommy (Roko Belic), and lesbian partners Michele (Susan Behshid) and Patricia (Jenee Gill). The group openly talks about their sexual experiences and desires, sharing a comfort with one another that demonstrates their security and loyalty: they discuss their cynicism and fantasies about romance, elaborate on their idols (all heterosexual movie stars who they suspect are gay, such as Tom Cruise), believe that AIDS is a government conspiracy, and sometimes masturbate together (while watching porn, or at a party, where the girls asks the guys to ejaculate into a bowl so they can try artificial insemination with a turkey baster).

The narrative begins (and Araki patently signals it as such) when Andy meets and slowly falls in love with a young man and Steven cheats on Deric with another guy, leading Deric to leave him; worse yet, he is later beaten up by gay-bashers. Tommy's parents realize that he is gay and throw him out of the house (no parents actually appear in the film). Michele and Patricia, who are the haziest characters, face no tumult like the boys; Tony Rayns argues that "the girls are all too clearly present for PC reasons of balance and solidarity, but the only problems Araki can think of giving them are those of shopping and prospective lesbian parenting; most of the time they are there only as confidantes for the screwed-up boys."[55] Steven tries to apologize to Deric for his indiscretion, and the loyal friends bond when Deric is beaten, but the film makes its sharpest statement after Andy's boyfriend leaves him for another guy, sending him into a depression that leads to his suicide.

The film actually begins with a statistic that 30 percent of teenage suicides are homosexuals, and with this ending the film somberly portrays its otherwise fun-loving and pleasure-seeking characters as tragically tormented. The image of Andy falling into his wealthy parents' pool and drowning is a statement on the indifference of class to alleviate the "teen angst" that the film portends in its subtitle. Still, *Totally Fucked Up* remains a balanced, normalizing image of teen homosexuality, depicting its characters as afflicted with many of the same dilemmas as all youth—parental and

relationship crises, boring jobs, drugs, sexual curiosities, career anxieties—
which are made more pressurizing by the fact that these individuals live in
a generally homophobic society that does not tolerate one common aspect
of their identities, their sexual preferences. Kevin Thomas points out that
none of the characters are presented "as gay stereotypes but rather as indis-
tinguishable in dress and mannerisms from other L.A. teenagers. (Only one
of the actors is actually gay.) The irony is that if any of these young men
had been even slightly obviously homosexual, they might have developed
lots more resiliency."[56]
    This is a point worth interrogating, for it is not sustained in the de-
piction of queer teens in following films: overtly homosexual youth may
show signs of resolve but they are nonetheless vulnerable to attack, and
youth who are either more subtle in their "queerness" or still questioning
their sexuality are no less tough and no more vulnerable. Thomas's claim
about *Totally Fucked Up* does not apply so well to the lesbian characters, nor
to Tommy, whose confidence seems rooted, perhaps not ironically, in his
buff jock body and good looks, and other films would assess how issues like
appearance and class indeed complicate characters' handling of their homosexuality. Indicating that images of queer youth were becoming more
common but not more popular, five other films were made about gay boys
in the later '90s that received little attention: *Parallel Sons* (1995) features an
intriguing story about a white teenager coming to grips with his African
American affinities while he administers to a wounded black criminal and
fosters an attraction to him; *Johns* (1996) is the bleak tale of a teenage hustler
who falls in love with a twentysomething hustler and learns the dangers of
working the streets; *The Delta* (1997) explores the life of a closeted teenager whose relationship with a frustrated Vietnamese immigrant leads to a
random murder; *The Toilers and the Wayfarers* (1997) is a mild drama about a
cast-off German American teen coming to terms with his emerging homosexuality and cultural identity; and the excellent *Edge of Seventeen* (1999)
tells the story of an '80s teen facing the complexities of coming out to his
girlfriend after sleeping with her, falling for a rather rakish boyfriend, and
trying to fit into his local gay community.
    Two mid-'90s independent films about young lesbians were somewhat
more visible, and depicted the topic as relatively normalized. Joe Brown
rightly observed of *The Incredibly True Adventure of Two Girls in Love* (1995)
that it depicts "a tentative, coltish courtship, simultaneously spoofing and
reveling in all the romantic movie clichés taken for granted in 'straight'
love stories."[57] Randy Dean (Laurel Holloman) is a high school senior who
fancies herself a rebel like James Dean—tough, removed, cool, and also like

the real Dean, gay. The locals mostly think of Randy as some kind of alienated tomboy: she wears primarily masculine clothes, sports a short haircut, and has a kissing affair going with a married woman. The story concentrates on Randy's brewing relationship with Evie (Nicole Parker), an attractive and popular girl at her school on whom she forms a sensitive crush. Despite knowing the adversities that could arise, Randy carefully pursues Evie, and to her relief Evie (who has just broken up with her whiny boyfriend) is receptive to her advances.

The film makes Evie's reciprocal attraction to Randy rather effortless. The two characters have distinct differences—Evie lives with her wealthy mother and Randy lives with her working-class lesbian aunt and her girlfriend; Evie is well read and intellectual while Randy struggles in her studies; Evie is black, Randy white (the interracial and cross-class relationships between queer characters in youth films suggests that their sexual tolerance carries over to racial and class tolerance); Randy is confident in her sexual preference, and Evie is just starting to question hers—but these differences are cast aside in their mutual attraction. When Randy reveals her interest in Evie she even tells her how dangerous the situation could become, but inexperienced Evie throws that caution to the wind. The film thus portrays Evie's choice of Randy as part of the natural romantic growth of a teenager, marked by the usual excitement and confusion that characterize young heterosexual relationships. In many ways this may appear idealistic, yet the film never raises the stakes for these characters so high that the long-term repercussions of their acts are seriously questioned. (An end credit implies that the story is the semi-autobiographical account of filmmaker Maria Maggenti, who apparently wanted to keep the story within the realm of comfortable plausibility.) The film concludes with another classic rite of passage for teens, when Evie invites Randy to her house for a weekend while her mom is away: the two concoct a messy dinner, get drunk, and make love—the first time either actually has sex with another woman. Evie's mom catches them, however, and a chaotic chase ensues in which various characters end up cornering the two girls at a motel, who agree to emerge after they swear to love each other forever.

To be sure, *Incredibly True Adventure* is full of significant issues about the social troubles of being young and gay, as when locals taunt Randy, and Evie's friends reject her when she tries to explain her new relationship: "I didn't say I was gay. I said I was in love." Yet the film is filled just as much with otherwise typical teen turbulence: school trouble, overbearing parents, the indefinite future. Like *Totally Fucked Up*, the film makes clear that homosexual youth have much in common with their heterosexual counterparts, but by leaving Evie's sexual identity ambiguously bisexual, and by eschewing excessive drama, the film presents an even more neutral portrait of queer youth, whose sexuality is one part of their identity and not their defining quality.

Another examination of young lesbianism is offered in *All Over Me* (1996). Where the conflicts in *Incredibly True Adventure* primarily revolve around the characters' choice of a same-sex partner, here the queer issue itself is subtler. Claude (Alison Folland) is a fifteen-year-old growing up in New York City, trying to finish tenth grade and enjoy the summer with her best friend Ellen (Tara Subkoff), with whom she plays guitar in hopes of forming a rock band. Claude has misgivings about her weight and appearance, especially in comparison to waifish Ellen, but still the two have a physically comfortable intimacy with each other: they fake fucking in front of a fun-house mirror for laughs, and after Ellen loses her virginity to her new boyfriend Mark (Cole Hauser), Claude invites her to show her how it felt, whereupon the two girls tenderly hump and kiss. The occurrence of this scene just after Ellen has first had sex with a man is significant, if only because it signals the apparent end of the intimacy that Claude and Ellen have shared and marks the beginning of Claude's futile attempt to save Ellen from Mark's mean, macho clutches. Each girl tells the other she loves her, but Claude is almost masochistically devoted to Ellen, helping her through a series of bad drug experiences and fights with Mark. Such devotion nonetheless shifts the power of the relationship from Ellen to Claude, and as Nell Bernstein noted, "Claude isn't quite sure who she wants to be yet, but you can see a more certain self straining to break through, and it makes her beautiful."[58]

The plot takes its most dramatic turn when one of Claude's gay friends is killed by the homophobic Mark, and another of her gay friends warns that she could be next, pointing to her emergent homosexual leanings, which she soon thereafter declares further by going to a club and picking up a cute riot grrrl guitarist named Lucy (Leisha Hailey). Claude's shift of affection to Lucy is gradual: she tries to remain loyal to Ellen but becomes disgusted by her self-destructive behavior with Mark, urging her to tell the police of his role in the murder. Ellen's protection of Mark is simply too much for Claude to bear—after all, he killed her friend and stole her girlfriend—and in the end Claude herself turns Mark in. In contrary closing shots, Claude practices guitar with the more talented and receptive Lucy and then kisses her in public, providing a social recognition of her lesbian identity, and Ellen later sees Claude burying a coin that her murdered friend had given her, symbolically putting to rest that darker, more confusing part of her life.

While Claude does struggle in her relationships with Ellen and Lucy, her choice of both of them as potential partners is not disputed in itself, save by the bigoted Mark. *All Over Me* simply portrays Ellen as a more insecure, selfish, and inappropriate partner for Claude, not solely on the grounds of her heterosexuality—which remains in question—but because of her abusive, morally irresponsible actions.[59] For Ellen, the queer issue remains distressing and uncertain, while Claude handles her homosexuality quite confidently by the end of the film, and is apparently better for getting away from the bad influence of Ellen. The story is edifying but not preachy, showcasing a possible queer scenario for youth without exploiting it through mystique or alienation.

Given this handful of queer youth roles in films of the '90s, teenage homosexuality had become somewhat more acceptable while still being complicated, and its often sensitive, non-extreme representation provided an image of queer youth as increasingly common, striving for identity like all young people, on their own terms. A breakthrough picture featuring a gay girl in an otherwise everyday high school role, *Election* (1999) showed that a teen character's queerness could be portrayed without destructive consequence, although even she impugns classification: "It's not like I'm a lesbian or anything. I'm attracted to the person. It's just that all the people I've been attracted to happen to be girls." The Oscar-winning *Boys Don't Cry* (1999) drew further attention to non-straight sexuality issues for youth with its true story of a cross-dressing girl posing as a boy who falls in love with a small-town girl and is raped and murdered by the girl's viciously homophobic friends.

In 2000, *Scary Movie* still indulged in tired yarns about teens' sexual confusion for the sake of a few cheap laughs, yet the tide that began turning in the '90s became a wellspring of many more positive queer youth depictions over the next decade, with over two dozen films appearing about gay and lesbian teens.[60] *The Journey of Jared Price* was little seen in 2000, and then another film that year, *But I'm a Cheerleader*, was widely applauded for its witty and supportive satire of hokum reparative therapy programs for queer youth, which was a more serious subject in *And Then Came Summer* later that year. Other surveys followed, and in another divergence from the '90s, the films focused largely on gay boys: *The Deep End* (2001), with a boy suspected of killing his lover; *Play Dead* (2001), which actually mines humor from same-sex necrophilia; *The Trip* (2002), about a gay-rights activist daunted by his lover's ideology; *Latter Days* (2003), dealing with a young Mormon missionary facing devastating penalization for being discovered in a gay relationship; *The Mudge Boy* (2003), featuring a farm boy discovering his sexuality; *Crutch* (2004), a story that takes on sexual confusion and substance abuse; *Harry and Max* (2004), managing to tackle incest and pedophilia between two brothers; *A Home at the End of the World* (2004), with a homo–hetero love triangle; *Brother to Brother* (2004), considering racial and fraternal conflicts for its black protagonist; *Dorian Blues* (2004), depicting a boy's troubles coming out to his father; *Colma: The Musical* (2006), using genre conventions to comment on race and sexuality; *Vacationland* (2006), about a boy with competing desires for his best friend and leaving his small town; *Wild Tigers I Have Known* (2006), featuring a thirteen-year-old discovering his homosexual urges; and *Shelter* (2007), portraying an art student surfer who falls for his best friend's older brother. Other movies offered comical alterations to queer youth plots, such as *Freshman Orientation* (2004), with its story of a teen going to college and posing as gay to win a girl, *Almost Normal* (2005), with its fantasy swap of gay and straight social realities for a high school student, and *Another Gay Movie* (2006), with numerous sendups of gay and straight youth sex films throughout, particularly *American Pie*. Girls remained inexplicably minimized in queer youth films up to this point in the decade, even with titles like *Fat Girls* (2006), which focuses on a gay boy more than his rotund female friend, and *She's the Man* (2006), which updates the switching gender ploys of *Just One of the Guys* with a girl passing as a boy to play soccer. The lesbian perspective at last resurfaced in 2007 with *Itty Bitty Titty Committee*, about a girl who joins a radical feminist group.

The queer youth film that gained the most attention during this time, due to its star cast and literary derivation, was *Running with Scissors* (2006), the true story of a teenager who comes of age with a mentally ill mother in the late '70s. Given the time period, gay culture is quite repressed, and Augusten (Joseph Cross) struggles with his emerging homosexuality as his mother becomes involved with a hack psychologist for asinine treatment. Yearning for something like normality since he has been surrounded by apparent lunacy for so long, Augusten finds specious relief in his first lover, the doctor's adopted son, a thirty-five-year-old psychotic drifter. Augusten seeks solace in journal writing while his mother maintains delirium through drugs and troubled lesbian partners, and as his maternal and romantic authorities become more unhinged, he realizes he needs to move away, then simply does. Aside from the sympathetic protagonist, the film is blighted by its self-absorbed supporting characters and pretentious style, making it an unfortunately hollow depiction of young gay life in a vital era just before AIDS.

In contrast, just two years earlier a much more powerful and important film appeared about a gay teen, the critically acclaimed *Mysterious Skin* (2004). A decade after *Totally Fucked Up*, Gregg Araki tells this tale of entangled sexual abuses among teens in a more fertile style and with an astonishingly tactful tone. Neil (Joseph Gordon-Levitt) is a teenage hustler disenchanted with his small Kansas town, where he services local middle-aged men, while his childhood friend Brian (Brady Corbet) has grown up apart from him, yet still haunted by a summer when they were kids and played Little League baseball together. That summer holds intense memories for Neil, as we learn through flashbacks that his coach systematically lured him into sexual acts, whereas Brian is riled by forgetting five hours of one day then, during which he is convinced he was abducted by aliens. Araki obfuscates any cause-and-effect nexus between Neil's nauseating abuse and his gay sexuality, which was already affirmed as a child, rather suggesting on a more psychic level that the affection Neil's coach bestowed on him was meaningful beyond—and really, before—the abuse. His contemporary work as a prostitute for older men is in a failed effort to reincarnate his absent father through the original adoring figure of his coach; it is also a repetitive confirmation that he will never find such a figure again. Even as Neil goes off to New York City and continues hustling for more severe clientele, "it still comes as a shock to realize," Dennis Lim argues, "that for Neil, the man who once abused him remains the first love he can't get over."[61]

Neil and Brian do not reconnect until the end of the film, after a decade in which the latter has evolved into a nose-bleeding asexual nerd, resisting the advances of a local disabled woman who believes she, too, was abducted by aliens. Brian has a sense that Neil could uncover the mystery behind his stolen memory, and cautiously refriends him after Neil returns from New York, having been raped by one of his johns. Neil's agonizing endurance of this ferociously dehumanizing violation is cast in stark juxtaposition with his embryonic experiences with the coach, which remain memories of candy-colored explorations into male pleasures. A similarly overwhelming mix of sensations leads Brian to ask Neil about their little league summer, and in one of the most disturbingly direct and emotionally responsible scenes in teen cinema history, Neil slowly explicates that shattering evening they spent with the coach at his house, when Neil, already familiar with how to obey, encouraged Brian to succumb to his own sodomizing. Unlike Neil, who has for so long subconsciously channeled his abuse into a dangerous exchange of fake intimacy with men, Brian only then realizes why he has felt so incessantly damaged. Roger Ebert points out that Brian "was unable to process what happened to him, has internalized great doubts and terrors, and may grow up neither gay nor straight, but forever peering out of his great big glasses at a world he will never quite bring into focus."[62] *Mysterious Skin* in no way exonerates the coach, recognizing that there is no justice to be brought to his victims, who, as an eloquent closing shot illustrates, will be hereafter isolated in their own unique world of disorder. Their solitary consolation, also suggested by this shot, is that they have formed a new bond together, not in sexual exchange, but in their mutual understanding of each other.

By the end of the '00s, the sheer volume of queer youth films presented abundant evidence that the heteronormative traditions of teen cinema from previous decades were no longer an impediment to portrayals of nonheterosexual adolescent experiences. The growing support for marriage equality laws allowing same-sex marriages in some states was also a factor in wider public acceptance of homosexuality, although in terms of audience reach, the vast majority of queer youth films remained relatively marginalized within the independent market. Even the studio support of *Running with Scissors* did not prevent the film from languishing at the box office, and the extolled *Mysterious Skin* earned less than $1 million before moving to video.

Subsequent queer youth films, while still more prolific, tended to be relegated to small film festivals — many with GLBT themes — or found their following on DVD and through websites. At least five appeared in 2008, including *The Sensei*, a startling genre bender about a bullied gay student who learns martial arts from a dedicated woman; *Tru Loved*, with a girl posing as the beard of a closeted high school quarterback; and *Were the World Mine*, a fantasy about a boy turning most of his town gay. Five more queer youth films came out in 2009, featuring a sexually curious twelve-year-old in *Night Fliers* and another homo–hetero love triangle in the upscale *Dare*. The turn to the '10s indicates further momentum for queer youth roles, with at least ten premiering in the first three years of the decade through distinctive films including *Dirty Girl* (2010), *Private Romeo* (2011), and *Nate and Margaret* (2012). Further examples include *Spork* (2010), an unpredictably inventive dance comedy about an outcast hermaphrodite caught up in class and race conflicts, *Gun Hill Road* (2011), featuring a transgendered Latino who identifies as a girl, and *Jack and Diane* (2012), with a quirky butch–femme lesbian couple that presumably would have been more common in the past plethora of queer love stories.

Another rare lesbian character is the protagonist of *Pariah* (2011), Alike (Adepero Oduye), a black Brooklyn teen increasingly ostracized by many around her, as the title suggests. Alike is a high school virgin rather assured of her attraction to girls, although she keeps this from her religious mother, even while she often appears androgynous and is close with her best friend Laura (Pernell Walker), who is clearly out. Alike's mother promotes a girl in her church as a preferred alternative, the supposedly pious Bina (Aasha Davis), essentially a polar opposite to Laura. Where Alike finds in the brash yet tender Laura a confidant with whom she can seek out girlfriends at clubs, and even entrusts her to procure a strap-on dildo, she is initially resistant to any shared interests that could cultivate a friendship with Bina. As she expresses her teen angst in compelling poetry, Alike reveals an inner artist longing for a kindred spirit, such as she surprisingly begins to find in Bina, who divulges through a kiss that she, too, likes girls.

Alike is a bright student with turmoil surrounding her at home, as her mother pressures her to be more feminine and forbids Laura's presence, and her more suspicious father will not fully support her. Alike's younger sister seems to be comfortable with her sibling's sexuality, but does not have the familial stature to provide endorsement. Then, setting off a series of greater woes, Bina sweetly seduces Alike only to immediately thereafter reject her, leaving her miserable and returning to Laura for succor. Her mother, forcing the issue, reacts to Alike's confession that she is a lesbian with a battering outburst, followed by further banishing of her daughter that appears permanent. Through her deeply affecting response to these events, Alike manages to reveal more than aching for acceptance as a lesbian, she unearths an unknown complexity to her character that she had previously feared and now liberates, as conveyed though a poem that closes, "I am not broken, I am free." And as Mary Pols concludes, "When Alike finally confronts what it means to be an outcast, she finds other doors beyond those she's always known, and the courage to walk through them."[63]

The progress that has been made in depicting queer youth in diverse and realistic ways is perhaps the most promising development in youth cinema since the turn of the century. Dominant American culture has been coming to terms with nonheterosexual people, and a film like *Pariah* demonstrates that conservative and regressive treatment of queerness is far more destructive than reparative. Further, recent films about queer youth, such as the widely praised *The Perks of Being a Wallflower* (2012), exemplify wholesome means by which heterosexual youth have integrated with and come to appreciate peers with other gender identities, a model of understanding and tolerance for youth in terms of all differences.

This ad campaign for Pariah *(2011) celebrates the performance of Adepero Oduye with no reference to her character being a lesbian teenager.*

PREGNANCY

Considering the relative frequency with which teenage pregnancies have occurred in reality, in youth films teen pregnancies have been rather intermittent. In films before the legalization of abortion in 1973, almost all "illegitimate" pregnancies resulted in the mother giving birth to the child, sometimes leaving the child for adoption as in the Oscar-winning *To Each His Own* (1946).[64] In another 1946 film, *That Brennan Girl*, a pregnant teenager widowed by the war has a baby but quickly reveals her difficulty raising the child on her own. Forty years later, even with the right to abortion, even after the advent of safe sex programs, even in the face of puritanical efforts to promote abstinence-only education in schools, teenage girls in movies were still having babies and enduring the difficulty of raising them. As recently as 2011, a study concluded, "Teen-centered films, as a source for sexual socialization, are relatively impoverished when it comes to responsible messages dealing with abstinence, safe sex practices, and the health risks associated with sex."[65]

Teenage pregnancies in movies remained scarce until postwar fears of juveniles brought the topic back to the screen in exploitation fare like *The Violent Years* (1956), in which a girl becomes pregnant from raping a man. Much more famously, teen starlet Sandra Dee played a girl who becomes pregnant in the slightly scandalous *A Summer Place* in 1959, although a less visible film from that year did address the possibility of abortion for its pregnant protagonist. In *Blue Denim* (1959), after a girl becomes pregnant from her boyfriend, he valiantly raises the money for her to have an abortion, and only minutes before the dreaded clandestine event — about to be performed illegally by a doctor with dubious morals — she is saved by both the boy's father and her own. At the end of the film, because her family cannot bear the shame, and implicitly believe she should bear the punishment, the girl is sent away to have the child in secrecy, and against his parents' warnings that he is throwing his life away, the boy goes after the girl so that they may sustain a family of their own and perhaps live happily ever after.

Films continued to feature more pregnant girls as second-wave feminism promoted equal rights for women and the Supreme Court moved closer to the landmark *Roe v. Wade* case in 1973. Some examples continued to reach for social commentary as in *Susan Slade* (1961), *Billy Jack* (1971), *The Carey Treatment* (1972), and *Our Time* (1974), with the latter two portraying tragic abortions for teenagers. Other films rose little higher than the grind house with *Teenage Mother* (1967), *The Hard Road* (1970), and *To Find a Man* (1972), which purported to make teenage abortion a comical matter.

One minor 1980 film, *Seed of Innocence*, did depict a teenage couple having a child, as did the far more conspicuous nineteenth-century story *The Blue Lagoon* that same year. For some time thereafter, contemporary characters who became pregnant went to clinics for legal, safe abortions. Even in two films set before the national legalization of abortion, girls went through with the procedure: *Racing with the Moon* (1984), with characters during WWII whose concerns are more financial than moral or medical, and *Dirty Dancing* (1987), set in 1963, with a minor character whose abortion is medically dangerous and morally impactful for the protagonists. Emotional and ethical issues were often raised by these situations, but the availability of abortion, and more so its discretion, kept the pregnant characters from facing the longer-term consequences of going to term and having a child. This was the case in films such as *The Last American Virgin, Fast Times at Ridgemont High* (both 1982), and *Teachers* (1984).[66] Yet these depictions persisted only until the mid-'80s; by the late '80s, with abortion becoming an ever more controversial topic, and publicized scandals involving teen pregnancies and risky adoptive parenting, the few films that did depict teen pregnancy showed their characters having the child (as with a married teen couple in *Parenthood*, and even the monstrous titular offspring in *A Nightmare on Elm Street 5: The Dream Child*, both 1989). In the teen pregnancy films of the '90s, most of the characters decide to have their babies, and in some cases raise them on their own despite a lack of income. This change in images of teen pregnancy corresponded with the conservative influence on American films after the more sexually liberal era of the early '80s.

In *Fast Times*, the narrative tone of Stacy's predicament is not condemning or condescending, but her relatively uneventful abortion is perhaps a bit too emotionally casual: she's more upset that Mike fails to help her than that she's aborting a child after only two sexual contacts. The abortion is depicted somewhat positively, at least in as much as Stacy has the procedure done at a legal clinic, suffers no apparent pain, and is happier for having it done. In *Last American Virgin*, Gary seizes on Karen's need for an abortion as an opportunity to declare his love for her, even though he is not the father. Gary is effectively trying to show Karen that he can be caring and affectionate through accommodating her in her time of crisis, only she returns to her despicable boyfriend at the end, leaving Gary as a mere tool for her to help endure the abortion. Gary's lack of having sex makes his realization indeed more pathetic, and the film thus shows abortion in a strikingly cavalier light. The matter is taken somewhat more seriously in *Teachers* when student Diane (Laura Dern) becomes pregnant from an unscrupulous gym teacher. Another teacher's role in helping Diane have an abortion—he takes her to a clinic and keeps the secret about his colleague—is then questioned from the perspective of how much a teacher should assist a student in her personal life. The issue of whether Diane should have the baby is not raised, nor is her moral culpability in maintaining the dalliance that led to her pregnancy.

By 1988, *"For Keeps"* presented an entirely different image of teenage pregnancy. Darcy (Molly Ringwald) and Stan (Randall Batinkoff) are high school sweethearts just beginning to have sex.[67] Darcy has ambitions to become a newspaper editor and Stan is gunning for a scholarship to Caltech, but their futures are thrown in jeopardy when Darcy realizes she's pregnant. When their parents find out, Darcy's single mother pushes her to have an abortion while Stan's parents insist that she have the baby and put it up for adoption, shutting out Darcy and Stan's eventual plan of having the child. The tone of the film is decidedly comic, at least at first: the parents are portrayed as bumbling and detached from their children's own interests, much like those in John Hughes's films, and most of the tension between the families is portrayed satirically. What Darcy and Stan begin to realize is that they have acquired a certain autonomy in making their decision to keep the baby, and they move into a squalid apartment, determined to raise their daughter and show their parents that they can subsist on their meager income. The film thereby plays to a middle-class mythology for youth, who resist their parents' humble privilege to stake out their own.

One of the most captivating aspects of Darcy and Stan's relationship is how nonsexual they are: their sixth and last sexual experience results in the pregnancy, as if to demonstrate that pregnancy is possible with minimal effort and while on birth control (Darcy was on the pill). Darcy doesn't even see Stan naked until after they're living together, an improbable scenario perhaps meant to demonstrate their previous innocence; as Janet Hawken claimed, "The lack of sex—or rather sex within a once-in-a-lifetime monogamous relationship—is another lesson for post-AIDS youth."[68] Ironically, the moment that Darcy does see Stan naked, he proposes to her—as if they had never considered marriage an option before—and they run off to an ersatz ceremony at a strange chapel. Darcy is forthright about this upheaval in her life, later pondering about her delivery, "I felt like when she was being ripped out from inside of me that everything I loved about being young was being ripped out at the same time." The rest of the film portrays the problems with having and raising a child as teenagers: the couple is constantly struggling for money, Darcy is forced to drop out of school and becomes depressed, Stan begins to drink and almost has an affair. Stan is otherwise a remarkably well-adjusted young father, caring for the baby while Darcy is postpartum, and rejecting an imperative scholarship so that they can stay together. Darcy, however, realizes that their youthful dreams are being destroyed, and fakes a fight with Stan to demand a "divorce" (their marriage wasn't legal) and convince him to go to Caltech.

By this point the film has presented Darcy as the more irresponsible of the two, until her sacrificial gesture of turning away Stan reveals her apparent pragmatic altruism: she plans to live with her mother and get a job so that at least Stan can have the future he wanted. However, the film sells out its own foreboding of teen parenting with a saccharine happy ending in which Stan secures scholarships for both of them to attend college locally and Darcy accepts his proposal to get married again, this time for real. For all of its demonstrations of the difficulties of pregnancy and raising children, *"For Keeps"* preserves the romantic ideal of love conquering all obstacles, holding out to youth the very fantasy that many believe is possible under such daunting circumstances. Roger Ebert wryly noted that the movie lacks "a notice at the end advising teenagers that for every young couple like this one, there are a thousand broken hearts."[69] This is because the film is a conservative recuperation of nuclear family values and tradition for two young people who temporarily threaten to have a premature family outside of legal wedlock and almost break up that family for their own interests, sustained by a deceptive vision of personal and parental success.

Immediate Family (1989) presents a teenage girl's pregnancy from a deliberately adult point of view (it has a blatant "ripped-from-the-headlines" feel to it, given the similar "Baby M" controversy of the previous year). Linda (Glenn Close) and Michael (James Woods) are a well-off thirtysomething couple who cannot have children, so they enter into an open adoption with impoverished young Lucy (Mary Stuart Masterson), who has a relatively loyal boyfriend in Sam (Kevin Dillon). The open adoption procedure means that the married couple gets to know the mother of their child and support her through the pregnancy, which makes for a fragile bonding at first that becomes all the more painful when Lucy decides to keep her baby. Like *"For Keeps,"* this film shows teenage parenting to be arduous and symptomatic of a white trash destiny, but it does not alleviate that condition with a happy ending for the teen. Rather, the happy ending is shifted to the older couple: after trying to raise the child with Sam and running into expected financial difficulties, Lucy emotionally returns the baby to Linda and Michael, saying she's not ready to be a mom. Then, over an essentially upbeat montage, the baby grows up healthy and happy as Lucy receives updates from Linda and Michael; she is now attending beauty school and still seeing Sam, with no apparent plans for marriage or children.

As Margaret Tally points out in her study, young women with low-income backgrounds are more likely to carry a baby to term if they get pregnant, which is relevant to many youth pregnancy stories.[70] The two teens in *Immediate Family* are not portrayed unsympathetically, although an unmistakable class critique is implicit in the narrative's resolution: Lucy and Sam are simply not wealthy enough to raise a child like Linda and Michael can, even though the "adults" seem so remote and superficial compared to the spirited and tough teens. Lucy's admission of being unprepared to raise a child is honest, and appears to be based as much on her lack of money as on her need for more maturity to handle such a responsibility. This seems to be a responsible message itself, yet the film simply inverts the reactionary perspective of *"For Keeps"* so that family values are sustained in the older characters, becoming a corrective of the "Baby M" case in which the infertile parents were required to give their adopted child to its real mother. Within the context of working-class struggle and inferiority that the film presents, its message is "that in spite of biology, certain people should have children and others (the lumpen) shouldn't," as David Edelstein argues.[71] The younger characters in this case are able to abandon the seriousness of their decision to keep the baby by getting rid of it after a trial basis, thereby commodifying the child—a notion made explicit in the adoption selection process—and depicting the teens as conscious of the liability that a child represents and shirking away from it accordingly.

An increasing number of '90s films featured teen pregnancies, including *Return to the Blue Lagoon* (1991), the doomed sequel about a couple rejecting civilization to raise their baby in the wild, and *That Night* (1992), set in the '60s with a protagonist relegated to a common practice of the day, having her child in a maternity hospital for unwed mothers. *Trust* (1991) was then the first youth film in six years to feature a teenager having an abortion, and has remained one of the last to actually depict the character preparing for the procedure. After careful thought about her future with a brooding new boyfriend who isn't the father of the child, Maria's decision to abort does not come easily, especially with the pro-life protesters outside the clinic chanting epithets—nowhere to be seen in '80s films—a scene that was only becoming more prominent in real life at the time. Yet foreseeing the hardships ahead, Maria has the abortion on her own rather than taking Matthew's offer of marriage, thus preserving her freedom. A further political statement in the film is the hardened but caring nurse who works at the clinic and consoles Maria. In a touching moment, Maria describes to the nurse how she thinks her impregnating estranged ex-boyfriend saw her during the act of sex, as collective body parts for his sexual pleasure, dejectedly summing up the considerably different consequences of pregnancy for girls than boys.

Gas, Food Lodging (1992) also features a pregnant teenager abandoned by her lover, only Trudi (Ione Skye) has the child. In somewhat similar fashion to past tradition, she drops out of school and goes away from home to give birth, yet ultimately gives the child up for adoption. An altogether different scenario plays out in *Just Another Girl on the I.R.T.* (1993) with Chantel

(Ariyan Johnson), a street tough, academically smart Brooklyn eleventh grader filled with racial pride. The film follows her through what could have been another uneventful high school year, until she becomes pregnant from her boyfriend. For all of Chantel's ambition and intelligence, she cannot decide what to do about her pregnancy. At first her boyfriend offers her money for an abortion, which is eventually ruled out as an option after she hesitates for too long. She then tries to ignore and hide her condition by dressing in baggy clothes. When she finally does give birth at her boyfriend's apartment, the film shows her labor pain with graphic intensity, made all the more unsettling by her decision to abandon the newborn immediately thereafter.[72] However, her boyfriend, who was preparing to leave the infant in a curbside garbage bag, is struck by his conscience and saves the child, encouraging Chantel to help raise the baby properly with his help. In the last scene, she declares her plans to be a good mother while she pursues her career goals. Like so many other rebellious teens, Chantel has the requisite issues with authority that empower her resistance to conformity, and thus her new role seems to come to her naturally. Jami Bernard found a deeper political parallel in this role: "Chantel is smart, quick, opinionated, and can mow down the competition with her big mouth. But on the subway, and outside her own insulated world, she is perceived by the rest of society as either invisible or a nuisance—just as black women have been depicted for the most part in all movies, including those made by black men."[73]

Indeed, since this African American female rebel personification was essentially unique in youth films to that time, one can easily apply pressure to the film's less-than-positive message about its protagonist. But the question of why such an otherwise aware and assertive girl would become so desperate as to commit infanticide demands closer consideration, if only because the film *is* calling attention to the difference between the academic and social struggles of high school and the more ambiguous and consequential struggles of adult life, which Chantel is not set to accept. Chantel is in her insular element mouthing back to her teachers and talking trash with her girlfriends, but no teenager, regardless of race, is ready to handle the independence and responsibilities of parenthood—or so the film initially seems to stress. With its ending, *Just Another Girl* then implies that while the transition to adulthood is tough, one simply has to live up to it, and thus Chantel, as David Denby observed, "manages to triumph without losing or learning anything."[74] The narrative contrasts Chantel's strong will and rebelliousness with her overwhelming confusion and lack of moral direction brought on by the pregnancy, and while rationality prevails, the film paints an ultimately questionable portrait of the very desperation that many real youth face in the same situation (as witnessed by a number of real-life news stories of teens killing their newborns), for which there is no clear resolution.

Manny & Lo (1996) offers a quite unconventional teen pregnancy tale. Sixteen-year-old Lo (Aleksa Palladino) and her younger sister Manny (Scarlett Johansson) are on the run from their different foster parents so they can be together, when one day Lo, who has occasional unprotected sex with boys she meets on the road, discovers that she's pregnant. Lo is refused by an abortion clinic after she has carried the pregnancy for too long, so she and Manny stumble on the idea of kidnapping a knowledge-able maternity store worker, Elaine (Mary Kay Place), who happens to be shielding some secrets of her own. The girls take Elaine to a mountain cabin they've invaded and slowly reveal to her their expectation of having her help deliver Lo's baby. At first Elaine is indignant toward the girls, but after she realizes Lo's needs she agrees to help, providing Elaine with a complex maternal role—to Lo, her unborn baby, and the mother-longing Manny—which had been denied her earlier in life when she found she was unable to have children herself.

Elaine's devotion to the girls then becomes unexpectedly maniacal: when the cabin's owner returns, Elaine secretly ties him up in a barn so as not to ruin the fulfillment of her new identity. Upon learning this, Lo be-comes suspicious of Elaine and abandons her, moving on with Manny until her labor sets in, whereupon Manny takes Lo back to Elaine, who remains not far from where they left her, waiting and willing to deliver Lo's baby. During the preceding confrontation, Lo challenges Manny about whether she wants to stay with Elaine, pointing out her noticeable affection for her, but the younger sister stays with her blood. This gesture of family preser-vation is then given further emphasis at the end, with Elaine apparently staying with the two girls after Lo's delivery, as if she will carry on her af-firming familial matriarchy. Lo's reluctance to deal with her pregnancy is indicative of her need to keep moving, and given their fugitive status, Lo's mobility and already parental care of Manny preclude her from being able to raise a child. Yet Manny's less nervous wisdom prevails, for both girls' greatest need is for just such a family arrangement that Elaine and a new child offer. The ending suggests that the characters' lives have been difficult enough on their own, and will be better if they stay together.

Gas, Food Lodging, Just Another Girl, and *Manny & Lo* were made by women, as were the rather obscure *Bellyfruit* (1999) and the mildly notable *Polish Wedding* (1998), about a pregnant girl whose imminent fate is predictable from the title. Perhaps these female filmmakers by the '90s had wanted to depict their protagonists' predicaments as more enduring than a conclusive abortion, since each girl faces a life of struggle ahead, yet they are determined to persevere like most teen mothers in other films.[75] Kelly Oliver speculates that "*Manny & Lo* may have started the turn in Hollywood to viewing teenage pregnancy as cute and funny," and goes on to claim, "Teenage pregnancy looks cool in films like *The Opposite of Sex* (1998)," wherein the wandering Dedee (Christina Ricci) decides to have her baby and give it to her gay brother and partner so that she can still work out the issues of her complicated life.[76] The same coolness could be seen in *Where the Heart Is* (2000), when the abandoned Novalee (Natalie Portman) finds a supportive community of eccentric characters to help her raise her child after she notoriously gives birth in a store, one of whom she eventually does marry. These depictions give their young women a noble sense of strength, achieved after overcoming their troubling pregnancies, and change the image of teenage pregnancy itself from degrading to potentially empowering. The assumed misfortune of being a teen mother, married or not, is alleviated with the intention of celebrating independent female capability and solidarity. Sarah Hentges sees positivity in these depictions as well: "The characters don't get abortions not because of politics, but because pregnancy allows these films to explore the complications and tribulations that accompany childbirth, and, more generally, coming of age. These celluloid girls' solutions may not work in real life, but they are still valid commentaries on a real problem; and they are solutions that don't undermine, expose, or attempt to define and confine the girl."[77]

This potent perspective would carry on in most of the succeeding productions about pregnant girls, with abortion remaining increasingly scandalous, even in *The Cider House Rules* (1999), with its teenage boy who learns how to deliver babies but refuses to terminate pregnancies. More than twice as many films appeared in this category in the '00s compared to the '90s. Some stories were sobering without being didactic: *Our Song* (2000) became the first significant film in seven years to deal with a pregnant African American teen; *On the Outs* (2004) portrays a girl pregnant from a much older drug dealer; and two period films, *Skipped Parts* (2000) and *Riding in Cars with Boys* (2001), each depict fifteen-year-olds having babies in the mid-'60s, the latter rendering an anomalous embellishment of the mother's endeavors to raise her child against formidable burdens. Other films were more extreme: *Sugar and Spice* (2001) features a cheerleader squad robbing a supermarket bank to support their captain's forthcoming twins; *American Girl* (2002) leaves vague whether a girl's overdose on children's vitamins is a suicide attempt or an intended abortion; *Palindromes* (2004) is an audaciously failed attempt at social commentary with a girl who intentionally gets pregnant and is then forced to have an abortion that results in a hysterectomy; and the supporting roles of pregnant teens in *Crossroads* (2002) and *How to Deal* (2003) are squashed by the presence of their pop star protagonists, respectively Britney Spears and Mandy Moore.[78] Oddly, stories with girls supposedly impregnated by immaculate means became a small trend with *Virgin* (2003), *Absent Father* (2008), and *Electrick Children* (2012). Spiritual matters of pregnancy and birth were also germane to the pleasing film *Saved!* (2004), in which a Christian schoolgirl becomes pregnant after a failed effort to convince her boyfriend that he is not gay. The narrative's sweeping exploration of serious religious issues is rare within teen cinema, as it compassionately yet humorously critiques certain conservative tenets—the repression of sexual desire, the condemnation of homosexuality, the promotion of separation between faiths—while skirting the abortion issue when the protagonist's motherhood is a *fait accompli*. And by the time her baby is born, she has assembled a diverse group of allies to help her with child rearing, whereupon the film abruptly ends like so many teenage pregnancy films, with no depiction of the labors that still lie ahead.

By the second half of the '00s, pregnancy had become a veritable staple of youth cinema as the condition of minor characters or the subject of minor plot points in *Coach Carter* (2005—where a pregnant girl can only mention "taking care of it" to refer to abortion), *Black Irish* (2007), *Mother and Child*, *What Goes Up*, *17 Again* (all 2009), *The Last Exorcism* (2010), and *On the Ice* (2011), and while not a topic throughout each film in *The Twilight Saga* (2008–2012), *Breaking Dawn—Part 1* (2011) did primarily focus on the protagonist's supernatural gravidity.[79] Youth films focusing on the subject were nonetheless met with mixed results, as with *Stephanie Daley* (2006), which drew minimal box office attention despite its star cast and extraordinary legal mystery about a girl accused of intentionally terminating her pregnancy. The exact opposite was the case with the modest film *Juno* (2007), whose plucky and pregnant title character brought Ellen Page an Oscar nomination and whose idiosyncratic story led to blockbuster success, leading Ty Burr to observe that the film had certified a "peculiar minigenre, the coming-to-term pregnancy comedy."[80]

Juno discovers she is pregnant in the opening scenes, and a quick flashback reveals the father is Paulie Bleeker (Michael Cera), who is always called by his last name, and whose delicate timidity clashes considerably with the sangfroid of his brashly assured sixteen-year-old gal pal. Bleeker

The pregnant title character of Juno *(2007), played by Ellen Page, invites the father of her child, Paulie Bleeker (Michael Cera), to touch her belly, with their bemused expressions betraying their efforts to assuage their situation.*

is surprised that her singular seduction of him occasioned her pregnancy, though he supports her choice to have an abortion, after she irreverently explains, "I was thinking I'd just nip it in the bud before it gets worse. Because they were talking about in health class how pregnancy . . . can often lead to an infant." That tenacity then collapses readily once she is confronted by a lone classmate pitiably protesting at the abortion clinic, which Andrew Sarris coldly called "a last-minute change of heart brought on by the emotional reality of a new life entering the universe."[81]

The narrative moves even faster to Juno's next decision, to give up the baby for adoption to a young infertile couple she saw advertising for a donor in a local paper, and she defies their assumption that she wants an open adoption by insisting she does not want to know the child. An almost immediate tension ensues between Juno and the couple, since she and the husband spend time together bonding over their shared music interests while the wife becomes increasingly nervous about the deal working out. This tension at once signals the husband's lack of enthusiasm for becoming a parent as it demonstrates Juno's lack of recognition for the fragility of their situation, which she conveys through much of the film with her flippant attitude and mordant repartee, telling the couple, "I am giving you the gift of life, screaming, pooping life, and you don't even have to be there when it comes out all covered in blood and guts." Juno also keeps herself deliberately detached from Bleeker as her affection for him becomes evident. Circumstances grow direr when the married couple acquiesce to divorce, although Juno is confident enough to maintain her agreement with the wife, and after a relatively ordinary delivery she gives birth to a baby boy that she and Bleeker refuse to see, keeping their childish nescience intact. In a tentative yet tender coda, she ruminates over how she fell in love with Bleeker after becoming pregnant with his spawn, attesting to her happy abnormality.

Another positive pregnancy chronicle is *Expecting Mary* (2010), in which the sixteen-year-old title character leaves home after her wealthy mother glibly expects her to have an abortion. She embarks on a runaway odyssey to find her father, who is equally inimical, and meets many quirky characters along the way who eventually inspire her to have her baby and give it up for adoption to a couple who suffered a sterilizing miscarriage. The gripping *South Dakota* (2013) also assesses the decision-making process of two pregnant protagonists, one of whom has been raped. This crime becomes a more problematic case in *Precious* (2009), definitely one of the most harrowing teen tragedies ever depicted in American cinema.

The story of Precious (Gabourey Sidibe) unfolds through spasmodic memories of the unspeakable abuse she has suffered at the hands of her mother and father since childhood. Her mother has allowed her father to rape her continually through those years, resulting in a previous child before her current confinement, and further adding to the welfare checks that come in. Precious is also sixteen, overweight, poor, African American, and illiterate, floating through a high school that cares little about her education, and denied access to her first child with Down syndrome, who now lives with a disconnected grandmother. Precious somehow survives with quiet dignity against the obviously enormous strain of her home life, compounded by her mother's cruel assaults on her, but the chance to attend an alternative school begins to give her potential for change. At one point she tells herself, "I'm gonna break through or somebody gonna break through to me," and both breakthroughs begin to happen when her firm yet understanding teacher works to improve her literacy, and even takes on temporary guardianship after Precious has her baby and finally escapes the murderous clutches of her mother.

Given the concern the narrative invests in promoting new opportunities for Precious—her toxic memories are countered with rich fantasies, and she begins making friends in her new school—her pregnancy is in many ways downgraded to just another symptom of her hopeless life. And as if those symptoms were not plentiful, Precious learns she is HIV-positive. Yet her spirit slowly emerges through her determination to keep her second child and regain her first, as she excels at school and finds more effective helpers in the social service system. In an utterly devastating climax, her mother tries to explain to a case worker why she vouchsafed her husband raping Precious since the age of three, then began sexually molesting her daughter herself, and because there can be no explanation, Precious finally rejects her mother altogether and walks away with her two children. Just as Precious has progressed through tests to verify her increasing knowledge, she now takes on the trial of raising two babies on her own—having overcome such an incredible amount of pain to endure it, having achieved the wisdom to know it is necessary, and having found enough resources to make it happen, that now this test feels manageable.

Some girls in this category at least appear to have an ongoing relationship that results in their unplanned pregnancy—as in *Immediate Family*, *Just Another Girl on the I.R.T.*, and *Coach Carter*—yet more often than not, pregnancies result from single and/or random encounters, as in *Gas, Food Lodging*, *Manny & Lo*, *Our Song*, *Riding in Cars with Boys*, *Palindromes*, *Saved!*, *Stephanie Daley*, *Juno*, *Expecting Mary*, *Breaking Dawn—Part 1*, *South Dakota*, and *The Greatest* (2009), in which a boy is killed almost immediately after he consummates his relationship with his girlfriend. These results not only indicate a lack of sensibility about birth control—which is rarely used by either partner—they goad the cynicism of young viewers who may rightly question whether so many girls in real life become pregnant from just one exchange. Of course, pregnancy is almost always a possible outcome of sex, but as with the excessive drama of several films about drugs and crime, youth may be resistant to believing these less probable consequences. And the fact that so many girls in these films are abandoned by the fathers of their children without any responsibility, and with no protest from the mother, misrepresents the legal obligations that even minors have for their offspring, further exaggerating a perception of boys as uninterested in their own progeny.

Just as we seldom see the intercourse that leads to pregnancies, films often neglect scenes of girls delivering their babies, and more often close the narrative within a very short time after birth, shirking elaboration on how girls move on with their decisions to give up their children for adoption (*Gas, Food Lodging, The Opposite of Sex, Juno, Expecting Mary*) or raise their children on their own (*Manny & Lo, How to Deal, Saved!, Precious*). This pattern not only dismisses the temporary yet significant pain of childbirth—and its potential medical complications—it allows stories of teenage pregnancy to persist within a vacuum that mutes the psychological, financial, and political magnitude of these girls' choices to give birth. With abortion so rarely considered as an option, much less often pursued, girls are customarily granted the fulfilling experience of maternity in these films while being relieved of its subsequent conditions. Those conditions can certainly be wonderful, even for children who have children, but only two films since 1980— *"For Keeps"* and *Riding in Cars with Boys*—have gone on to explore those conditions for their characters. Given how often the film industry promotes pregnant girls giving birth, their products purvey minimal support in providing models that illuminate how they may *live* with their children, for so many girls in these films and in real life continually face a need for support starting the moment they conceive.

CONCLUSION

Where youth in school films struggle for identity in their educational surroundings and delinquents do so through rebellion, youth in romance movies inevitably discover their identities through their pursuits of affection and pleasure. In love stories, youth strive to find the other who will make them significant, the other who will give them a sense of purpose and meaning, who will complete who they are. In sex stories, even when sex is disappointing and dull, youth seek affirmation of their desirability and fulfillment of their desires. In many cases, however, these goals go unfulfilled or are compromised.

The image of youth in films about sex in the '80s changed from melodramatic and carefree to serious and concerned, and also exposed an increasing vilification of young sexuality. The processes of falling in love and having sex became ever more complex under the specter of AIDS that persisted into the '90s (although to this day remarkably few youth films address any sexually transmitted diseases), and the general dominance of negative youth depictions in the '90s reflected social tensions around teen promiscuity and irresponsibility, not to mention hedonism.

At least by the '00s the subgenre had managed to engender some encouraging depictions of the often inexplicable erosphere of youth. Adolescents still struggle with their appearance and attractiveness, as more movies assure them that they can indeed manage to cope with the mysteries of sexual impulses and behavior. The subgenre has been successful at preserving some of the traditional rites of adolescence like falling in love, losing virginity, and going to prom, while carefully considering the more liberating potential of questioning sexual orientation altogether. As a form of entertainment, youth cinema has been paradoxically productive at teaching youth lessons in love and sex that they may not want to know, the highs *and* the lows, because the entire cycle of development that youth engage in—from curiosity to longing to practice to procreation—is not only vital to human survival, it is endlessly fascinating.

Six   C O N C L U S I O N

Youth Cinema into a New Century

There have been two primary goals of this study: to examine how the image of youth developed in American cinema since 1980, and to demonstrate that such an examination must be founded on an analysis of various generic conventions pertaining to films about youth. I will speak to this second aim first, because it has been more implicit.

One of my arguments that has been established from the start is that depictions of teenagers in cinema are characterized by and rely on certain generic elements, for many of the same reasons that all films are produced within certain generic traditions and styles. The generic identification of any movie makes it more marketable by the film industry and thus conditions a set of expectations in its audience, yielding a codified system of standards that producers, critics, and viewers employ in evaluating a film's quality. A film is commonly considered to be most appealing when it dynamically fulfills the codes of its genre, and perhaps more so, when it integrates past codes and introduces new ones, developing further genres and subgenres in an evolutionary cycle.

When a given social population is portrayed through existing and emerging genres, a consequential set of standards and expectations is developed over time by the film industry and the audience. The population in question is depicted as acting within an evident range of behaviors and having a limited number of concerns. In this way character paradigms are generated, easily identifiable figures who have an indexical—if not necessarily representative—connection to their real-life referents. Genres of human types can thereby be formed.

These character types are most fruitfully studied within an analysis of the generic styles of the films in which they appear. Because these types cross over and intertwine with more than one genre, yet retain a clear coherence within the genres in which they are portrayed, specific subgenres emerge, as do further categories within those subgenres. The generic traditions of horror that some youth films work under, for instance, are integrated with certain concerns and conventions of youth cinema as its own genre, producing a hybrid set of combinative plot elements, narrative motifs, and styles of representation that make the "youth horror film" a specific subgenre unto itself. Then, within that subgenre, further subgeneric categories of the horror film can be located, such as the slasher film and the supernatural film, and how youth are portrayed in relation to these styles is generally indicative of larger issues of youth representation.

Another case may better illustrate the point. Within youth delinquency films, a spectrum of delinquent styles is utilized, spanning a range of moral concerns and actual types of rebellion. Within each of these styles, which borrow from other generic traditions (such as the beach movie, musicals, family dramas, and crime stories), clear processes of representing youth are discernable in relation to that style's conventions. The dance-loving youth, for example, win respect by engaging everyone else in dancing; children who care for animals tend to find love and validation they could not find in people; tough girls struggle for an identity free from patriarchal and age-based discriminations. The diversity of delinquency in films about teenagers is not only indicative of the diverse motivations and means of delinquency of teenagers in reality, but it points to the many different identities of youth that are represented by these films.

Given that diversity, within the delinquency subgenre and others, the method of studying these films must necessarily be as inclusive as possible. This inclusiveness has been a major methodological campaign of my research. Many genre researchers select films in a hit-or-miss fashion, rendering their analysis arbitrary or assumptive. Thus I took the position that I would address as many films as were relevant within each youth subgenre, giving additional attention to films that merited it.

This procedure of course raised a new set of problems as it alleviated old ones. First and foremost, I could not see *all* of the films within each subgenre, because some were simply unavailable. In trying to make comprehensive claims about individual subgenres then, I found myself still relying on repeated assumptions, which I tried to resolve by at least reading about the films that I could not view. This aspect of the research was humbling, and exposed another dilemma in current film research—the lack of access to all texts. Rarely do contemporary literary scholars ever suffer to locate recent books or magazines, but many films continue to be difficult if not impossible to find, even in today's video/digital movie climate. I inevitably had to accept the limitations of access placed on me by available distribution sources, although I know that given time, many of the titles that

I have thus far been unable to locate may become available for viewing and incorporated into a future study. Partially as a consequence of these limitations, and more so as a symptom of personal bias, I also found myself inevitably giving more attention to the films that I enjoyed the most and found the most significant, which in many ways seems appropriate, but begs the question of how subjectively a film's "merit" is determined.

Another problem with my approach was that by trying to be so comprehensive, I initially developed an overambitious set of "rules" that I thought these films followed, which is a classic defect of much genre research. Despite the similarities of films within each subgenre, they were made by different studios under different conditions and over time, and are thus not as rule-bound as other phenomena of film history (such as the use of specialized equipment). Genre study is indeed an inexact science, regardless of how exact we scholars would like to make it. I have attempted to be as precise as possible while still appreciating that the codes and patterns I am studying are quite malleable and arguable. I have worked from the most informed foundation possible, both in terms of my knowledge of the films I have studied and my curiosities about the films I have not.

I believe that such a foundation is required for any serious genre study. The genre researcher must strive for maximum comprehensiveness while developing an analytically reliable understanding of the films in question. Research can still focus on particular aspects of a genre, such as its aesthetic style or plot development, but these aspects must be studied against as inclusive a background as possible—even when limits imposed by publishers prevent full discussion of all aspects and examples in all texts. This background is ideally achieved by studying the maximum number of films within that genre, and the social, industrial, and/or aesthetic conditions under which they were released. My subject has been the image of youth between the ages of twelve and twenty in American films released since 1980; in studying that subject I have incorporated an understanding of youth trends, public politics, and film industry operations during that same time. I do not feel that my study is nearly as far-reaching as it could be, but given my particular focus on the generic development of youth images, I feel that I have covered an optimal number of relevant examples and contextual issues.

This book further reveals the difficulty of doing social representation research within film studies. Mine is but one perspective on the vast array of films about youth, and I am no longer a member of the audience to whom these films are directed. I bring to my analysis a bundle of personal experiences that influence even my most rigidly objective readings (if indeed any reading can be objective). My tacit effort as a social image researcher has been to recognize and minimize the influences of my past that limit me from understanding social experiences that are not similar to my own. To assume that films can aid me in that goal is treacherous, because they are the already limited representations of an elite industry that is maintained by the dominant interests of culture. Finding a space in which to consider these films that is both subjectively reflective *and* socially responsive is thus remarkably difficult, yet again, by considering the widest range of examples against the most inclusive set of contextual issues does take us farther in producing an informed analysis. The truth will remain that regardless of how informed a social researcher is, the research will always be imbued with the problematics of her or his personal ideological positions.

In terms of studying youth, these problematics are especially crucial to remember. Essentially all academic researchers have passed their teenage years, and are no longer able to view themselves as part of the youth population. This factor is an advantage in terms of maintaining one's distance from the subject being studied, and presumably ensures a reliable amount of wisdom gained past the teen years. Yet, all too often, youth films are viewed and studied by adult critics in a condescending manner, toward their themes as well as their characters. Scholars like David Considine, Thomas Doherty, Jon Lewis, Stephen Tropiano, and Catherine Driscoll demonstrate that the youth film can be studied seriously within various legitimate academic frames without positioning youth—characters or viewers—as necessarily inferior subjects.

Youth films, as has been argued throughout this book, reveal an enormous amount about who we are, and despite their limitations, they are just as cinematically rich—in terms of aesthetics, politics, and social imaging—as the dominant cinema about adults. In fact, given their limitations, and the assumptions that are often made about them, American youth films since the 1980s have depicted a generally diverse and most often positive image of teenagers. In most cases, youth are portrayed as stoic, resilient, strong, inquisitive, hopeful, and/or creative. Consider how many different types of characters have been introduced in the various subgenres of youth cinema during this time, and the variety of themes that these characters have addressed. Virtually all real-life teen experiences are available in youth films, albeit some with much more prominence than others. The increasing roles for teenage girls and African Americans, while not without flaws, have been a progressive change over the white male dominance of teen films up through the 1980s.

All the same, many images and themes have yet to be covered, or covered adequately, in American youth cinema. Girls are still not represented with the same frequency as boys. The number of noncriminal roles for African American and Latino/a characters, while improving, remains shamefully small. Teenage plights with drugs, depression, divorce, and disability have received relatively little attention. Pregnancy, abortion, and parenting in youth films are far rarer than they are in real life. The incidence of sexually transmitted diseases among youth has been virtually ignored. The fact that more teens are entering college than ever before, and facing changing pressures accordingly, has barely been reflected in recent youth films. The wide involvement of youth in community and religious organizations could be honored more often, and beyond the handful of specifically Christian films geared to adolescents, youth rarely have political affiliations, even if they have clearly political ideas.

What has been covered in youth films since 1980, from a generic and representational perspective, is the following (appendix A provides a chronological filmography of youth films that relate to these trends):

Of the five basic school characters, the intellectual nerd is slowly gaining a higher degree of acceptance, the delinquent has become less visible, the rebel has more reasons to revolt, the popular student has become more vulnerable, and athletes are more sensitive. The nerd character remains subject to humiliation by his or her peers, yet most nerds in school films succeed in proclaiming a sense of self-identity and assurance that other characters do not, and gain their acceptance through proud perseverance. Delinquents in school films have gradually faded away since the turn of the century, while the films about them have pointed to an increasing array of social and educational sources for their misguided behavior. Likewise, rebels are more aware of their surroundings and the oppositions they face, and usually address ever more serious issues. Popular students, whom youth films have traditionally held in some contempt for their wide acceptance, have been shown struggling with many of the same identity issues as their less accepted counterparts. And athletes, while maintaining their prominence in real American high schools, have seen their screen image become one of greater sincerity and sympathy.

Within the delinquency subgenre, as with the delinquent school character, there are now more reasons for youth to rebel, and more means with which to do so. The most visible shift within this subgenre has been in its moral addresses toward its characters: many early to mid-'80s delinquency films made deviance look fun and ultimately harmless, but by the early '90s the dominant image of youth delinquency was the dangerous African American hoodlum, and in the later '90s delinquent roles incorporated both moral poles to neutralize the potency of youth rebellion accordingly, until the Columbine killings in 1999 made the industry all but abandon blatant images of delinquency altogether. The delinquency subgenre has offered the clearest developments in the depiction of female and minority youth, although naturally under typically negative terms.

The youth horror subgenre has continued fluctuating in popularity. The boom that buoyed slasher films in the early '80s lasted just a few years, while numerous supernatural films continued to be made. Many films in the subgenre continued to be very revealing of youth issues on a metaphorical level, pointing to shifts in concerns about sexuality, drug use, spirituality, and social oppression. The teenage characters in these films have become more authoritative and less victimized by the forces of evil they confront and the flights of fancy they pursue, to the point that a number of youth horror films by the '90s had become reflexive and revisionist, and by the '00s the dominant interest within the subgenre was fantasy more than fear.

Films about youth falling in love and having sex remain the most difficult to classify. During the early '80s, when the abundance of teen sex films reveled in the liberation of portraying the sexually adventurous teenager, young romance was the exception. But by the mid-'80s, after the sex stories had become so routine and social concerns over teen pregnancy, AIDS, and other sexually transmitted diseases rendered the teen "sex quest" film unpalatable, youth began finding love again. By the '90s, an increasing variety of teen romantic and sexual experiences were represented: interracial, homosexual, passionate, dysfunctional, dangerous, redemptive. The "threats" of young love and sex are as present as ever, but teens have been given more credit for handling their affairs, even to the point of having children more often, and '00s films implicitly offered far greater rewards (and punishments) for teens' amorous pursuits than the sex act itself.

Overall, American youth films since 1980 have depicted teenagers as an increasingly self-aware and insightful group, who are still learning much about life and who they are, yet who are usually doing so with energy and intelligence. This general positivity has not prevented a number of films from vilifying youth or making them appear irresponsible and stupid, yet these films are the exception. Most often, even within condemning films, at least one teenage character retains some sense of integrity or morality. An argument can be made that adult filmmakers are only producing such images of youth to appeal to young audiences who patronize the films, and that these images are based on the social realities and fantasies of most youth, or else the films would not find an audience. This argument helps to explain the decline of many styles of youth film, as with the slasher and sex quest films. Why other realistic conditions such as those listed above have yet to be depicted more often is based on a complicated series of reasons, ranging from simple conservatism on the part of the film industry to a potentially more sinister social concern that youth (or even adults) cannot handle seeing all of their realities incorporated into the entertainment of going to the movies. If this latter possibility is true, it speaks to the film industry's failure to give youth enough credit for handling a more complete range of narratives about themselves.

As stated in the introduction, a split image of youth has been presented in American films since the 1950s: good kids and bad kids. Youth films since the 1980s have questioned that traditional division and problematized the image of youth having inherent values. By giving youth more powers of self-identification, recent youth films have placed more responsibility on their protagonists to deal with their ascent through adolescence, an ascent that can take any number of directions en route to maturity. With the formation of the Generation X identity in the '90s, young people were told that the path to adulthood is longer and less secure than ever before, and that they must resist the temptation to "slack" lest they remain in a permanent state of adolescence. Most youth films of the millennial '00s further encouraged such resistance, albeit through often more metaphorical scenarios.

Any future study of the image of youth in cinema should continue to trace established and new subgeneric divisions and their developments, and should expand to an even more complete sampling of relevant films. Greater access to film texts through digital technology should allow for the inclusion of virtually all youth films, and will demand more extensive analysis than that which can be offered here. Contextualizing youth films within social and cultural conditions will continue to be vitally important to understanding how the images of youth are generated by cinema; and with the growing presence of youth on television, the Internet, and in music, future studies of youth representation will need to more often employ multimedial perspectives. Above all, a trusting support and sympathy for youth must be the foundation for studying their media representations, at least as long as they remain excluded from the systems that generate their representations. The access youth have to technology will not only change their senses of identity, but it should provide them with the means to take greater control over the production of their images, which will be a radical development indeed.

Meanwhile, we adults can do more for our children to become more critical consumers of texts. Young people need not be the mere *tabula rasae*

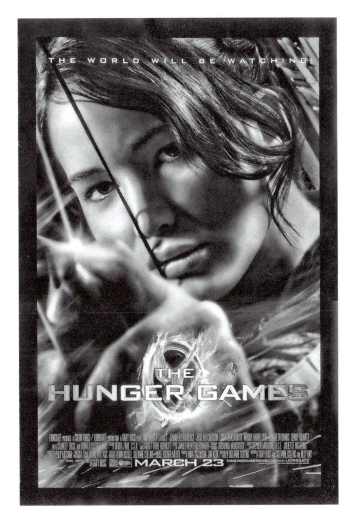

The Hunger Games *started as a trilogy in 2012 and is poised to become another successful American youth film franchise after* The Twilight Saga *(2008–2012). There will likely be many more.*

that conservative capitalism would prefer, ingesting information with little analysis. The increasingly expanding exposure to screen media that industry and even educators promote means that youth are eager to partake in—and purchase—massive amounts of narratives about their lives and culture, with an enthusiasm that shows no signs of receding, ever.[1] Yet youth also need to see a definite amount of attractive pleasure in challenging the media system and they need to be assured that they will become stronger as a result of their knowledge. If we are going to foster a true sense of media literacy for future generations, we need to use the media products that appeal to young people to question how they are being targeted and manipulated by these media. And above all, we need to empower young people themselves to comprehend the media in more critical ways and to make their use of media more informed and sophisticated.

This book has been an attempt to show how images of youth in American cinema at the turn of the millennium are evolving, and its main argument has been that adolescent depictions are becoming increasingly complex, dynamic, and revealing. My intention has been to direct greater attention to the study of youth as a social group in media, and to lend legitimacy to that endeavor by demonstrating how sophisticated are the ways that youth have been portrayed. As a global culture, we must be especially concerned with how we tell youth who they are, because their impressionability allows them to utilize a wide range of images that can induce them to both achieve greatness and falter in despair. With succeeding generations of young people becoming the adults of each tomorrow, the media that define them will be largely responsible for their roles in the world. We can just hope that media-making will continue to become an increasingly democratic and accessible process, and that those people who make and study future media will respect and *celebrate* all of the discoveries, anxieties, opportunities, pains, wonders, and joys of what it means to be young.

Catherine Driscoll

AFTERWORD

Imagine Becoming Someone

W hen I set out to research scholarship on teen film in 2010, I was drawing on more than a decade of teaching teen film across a range of courses—on popular culture, youth culture, girlhood, gender and media, genre studies, and cultural studies—and thus framed by ends that were never confined to describing the teen film genre. It was quickly clear to me that Timothy Shary was the standard film studies and genre studies authority when it came to describing the field of teen film and a core reference for understanding how teen film fits within American cultural history. It was just as clear to me that how Shary and I approached teen film was very different. Across three books and a number of related essays, his work provided me with the most comprehensive overview of what American teen film looks like to a U.S. expert on the subject. Of those books, *Generation Multiplex* was always the most comprehensive, and this revised edition adds to its already fulsome catalog of U.S. films about teenagers another decade's worth of examples. It has also updated Shary's account of the shifting dominant themes of mainstream U.S. teen film and I immediately see its value for my next groups of students. But how we approach the genre remains very different.

Shary and I are equally interested in the cultural context of teen film as a changing genre and in the cultural commentaries manifest in teen film. However, coming from outside both film studies as a field and genre theory as an approach, I am far less inclined to search for a descriptive taxonomy of teen films—even one that is, as in Shary's case, nuanced enough to encompass change. Moreover, coming from outside the United States, I was never likely to see "America" as the exclusive source for any account of the genre. There is much to be learned from such an excellent account of American cinematic images of youth, but viewing teen film from a perspective not confined to U.S. examples demands, I think, a different account of what establishes its popular recognizability. Coming instead from the field of cultural studies, and thus with a central focus on continuity between forms and practices of representation that link film to culture more broadly and understanding representation as producing as well as reflecting our sense of the world, for me teen film is one significant part of a field in which our ideas about adolescence (and thus citizenship, development, identity, sex, and so on) are made manifest. Although age is clearly very important to teen film, for me it is "adolescence" rather than age that lies at the center of teen film—not teenagers *per se* but the process of becoming a recognizable adult subject. Becoming *someone*. Finally, coming from Australia also means my sense of a teen film canon, and what its component texts can signify, both overlaps with and differs from Shary's. This is not only about what films should be included—though it's true I cannot imagine a teen film genre that excludes *Puberty Blues* (Australia, 1981), *Akira* (Japan, 1988), or *Bend It Like Beckham* (UK, 2002)—but also about what historical and cultural contexts we should situate them in and how international trade and transnational negotiations of ideas about adolescence should be factored into their analysis.

A more detailed account of the above points can be found in my book *Teen Film: A Critical Introduction*, and further context for them can be found in my more theoretically oriented earlier books on girls (*Girls: Feminine Adolescence in Popular Culture and Cultural Theory*), which includes some discussion of "teen" and "youth" film, and on modern "culture" (*Modernist Cultural Studies*), which considers the related modernity of both cinema and adolescence.[1] But in this context I want to focus instead on where Shary and I clearly agree. I can't be exhaustive about this but I want to consider three closely related and equally significant tendencies in teen film as a genre which also offer crucial opportunities for scholarship on teen film: cross-media dialog, transnational standardization of the idea of adolescence, and the continual renegotiation of gendered sexual development. These indicate for me some of the important interdisciplinary contributions being made by contemporary scholarship on teen film, including in this book.

It might be tempting to refer to the cross-media dialog characterizing teen film as "transmedia storytelling" or "cultural convergence," which are presently popular critical concepts for media and film analysis, but in fact I do not principally mean here the sale of particular commodities across different media forms, however important that has been to teen film, especially since the 1950s.[2] In his *Teenagers and Teenpics*, Thomas Doherty stressed the way teen film "exploited" a marketplace that it helped produce by cross-promoting film, music, and other media forms, and this aspect of the genre has certainly continued.[3] But as Shary's reference to the Internet in this edition suggests, teen film now far more dramatically speaks to and draws from other media forms, including not only music and fashion but also, for example, digital games and online platforms and practices. We shouldn't see this as a matter of technologically determined challenges to cinema, however, because the relationship between teen film and television or literature has also continued to change. Films like *Twilight* (2008) or *Pitch Perfect* (2012) certainly must now promote themselves through television ads and programming and online social networking sites, as well as typically also using radio spots, traditional movie posters, and dedicated websites. But they also must belong to a cross-media generic conversation. If *Twilight* is obviously adapted from fiction particularly successful with girls it also draws heavily on the success of series like *Buffy the Vampire Slayer* (1997–2003) and *Supernatural* (2005–), which led the way in redirecting fantasy television to young audiences; further, *Pitch Perfect* draws heavily on the success of the *High School Musical* films (2006–2008) and *Glee* (2009–) in resurrecting the genre of school song and dance.

The fact that *Pitch Perfect* and *Supernatural* would be excluded from Shary's taxonomy of "teen" texts because they deal with "college age" characters (the lead "boys" in *Supernatural* begin the series at age twenty-two and twenty-six) is worth noting here. While *High School Musical* specifically ends its film series with graduation, both the *Buffy* and *Glee* series trace their characters' ongoing dramas of identity formation and social placement into post–high school lives, and *Pitch Perfect* revamps the *Fame* (1980, 2009) and *Glee* standards for a college narrative that still includes expected high school elements like peer pressure, popularity contests, and parental expectations. These texts exemplify the way ideas about adolescence refined in teen film have bled out into other media and hybridized with other genres but then also fed back into texts centrally addressed to and about teenagers.

And this points to the second tendency I want to foreground here. Teen film centrally depends on a set of ideas about growing up, maturing, finding one's place in the world, or developing one's own unique identity (i.e., ideas about adolescence). While Shary and I differ on whether such plots and motifs circulating around non-teenage characters should be called "teen film," we both recognize the influence of the way such ideas about adolescence are shared by older (and younger) as well as teenage characters. We both also recognize that these are not exclusively American ideas. While his focus is on American texts (predominantly U.S. with some Canadian and British interlopers), Shary's lists of teen films include many that are produced across international borders, from *Harry Potter and the Sorcerer's Stone* (2001) to *Life of Pi* (2012), and many more that adapt non-American stories to American film, from *The Last American Virgin* (1982) to *10 Things I Hate About You* (1999), or otherwise seamlessly incorporate the adolescence of non-American youth or successfully communicate adolescent stories to non-American audiences. So how are such highly mobile ideas produced?

Researchers in film and cultural studies have been discussing how it is that some genres and films succeed internationally while others do not for a very long time. But for no genre do we have a clearer picture of the cultural affordances of and limits on such success than for teen film. My special area of interest in teen film at present is in its very close ties to the development and dissemination of media classification systems as a transnational dialogue about adolescence. While the same film text can be assigned to a range of different appropriate ages based on state-based cultural expectations, it is equally clear that the distribution of teen film, since the early twentieth century, has helped both communicate and form ideas about physical, psychological, and sexual development, about citizenship and cultural identity, about productive adult lives and desirable relations to social norms. While Shary's focus on the United States allows him to offer importantly specific cultural context, for example about school ages and institutional practices, an Indian story about the emergence of teen film in relation to citizenship norms, classification practices, and representations of education would be just as telling. The importance of adolescence on screen is apparent in many countries that had no dominant youth culture expressed through shopping mall multiplexes in the 1980s, and in every one a sense of the importance of guiding adolescence shapes cinema production through limits on film distribution tied to other ways of guiding adolescence. The cultural importance of teen film is manifest in the way it centrally explains the how, why, what, and who of institutions for guiding adolescence, to which media classification is no less important than the equally transnational concept of high school.

If the cross-media intertextual dialogue characterizing teen film on an international terrain has produced some very clear generic conventions clustering around a set of developmental tropes, the available media classification systems, and the censorship systems closely tied to them, stress the importance among them of gendered narratives about sex. This offers one timely example of the way teen film responds to and itself furthers cultural change. Few things seem more central than sexuality to the idea of adolescence at the heart of modern subjectivity, and teen film has played a particularly prominent role in communicating and developing an idea of adolescence as an identity crisis bound simultaneously to emerging sexuality and training in citizenship. The relations between sex, sexuality, and dominant cultural norms are once again a particularly significant theme in contemporary teen film. I say "once again" because it would be a major error not to notice that teen film's emphasis on sexuality comes to the foreground in waves. This prominence is tied this time around to international debates about the sexualization of childhood, and girlhood in particular, and to equally international debates and changes regarding the status of "gay marriage" and thus possible relations between adolescence and homosexuality.[4] Different cultural touchstones were involved when teen sexuality was a sensational danger in the late 1950s, as in *Blackboard Jungle* (1955), *Gidget* (1959), or *Where the Boys Are* (1960). And, as Shary indicates in this volume, different ones were involved when celebrating teen sexuality was a crucial generic component of teen film in the late 1970s and early 1980s, or when new, more prudential forms of sexuality came to the fore in the late 1980s and early 1990s. But of course we must avoid sweeping causal narratives about changes to teen film conventions, and so in closing I want to stress consistency once more. Despite the responsiveness of teen film to precise cultural conditions demanded by its place in a broader youth culture, the genre remains invested in and indeed important to defining modern adolescence.

In this volume Shary particularly emphasizes the way '90s U.S. teen films replied to and shifted the conventions of the '80s, and taking this as a starting point, twenty-first-century teen film can seem to represent adolescence—including adolescent sexuality—as highly uncertain, as no longer privileging the same recognizable narratives about young people's motivations. For Shary's analysis, which stresses that teen film can be ethical as well as entertaining—narratively satisfying in a moral sense—teen films fail to satisfy when rebellion does not have a sufficient cause and rebel characters fail to ethically engage their viewers. As I suggested above, there certainly are changes in the ethical framework of teen film—in, for example, how teen film maps acceptable and expected forms of sexuality for adolescents and for adults. But the morality of teen film has never been homogenous, and neither natural justice nor aesthetics much help us understand the very broad attraction of youthful rebellion and risk taking or the youthful pursuit of desirable self-production. We need to stress the material conditions—the simultaneously physical and discursive institutions—within which adolescence is experienced and which allow teen cinema to not only represent the close guidance of adolescents in practice, but also imagine escape from those limiting forces. In the challenges of popularity and of marginalization, in the quest for true love or the right sex, in the conflict between expectations of individual success and sufficient obedience, in the dynamic of both keeping up with constant change and finding a place in the world, and in proliferating fantasies of individual worth and questions about what really counts as mature or valuable, teen film is first and last an invitation to imagine becoming someone. A teen film is thus not only a story for or about teenagers, and therefore it is vitally important that at the end of any teen film the story has only just begun.

Appendix A FILMOGRAPHY OF YOUTH
FILMS, 1980–2013

The following films constitute the universe of American feature films about youth released (theatrically or straight-to-video) in the last thirty-plus years — at least all of those that I was able to verify and evaluate for inclusion in this study. Films that were not part of the analysis: documentaries, made-for-TV movies, animation, and pornography intended for the adult market. Notice that some films from the first edition have been eliminated due to closer evaluation, some have been added through further research, and some have been relocated to other years by corroborating release dates.

The criteria for inclusion are: (1) feature films made and released in the United States starting in 1980 and partially into 2013, which (2) significantly portray at least one character between the ages of twelve and twenty, and (3) are supportable with viable external reviews. Films about college-aged characters are not included unless they distinctly feature teenagers.

1980

Alien Dead
The Apple
The Blue Lagoon
Carny
Cutting Loose
Fade to Black
Fame
Foxes
Friday the 13th
The Great Santini
Happy Birthday, Gemini
The Hollywood Knights

The Idolmaker
Little Darlings
Mother's Day
My Bodyguard
Ordinary People
Out of the Blue
Seed of Innocence
Times Square
To All a Good Night
Up the Academy
The Watcher in the Woods

1981

Blood Beach
The Burning
Carbon Copy
Choices
The Chosen
The Dark End of the Street
Endless Love
Eyes of a Stranger
Fear No Evil
Four Friends
Friday the 13th Part 2

The Funhouse
Graduation Day
Halloween II
Hollywood High Part II
Longshot
Only When I Laugh
Private Lessons
Rivals
Student Bodies
Taps
Wacko

1982

Abuse
Beach House
The Beast Within
Class of 1984
The Escape Artist
E.T. The Extra-Terrestrial
Fast Times at Ridgemont High
Forty Deuce
Friday the 13th Part 3
Full Moon High
Goin' All the Way!
Grease 2
Homework

Honkytonk Man
I Ought to Be in Pictures
Ladies and Gentlemen, The Fabulous Stains
The Last American Virgin
Liar's Moon
Madman
Midnight
Night Warning
Slumber Party Massacre
Tex
The Vals
Zapped!

1983

All the Right Moves
Angelo My Love
Baby It's You
Bad Boys
Boogeyman 2
Christine
Class
The First Turn On!
Getting It On

I Am the Cheese
Joysticks
The Lords of Discipline
Losin' It
The Loveless
Max Dugan Returns
My Tutor
The Outsiders
Private School

Risky Business
Rumble Fish
Scarred
Sleepaway Camp

Sweet 16
Valley Girl
WarGames
Wild Style

1984

Alphabet City
American Taboo
Angel
Beat Street
Birdy
Blame It on the Night
Blame It on Rio
Blood Theater
Children of the Corn
City Limits
Delivery Boys
Desperate Teenage Lovedolls
Fatal Games
First Born
The Flamingo Kid
Footloose
Friday the 13th: The Final Chapter
Gimme an F!
Going Back
Grandview, U.S.A.
Gremlins
Hadley's Rebellion
Hollywood Hot Tubs
Hot Dog . . . The Movie
Hot Moves
Joy of Sex
The Karate Kid
Kidco

The Last Starfighter
Lovelines
Making the Grade
Meatballs Part II
Nickel Mountain
Night of the Comet
A Nightmare on Elm Street
No Small Affair
Old Enough
The Power
The Prey
Racing with the Moon
Reckless
Red Dawn
Repo Man
Running Hot
Savage Streets
Sixteen Candles
Snowballing
The Stone Boy
Stranger Than Paradise
Suburbia
Surf II
Teachers
Voyage of the Rock Aliens
Where the Boys Are '84
The Wild Life

1985

Back to the Future
The Beniker Gang
Better Off Dead

The Boys Next Door
The Breakfast Club
Cave Girl

Evils of the Night

Explorers

Fast Forward

Friday the 13th Part V: A New Beginning

Fright Night

Girls Just Want to Have Fun

The Goonies

Hard Choices

Heaven Help Us

The Heavenly Kid

Hot Chili

Hot Resort

I Was a Teenage TV Terrorist

The Journey of Natty Gann

Just One of the Guys

The Legend of Billie Jean

Mask

Mischief

The Mutilator

My Science Project

The New Kids

A Nightmare on Elm Street Part 2:
    Freddy's Revenge

Once Bitten

Out of Control

Paradise Motel

Pink Nights

Private Resort

Radioactive Dreams

Real Genius

Return of the Living Dead

Screen Test

Secret Admirer

Seven Minutes in Heaven

Silver Bullet

Smooth Talk

Sylvester

Teen Wolf

That Was Then, This Is Now

Tomboy

Tuff Turf

Vision Quest

Weird Science

Young Sherlock Holmes

The Zoo Gang

1986

The Abomination

At Close Range

Bad Girls Dormitory

The Big Bet

Blue Velvet

Born American

Brighton Beach Memoirs

Chopping Mall

The Class of Nuke 'Em High

Critters

Dangerously Close

Deadly Friend

Desert Bloom

Ferris Bueller's Day Off

Fire with Fire

Flight of the Navigator

Free Ride

Jason Lives: Friday the 13th Part VI

Hoosiers

Iron Eagle

The Karate Kid Part II

Labyrinth

Lucas

The Manhattan Project

The Mosquito Coast

Neon Maniacs

One Crazy Summer

One More Saturday Night

Out of Bounds

Peggy Sue Got Married

Platoon

Playing for Keeps

Pretty in Pink
Rad
Reform School Girls
Revenge of the Teenage Vixens
     from Outer Space
Running Mates
Slaughter High
Solarbabies
SpaceCamp
Spookies

Stand by Me
Thinkin' Big
Thrashin'
3:15
Trick or Treat
Twisted
Wildcats
Willy/Milly
Wired to Kill
Youngblood

1987

Adventures in Babysitting
Amazing Grace and Chuck
Back to the Beach
La Bamba
Big Bad Mama II
Blood Lake
Can't Buy Me Love
China Girl
The Curse
Dirty Dancing
Doom Asylum
Gaby: A True Story
The Gate
Hell on the Battleground
Hiding Out
Hot Pursuit
In the Mood
I Was a Teenage Zombie
Kidnapped
Less Than Zero
Like Father, Like Son
The Lost Boys
Maid to Order
The Majorettes
Masters of the Universe
The Monster Squad
Morgan Stewart's Coming Home
My Little Girl

Nice Girls Don't Explode
Night of the Demons
A Nightmare on Elm Street 3:
     Dream Warriors
Night Screams
North Shore
O.C. and Stiggs
Party Camp
Pretty Smart
The Principal
Return to Horror High
River's Edge
Slaughterhouse
Slumber Party Massacre II
Some Kind of Wonderful
Square Dance
Summer Camp Nightmare
Summer School
Sweet Lorraine
Terminal Entry
Three for the Road
Three O'Clock High
A Tiger's Tale
Welcome to 18
White Water Summer
The Wraith
Zombie High

1988

Aloha Summer
Beach Balls
The Beat
Big
Biloxi Blues
Black Roses
The Blob
Bloody Pom Poms
The Boy from Hell
Cannibal Campout
The Chocolate War
Clownhouse
Colors
Critters 2: The Main Course
Curfew
Cutting Class
Dakota
Death by Dialogue
Defense Play
Doin' Time on Planet Earth
Dudes
18 Again!
Flesh Eating Mothers
"For Keeps"
Friday the 13th Part VII: The New Blood
The Great Outdoors
Hairspray
Halloween 4: The Return of Michael Myers
Hide and Go Shriek
Hollow Gate
The In Crowd
The Invisible Kid
Johnny Be Good
The Kiss
The Last Slumber Party

Leader of the Band
License to Drive
Little Nikita
Lone Wolf
My Best Friend Is a Vampire
Mystic Pizza
The Night Before
A Night in the Life of Jimmy Reardon
A Nightmare on Elm Street 4:
      The Dream Master
976-EVIL
1969
Permanent Record
Phantasm II
Phantom Brother
Plain Clothes
The Prince of Pennsylvania
Pumpkinhead
The Rescue
Return of the Living Dead Part II
Running on Empty
Satisfaction
Senior Week
Sleepaway Camp II: Unhappy Campers
Stand and Deliver
Student Affairs
Survival Quest
Teen Vamp
Terror Squad
Valentino Returns
Vice Versa
Watchers
Waxwork
The Wizard of Loneliness

1989

Back to the Future 2
Beverly Hills Brats

Beware: Children at Play
Beyond the Stars

Bill and Ted's Excellent Adventure
Blueberry Hill
Catch Me If You Can
Cemetery High
C.H.U.D. II: Bud the Chud
Dead Poets Society
Deadly Innocents
Deadly Weapon
Dream a Little Dream
Far from Home
Forbidden Sun
Friday the 13th VIII: Jason Takes
  Manhattan
Girlfriend from Hell
Gleaming the Cube
The Gumshoe Kid
Halloween 5: The Revenge of Michael Myers
Heathers
Hell High
Hot Times at Montclair High
How I Got into College
Immediate Family
In Country
The Karate Kid Part III
Kinjite: Forbidden Subjects
Lean on Me
Lost Angels
Memorial Valley Massacre
Misplaced

Monster High
Morgan's Cake
My Mom's a Werewolf
Night Children
Night Life
Night Visitor
A Nightmare on Elm Street 5:
  The Dream Child
Nowhere to Run
Offerings
Parenthood
Pet Sematary
Rooftops
Say Anything . . .
See You in the Morning
Shag
She's Out of Control
Sing
Sleepaway Camp III: Teenage Wasteland
Society
Staying Together
Teen Witch
Troop Beverly Hills
True Blood
Uncle Buck
Under the Boardwalk
War Party
Who Shot Pat?
Wizards of the Lost Kingdom II

1990

Back to the Future 3
Book of Love
Buried Alive
Class of 1999
Coupe de Ville
Courage Mountain
Cry-Baby
A Cry in the Wild
Daredreamer
Dead Girls

Diving In
Edward Scissorhands
The Forbidden Dance
Getting Lucky
Harley
House Party
The Invisible Maniac
Kid
Lambada
Lisa

Lord of the Flies
Mermaids
Mirror Mirror
Monday Morning
The Natural History of Parking Lots
Pump Up the Volume
Riding the Edge
Rockula
Slumber Party Massacre III
Soultaker

Stella
Streets
There's Nothing Out There
Think Big
The Unbelievable Truth
Welcome Home, Roxy Carmichael
The Willies
Witchcraft II: The Temptress
Zapped Again

1991

Across the Tracks
All I Want for Christmas
An American Summer
And You Thought Your Parents Were Weird
Bill and Ted's Bogus Journey
Billy Bathgate
Boyz N the Hood
Child's Play 3
Class Act
Class of Nuke 'Em High Part II:
  Subhumanoid Meltdown
Convicts
Cool as Ice
Critters 3
December
Dogfight
Don't Tell Mom the Babysitter's Dead
Dutch
Family Prayers
Fast Getaway
Freddy's Dead: The Final Nightmare
The Haunting of Morella

Heaven Is a Playground
If Looks Could Kill
Infinity
Lunatic
The Man in the Moon
My Own Private Idaho
No Secrets
The People Under the Stairs
Popcorn
Prayer of the Rollerboys
Rambling Rose
Return to the Blue Lagoon
Rock 'n' Roll High School Forever
Shout
Straight Out of Brooklyn
Toy Soldiers
Trust
Up Against the Wall
Virgin High
White Fang
Wild Hearts Can't Be Broken

1992

Adventures in Dinosaur City
Alan & Naomi
Big Girls Don't Cry . . . They Get Even

Body Waves
Brutal Fury
Buffy the Vampire Slayer

Children of the Corn II: The Final Sacrifice
Children of the Night
Crisscross
Crossing the Bridge
Dark Horse
Dr. Giggles
Encino Man
Gas, Food Lodging
Gate 2
Gladiator
Journey to Spirit Island
Judgement
Juice
Ladybugs
Meatballs 4

Newsies
Pet Sematary 2
Poison Ivy
Scent of a Woman
School Ties
Second Glance
Sleepwalkers
Split Infinity
Terminal Bliss
This Is My Life
3 Ninjas
Twin Peaks: Fire Walk with Me
Wayne's World
Where the Day Takes You
Zebrahead

1993

Airborne
An Ambush of Ghosts
American Heart
Arcade
Body Snatchers
A Bronx Tale
Calendar Girl
Class of 1999 II: The Substitute
Coneheads
The Crush
The Day My Parents Ran Away
Dazed and Confused
The Double O Kid
A Far Off Place
Free Willy
Guncrazy
Hocus Pocus
A Home of Our Own
Jack the Bear
Jason Goes to Hell: The Final Friday
Just Another Girl on the I.R.T.
Just One of the Girls
King of the Hill
The Liar's Club

Lost in Yonkers
Made in America
The Man Without a Face
Matinee
Menace II Society
My Boyfriend's Back
Only the Strong
Pocket Ninjas
Remote
Rescue Me
Return of the Living Dead 3
Rich in Love
The Sandlot
The Seventh Coin
Showdown
Sidekicks
Sister Act 2: Back in the Habit
The Skateboard Kid
Surf Ninjas
Swing Kids
Teenage Bonnie and Klepto Clyde
Teenage Exorcist
That Night
This Boy's Life

3 Ninjas Knuckle Up
Ticks
Trauma
Unbecoming Age
Warlock: The Armageddon

Watchers 3
Wayne's World 2
What's Eating Gilbert Grape
White Wolves: A Cry in the Wild II

1994

Above the Rim
Blank Check
Brainscan
Camp Nowhere
Class of Nuke 'Em High 3: The Good,
    the Bad and the Subhumanoid
A Dangerous Place
Double Dragon
Ernest Goes to School
Foreign Student
Fresh
Fun
Heaven Sent
Holy Matrimony
Imaginary Crimes
The Inkwell
Lassie
Little Big League
Little Women
Magic Kid II
Milk Money
Mi Vida Loca (My Crazy Life)
Mirror Mirror 2: Raven Dance
Mod Fuck Explosion

My Father the Hero
My Girl 2
Natural Born Killers
The Next Karate Kid
Night of the Demons 2
Phantasm III: Lord of the Dead
A Pig's Tale
Pumpkinhead II: Blood Wings
Return of the Texas Chainsaw Massacre
Richie Rich
Safe Passage
Shrunken Heads
The Skateboard Kid 2
Spanking the Monkey
Spitfire
The St. Tammany Miracle
The Stoned Age
Tammy and the T-Rex
There Goes My Baby
3 Ninjas Kick Back
To Die, To Sleep
Totally Fucked Up
White Fang 2: Myth of the White Wolf
Windrunner

1995

. . . And the Earth Did Not Swallow Him
Angus
Animal Room
Art for Teachers of Children
The Babysitter
The Baby-Sitters Club

The Basketball Diaries
Billy Madison
Bleeding Hearts
Born to Be Wild
A Boy Called Hate
The Brady Bunch Movie

The Break
Breaking Free
Captain Nuke and the Bomber Boys
Casper
Children of the Corn III: Urban Harvest
Clockers
Clueless
Dangerous Minds
Dead Beat
Demolition High
Evolver
The Fantasticks
Far from Home: The Adventures of
    Yellow Dog
Freeway
Free Willy 2: The Adventure Home
Gold Diggers: The Secret of Bear Mountain
Hackers
The Incredibly True Adventure of Two Girls
    in Love
A Kid in King Arthur's Court
Kids
The Love Lesson
Mad Love
Mighty Morphin Power Rangers: The Movie

Mr. Holland's Opus
Mommy
Monster Mash: The Movie
My Teacher's Wife
New Jersey Drive
Now and Then
Once Upon a Time . . . When We
    Were Colored
Other Voices, Other Rooms
Parallel Sons
Poison Ivy 2: Lily
Powder
The Power Within
Raging Angels
Sacred Hearts
Senior Trip
S.F.W.
Tales from the Hood
Tall Tale
Test Tube Teens from the Year 2000
To Die For
Tom and Huck
True Crime
Unstrung Heroes
White Wolves II: Legend of the Wild

1996

Alaska
All Over Me
American Buffalo
Before and After
Boys
Carried Away
Children of the Corn IV: The Gathering
The Craft
The Crucible
Don't Be a Menace to South Central While
    Drinking Your Juice in the Hood
The Doom Generation
Fathers' Day
Fear

First Kid
Flipper
Fly Away Home
Foxfire
Girls Town
High School High
House Arrest
Illtown
Johns
Little Witches
Manny & Lo
Marvin's Room
Mirror Mirror III: The Voyeur
Mommy 2: Mommy's Day

Mrs. Winterbourne
My Uncle: The Alien
The Offering
The Paper Brigade
Past Perfect
Phat Beach
Provocateur
Race the Sun
Reggie's Prayer
Ripe
Romeo + Juliet
Scream
Sleepers

Sometimes They Come Back . . . Again
Sticks and Stones
The Substitute
Sunchaser
Sunset Park
Telling Lies in America
That Thing You Do!
Tiger Heart
Timeless
To Gillian on Her 37th Birthday
Tromeo and Juliet
Welcome to the Dollhouse
White Squall

1997

Address Unknown
Air Bud
Anarchy TV
A Better Place
Black Circle Boys
Campfire Tales
Cries of Silence
The Delta
Eight Days a Week
Eye of God
Free Willy 3: The Rescue
Good Burger
Gummo
Hurricane Streets
The Ice Storm
I Know What You Did Last Summer
Inventing the Abbotts
Jungle 2 Jungle
Little Boy Blue
Lover Girl
Magenta

Masterminds
Niagara, Niagara
Night of the Demons 3
Nowhere
187
Poison Ivy III: The New Seduction
Scream 2
Six Ways to Sunday
Somebody Is Waiting
Squeeze
Star Kid
Starship Troopers
That Darn Cat
Titanic
The Toilers and the Wayfarers
Trading Favors
Trojan War
Turbo: A Power Rangers Movie
Warriors of Virtue
Wild America

1998

The Adventures of Sebastian Cole
Air Bud: Golden Receiver
American History X
Another Day in Paradise
Apt Pupil
Around the Fire
Bloodsuckers
Buffalo '66
Can't Hardly Wait
Children of the Corn V: Fields of Terror
Dancer, Texas Pop. 81
Disturbing Behavior
Eden
The Faculty
Girl
Halloween H$_2$O: 20 Years Later
He Got Game
The Horse Whisperer
If I Die Before I Wake
I Still Know What You Did Last Summer
Little Men
Lolita
Mel
The Mighty
Nowhere to Go
The Opposite of Sex
Pamela's Prayer

Pecker
Pleasantville
Polish Wedding
P.U.N.K.S.
Richochet River
Ringmaster
Rushmore
17 & Under
Simon Birch
Slums of Beverly Hills
Small Soldiers
A Soldier's Daughter Never Cries
Strangeland
Superstar
Sweet Jane
Talisman
3 Ninjas: High Noon at Mega Mountain
Tiger Street
True Friends
200 Cigarettes
Whatever
Wicked
Wilbur Falls
Wild Horses
Wild Things
Wrestling with Alligators
Yellow

1999

American Beauty
American Pie
American Virgin
Anywhere But Here
Bellyfruit
Blue Ridge Fall
Born Bad
The Boy with the X-Ray Eyes
Boys Don't Cry

Brokedown Palace
Children of the Corn 666: Isaac's Return
The Cider House Rules
Coming Soon
Coyotes
Crazy in Alabama
Cruel Intentions
Deal of a Lifetime
Desecration

Desert Blue
Detroit Rock City
Dick
Drive Me Crazy
Drop Dead Gorgeous
Edge of Seventeen
Election
Freeway II: Confessions of a Trickbaby
Getting to Know You
Girl, Interrupted
Go
Idle Hands
Jawbreaker
Joe the King
The Joyriders
Just Looking
The Last Best Sunday
Liberty Heights
Light It Up
The Mod Squad

Never Been Kissed
October Sky
Outside Providence
Passport to Paris
The Prince and the Surfer
Pups
The Rage: Carrie 2
The Secret Life of Girls
She's All That
Story of a Bad Boy
Teaching Mrs. Tingle
10 Things I Hate About You
Trash
Trippin'
Tumbleweeds
2 Little, 2 Late
Varsity Blues
Walking Across Egypt
Whiteboyz
The Wood

2000

The After School Special
Air Bud III: World Pup
All I Wanna Do
Almost Famous
And Then Came Summer
Big Monster on Campus
Black and White
Blast
Boricua's Bond
Bring It On
The Bumblebee Flies Anyway
But I'm a Cheerleader
Can't Be Heaven
Castle Rock
Center Stage
Cherry Falls
Crime + Punishment in Suburbia
The Debut

The Dream Catcher
Double Parked
Final Destination
Finding Forrester
George Washington
Girlfight
Here on Earth
The Hi-Line
The Journey of Jared Price
Living the Life
Love & Basketball
Lover's Lane
Mad About Mambo
Our Lips Are Sealed
Paranoid
Pay It Forward
Pep Squad
Psycho Beach Party

Remember the Titans
Ricky 6
Scary Movie
Scream 3
Shriek If You Know What I Did Last
    Friday the 13th
Skipped Parts
Sleepy Hollow High
The Smokers
Snow Day
Swimming
Tadpole

Taliesin Jones
Terror Tract
The Tic Code
Tigerland
Traffic
Whatever It Takes
Where the Heart Is
The Vault
The Virgin Suicides
Walking Across Egypt
White Wolves III: Cry of the White Wolf
Wildflowers

2001

American Pie 2
An American Rhapsody
Baby Boy
The Brotherhood 2: Young Warlocks
Buck Naked Arson
Bully
Campfire Stories
Children of the Corn 7: Resurrection
Children on Their Birthdays
Close Call
Crazy/Beautiful
The Deep End
Donnie Darko
18
Extreme Days
Flossin
Get Over It
Ghost World
The Glass House
Gypsy 83
Happy Campers
Hedwig and the Angry Inch
Igby Goes Down
Jacked
Josie and the Pussycats

L.I.E.
Life as a House
Little Secrets
Manic
Max Keeble's Big Move
Mockingbird Don't Sing
My First Mister
Nikita and the Blues
Not Another Teen Movie
O
Our Song
Play Dead
The Princess Diaries
Reversal
Riders
Riding in Cars with Boys
Save the Last Dance
Scary Movie 2
Spy Kids
Storytelling
Sugar and Spice
Tart
Wet Hot American Summer
Winning London
The Young Girl and the Monsoon

2002

American Girl
Bang Bang You're Dead
Better Luck Tomorrow
Big Fat Liar
Blind Spot
Blue Car
Catch Me If You Can
Crossroads
The Dangerous Lives of Altar Boys
Dead Above Ground
The Emperor's Club
The Frightening
Heart of America
Home Room
Hometown Legend
The Hot Chick
ken park
The Kingston High
Like Mike

Murder by Numbers
The New Guy
Orange County
Real Women Have Curves
Roger Dodger
Slap Her, She's French
The Slaughter Rule
The Source
Spider-Man
Spy Kids 2: Island of Lost Dreams
Swimfan
The Trip
Try Seventeen
Tuck Everlasting
A Walk to Remember
When in Rome
White Oleander
Wishcraft

2003

Agent Cody Banks
All the Real Girls
American Wedding
The Battle of Shaker Heights
Biker Boyz
The Brotherhood III: Young Demons
Camp
Chasing Holden
Cheaper by the Dozen
Detention
Dumb and Dumberer: When Harry
    Met Lloyd
Elephant
Final Destination 2
Freaky Friday
Freddy vs. Jason

Grind
Hangman's Curse
Holes
How to Deal
Latter Days
Levelland
The Lizzie McGuire Movie
Love Don't Cost a Thing
The Mudge Boy
Scary Movie 3
Spy Kids 3-D: Game Over
Thirteen
Virgin
United States of Leland
What a Girl Wants
Zero Day

2004

Admissions
Agent Cody Banks 2: Destination London
America Brown
American Yearbook
Brother to Brother
Catch That Kid
Chasing Liberty
A Cinderella Story
Close Call
Confessions of a Teenage Drama Queen
Cotton Flowers
Crutch
Dandelion
Dirty Dancing: Havana Nights
The Door in the Floor
Dorian Blues
The Dust Factory
Ella Enchanted
Fat Albert
First Daughter
Freshman Orientation
Friday Night Lights
Funky Monkey
The Girl Next Door

Harry and Max
A Home at the End of the World
Imaginary Heroes
Mean Creek
Mean Girls
Mysterious Skin
Napoleon Dynamite
New York Minute
On the Outs
Palindromes
The Perfect Score
The Prince and Me
Purgatory House
Raise Your Voice
Runaways
Saved!
Serial Killing 4 Dummys
Sleepover
Speak
Stateside
13 Going on 30
Undertow
Winter Solstice

2005

Almost Normal
An American Haunting
American Pie Presents Band Camp
Away Awake
Bad Girls from Valley High
Bad Reputation
The Ballad of Jack and Rose
Brick
Chaos
The Chumscrubber
Coach Carter

Come Away Home
Cry_Wolf
Cursed
The Derby Stallion
Dirty Deeds
Down in the Valley
Duma
The Good Humor Man
Happy Endings
Hard Candy
Havoc

High School Record
Ice Princess
Infection
The Kid & I
Kids in America
Lords of Dogtown
Me and You and Everyone We Know
Nearing Grace
One Last Thing . . .
Our Very Own
The Perfect Man
Pop Star
Pretty Persuasion
The Quiet
Racing Stripes
Rebound

Reefer Madness: The Movie Musical
Return of the Living Dead: Necropolis
River's End
Roll Bounce
The Sisterhood of the Traveling Pants
Sky High
Smile
The Squid and the Whale
Strangers with Candy
Tamara
Thumbsucker
Twelve and Holding
The 12 Dogs of Christmas
Underclassman
The Upside of Anger
Yours, Mine and Ours

2006

Accepted
All You've Got
Always Will
American Pie Presents The Naked Mile
Another Gay Movie
Aquamarine
ATL
Automaton Transfusion
Beautiful Ohio
Believe in Me
Colma: The Musical
The Conrad Boys
The Covenant
Die and Let Live
Eye of the Dolphin
The Fast and the Furious: Tokyo Drift
Fat Girls
Final Destination 3
Fingerprints
Five Across the Eyes
Flicka
The Good Student
The Grudge 2

A Guide to Recognizing Your Saints
Half Nelson
Hoot
John Tucker Must Die
The Legend of Tillamook's Gold
Loren Cass
The Lost
Material Girls
Mini's First Time
Pathogen
Pope Dreams
Pretty Cool
Running with Scissors
The Sasquatch Gang
Saving Shiloh
She's the Man
Southern Justice
State's Evidence
Stay Alive
Step Up
Stephanie Daley
Stick It
Surf School

Take the Lead
Unaccompanied Minors
Vacationland
A Very Serious Person

When a Stranger Calls
Whirlygirl
Wild Tigers I Have Known
Zoom

2007

An American Crime
American Pie Presents Beta House
The Babysitters
Black Irish
Bratz
Charlie Bartlett
Cherry Crush
Choose Connor
Disturbia
Dribbles
Feel the Noise
Freedom Writers
Full of It
Georgia Rule
The Girl Next Door
The Go-Getter
Gracie
Hairspray
Halloween
Her Best Move
Home of the Giants
Hounddog
How She Move
The Invisible
Itty Bitty Titty Committee
Juno
King of California
The Life Before Her Eyes

Man in the Chair
Mo
Moondance Alexander
Nancy Drew
Normal Adolescent Behavior
Paranoid Park
A Plumm Summer
Pretty Cool Too
Pride
Remember the Daze
Resurrection Mary
Rocket Science
Rolling
Sarah London and the Paranormal Hour
Shanghai Kiss
Shelter
Snow Angels
Stomp the Yard
Superbad
Sydney White
Tammytown
Teeth
Tournament of Dreams
Towelhead
Trade
Transformers
War Eagle, Arkansas

2008

Absent Father
The Adventures of Food Boy
Afterschool

All Roads Lead Home
Assassination of a High School President
Bart Got a Room

City of Ember
College
College Road Trip
Dakota Skye
Dance of the Dead
Deadgirl
Dog Gone
Dream Boy
Extreme Movie
The Flyboys
The Forbidden Kingdom
Foreign Exchange
For the Love of a Dog
Gardens of the Night
Gran Torino
Half-Life
Hamlet 2
Harold
High School Musical 3: Senior Year
Journey to the Center of the Earth
Keith
Lost Stallions: The Journey Home

Lymelife
Make It Happen
Make-Out with Violence
Middle of Nowhere
Never Back Down
Nick and Nora's Infinite Playlist
Prom Night
Return to Sleepaway Camp
The Secret Life of Bees
The Sensei
Sex Drive
Speed Racer
Spy School
Step Up 2: The Streets
Superhero Movie
Tru Loved
Twilight
Under the Influence
The Wackness
Watercolors
Were the World Mine

2009

According to Greta
An American Affair
American Bully
American Pie Presents The Book of Love
American Virgin
Amreeka
Balls Out: Gary the Tennis Coach
Bandslam
The Blind Side
The Brotherhood V: Alumni
Cabin Fever 2: Spring Fever
Dance Flick
Dare
Dear Lemon Lima
Dragonball: Evolution
Fame
Fired Up!

The Gold Retrievers
The Greatest
Halloween II
Hannah Montana: The Movie
Hooking Up
Hotel for Dogs
Hurricane Season
I Love You, Beth Cooper
Jennifer's Body
Just Peck
Knock 'Em Dead, Kid
The Lovely Bones
Minor Details
My One and Only
Mystery Team
Night of the Demons
Night Fliers

Paper Man

Precious

Push

Rivers Wash Over Me

A Serious Man

17 Again

Shannon's Rainbow

16 to Life

Teenage Dirtbag

Tenderness

The Twilight Saga: New Moon

We Are the Mods

What Goes Up

Whip It

Wild About Harry

Wild Cherry

The Wild Stallion

The Winning Season

World's Greatest Dad

Wrecked

Youth in Revolt

Zombieland

2010

@urFRENZ

Adventures of a Teenage Dragonslayer

Alice in Wonderland

Anderson's Cross

Beware the Gonzo

Chasing 3000

Darren & Abbey

Dirty Girl

Easy A

Expecting Mary

The Final

Flipped

Friction

Hanna's Gold

High School

Ice Castles

It's Kind of a Funny Story

Janie Jones

The Karate Kid

Kick-Ass

The Last Exorcism

The Last Song

Legendary

Let Me In

Logan

Mad World

Memoirs of a Teenage Amnesiac

More Than Diamonds

My Soul to Take

A Nightmare on Elm Street

Percy Jackson & the Olympians:
*   The Lightning Thief*

The Prankster

The Runaways

Spork

The Spy Next Door

Standing Ovation

Trust

Twelve

The Twilight Saga: Eclipse

Vampires Suck

Winter's Bone

Woodshop

2011

Abduction

The Absent

After the Wizard

Another Earth

The Art of Getting By
Beastly
Beautiful Wave
A Better Life
The Chaperone
Decision
Detachment
Detention
Diary of a Wimpy Kid: Rodrick Rules
The Dynamiter
Ecstasy
Footloose
God Bless America
The Greening of Whitney Brown
Gun Hill Road
Hick
Hugo
I Am Number Four
The Ideal
Mangus!
Margaret
Montana Amazon

Mooz-Lum
My Sucky Teen Romance
October Baby
The Odds
On the Ice
Pariah
Private Romeo
Prom
Restless
Rosewood Lane
Someday This Pain Will Be Useful to You
Soul Surfer
Spy Kids: All the Time in the World in 4D
Super 8
Terri
That's What I Am
Touchback
The Twilight Saga: Breaking Dawn—Part 1
A Warrior's Heart
Win Win
The Wise Kids
Yelling to the Sky

2012

The Amazing Spider-Man
Bad Kids Go to Hell
Camp Virginovich
Chronicle
Claire
Cowgirls 'n' Angels
Detention of the Dead
Diary of a Wimpy Kid: Dog Days
Dropping Evil
Electrick Children
Emoticon;)
The Falls
The First Time
The Forger
The Frontier Boys
Future Weather
Girl in Progress

Hardflip
Hello I Must Be Going
The Hunger Games
Jack and Diane
Journey 2: The Mysterious Island
Life of Pi
LOL
The Mine
Moonrise Kingdom
Nate and Margaret
The Perks of Being a Wallflower
Project X
Red Dawn
Rock of Ages
Sassy Pants
Secrets in the Snow
16-Love

Sleepaway Camp IV: The Survivor
Smitty
So Undercover
Struck by Lightning
Thunderstruck

Tiger Eyes
12 Dogs of Christmas: Great Puppy Rescue
21 Jump Street
The Twilight Saga: Breaking Dawn—Part 2
Wolf

2013

After Earth
All the Boys Love Mandy Lane
American Cliché
Ashley
Beautiful Creatures
Black Nativity
The Bling Ring
Carrie
Chastity Bites
Chilling Visions: 5 Senses of Fear
Crush
Death to Prom
Devil's Knot
Disconnect
Dreams of the Wayward
Ender's Game
The Family
First Period
Geek USA
Grow Up, Tony Phillips
Heaven's Door
The Hunger Games: Catching Fire
It Felt Like Love
Joe
Kick-Ass 2
The Kings of Summer

The Last Keepers
Mindscape
The Mortal Instruments: City of Bones
Mud
1 Chance 2 Dance
Percy Jackson: Sea of Monsters
Short Term 12
South Dakota
Space Warriors
Spaz
The Spectacular Now
Spirit of Love
Spot Check
Standing Up
Stoker
A Talking Cat!?!
A Teacher
Teacher's Day
The To Do List
Truth or Dare
Us & Them
Violet & Daisy
Warm Bodies
The Way Way Back
We're the Millers

Appendix B S U B J E C T I V E

S U P E R L A T I V E   L I S T S

As a way of closing this lengthy study, I offer the following lists of various subjective categories for the youth films I have examined from 1980 to 2013. These lists are meant to be entertaining as well as informative. All titles are in alphabetical order.

MOST ENJOYABLE FILMS

Adventures in Babysitting
American Pie
Back to the Future
Better Off Dead
Bill and Ted's Excellent Adventure
The Brady Bunch Movie
But I'm a Cheerleader
Can't Hardly Wait
Catch Me If You Can (2002)
Clueless
Dead Poets Society
Dirty Dancing
Easy A
The Faculty
Ferris Bueller's Day Off
Flight of the Navigator
Fly Away Home
Heathers

House Party
The Incredibly True Adventure of Two Girls in Love
License to Drive
Lucas
Mr. Holland's Opus
Parenthood
The Perks of Being a Wallflower
Pretty in Pink
Rambling Rose
Real Genius
Real Women Have Curves
Risky Business
Say Anything . . .
Stand by Me
Superbad
Valley Girl
What's Eating Gilbert Grape

LEAST ENJOYABLE FILMS

American Bully
Assassination of a High School President
Automaton Transfusion
The Babysitter
Chaos
Cool as Ice
Every *Children of the Corn* film
The Doom Generation
Endless Love
Foxes
Gummo
Hackers
Every *Halloween* sequel

Johnny Be Good
ken park
Less Than Zero
Lolita
O.C. and Stiggs
Out of Control
Palindromes
The Runaways
Sing
The Smokers
Solarbabies
Twin Peaks: Fire Walk with Me

BEST ACTORS

Matthew Broderick
John Cusack
Claire Danes
Leonardo DiCaprio
Matt Dillon
Joseph Gordon-Levitt
Jake Gyllenhaal
Scarlett Johansson
Jennifer Lawrence
Heather Matarazzo
Chloë Grace Moretz
Sean Nelson

Sean Penn
Lou Diamond Phillips
River Phoenix
Natalie Portman
Christina Ricci
Winona Ryder
Gabourey Sidibe
Eric Stoltz
Hilary Swank
Lili Taylor
Reese Witherspoon

MOST UNDERRATED FILMS

Angus
Bad Kids Go to Hell
Brick
Dear Lemon Lima
Dogfight
Fire with Fire
"For Keeps"
Ghost World

Girls Town
He Got Game
I Am the Cheese
The Last Starfighter
Latter Days
The Man in the Moon
The Mighty
My Bodyguard

Night of the Demons   *Swing Kids*
Pariah   *Tex*
Seven Minutes in Heaven   *Tumbleweeds*
Sleepaway Camp   *War Party*
Speak   *Zebrahead*
Spork

MOST OVERRATED FILMS

The Blue Lagoon   *Mystic Pizza*
Edward Scissorhands   *Newsies*
Elephant   *Nick and Nora's Infinite Playlist*
Encino Man   *Red Dawn* (1984)
Every *Friday the 13th* sequel   *Running with Scissors*
Friday Night Lights   *Rushmore*
Hannah Montana: The Movie   *She's All That*
The Hunger Games   *Teen Wolf*
I Know What You Did Last Summer   *The Twilight Saga: New Moon*
Kids   *Varsity Blues*
Lords of Dogtown

SPECIAL TRUE STORIES

An American Rhapsody   *La Bamba*
The Blind Side   *Lean on Me*
Boys Don't Cry   *Mask*
Catch Me If You Can (2002)   *October Sky*
Coach Carter   *Pride*
Duma   *Race the Sun*
Freedom Writers   *Remember the Titans*
Gaby: A True Story   *Soul Surfer*
Girl, Interrupted   *Stand and Deliver*
Gracie   *This Boy's Life*
Hurricane Season   *Wild Hearts Can't Be Broken*
In the Mood   *White Squall*

MOST AESTHETICALLY AMBITIOUS

American Beauty
Brick
Donnie Darko
Fly Away Home
Fresh
Fun
George Washington
Go
Hedwig and the Angry Inch
Hugo
The Lovely Bones
Moonrise Kingdom

My Own Private Idaho
A Nightmare on Elm Street 4:
    The Dream Master
Pleasantville
Precious
Return of the Living Dead 3
Romeo + Juliet
Rumble Fish
Spork
Three O'Clock High
Totally Fucked Up
The Virgin Suicides

MOST BIZARRE

An American Crime
Apt Pupil
The Ballad of Jack and Rose
Buffalo '66
Dangerously Close
Deadgirl
Freeway
Jawbreaker
Niagara, Niagara
Night of the Comet
Nowhere

Pecker
Powder
The Quiet
Repo Man
Return to Horror High
Society
Spanking the Monkey
Starship Troopers
Teeth
Willy/Milly
Zapped

MOST SURPRISINGLY CURIOUS

American Virgin (1999)
Angel
Art for Teachers of Children
Black Roses
Bleeding Hearts
Cherry Falls
China Girl
Coming Soon
Deadly Friend
Detachment

Expecting Mary
Foreign Student
The Funhouse
Getting to Know You
The Girl Next Door (2004)
Just One of the Girls
Just One of the Guys
Kids in America
Lambada
Once Bitten

The People Under the Stairs
Only the Strong
Pups
Purgatory House
Restless

The Sensei
Smooth Talk
Square Dance
Tales from the Hood
There's Nothing Out There

BEST / WORST TITLES

. . . And the Earth Did Not Swallow Him
And You Thought Your Parents Were Weird
Bloody Pom Poms
Chopping Mall
Desperate Teenage Lovedolls
Don't Be a Menace to South Central While Drinking Your Juice in the Hood
Don't Tell Mom the Babysitter's Dead
Gimme an F!
Gleaming the Cube
Hide and Go Shriek
I Was a Teenage TV Terrorist
Make-Out with Violence

Mod Fuck Explosion
My Best Friend Is a Vampire
My Mom's a Werewolf
My Uncle: The Alien
Nice Girls Don't Explode
Revenge of the Teenage Vixens from Outer Space
Shriek If You Know What I Did Last Friday the 13th
Teenage Bonnie and Klepto Clyde
10 Things I Hate About You
Test Tube Teens from the Year 2000
Tromeo and Juliet

MOST NEGATIVE REPRESENTATIONS OF YOUTH

The Big Bet
Bully
Class of 1984
Cruel Intentions
The Crush
Fear
The Girl Next Door (2007)
Gummo
ken park
Kids
Lord of the Flies

Natural Born Killers
Nowhere
O
187
Poison Ivy
Pretty Persuasion
The Principal
The Rage: Carrie 2
River's Edge
Swimfan
Wild Things

MOST POSITIVE REPRESENTATIONS OF YOUTH

Alaska

Amazing Grace and Chuck

The Blob

Coach Carter

Dakota

Dear Lemon Lima

Flicka

The Forbidden Dance

Freedom Writers

Gold Diggers: The Secret of Bear Mountain

Light It Up

Little Women

Lucas

Mask

October Sky

Pay It Forward

Pump Up the Volume

Say Anything . . .

Sidekicks

The Sisterhood of the Traveling Pants

Soul Surfer

Stand and Deliver

Winter's Bone

MOST INFLUENTIAL TO OTHER YOUTH FILMS

Beat Street

Big

Boyz N the Hood

The Breakfast Club

Dead Poets Society

Fast Times at Ridgemont High

Footloose

Free Willy

Heathers

Juno

The Karate Kid

Mean Girls

My Own Private Idaho

Napoleon Dynamite

The Next Karate Kid

A Nightmare on Elm Street

Not Another Teen Movie

The Outsiders

Risky Business

Scary Movie

Scream

Sixteen Candles

Slumber Party Massacre

SpaceCamp

Step Up

Superbad

Taps

Twilight

WarGames

MY PERSONAL FAVORITES

All the Real Girls

Birdy

Blue Velvet

The Breakfast Club

The Chocolate War

Coming Soon

Diary of a Wimpy Kid: Rodrick Rules

Edge of Seventeen

Election

Fun

Gran Torino

Heathers

Hugo

Kick-Ass

The Legend of Billie Jean

Let Me In

Lucas

Mirror Mirror

My First Mister

Mysterious Skin

Pump Up the Volume

Reckless

Saved!

Society

Thirteen

Trust (1991)

Welcome to the Dollhouse

NOTES

FOREWORD

1. Thomas Schatz, "Film Genre and the Genre Film" (1981), reprinted in *Film Theory and Criticism*, 7th ed., ed. Leo Braudy and Marshall Cohen (New York: Oxford University Press, 2009), 564.

2. Ibid.

CHAPTER 1. INTRODUCTION:
THE CINEMATIC IMAGE OF YOUTH

1. See Thomas Doherty, *Teenagers and Teenpics: The Juvenilization of American Movies in the 1950s* (Boston: Unwin Hyman, 1988), 1–16.
The number of feature films actually written and/or directed by teenagers at the time of their release is minuscule, although an early claim can be made by Matty Rich, who was nineteen when he premiered *Straight Out of Brooklyn* (1991). Younger still was Celeste Marie Davis, who was fourteen when she remarkably wrote and starred in *Purgatory House* (2004). Rich made only one more feature, *The Inkwell* (1994), and Davis has made none, so the most auspicious career overall has been that of Emily Hagins, who wrote and directed the well-received *Pathogen* (2006) at the age of *twelve*. She went on to make *The Retelling* (2009) before receiving her widest acclaim yet for *My Sucky Teen Romance* in 2011, which she wrote and directed at just eighteen. Believe it or not, her *fourth* feature by the age of twenty, *Grow Up, Tony Phillips*, is in limited release as of this writing, and *Chilling Visions: 5 Senses of Fear*, an omnibus feature, is due for release by the end of 2013.

2. In my 1998 dissertation at the University of Massachusetts ("Generation Multiplex: The Image of Youth in American Cinema, 1981–1996"), I analyze hundreds more films than can be included here, and provide more analyses of some specific teen subgenre categories that are here minimized to brief descriptions for the sake of concision and relevance.

3. Kenneth Keniston, "Youth: A 'New' Stage of Life," in *Youth and Culture: A Human-Development Approach*, ed. Hazel V. Kraemer (Monterey, CA: Brooks/Cole Publishing, 1974), 103.

4. An excellent analysis of early legislation on juvenile delinquency can be found in *Juvenile Delinquency: An Integrated Approach*, 2nd ed., by James Burfeind and Dawn Jeglum Bartusch (Sudbury, MA: Jones and Bartlett, 2010), 15–28.

5. A classic example of the moral concerns raised about children's exposure to movies in the early twentieth century is Jane Addams's "The House of Dreams" from her book *The Spirit of Youth and the City Streets* (1909), reprinted in *The Movies in Our Midst: Documents in the Cultural History of Film in America*, ed. Gerald Mast (Chicago: University of Chicago Press, 1982), 72–78.

A plethora of studies claiming the negative influence of movies on children then appeared throughout the 1920s and 1930s, including the infamous Payne Fund Studies, although rarely did these analyses consider the image of youth presented in film, being more concerned with how youth could emulate supposedly immoral behaviors of adults on screen. These studies were conducted and published during a wave of moral panics that led to the foundation of the Motion Picture Production Code in 1930 and an overall crackdown on the moral looseness or ambiguity of American films. Nonetheless, many of these studies used often dubious methods and made often spurious claims (see bibliography for full citations): Alice Mitchell, *Children and Movies* (1929); Ruth Peterson and L. L. Thurstone, *Motion Pictures and the Social Attitudes of Children* (1933); Herbert Blumer and Philip Hauser, *Movies, Delinquency, and Crime* (1933); Wendell Dysinger and Christian Ruckmick, *The Emotional Responses of Children to the Motion Picture Situation* (1933); Henry James Forman, *Our Movie Made Children* (1933); P. G. Cressey and F. M. Thrasher, *Boys, Movies, and City Streets* (1934); Richard Ford, *Children in the Cinema* (1939).

For a contemporary analysis of these studies and the attitudes that fueled them, see Garth S. Jowett, Ian C. Jarvie, and Kathryn H. Fuller, eds., *Children and the Movies: Media Influence and the Payne Fund Controversy* (New York: Cambridge University Press, 1996). See also Georganne Scheiner, *Signifying Female Adolescence: Film Representations and Fans, 1920–1950* (Westport, CT: Praeger, 2000).

6. See William S. Loiry, *The Impact of Youth: A History of Children and Youth with Recommendations for the Future* (Sarasota, FL: Loiry Publishing House, 1984), 135; and Christine Griffin, *Representations of Youth: The Study of Youth and Adolescence in Britain and America* (Cambridge, UK: Polity Press, 1993), 18–23.

7. The actual Paramount ruling can be found in *United States v. Paramount Pictures, Inc.*, 334 U.S. 131, 166 (1948). The "Miracle Decision" is 1952 U.S. Supreme Court case *Burstyn v. Wilson*, 343 U.S. 495 (1952).

8. Evidence of Dean's legacy from *Rebel* was the publication of a collection about the film on September 30, 2005, the fiftieth anniversary of his death: *"Rebel Without a Cause": Approaches to a Maverick Masterwork*, ed. J. David Slocum (Albany: State University of New York Press, 2005).

9. See David Baker, "Rock Rebels and Delinquents: The Emergence of the

Rock Rebel in 1950s 'Youth Problem' Films," *Continuum* 19, no. 1 (March 2005): 39–54.

10. For an account of these films, see Alan Betrock, *The I Was a Teenage Juvenile Delinquent Rock 'n' Roll Horror Beach Party Movie Book: A Complete Guide to the Teen Exploitation Film, 1954–1969* (New York: St. Martin's Press, 1986). See also Lesley Speed, "Tuesday's Gone: The Nostalgic Teen Film," *Journal of Popular Film and Television* 25, no. 1 (Spring 1998): 24–32; and Aniko Bodroghkozy, "Reel Revolutionaries: An Examination of Hollywood's Cycle of 1960s Youth Rebellion Films," *Cinema Journal* 41, no. 3 (Spring 2002): 38–58.

11. Barbara Jane Brickman offers a strikingly thorough analysis of youth culture and cinema in the decade in *New American Teenagers: The Lost Generation of Youth in 1970s Film* (New York: Continuum, 2012).

12. See Geoffrey T. Holtz, *Welcome to the Jungle: The Why Behind "Generation X"* (New York: St. Martin's Griffin, 1995), 69–70.

13. To understand just how significant the '80s were as *anni mirabiles* of American youth cinema, and what a demarcation 1980 itself offered, consider just the following recent books, articles, and theses (see the bibliography for full citations): Christina Lee, "Going Nowhere? The Politics of Remembering (and Forgetting) Molly Ringwald" (2007); Emily Bennion, "Sexual Content in Teen Films: 1980–2007" (2008); Erik Bernasek, "Does Barry Manilow Know You Raid His Wardrobe? Themes of Authority and Rebellion in American Movies About High School" (2008); Tom Robinson, Mark Callister, and Dawn Magoffin, "Older Characters in Teen Movies from 1980–2006" (2009); Thomas A. Christie, *John Hughes and Eighties Cinema: Teenage Hopes and American Dreams* (2010); Susannah Gora, *You Couldn't Ignore Me If You Tried: The Brat Pack, John Hughes, and Their Impact on a Generation* (2010); Mark Callister, Lesa Stern, Sarah Coyne, Tom Robinson, and Emily Bennion, "Evaluation of Sexual Content in Teen-Centered Films from 1980 to 2007" (2011); Tony Pichaloff and Doug Pichaloff, *Hollywood Teen Movies: 80 from the '80s: The Good, the Bad, and the Forgotten* (2011); Mark Callister, Sarah Marie Coyne, Tom Robinson, John J. Davies, Chris Near, Lynn Van Valkenburg, and Jason Gillespie, "'Three Sheets to the Wind': Substance Use in Teen-centered Film from 1980 to 2007" (2012).

14. *Entertainment Weekly* identified the flourishing youth media market in two feature articles at the end of the decade: Chris Nashawaty, "The New Teen Age," Nov. 14, 1997, 24–35; and Josh Young, "They're All That," March 12, 1999, 20–29. The ubiquity of teen media has led to numerous cautionary guides such as Candice Kelsey, *Generation MySpace: Helping Your Teen Survive Online Adolescence* (New York: Marlowe & Co., 2007), and the expansion of teen television has even attracted the academic field, resulting in books such as Sharon Marie Ross and Louisa Stein, *Teen Television: Essays on Programming and Fandom* (Jefferson, NC: McFarland, 2008), and Glyn Davis and Kay Dickinson, *Teen TV: Genre, Consumption, and Identity* (London: British Film Institute, 2008).

15. Molly Haskell, *From Reverence to Rape: The Treatment of Women in the Movies*

(New York: Holt, Rinehart and Winston, 1974); Thomas Cripps, *Slow Fade to Black: The Negro in American Film, 1900–1942* (New York: Oxford University Press, 1977); Ralph Friar and Natasha Friar, *The Only Good Indian: The Hollywood Gospel* (New York: Drama Book Specialists, 1972); Lester Friedman, *The Jewish Image in American Film* (Secaucus, NJ: Citadel Press, 1987); Martin Norden, *Cinema of Isolation: A History of Physical Disability in the Movies* (New Brunswick: Rutgers University Press, 1994).

16. Paul Willemen, "Presentation," in Stephen Neale, *Genre* (London: British Film Institute, 1983), 1.

17. Andrew Tudor, "Genre" (1973), reprinted in *Film Genre Reader IV*, ed. Barry Keith Grant (Austin: University of Texas Press, 2012), 4.

18. Thomas Schatz, *Hollywood Genres: Formulas, Filmmaking, and the Studio System* (New York: Random House, 1981), 3.

19. Stephen Neale, *Genre and Hollywood* (London: Routledge, 2000), 28.

20. Barry Keith Grant, *The Hollywood Film Musical* (West Sussex, UK: Wiley-Blackwell, 2012), 4.

21. Daniel Lopez, *Films by Genre: 775 Categories, Styles, Trends, and Movements Defined, with a Filmography for Each* (Jefferson, NC: McFarland, 1993), 332.

22. Ibid., 390.

23. *The Moving Image Genre-Form Guide*, compiled by Brian Taves (chair), Judi Hoffman, and Karen Lund, Library of Congress Motion Picture/Broadcasting/Recorded Sound Division report, Feb. 12, 1997. My thanks to Brian Taves for providing me with this report. Work on genre designations continues in the same division under the Acquisitions and Bibliographic Access Directorate; in 2009 the division began using new genre-form headings after an initiative by the library's Policy and Standards Division. See http://www.loc.gov/rr/mopic/migintro.html.

24. Ibid., 60.

25. Janet Staiger refers to this dilemma as the "purity hypothesis" in "Hybrid or Inbred: The Purity Hypothesis and Hollywood Genre History," *Film Criticism* 22, no. 1 (Fall 1997): 6. Further valuable genre theories since then have been advanced by Torben Grodal, *Moving Pictures: A New Theory of Film Genres, Feelings, and Cognition* (New York: Oxford University Press, 1997); Nick Browne, ed., *Refiguring American Film Genres: History and Theory* (Berkeley: University of California Press, 1998); Rick Altman, *Film/Genre* (London: British Film Institute, 1999); and Barry Langford, *Film Genre: Hollywood and Beyond* (Edinburgh: Edinburgh University Press, 2005).

26. David M. Considine, *The Cinema of Adolescence* (Jefferson, NC: McFarland, 1985).

27. Mark Thomas McGee and R. J. Robertson, *The J. D. Films: Juvenile Delinquency in the Movies* (Jefferson, NC: McFarland, 1982). I argue for and against different practices in "The Teen Film and Its Methods of Study," *Journal of Popular Film and Television* 25, no. 1 (Spring 1997): 38–45.

28. The Young Artist Awards do not enjoy nearly the hype of the Oscars, but they have been successful for over three decades in awarding future Oscar nominees

and winners, such as Diane Lane (*A Little Romance*, 1979), Elisabeth Shue (*The Karate Kid*, 1984), River Phoenix (*Explorers*, 1985), Winona Ryder (*Great Balls of Fire*, 1989), Reese Witherspoon (*Jack the Bear*, 1993), Haley Joel Osment (*Forrest Gump*, 1994), Abigail Breslin (*Little Miss Sunshine*, 2007), and Hailee Steinfeld (*True Grit*, 2011).

29. See Wiley Lee Umphlett, *The Movies Go to College: Hollywood and the World of the College-Life Film* (Rutherford: Fairleigh Dickinson University Press, 1984); David Hinton, *Celluloid Ivy: Higher Education in the Movies, 1960–1990* (Metuchen, NJ: Scarecrow, 1994); and John E. Conklin, *Campus Life in the Movies: A Critical Survey from the Silent Era to the Present* (Jefferson, N.C.: McFarland, 2008).

30. The 2003 film *Matchstick Men* is probably the best example of a taxonomic imbroglio for identifying a "youth movie": a man discovers the fourteen-year-old daughter he never knew, and for most of the story, he and we believe her to be a teenager, until the twist ending, when she is revealed to be a young woman beyond her teen years. The film has some curious commentary on "playing at" being a teen in the early '00s, given the character's attire and accessories, as well as her demeanor. All the same, to call it a movie about a teenage character would be inaccurate. A different dilemma is *Marie Antoinette* (2006), which follows the eighteenth-century French queen throughout her teens for about half of the film, while she ages into her twenties in the second half, and only partially pertains to youth as defined here; however, despite its period and location, it is a product of its time, and of a youthful director, and thus could be argued as relevant to contemporary American youth.

31. G. Stanley Hall, *Adolescence: Its Psychology, and Its Relations to Physiology, Anthropology, Sociology, Sex, Crime, Religion, and Education* (New York: Appleton & Company, 1904). Scholars who credit Hall with some variety of "discovering" adolescence are Johan Fornas in "Youth, Culture, and Modernity," in *Youth Culture in Late Modernity*, ed. Johan Fornas and Goran Bolin (London: Sage, 1995), 5; Griffin, 11; and John R. Gillis in *Youth and History: Tradition and Change in European Age Relations, 1770–Present* (New York: Academic Press, 1981), 118.

32. Griffin, 18–26.

33. Robert Havighurst traced developmental ascents through adolescence to adulthood in *Developmental Tasks and Education* (New York: Longman, 1948). Jean Piaget's contribution, among others, was a theory of cognitive development during adolescence in *The Growth of Logical Thinking*, written with Bärbel Inhelder (New York: Basic Books, 1958). Erik Erikson mapped out psychological development according to age, in which adolescence was a stage for young people to negotiate their ego identity to achieve adulthood, which he discussed in books such as *The Challenge of Youth* (Garden City, NY: Anchor Books, 1963) and *Identity, Youth, and Crisis* (New York: Norton, 1968). D. W. Winnicott proposed a variety of theories about the roles of play in child development in *The Child, the Family, and the Outside World* (Baltimore: Penguin, 1964), and *Playing and Reality* (New York: Tavistock Publications, 1971). Anna Freud was an advocate of children's rights based on her psychological research, which is collected in *Beyond the Best Interests of the Child*,

written with Joseph Goldstein and Albert Solnit (New York: Free Press, 1979), and *A Child Analysis with Anna Freud* by Peter Heller (Madison, CT: International Universities Press, 1990). David Considine discusses other adolescent research developments in his dissertation, "The Depiction of Adolescent Sexuality in Motion Pictures: 1930–1980," (University of Wisconsin, Madison, 1982), 8–18. See also Morton Hunt, *The Story of Psychology* (New York: Doubleday, 1993), 350–395.

34. Kenneth Keniston, *Youth and Dissent* (New York: Harcourt Brace Jovanovich, 1960).

35. Philippe Ariès, *Centuries of Childhood: A Social History of Family Life* (New York: Random House, 1962).

36. James Coleman, *The Adolescent Society: The Social Life of the Teenager and Its Impact on Education* (New York: Free Press of Glencoe, 1961); Stuart Hall and Tony Jefferson, eds., *Resistance Through Rituals: Youth Subcultures in Post-War Britain* (London: Hutchinson, 1976); Angela McRobbie, *Feminism and Youth Culture: From "Jackie" to "Just Seventeen"* (London: Macmillan, 1991); Dick Hebdige, *Subculture: The Meaning of Style* (London: Methuen, 1979), and *Hiding in the Light* (London: Methuen, 1993).

37. Griffin, 196–214.

38. Geoffrey Pearson, *Hooligan: A History of Respectable Fears* (New York: Schocken Books, 1983); Jon Lewis, *The Road to Romance and Ruin: Teen Films and Youth Culture* (New York: Routledge, 1992).

39. Grace Palladino, *Teenagers: An American History* (New York, Basic Books, 1996). Michael Barson and Steven Heller offer a somewhat sensational approach to teen history in *Teenage Confidential: An Illustrated History of the American Teen* (San Francisco: Chronicle Books, 1998). See also Lucy Rollin, *Twentieth-Century Teen Culture by the Decades: A Reference Guide* (Westport, CT: Greenwood Press, 1999).

40. Murray Milner, *Freaks, Geeks, and Cool Kids* (New York: Routledge, 2006).

41. Loiry, 223–245.

42. Douglas Coupland, *Generation X: Tales for an Accelerated Culture* (New York: St. Martin's Press, 1991). Perhaps the most personal examination of the emergent twentysomething population can be found in the unique oral history written by Michael Lee Cohen, *The Twenty-Something American Dream: A Cross-Country Quest for a Generation* (New York: Dutton, 1993). See also David M. Gross and Sophfronia Scott, "Proceeding with Caution," *Time*, July 16, 1990, 56–62.

43. This elongation of youth, or more specifically the delay of adulthood, is discussed in broader social terms in "The Rocky Road to Adulthood," by Marcia Mogelonsky, *American Demographics*, May 1996, 26–35, 56.

44. Susan Littwin, *The Postponed Generation: Why America's Grown-Up Kids Are Growing Up Later* (New York: Morrow, 1986). Barbara Schneider and David Stevenson conducted an extensive longitudinal study that questions the Generation X notion of youth in *The Ambitious Generation: America's Teenagers, Motivated but Directionless* (New Haven: Yale University Press, 2000).

45. Karen Ritchie, *Marketing to Generation X* (New York: Lexington Books, 1995); Holtz.

46. Thomas Hine, *The Rise and Fall of the American Teenager* (New York: Harper Perennial, 2000).

47. Christina Lee, *Screening Generation X: The Politics and Popular Memory of Youth in Contemporary Cinema* (London: Ashgate, 2010).

48. Alissa Quart, *Branded: The Buying and Selling of Teenagers* (New York: Basic Books, 2003); Deron Boyles, ed., *The Corporate Assault on Youth: Commercialism, Exploitation, and the End of Innocence* (New York: Peter Lang, 2008); Henry Giroux, *Youth in Revolt: Reclaiming a Democratic Future* (Boulder, CO: Paradigm, 2012).

49. Kerry Mallan and Sharyn Pearce, eds., *Youth Cultures: Texts, Images, and Identities* (Westport, CT: Praeger, 2003); Neil Campbell, ed., *American Youth Cultures* (New York: Routledge, 2004), previously published as *The Radiant Hour: Versions of Youth in American Culture* (Exeter: University of Exeter Press, 2000); Mary Jane Kehily, *Understanding Youth: Perspectives, Identities, and Practices* (London: Sage, 2007); Siân Lincoln, *Youth Culture and Private Space* (London: Palgrave Macmillan, 2012).

50. Considine wrote the first book-length study of teens in American cinema in 1985; at the same time, Kathy Merlock Jackson was working on her dissertation at Bowling Green State University, which became the first book-length study of children in American cinema, *Images of Children in American Film: A Sociocultural Analysis* (Metuchen, NJ: Scarecrow Press, 1986).

51. Considine, *Cinema of Adolescence*, 9.

52. For a cursory study of the topic, see Caroline Clayton Clark, "Film Families: The Portrayal of the Family in Teen Films from 1980 to 2007" (M.A. thesis, Brigham Young University, 2008).

53. Lewis, 3.

54. Ibid., 150.

55. Jonathan Bernstein, *Pretty in Pink: The Golden Age of Teenage Movies* (New York: St. Martin's Griffin, 1997).

56. Murray Pomerance and John Sakeris, eds., *Pictures of a Generation on Hold: Selected Papers* (Toronto: Media Studies Working Group, 1996); some of the articles from this collection, and other new essays on youth, have been published in the anthology *Popping Culture*, also edited by Pomerance and Sakeris, now in its seventh edition (New York: Pearson, 2012).

57. Murray Pomerance and Frances Gateward, eds., *Sugar, Spice, and Everything Nice: Contemporary Cinemas of Girlhood* (Detroit: Wayne State University Press, 2002); Pomerance and Gateward, eds., *Where the Boys Are: Cinemas of Masculinity and Youth* (Detroit: Wayne State University Press, 2005). For another overview of American teen cinema primarily focused on girls, see Roz Kaveney, *Teen Dreams: Reading Teen Film from "Heathers" to "Veronica Mars"* (London: I. B. Tauris, 2006).

58. Timothy Shary and Alexandra Seibel, eds., *Youth Culture in Global Cinema* (Austin: University of Texas Press, 2007); Patrick Jamieson and Daniel Romer, eds., *The Changing Portrayal of Adolescents in the Media Since 1950* (New York: Oxford University Press, 2008).

59. Anne Hardcastle, Roberta Morosini, and Kendall Tarte, eds., *Coming of Age on*

Film: Stories of Transformations in World Cinema (Winston–Salem: Wake Forest University Romance Languages Film Symposium, 2006).

60. Timothy Shary, *Teen Movies: American Youth on Screen* (London: Wallflower, 2005); Stephen Tropiano, *Rebels & Chicks: A History of the Hollywood Teen Movie* (New York: Back Stage Books, 2006).

61. Tropiano, 278.

62. Catherine Driscoll, *Teen Film: A Critical Introduction* (New York: Berg, 2011).

63. Shorter and more focused overviews of youth films worth noting include the following (see bibliography for full citations): Armond White, "Kidpix" (1985); Thomas Leitch, "The World According to Teenpix" (1992); Randall Clark, "Teenage Films" (1995); Peter Henne, "Teen Days That Shook the World" (1999); Elayne Rapping, "Youth Cult Films" (1999); Wheeler Winston Dixon, "'Fighting and Violence and Everything, That's Always Cool': Teen Films in the 1990s" (2000); Henry Giroux, "Hollywood Film and the War on Youth" (2002); John Stephens, "'I'll Never Be the Same After That Summer': From Abjection to Subjective Agency in Teen Films" (2003); Robin Wood, "Party Time or Can't Hardly Wait for That American Pie: Hollywood High School Movies of the '90s" (2005); Bradley Schauer, "Dimension Films and the Exploitation Tradition in Contemporary Hollywood" (2009).

64. Neale, *Genre and Hollywood*, 125.

65. Pam Cook, *The Cinema Book*, 3rd ed. (London: British Film Institute, 2008).

66. Amanda Ann Klein, *American Film Cycles: Reframing Genres, Screening Social Problems, and Defining Subcultures* (Austin: University of Texas Press, 2011), 101.

67. Richard Nowell, *Blood Money: A History of the First Teen Slasher Cycle* (New York: Continuum, 2011).

68. Indulgent yet telling appreciations of the genre continue to appear, such as Nikki Roddy, *How to Fight, Lie, and Cry Your Way to Popularity (and a Prom Date): Lousy Life Lessons from 50 Teen Movies* (San Francisco: Zest Books, 2011).

69. Ruth M. Goldstein and Edith Zornow, *The Screen Image of Youth: Movies About Children and Adolescents* (Metuchen, NJ: Scarecrow Press, 1980); Vincent Canby, "Stop Kidding Around," *New York Times*, July 23, 1972, sec. 3, 1.

CHAPTER 2. YOUTH IN SCHOOL: ACADEMICS AND ATTITUDE

1. Jonathan Bernstein, *Pretty in Pink: The Golden Age of Teenage Movies* (New York: St. Martin's Griffin, 1997), 158.

2. "Popularity" in this case, as in most others, is somewhat subjectively measured, although my research and experiences support the claim that *The Breakfast Club* and *Heathers* were undoubtedly the most seen and influential school films between 1985 and 1990 (and along with *Say Anything . . .* and *Dirty Dancing*, the most popular teen films of this time in general). Yet to demonstrate the specious value of box office earnings as an indicator of popularity—and to explain why I use them

sparingly to support social/aesthetic claims— *The Breakfast Club* earned $38.1 million in its U.S. theatrical release compared to the flop-like numbers of *Heathers*, only $1.1 million. The latter film became much more successful on cable and video, and has seen further recognition through VHS and DVD rereleases, making an assessment of its true audience reach more difficult to determine. Further, reports of domestic box office earnings often vary widely from source to source, and grosses can still be based on faulty approximations (even at the studio level); to this day, debate persists over distributors and studios inflating their earnings numbers, while straight-to-video films have essentially no way to measure their viewers, despite their potential impact.

Unless otherwise noted, all box office figures in this book are based on U.S. theatrical earnings and are gathered from the Internet Movie Database at http://www.imdb.com/.

3. These characters have been more thoroughly studied in *The Hollywood Curriculum: Teachers in the Movies*, 2nd rev. ed., by Mary M. Dalton (New York: Peter Lang, 2010). For a broader view of teachers and students from a sociological perspective, see Robert C. Bulman, *Hollywood Goes to High School: Cinema, Schools, and American Culture* (New York: Worth, 2004).

4. Katy J. Wolfrom, "Reel Principals: A Descriptive Content Analysis of the Images of School Principals Depicted in Movies from 1997–2009" (D.Ed. diss., Indiana University of Pennsylvania, 2010).

5. Another approach to the subgenre could entail focusing on the various rituals that schools reproduce and students endure, such as science fairs, sporting events, dances, and the college-application process. The last of these alone tends to generate a notable example every year or two, since college is easily portrayed as the next bastion of acceptance that students must surmount. A short list would include *Risky Business* (1983), *How I Got in to College* (1989), *He Got Game* (1998), *Coming Soon* (1999), *Orange County* (2002), *Accepted* (2006), and *College Road Trip* (2008). While my focus is on character types since I am studying representation, this approach warrants further consideration.

6. *Lucas* review, Joseph Gelmis, *Newsday*, March 28, 1986, Part III, 5.

7. Three increasingly inconspicuous sequels followed, which effectively offered more of the same: *Revenge of the Nerds 2: Nerds in Paradise* (1987), *Revenge of the Nerds 3: The Next Generation* (1992), and *Revenge of the Nerds 4: Nerds in Love* (1994), which was made for TV.

8. *The Breakfast Club* review, David Denby, *New York*, Feb. 18, 1985, 95.

9. *Lucas* review, David Edelstein, *Village Voice*, April 15, 1986, 64.

10. *Lucas* review, David Denby, *New York*, April 28, 1986, 93.

11. Some critics pointed out that the film, which was directed by convicted child molester Victor Salva, also speaks to the tensions of pedophilia.

12. *Class Act* review, David Denby, *New York*, June 22, 1992, 56.

13. *Class Act* review, Jami Bernard, *New York Post*, June 5, 1992, 25.

14. The Cinderella mythology flourishes in literal adaptations (*Ever After: A Cin-*

derella Story [1998], *A Cinderella Story* [2004], *Ella Enchanted* [2004]) and more implicit interpretations (*She's All That* [1999], *What a Girl Wants* [2003], *The Prince and Me* [2004] *Aquamarine* [2006]).

15. There is apparently an argument as to whether Dawn is eleven or twelve years old. Many reviews list her as eleven, but most American school students do not start seventh grade until the age of twelve. I include *Welcome to the Dollhouse* because it is about junior high school, and clearly addresses school issues for adolescents.

16. *Welcome to the Dollhouse* review, Lisa Schwarzbaum, *Entertainment Weekly*, May 31, 1996, 43.

17. *She's All That* review, Jane Ganahl, *San Francisco Examiner*, Jan. 29, 1999, D3.

18. *Dear Lemon Lima* review, Christopher Campbell, *Indiewire*, Feb. 28, 2011, http://blogs.indiewire.com/spout/dear_lemon_lima_review.

19. The director of *Class of 1984*, Mark Lester, was also responsible for *Truck Stop Women* (1974) and *Roller Boogie* (1979), so his possible foray into docudrama is questionable indeed.

20. *Lean on Me* review, Charles Epstein, *Films in Review*, June–July 1989, 361.

21. The sequel to this sequel, *Class of 1999 II: The Substitute* (1993), lacks the gangs and grand sociopolitical gestures of the first film, and becomes a violent contest between bad students and a sadistic teacher *posing* as an android. What the film illogically omits from the original is the near-futuristic image of schools overrun by organized delinquents—in fact, the students' presence in the film is quite small—and its already empty statement on youth violence is cast aside as all culpability for violence and delinquency is passed on to teachers, leaving the students conspicuously unmotivated in raising the trouble that their teachers are trying to eradicate.

22. Jeannette Sloniowski, "A Cross-Border Study of the Teen Genre: The Case of John N. Smith," *Journal of Popular Film and Television* 25, no. 3 (Fall 1997): 132.

23. The film's sequel was made for TV: *The Substitute 2: School's Out* (1998) did little to improve on the original. *The Substitute 3: Winner Takes All* (1999), and the unnumbered fourth film, *The Substitute: Failure Is Not an Option* (2001), went straight-to-video.

24. *The Breakfast Club* review, David Edelstein, *Village Voice*, Feb. 26, 1985, 52.

25. The screenwriter of *Tuff Turf*, who is listed as "Jette Rinck," likely used a pseudonym: this is the same name as the James Dean character in *Giant* (1956).

26. *Tuff Turf* review, Michael Wilmington, *Los Angeles Times*, Jan. 11, 1985, Calendar, 15.

27. *Pretty Persuasion* review, Roger Ebert, *Chicago Sun-Times*, Aug. 26, 2005, C1.

28. A subplot of *Kids in America* leads to the film deliberately breaking a record in film history that had stood for over sixty years, which I will not reveal here. However, I will point out that the film currently cited most often for holding this record, *Elena Undone* (2010), is well short of the very high standard set here.

29. *All I Wanna Do* is only one of many youth period films set in 1963, the year of

Kennedy's assassination, which seems to mark the division of the prosperous post–World War II '50s from the cynical Vietnam War '60s (many more youth films take place in 1962 and 1964). Also set in 1963 are *The Flamingo Kid*, *Hoosiers*, *Dirty Dancing*, *Mermaids*, *Coupe de Ville*, *Shag*, *Skipped Parts*, and *Flipped*.

30. *The Chocolate War* review, Hal Hinson, *Washington Post*, Jan. 20, 1989, D1.

31. *Rushmore* review, Kevin Courrier, *Box Office Magazine* 134 (Nov. 1998): 135.

32. James C. McKelly offers a comparative reading of the rebel aspects of *Heathers* and *Rebel Without a Cause*, in "Youth Cinema and the Culture of Rebellion: *Heathers* and the *Rebel* Archetype," in *Pictures of a Generation on Hold: Selected Papers*, ed. Murray Pomerance and John Sakeris (Toronto: Media Studies Working Group, 1996), 107–114.

33. The film plays somewhat like *The Breakfast Club* in its plot of confined students who bond over their shared problems, a connection which is made clever by the casting of Judd Nelson as the students' favorite teacher. However, the 1985 film clearly showed the class and power issues that divided the students through the school caste system, and there is no similar division here. Further, these students' problems are far more pressing (though perhaps less common) than those of *The Breakfast Club* kids.

34. *Light It Up* review, Mick LaSalle, *San Francisco Chronicle*, Nov. 10, 1999, D1.

35. A long-standing argument among fans of the film revolves around this gesture and whether Claire and John consummated their relationship in the closet earlier. Some have interpreted Claire giving John the diamond as "payment" for relieving her of her virginity, with the closing shot of his jubilant fist pump to the air being a phallic celebration of having sex with her. A quarter century later, screenwriter Bert V. Royal offered some closure to the mystery in a montage sequence from *Easy A* (2010) during which the protagonist wishes her love life was like an '80s movie. Over the iconic closing shot of *The Breakfast Club*, she intones, "I want Judd Nelson thrusting his fist into the air because he knows he got me just once." At least this character, who would not have been born when the film appeared, and Royal, who would have been a seven-year-old, both believe that John and Claire did indeed copulate in the closet.

36. *Clueless* review, Owen Gleiberman, *Entertainment Weekly*, July 28, 1995, 42.

37. *Election* review, Cindy Fuchs, *Philadelphia City Paper*, http://www.citypaper.net/, May 6, 1999. See also Annie Nocenti, "Adapting and Directing *Election*: A Talk with Alexander Payne and Jim Taylor," *Scenario* 5, no. 2 (1999): 104–109, 189–190.

38. Stephen Holden, "A New Rule: The Beautiful Are the Bad," *New York Times*, Feb. 28, 1999, C3. David Denby also addressed this issue in his perceptive but sometimes stereotypical "High School Confidential," *New Yorker*, May 31, 1999, 94–98.

39. *Mean Girls* review, Jessica Winter, *Village Voice*, April 20, 2004, 57.

40. Elizabeth Behm-Morawitz and Dana E. Mastro, "Mean Girls? The Influence of Gender Portrayals in Teen Movies on Emerging Adults' Gender-Based Attitudes and Beliefs," *Journalism and Mass Communication Quarterly* 85, no. 1 (March 2008):

131–146. The findings in this article also suggest that the viewing of teen movies by college students is associated with negative stereotypes about female friendships and gender roles.

41. The 2002 book that screenwriter Tina Fey used as the basis for her story in *Mean Girls* was *Queen Bees and Wannabes: Helping Your Daughter Survive Cliques, Gossip, Boyfriends, and Other Realities of Adolescence* by Rosalind Wiseman (New York: Crown), which was revised and published with the slightly altered subtitle . . . *and the New Realities of Girl World* by the same press in 2009.

42. Emily Fox-Kales offers compelling comments about girls' body issues in *Mean Girls* and other films in "Teen Bodies: Valley Girls and Middle School Vamps," in *Body Shots: Hollywood and the Culture of Eating Disorders* (Albany: State University of New York Press, 2011), 119–140.

43. *Mean Girls 2* (2011) was a made-for-TV movie, essentially a remake rather than a sequel, that did not gain nearly the same popularity as the original.

44. Jason Beck, "A Comparison of Male Athletes with Teenage Peers in Popular Teen Movies" (M.A. thesis, Brigham Young University, 2011).

45. Oddly enough, one of the highest-earning youth sports films of the '80s was *Wildcats*, in which the teen characters were secondary to the star draw of Goldie Hawn—the film made $26.3 million at the box office. However, as any polling of '80s youth will reveal, *Wildcats* left far less of an impression than films like *All the Right Moves* and *Vision Quest*. By the '90s, youth sports films were still earning low numbers, such as $8.8 million for *The Next Karate Kid* and $10 million for *Sunset Park*, only by this point the films were indeed leaving smaller impressions.

46. The Disney studio (as Buena Vista Pictures) in the mid-'90s began releasing a number of youth-themed sports films after the success of their 1992 children's film *The Mighty Ducks*, one of which was the baseball fantasy remake *Angels in the Outfield* (1994) and others of which included *3 Ninjas* (1992; which yielded a martial arts franchise under TriStar from 1994 to 1998), weight-loss fitness-camp comedy *Heavyweights* (1994), soccer comedy *The Big Green* (1996), and three *Mighty Ducks* sequels: *The Mighty Ducks: D2* (1994), *D3* (1996), and *The Mighty Ducks: The First Face-Off* (1997). Films from other studios in this same vein included the baseball comedies *Rookie of the Year* (1993) and *Little Big League* (1994), pee-wee football comedy *Little Giants* (1994), and the military academy comedy *Major Payne* (1995). While some of these films featured some teenage characters, most are excluded from the present study because they are primarily about pre-teens and most are not about school sports. For an interesting discussion of distinctions in teen comedy, see Stephanie Zacharek, "There's Something About Teenage Comedy . . ." *Sight and Sound* 9, no. 12 (Dec. 1999): 20–22.

47. *Ladybugs* (1992) features a pre-teen girls' soccer team, but tellingly, the "star" of the team is a boy posing as a girl.

48. A Christian-themed film about a girl's basketball team, *The St. Tammany Miracle*, did appear in 1994, but was virtually unseen outside of church groups and faith-based broadcasting.

49. *Vision Quest* review, David Edelstein, *Village Voice*, Feb. 26, 1985, 52.

50. *Varsity Blues* grossed $52.9 million at the U.S. box office.

51. *Varsity Blues* review, Owen Gleiberman, *Entertainment Weekly*, Jan. 22, 1999, 72.

52. While the book is lacking in depth, and despite its title is virtually devoid of any discussion about school films, *Hollywood Films About Schools: Where Race, Politics, and Education Intersect*, by Robert Chennault (New York: Palgrave Macmillan, 2006), does offer an interesting argument about racial politics in government between 1980 and 2000 that bears on some of the films discussed in the present study.

CHAPTER 3. DELINQUENT YOUTH:
HAVING FUN, ON THE LOOSE, IN TROUBLE

1. As with all criminality, incidents can only become statistics when they are reported and recorded, so actual youth crime is inevitably more common than the social systems that verify it through arrest and conviction. Using such sources, all delinquency cases in U.S. juvenile courts peaked from 1995 through 1998 with 1.8–1.9 million, and by 2009 the number had steadily declined to 1.5 million; the proportion of these cases that were cataloged as violent crimes declined accordingly, from nearly 130,000 in 1995 (or 7.2 percent) to just over 80,000 in 2009 (or 5.3 percent). Figures taken from the U.S. Department of Justice, Office of Juvenile Justice and Delinquency Prevention, at http://www.ojjdp.gov/ojstatbb.

While his approach is primarily clinical, Scott Snyder did offer a considerable study of the topic in films over three journal essays (see bibliography for full citations): "Movies and Juvenile Delinquency: An Overview" (1991), "Movie Portrayals of Juvenile Delinquency: Part 1—Epidemiology and Criminology," and "Movie Portrayals of Juvenile Delinquency: Part 2—Sociology and Psychology" (both 1995).

2. The other four adult–child age-switching fantasies of this short period were *Like Father, Like Son* (1987), *18 Again!* (1988), *Vice Versa* (1988), and *Dream a Little Dream* (1989).

3. Hebdige explored wider cultural issues in *Subculture: The Meaning of Style* (London: Methuen, 1979); for actual movies, see the incredibly thorough *Destroy All Movies! The Complete Guide to Punks on Film*, ed. Zach Carlson and Bryan Connolly (Seattle: Fantagraphics, 2010).

4. The first edition of this book (2002) included a type of youth delinquency plot I labeled "Patriotic Purpose": nationalistic teen films from 1984 to 1988, during the height of the Reagan presidency and the last days of the Cold War, that featured youth fighting foreign enemies. The defiance in these films was not against mere parents and adults, but against the potential corruption threatened by any alien force; the conservation of American identity, not just youth identity, is the priority. These films peaked in popularity with the Oscar-winning success of *Pla-*

toon (1986), about a teenage soldier sent to fight in Vietnam, which was all but immediately remade as *Hell on the Battleground* (1987) by a low-budget studio. However, the genesis of the trend was in 1984 with a film that directly targeted fears of foreign attack, *Red Dawn*, in which youth band together in a futile effort to save their town from Russian invaders. Where *Platoon* questioned the validity of war and its damage to young people, other films pushed persuasive arguments for why their teen militants needed to fight: in *Iron Eagle* (1986) an aspiring air force cadet rescues his father from an Arab country by flying a fighter jet; *Born American* (1986) follows teen boys unjustly imprisoned by the Russian military who then escape; *Terror Squad* (1987) has students fighting off Libyans who take over their school; *Little Nikita* (1988) portrays a teen coping with the fact that his parents are Soviet spies; *The Rescue* (1988) uses a whole cadre of kids to infiltrate North Korea and rescue their navy fathers. The wave ended thereafter, as the Cold War closed and the industry redirected its image of youth fighting to urban African American teens, whose cultural plight and resulting criminality received abundant attention on screen in the early '90s.

5. The twin stars of *New York Minute*, Mary-Kate and Ashley Olsen, gained massive popularity in '90s television as children and released a made-for-video travel series as they went through adolescence: *Passport to Paris* (1999), *Our Lips Are Sealed* (2000), *Winning London* (2001), and *When in Rome* (2002). The Olsens had meanwhile built a massive merchandizing empire, although since this first theatrical feature failed at the box office in 2004 (grossing less than half of its production costs), they have not made another film together, and like so many child stars, their popularity faded drastically after they entered adulthood.

6. See Amy Best, *Fast Cars, Cool Rides: The Accelerating World of Youth and Their Cars* (New York: New York University Press, 2006).

7. While it does not focus exclusively on delinquency, consider "'Fighting and Violence and Everything, That's Always Cool': Teen Films in the 1990s" by Wheeler Winston Dixon, in *Film Genre 2000*, ed. Wheeler Winston Dixon (Albany: State University of New York Press, 2000), 125–142.

8. For a perspective on how drug use has been handled in films for teens, see "'Three Sheets to the Wind': Substance Use in Teen-Centered Film from 1980 to 2007," by Mark Callister, Sarah Marie Coyne, Tom Robinson, John J. Davies, Chris Near, Lynn Van Valkenburg, and Jason Gillespie, *Addiction Research and Theory* 20, no. 1 (2012): 30–41.

9. *Juice* review, Anne Billson, *New Statesman and Society*, Aug. 28, 1992, 28.

10. *Beat Street* review, J. Hoberman, *Village Voice*, June 19, 1984, 53.

11. *Footloose* review, Donald Greig, *Monthly Film Bulletin*, April 1984, 116.

12. *Dirty Dancing* grossed $63 million in its initial 1987 release, and earned about $1 million more in its tenth-anniversary rerelease in 1997. For a detailed collection about the film, see Yannis Tzioumakis and Siân Lincoln, eds., *The Time of Our Lives: "Dirty Dancing" and Popular Culture* (Detroit: Wayne State University Press, 2013).

13. *Salsa* (1988) is steeped in passion as well, although it isn't a film about teenagers *per se*, since the main characters are just over twenty. The film is a curious preview of Hollywood's attempt to capitalize on Latin music and dance with the lambada movies two years later, displacing sexual and ethnic tensions into its titular dance form.

14. *Dirty Dancing* review, Roger Ebert, *Chicago Sun-Times*, Aug. 21, 1987, C1.

15. The cancellation of the long-running popular television dance program *American Bandstand* in 1989 would be further evidence that media-based teen dancing would decline in the '90s.

16. There were two other aquatic animal films released in the mid-'90s that are not suited to the present study: *Andre* (1994), about a young girl's relationship with a seal, and *Magic in the Water* (1995), about a "bad dad" who becomes possessed by a mythical whalelike creature that teaches him how to love his kids better, very much in keeping with the theme of problem parents so prominent in '90s films.

17. *Free Willy* grossed $77.7 million at the box office.

18. *Free Willy* review, Hal Hinson, *Washington Post*, July 14, 1993, D1.

19. *Lord of the Flies* review, Gary Giddins, *Village Voice*, March 20, 1990, 66.

20. Mary Celeste Kearney, "Girlfriends and Girl Power: Female Adolescence in Contemporary U.S. Cinema," in *Sugar, Spice, and Everything Nice: Contemporary Cinemas of Girlhood*, ed. Murray Pomerance and Frances Gateward (Detroit: Wayne State University Press, 2002), 125.

21. Peggy Orenstein, "The Movies Discover the Teen-Age Girl," *New York Times*, Aug. 11, 1996, B1.

22. Ibid., B20.

23. Thomas Doherty, *Teenagers and Teenpics: The Juvenilization of American Movies in the 1950s*, rev. and exp. ed. (Philadelphia: Temple University Press, 2002), 123–127.

24. *Angel* review, Stanley Crouch, *Village Voice*, Feb. 7, 1984, 56.

25. *The Legend of Billie Jean* review, David Edelstein, *Village Voice*, July 23, 1985, 56.

26. *Mi Vida Loca* review, Kevin Thomas, *Los Angeles Times*, July 22, 1994, Calendar, 4.

27. *Mi Vida Loca* review, Leslie Felperin, *Sight and Sound* 5, no. 4 (April 1995): 48.

28. Kearney, 135.

29. *Girls Town* review, Emanuel Levy, *Variety*, Jan. 29, 1996, 77.

30. *Girls Town* review, Phil Riley, *Motion Picture Guide Annual, 1997*, 146.

31. Levy, 77.

32. Bernard Weinraub, "Who's Lining Up at Box Office? Lots and Lots of Girls," *New York Times*, Feb. 23, 1998, B4. In *Pictures of Girlhood: Modern Female Adolescence on Screen* (Jefferson, NC: McFarland, 2006), Sarah Hentges makes a cogent political argument about the correlation between girls' on-screen presence and their consumer value, that "girls do not have confidence in themselves as much as they have confidence in the products they consume, and in the eyes of mainstream culture, these products, and not the confidence, determine the girl" (9).

33. Yvonne Tasker, "Bodies and Genres in Transition: *Girlfight* and *Real Women Have Curves*," in *Gender Meets Genre in Postwar Cinemas*, ed. Christine Gledhill (Urbana: University of Illinois Press, 2012), 84.

34. "Vagilante" is a term that I thought was coined in my discussion of the film with Devin Griffiths, yet I have since learned that it is used as a slang word for any woman who demonstrates sexual control or revenge. The lone case in medical history of a woman with even a remotely parallel condition can be found in "Iatrogenic Vagina Dentata," a letter to the editor of the *American Journal of Forensic Medicine and Pathology* 10, no. 3 (Sept. 1989): 269, in which J. N. P. Davies reports of a woman whose postoperative genital pain was due to the protrusion of metal staples left in her vagina after gynecological surgery, "with the sharp ends sticking out in her vaginal vault." This publication was later cited numerous times, erroneously, as a genuine case of *vagina dentata*, and sources also erroneously cited a "benign embroid tumor containing teeth" as the cause of the phenomenon.

35. *Teeth* review, Steve Biodrowski, *Cinefantastique* 41, no. 1 (Jan. 21, 2009): 37.

36. The story bears a distinct resemblance to *Battle Royale*, a 2000 Japanese film in which high school students are placed on a deserted island with arbitrary weapons in a fight to the death.

37. As of this writing, the film's studio, Lionsgate, is developing a video game based on the film for commercial release. Meanwhile, a more traditional board game, *District 12*, has appeared, along with role-playing and card games.

38. As this book goes to press, the first sequel, *The Hunger Games: Catching Fire*, is scheduled to be released in fall 2013, again featuring Lawrence and Hutcherson in the lead roles. If it follows the trajectory of the novels, Katniss finds herself in a more precarious yet important leadership role for the districts. The third novel of the trilogy, *Mockingjay*, is scheduled to follow the recent trend established by the *Harry Potter* series and continued with *The Twilight Saga* by being broken into two films, the first to be released in 2014 and the second in 2015. Star Jennifer Lawrence, who won an Oscar for playing an adult character in *Silver Linings Playbook* (2012), will be twenty-five when the last *Hunger Games* film is released.

39. Another S. E. Hinton adaptation, *Tex* (1982), had already earned mild acclaim with its story of a boy who becomes increasingly troubled by life due to the misguidance of his father and older brother.

40. Richard Combs, *River's Edge* review, *Monthly Film Bulletin*, Oct. 1987, 294. See also the extensive analysis Vicky Lebeau gives to the film throughout *Lost Angels: Psychoanalysis and Cinema* (New York: Routledge, 1995).

41. Shirley Clarke's underground classic *The Cool World* (1963) was a notable exception—it provided a harsh portrait of a teen ghetto gang seriously involved in crime—yet its harshness may have been the very factor that prevented it from receiving wider distribution.

42. S. Craig Watkins referred to this trend as the "ghetto action film cycle" in his book *Representing: Hip Hop Culture and the Production of Black Cinema* (Chicago: University of Chicago Press, 1998), however, he does not use the term to distinguish

such non-teen action films as *New Jack City* from teen movies. He does concur that the cycle ran from 1991 to 1995. Amanda Ann Klein studies these films as a cycle in *American Film Cycles: Reframing Genres, Screening Social Problems, and Defining Subcultures* (Austin: University of Texas Press, 2011), 138–174.

43. One later film about African American youth that could arguably be claimed as part of this cycle was *Squeeze* in 1997, about three young teens on the verge of adopting delinquent lifestyles. However, the story's focus on the characters' psychological experiences and their as-yet minor criminality do not enlist it within the same tradition as the early '90s films.

44. *Boyz N the Hood* review, Jack Mathews, *Newsday*, July 12, 1991, part 2, 60.

45. Paula Massood, "Mapping the Hood: The Genealogy of City Space in *Boyz N the Hood* and *Menace II Society*," *Cinema Journal* 35, no. 2 (Winter 1996): 94. Murray Forman also offers commentary on the relationship between black identity and city space in "The 'Hood Took Me Under: Urban Geographies of Danger in New Black Cinema," in *Pictures of a Generation on Hold: Selected Papers*, ed. Murray Pomerance and John Sakeris (Toronto: Media Studies Working Group, 1996), 45–56.

46. Two other films appeared in 1992 that were somewhat a part of the trend in African American youth crime films, but do not properly belong in this category. *Zebrahead* was more formally a study of interracial dating, and its small amount of violence, while speaking to the volatility of racial tensions, does not enlist it within the same subgeneric classification as the films above. *South Central* is another compelling film about the plight of urban blacks, but its main character is an adult ex-convict who returns to his family in an effort to keep his ten-year-old son from the life of crime that derailed him as a younger man. The film continues the message of the need for strong paternal guidance in young black men's lives, although within the confines of this study it does not qualify as a youth film.

47. *Menace II Society* review, David Denby, *New York*, May 31, 1993, 54.

48. An interesting film using the basketball theme that is not very much about youth or crime but is worth citing all the same is *Heaven Is a Playground* from 1991. The story unfolds around public basketball courts, where hopeful African American youth aspire to college scholarships under the tutelage of a freelance scout. What is most compelling about the existence of this film—which was not well received in limited theatrical release—is that its positive image of the proud, non-criminal African American male youth who play basketball was lost in the attention paid to the more violent and distraught depictions of male African Americans in crime films of the same time. The athletes in the film may not be very well developed, yet it remains an important exception in the representation of African American youth in the early '90s.

49. *Clockers* review, James Berardinelli, *ReelViews*, 1995, http://www.reelviews .net/movies/c/clockers.html.

50. See Gregory M. Colón Semenza, "Shakespeare After Columbine: Teen Violence in Tim Blake Nelson's *'O*,'" *College Literature* 32, no. 4 (Fall 2005): 99–124.

51. A 2010 content analysis of ninety films (thirty each from the '80s, '90s, and

'00s) "aimed at adolescents" indicated that violence decreased over these three decades, specifically gun violence, "but other types of physical aggression (including indirect physical aggression) increased." In films about teenage characters, violence "was portrayed less frequently than expected." See "Yes, Another Teen Movie: Three Decades of Physical Violence in Films Aimed at Adolescents," by Sarah Coyne, Mark Callister, and Tom Robinson, *Journal of Children and Media* 4, no. 4 (2010): 387–401.

52. Murray Pomerance casually inserts the shower scene of the boys into this description to emphasize its banality: "While they sleep, while they eat breakfast in the kitchen, while they watch a documentary on Nazism in the living room and receive their gun shipment, while they practice shooting in the garage, and while they shower together, the camera explores the space they inhabit but essentially frames them as situated, comfortable, engaged, and static." In "Pachyderm's Progress," in *Youth Culture in Global Cinema*, ed. Timothy Shary and Alexandra Seibel (Austin: University of Texas Press, 2007), 215–216. Cynthia Fuchs is one of the few scholars to imply that the boys may actually have sex as they shower, because "the little bit of fear and desire evinced in their brief dialogue ('I've never even kissed anyone') suggests, gently, that they are confused and sad, seeking only to have sex before the death they know is coming." *Elephant* review, *PopMatters*, Nov. 10, 2003, http://www.popmatters.com/pm/review/elephant.

53. Jennifer Rich, "Shock Corridors: The New Rhetoric of Horror in Gus Van Sant's *Elephant*," *Journal of Popular Culture* 45, no. 6 (Dec. 2012): 1311.

54. Jessie Klein looks at the broader topic in *The Bully Society: School Shootings and the Crisis of Bullying in America's Schools* (New York: New York University Press, 2012).

55. *Brick* review, Michael Atkinson, *Village Voice*, March 21, 2006, 57.

CHAPTER 4. THE YOUTH HORROR FILM: SLASHERS AND THE SUPERNATURAL

1. David Cook, *A History of Narrative Film*, 3rd ed. (New York: Norton, 1996), 945. See also Richard Nowell's lengthy analysis of the boom-and-bust year of 1981 for the slasher film in *Blood Money: A History of the First Teen Slasher Cycle* (London: Continuum, 2011), particularly 187–242.

2. See Shelley Stamp Lindsey, "Horror, Femininity, and Carrie's Monstrous Puberty," *Journal of Film and Video* 43, no. 4 (Winter 1991): 33–44.

3. Carol Clover, *Men, Women, and Chain Saws: Gender in the Modern Horror Film* (Princeton: Princeton University Press, 1992), 35.

4. Cook, 944.

5. Cook claims that *Halloween* "returned sixty million dollars on an eight-hundred-thousand-dollar investment" (945).

6. *Student Bodies* begins with this caption: "Last year 26 horror films were re-leased. None of them lost money."

7. Chris Nashawaty, "Oh, the Horror," *Entertainment Weekly*, Jan. 17, 1997, 8. Nowell argues for three slasher cycles after the first in the early '80s, each marked by a landmark film: 1984 to 1989 (after *A Nightmare on Elm Street*), 1996 to 2000 (after *Scream*) and "beginning in 2005 and continuing unabated" with the releases of "re-inventions" such as *Black Christmas* (2006), *Halloween* (2007), *Prom Night* (2008), *Friday the 13th* (2009), and *A Nightmare on Elm Street* (2010): 11, 250.

8. In his study *Horror and the Horror Film* (London: Anthem, 2012), Bruce Kawin provides a comprehensive list of foes under the heading "Supernatural Monsters" including (in order of presentation): demons, doubles, vampires, witches, ghosts, zombies, mummies, others back from the dead, werewolves and other shape-shifters, legendary figures, nameless forces, and immortal slashers such as Michael, Jason, and Freddy (91–151). Kawin's reading of the mutant teen thriller *The Funhouse* (1981), which goes back to his first review of the film when it was released, is par-ticularly trenchant (86–87).

9. Clover, 5.

10. Ibid., 35.

11. Ibid., 40.

12. Vera Dika, *Games of Terror: "Halloween," "Friday the 13th," and the Films of the Stalker Cycle* (Toronto: Associated University Presses, 1990).

13. Ibid., 55. While Clover's book did not appear until 1992, she and Dika both published their foundational work on the subject in 1987, Dika in "The Stalker Film, 1978–81," in *American Horrors: Essays on the Modern Horror Film*, ed. Gregory Waller (Urbana: University of Illinois Press, 1987): 86–101, and Clover in "Her Body, Himself: Gender in the Slasher Film," *Representations* 20 (1987): 187–228.

14. Dika, 55.

15. Ibid., 56.

16. Ibid., 57.

17. Adam Rockoff, *Going to Pieces: The Rise and Fall of the Slasher Film, 1978–1986* (Jefferson, NC: McFarland, 2002; reprinted 2011).

18. Ibid., 5.

19. Nowell also published "'There's More Than One Way to Lose Your Heart': The American Film Industry, Early Teen Slasher Films, and Female Youth," *Cinema Journal* 51, no. 1 (Fall 2011): 115–140, which was revised into the first chapter of *Blood Money*.

20. Nowell, 4. Nowell's work further takes up the arguments of scholars such as James Weaver in "Are 'Slasher' Horror Films Sexually Violent? A Content Analysis," *Journal of Broadcasting and Electronic Media* 35, no. 3 (Summer 1991): 385–392. Weaver's study was later expanded on by Barry Sapolsky and Fred Molitor in "Content Trends in Contemporary Horror Films," in *Horror Films: Current Research on Audi-ence Preferences and Reactions*, ed. James Weaver and Ron Tamborini (Mahwah, NJ:

Lawrence Erlbaum Associates, 1996), 35–52, whose analyses clearly indicate that women are more often "seen in fear" than are men in slasher films of the 1980s (by an overwhelming margin), but that there is no significant difference between the number of male and female murder victims. The authors thus go on to conclude that, contrary to popular perception, "females have not been found to be the primary victims in slasher films," and more arguably, they claim that "sex and violence are not frequently connected in slasher films" (46). The authors suggest that political motives and faulty methodologies in other studies are explanations for why perceptions of the slasher film have become so zealous, at least in terms of female victimology and the "sex = death" link, although their approach does not single out or examine issues particular to youth. Nowell traces many of the gendered attitudes about slasher films to the film critics Gene Siskel and Roger Ebert, who he claims eliminated "clearly drawn generic boundaries between teen slashers and violence-against-women movies" (228) with their reviews in 1980, and through his analysis supports many of the observations advanced by Sapolsky and Molitor.

21. Robin Wood, "Introduction to the American Horror Film," in *The American Nightmare: Essays on the Horror Film*, ed. Robin Wood and Richard Lippe (Toronto: Festival of Festivals, 1979).

22. Ibid., 167.

23. For an alternative perspective on male representation in these films, see Klaus Rieser, "Masculinity and Monstrosity: Characterization and Identification in the Slasher Film," *Men and Masculinities* 3, no. 4 (2001): 370–392.

24. Wood, 170.

25. Jonathan Bernstein, *Pretty in Pink: The Golden Age of Teenage Movies* (New York: St. Martin's Griffin, 1997), 34.

26. Ibid., 37.

27. Ibid., 35.

28. Bernstein also singles out the "blob movie," although I subsume this variety within the "supernatural" heading since his one example — *The Blob* (1988) — does not constitute a category unto itself. Brigid Cherry offers further consideration of labeling teen horror categories in "Subcultural Tastes, Genre Boundaries, and Fan Canons," in *The Shifting Definitions of Genre: Essays on Labeling Films, Television Shows, and Media*, ed. Lincoln Geraghty and Mark Jancovich (Jefferson, NC: McFarland, 2008), 201–215.

29. In *Laughing Screaming: Modern Hollywood Horror and Comedy* (New York: Columbia University Press, 1994), William Paul examines the "gross-out" influences of a number of youth horror films and comedies. Less relevant to youth cinema but worth consulting for recent horror film research are Isabel Pinedo's "Postmodern Elements of the Contemporary Horror Film" and Scott R. Olson's "College Course File on Horror," both in a "Film Genres" edition of the *Journal of Film and Video* 48, nos. 1–2 (Spring–Summer 1996): 17–25 and 47–62 (respectively). See also *Nightmare on Main Street: Angels, Sadomasochism, and the Culture of the Gothic* (Cambridge: Harvard University Press, 1997) by Mark Edmundson, which

considers the gothic traditions of horror in film and literature from a wide range of cultural influences. Carol Siegel explores the goth culture in *Goth's Dark Empire* (Bloomington: Indiana University Press, 2005) and analyzes it through films such as *Boys Don't Cry* (1999), *The Sixth Sense* (1999), and *Crime + Punishment in Suburbia* (2000).

30. Youth moralities in these films are surveyed by Sarah Trencansky in "Final Girls and Terrible Youth: Transgression in 1980s Slasher Horror," *Journal of Popular Film and Television* 29, no. 2 (Summer 2001): 63–73.

31. *Friday the 13th: The Final Chapter* review, David Edelstein, *Village Voice*, April 24, 1984, 57.

32. Pat Gill, "The Monstrous Years: Teens, Slasher Films, and the Family," *Journal of Film and Video* 54, no. 4 (2003): 16.

33. Kelly Connelly discusses the empowerment of Laurie Strode as the Final Girl of *Halloween H₂O* in "From Final Girl to Final Woman: Defeating the Male Monster in *Halloween* and *Halloween H₂O*," *Journal of Popular Film and Television*, 35, no. 1 (2007): 12–21.

34. Ryan Lizardi, "'Re-imagining' Hegemony and Misogyny in the Contemporary Slasher Remake," *Journal of Popular Film and Television* 38, no. 3 (July–Sept. 2010): 121.

35. An extremely detailed account of the series is available in *Crystal Lake Memories: The Complete History of "Friday the 13th,"* by Peter Bracke (Los Angeles: Sparkplug Press, 2005).

36. Rhonda Hammer and Douglas Kellner offer a surprising reading of *Friday the 13th: The Final Chapter* with a wide context in "Movies and Battles over Reaganite Conservatism," in *American Cinema of the 1980s: Themes and Variations*, ed. Stephen Prince (New Brunswick: Rutgers University Press, 2007), 120–122.

37. *A Nightmare on Elm Street 3: Dream Warriors* review, Judith Williamson, *New Statesman*, Dec. 11, 1987, 24.

38. *A Nightmare on Elm Street* review, David Sterritt, *Christian Science Monitor*, Nov. 28, 1984, 34.

39. *A Nightmare on Elm Street* review, David Edelstein, *Village Voice*, Nov. 20, 1984, 55.

40. Douglas Rathgeb, "Bogeyman from the Id," *Journal of Popular Film and Television* 19, no. 1 (Spring 1991): 41. See also Jonathan Markovitz, "Female Paranoia as Survival Skill: Reason or Pathology in *A Nightmare on Elm Street*?" *Quarterly Review of Film and Video* 17, no. 3 (2000): 211–220; and James Kendrick, "Razors in the Dreamscape: Revisiting *A Nightmare on Elm Street* and the Slasher Film," *Film Criticism* 33, no. 3 (Spring 2009): 17–33.

41. Philip Kemp later claimed that the producers added this ending to facilitate sequels. *Freddy's Dead* review, *Sight and Sound*, Feb. 1992, 45.

42. Kyle Christensen, "The Final Girl Versus Wes Craven's *A Nightmare on Elm Street*: Proposing a Stronger Model of Feminism in Slasher Horror Cinema," *Studies in Popular Culture* 34, no. 1 (Fall 2011): 30.

43. As with the *Halloween* and *Friday the 13th* series, the original director did not direct any of the sequels, although Wes Craven did write and direct *New Nightmare*, the seventh in the series in 1994, and was a writer on the third film.

44. L. J. DeGraffenreid, "What Can You Do in Your Dreams? Slasher Cinema as Youth Empowerment," *Journal of Popular Culture* 44, no. 5 (2011): 954.

45. A vaguely connected straight-to-DVD sequel was made in 2003 called *Cheerleader Massacre*, which was itself loosely followed by *Cheerleader Massacre 2* in 2009.

46. *Scream* earned $103 million in its 1996–1997 release, *Scream 2* earned $101.3 million within the next year, and *Scream 3* earned $89.1 million at the U.S. box office in 2000, making these the highest-grossing teen horror films ever up to that time. *Gremlins* (1984) did earn $153 million on its own, although its distant sequel, *Gremlins 2: The New Batch* (1990), grossed only $41.5 million. The five *Twilight* films (2008–2012) now form the highest-grossing teen franchise in any subgenre, with over $1.4 billion in U.S. box office revenue; the most prolific franchise, *Friday the 13th*, with twelve editions from the 1980 original to present, has earned $381 million, or $736 million adjusted for inflation, according to BoxOfficeMojo.com.

47. See Kathleen Rowe Karlyn, "*Scream*, Popular Culture, and Feminism's Third Wave," in *Motherhood Misconceived: Representing the Maternal in U.S. Films*, ed. Heather Addison, Mary Kate Goodwin-Kelly, and Elaine Roth (Albany: State University of New York Press, 2009), 177–198.

48. For two studies of *Scream* in the context of the subgenre, see the work of Valerie Wee: "The *Scream* Trilogy: 'Hyper-postmodernism' and the Late-Nineties Teen Slasher Film," *Journal of Film and Video* 57, no. 3 (Fall 2005): 44–61; and "Resurrecting and Updating the Teen Slasher: The Case of *Scream*," *Journal of Popular Film and Television* 34, no. 2 (Summer 2006): 50–61.

49. *My Soul to Take* review, Marc Savlov, *Austin Chronicle*, Oct. 15, 2010, http://www.austinchronicle.com/calendar/film/.

50. Gill, 18.

51. *Christine* review, Sheila Johnston, *Monthly Film Bulletin*, March 1984, 77.

52. At least two critics found this revelation to be connotative of AIDS: Michael Wilmington in the *Los Angeles Times*, Aug. 5, 1988, Calendar, 10; and Julian Petley in *Monthly Film Bulletin*, June 1989, 170.

53. The original film was less intriguingly sequelized in 1994 with *Mirror Mirror 2: Raven Dance*, in which a teenage girl and her brother become victims of the mirror, and then *Mirror Mirror III: The Voyeur* in 1995 and *Mirror Mirror IV: Reflection* in 2000.

54. *Body Snatchers* review, John Powers, *New York*, Feb. 21, 1994, 48.

55. The cinematic depiction of teen witches in the three 1996 films stands in stark contrast to the mildly successful television show *Sabrina, the Teenage Witch*, which also started that same year, where the main character's association with the supernatural is portrayed in still mystical but altogether positive ways. While not a witch, the same could be said of the heroine in TV's more popular *Buffy the Vampire Slayer*, which started in 1997.

56. *The Craft* review, Roger Ebert, *Chicago Sun-Times*, May 10, 1996, C1.

57. Peg Aloi, "A Charming Spell: The Intentional and Unintentional Influence of Popular Media upon Teenage Witchcraft in America," in *The New Generation Witches: Teenage Witchcraft in Contemporary Culture*, ed. Hannah E. Johnson and Peg Aloi (London: Ashgate, 2007), 118.

58. In addition to the 1999 sequel, *Carrie* was remade for television in 2002, and Chloë Grace Moretz will star as the title heroine in a remake after this book goes to press in 2013.

59. See Christian Sellers and Gary Smart, *The Complete History of "The Return of the Living Dead"* (London: Plexus, 2011).

60. George Ochoa wrote the curious *Deformed and Destructive Beings: The Purpose of Horror Films* (Jefferson, NC: McFarland, 2011), in which he offers a detailed taxonomy of zombies (151–167), and an acerbic evaluation of *Zombieland* (114–115).

61. Jared Roberts provides pithy commentary on all of *The Brotherhood* films in *The Lair of the Boyg*, which includes this Nov. 26, 2011, posting: http://www.lairof theboyg.com/2011/11/guide-to-brotherhood-series.html#broth2.

62. Wes Craven had attempted to regain his eminence in the subgenre before the rise of *Twilight* with a monster tale that was quickly forgotten: *Cursed* (2005), about a teenage boy dealing with a werewolf incantation, barely registered with critics and audiences.

63. *Twilight* review, Cynthia Fuchs, *PopMatters*, Nov. 21, 2008, http://www.pop matters.com/pm/review/66011-twilight/.

64. *Twilight* review, Richard Corliss, *Time*, Nov. 20, 2008, 53.

65. *New Moon* review, Manohla Dargis, *New York Times*, Nov. 19, 2009, C1.

66. *New Moon* review, Mick LaSalle, *San Francisco Chronicle*, Nov. 21, 2012, D1.

67. Kelly Oliver, *Knock Me Up, Knock Me Down: Images of Pregnancy in Hollywood Films* (New York: Columbia University Press, 2012), 200.

68. *Breaking Dawn—Part 1* review, Todd McCarthy, *Hollywood Reporter*, Nov. 11, 2011, http://www.hollywoodreporter.com/movie/twilight-saga-breaking-dawn-part-1/review/260687.

69. Oliver, 197.

70. To illustrate the ongoing double standard the Code and Ratings Administration (CARA) of the Motion Picture Association of America (MPAA) still maintains between sex and violence, especially in youth films, the PG-13 rating card before *Breaking Dawn—Part 1* notes that the film contains "disturbing images, violence, sexuality/partial nudity." The gory birthing of Bella's baby in this scene—and the fact that it is performed through Edward biting open her skin, which is partially obscured—followed by Bella's agonizing death, is all far more brutally disturbing than the quiet sex and "partial nudity" of the characters that is primarily contained in a few shots of their bare legs and arms when they swim. Kelly Oliver adds, "The bloodstains between Bella's legs suggest that we have more fascination with—or anxiety over—blood associated with women's menstruation and reproduction than with blood-sucking vampires" (196). Perennial ratings critic Roger Ebert called this "without doubt the most blood-curdling scene of live childbirth

in a PG-13 movie," and went on to rightly suggest, "Probably the sight of Bella and Edward demolishing the bedroom [during sex] would have tipped it over into R territory" (*Breaking Dawn—Part 1* review, Roger Ebert, *Chicago Sun-Times*, Nov. 16, 2011, C1). In the commentary track on the DVD disc, director Bill Condon describes how they had shot a slightly more explicit sex scene but that the MPAA had "decided" the rating would require edits, including the reduction of a single thrust seen from behind Edward (00:36:26–00:37:04). The MPAA does not have a rubric of standards in advance of each rating, but rather only "advises" on ratings after a film has been submitted to CARA for review.

71. Renesmee is played in both films by no less than eleven different credited actresses, aging from her toddler years to young adulthood. Some reports claim that the baby Renesmee is a digital creation, while director Bill Condon claims on the DVD commentary track that the older Renesmee was the result of special effects artists who age-progressed the features of eleven-year-old actress Mackenzie Foy to estimate what she would look like at the age of eighteen. Foy plays Renesmee at the end of *Breaking Dawn—Part 1*, while Christie Burke is credited with playing Renesmee as a "young woman" in only the second film.

72. In referring to the climax of the film in his review, Michael Phillips gave a conclusive statement on the inconsistent hypocrisy of the films' ratings: "The touchingly misguided folks at the Motion Picture Association of America classification and ratings administration have allowed this melee of decapitations to get by with a PG-13. Presumably this is payback for all that earnest abstinence in the first few hundred minutes of the *Twilight* saga" (*Breaking Dawn—Part 1* review, *Chicago Tribune*, Nov. 15, 2012, http://articles.chicagotribune.com/2012-11-15/busi ness/sc-mov-1115-twilight-breaking-dawn-part-2-20121116_1_vampire-twilight -films-twilight-saga).

73. Mark Cotta Vaz has written a book about each film in the series, beginning with *"Twilight": The Complete Illustrated Movie Companion* (New York: Little, Brown, 2008). While it focuses almost entirely on Meyer's books, *Bitten by "Twilight": Youth Culture, Media, and the Vampire Franchise*, ed. Melissa A. Click, Jennifer Stevens Aubrey, and Elizabeth Behm-Morawitz (New York: Peter Lang, 2010) offers a wide perspective on the series in relation to youth. Casting slightly more attention on the films is *Genre, Reception, and Adaptation in the "Twilight" Series*, ed. Anne Morey (London: Ashgate, 2012). An entire cottage industry of books, music, and other products has emerged based on *Twilight*, similar to the *Harry Potter* phenomenon already in motion.

74. *Let Me In* review, Amy Biancolli, *San Francisco Chronicle*, Dec. 14, 2012, D1.

75. Denis Wood offers an interesting mythological reading of the film in "No Place for a Kid: Critical Commentary on *The Last Starfighter*," *Journal of Popular Film and Television* 14, no. 1 (Spring 1986): 52–63.

76. *Beetlejuice* (1988) was a success, but its story concentrated primarily on the antics of its eponymous "bio-exorcist" and less on the role of its rising teen star, Winona Ryder.

77. Christopher Falzon provides an unexpected dualist reading of the film in *Philosophy Goes to the Movies: An Introduction to Philosophy* (New York: Routledge, 2007), 75–77.

78. *Casper* review, Caryn James, *New York Times*, May 26, 2005, C13.

79. *Casper* engendered three sequels over the five years after its release, all of which went straight-to-video and inevitably landed in the "kid vid" sections of stores. The franchise also produced an entire line of toys and memorabilia, making the boy ghost one of the most conspicuous commodities among children for the rest of the decade. See more complete coverage of this phenomenon, and that of *Toy Story* the same year, in Timothy Shary, "1995: Movies, Teens, Tots, and Tech," in *American Cinema of the 1990s: Themes and Variations*, ed. Christine Holmlund (New Brunswick: Rutgers University Press, 2008), 137–156.

80. *Film Threat* magazine called *Purgatory House* the best film of 2004: http://www.filmthreat.com/features/1311/.

81. Arguments about the reason for the title change are inconsistent. Some sources claim that Scholastic feared young American youth would not buy a book with "philosopher" in the title, while others claim that the publisher wanted a greater emphasis on magic in the title, and conspiracy theories claim Scholastic actually wanted to generate controversy over the book's promotion of witchcraft for children. The truth behind the change is certainly proprietary to the press and thus may never be known.

82. Temple Northup and Carol M. Liebler, "The Good, the Bad, and the Beautiful," *Journal of Children and Media* 4, no. 3 (Aug. 2010): 265–282.

83. *Kick-Ass* review, Peter Travers, *Rolling Stone*, April 15, 2010, http://www.rollingstone.com/movies/reviews/kick-ass-20100415#ixzz2FdU1n4de.

84. An indicator of the double standard between profanity and violence in youth movies emerged after eleven-year-old Chloë Grace Moretz uttered this line to a roomful of dangerous criminals: "OK, you cunts, let's see what you can do now." As director Matthew Vaughn pointed out, "You know, her character wipes out just about everyone on screen, and that one word is where all the controversy is." The word is not said within a sexual context, but its etymology as a sexual term is certainly part of the problem. See Scott Bowles, "Chloe Moretz, 13, Can Kick Your You-Know-What," *USA Today*, April 15, 2010, http://usatoday30.usatoday.com/life/movies/news/2010-04-15-chloe15_ST_N.htm.

85. Jessica Robinson, *Life Lessons from Slasher Films* (Lanham, MD: Scarecrow Press, 2012).

86. Ibid., 193.

87. See Angela M. Cranon, "Rolfe Kanefsky's Creepy Thriller Nightmare Man Already Taking Home Awards!" *Hollywood Scriptwriter* 27, no. 5 (Oct. 2007): 4–9.

CHAPTER 5. YOUTH ROMANCE: FALLING
IN LOVE AND THE FALLOUT OF SEX

1. I employ this term "erosphere"—which has been used by previous authors—to refer to the entire wide realm of romantic and sexual experiences for youth.

2. Emily Bennion, "Sexual Content in Teen Films: 1980–2007" (M.M.C. thesis, Brigham Young University, 2008), 3. See also Marianne Sinclair's historical appreciation of girls' sexuality in films primarily before 1980, *Hollywood Lolitas: The Nymphet Syndrome in the Movies* (New York: Holt, 1988).

3. For an interesting examination of male sexuality in the youth films of John Hughes, see Marianne H. Whatley, "Raging Hormones and Powerful Cars: The Construction of Men's Sexuality in School Sex Education and Popular Adolescent Films," *Journal of Education* 170, no. 3 (1988): 100–121. Also see the genre and gender analysis Catherine Driscoll provides in her erudite explication "John Hughes: Teen Film, 1984–1987," in *Teen Film: A Critical Introduction* (New York: Berg, 2011), 45–56.

4. National Center for Health Statistics and Centers for Disease Control, cited in *The Adolescent and Young Adult Fact Book* by the Children's Defense Fund (Washington, DC, 1991).

5. David M. Considine, *Cinema of Adolescence* (Jefferson, NC: McFarland, 1985), 262. *The Last Picture Show* (1971), a more popular American film in release around the same time as *Friends*, was also a factor in the increasingly sexualized image of youth.

6. Director Franco Zeffirelli, who filmed the famous version of *Romeo and Juliet* in 1968, took advantage of loosening moral codes to show his young protagonists in lengthy nude lovemaking sessions, all without any form of birth control, including one scene in which David is shown coming to an ostentatious orgasm.

7. *Endless Love* review, Sheila Benson, *Los Angeles Times*, July 17, 1981, Calendar, 14.

8. See Elaine Roth, "'You Just Hate Men!' Maternal Sexuality and the Nuclear Family in *Gas, Food Lodging*," in *Motherhood Misconceived: Representing the Maternal in U.S. Films*, ed. Heather Addison, Mary Kate Goodwin-Kelly, and Elaine Roth (Albany: State University of New York Press, 2009), 111–124.

9. *Say Anything . . .* review, Roger Ebert, *Chicago Sun-Times*, April 14, 1989, C1.

10. Jonathan Bernstein, *Pretty in Pink: The Golden Age of Teenage Movies* (New York: St. Martin's Griffin, 1997), 105.

11. *Trust* review, J. Hoberman, *Village Voice*, July 30, 1991, 53.

12. *Trust* review, Philip Strick, *Sight and Sound* 1, no. 9 (Sept. 1991): 53.

13. Timothy Shary, "'The Only Place to Go Is Inside': Confusions of Sexuality and Class in *Clueless* and *Kids*," in *Pictures of a Generation on Hold: Selected Papers*, ed. Murray Pomerance and John Sakeris (Toronto: Media Studies Working Group, 1996), 162.

14. *Fear* review, Mick LaSalle, *San Francisco Chronicle*, April 12, 1996, D1.

15. Lisa Schwarzbaum commented on the release of *Fear* and *The Craft* in theaters and on video at the same time in a review titled "Demonic Youth," in which she noted "the conservatism of big-studio teen movies, now and forever," as "oh-so-sophisticated products of Hollywood" (*Entertainment Weekly*, Oct. 11, 1996, 99).

16. Richard Burt offers sundry commentary on this film, and *My Own Private Idaho*, in *Unspeakable ShaXXXspeares: Queer Theory and American Kiddie Culture*, rev. ed. (New York: Palgrave Macmillan, 1999).

17. Youth love stories are strewn with so-called assignments—punishments, bets, jobs—to make opposites attract, as here and in *My Tutor*, *Girls Just Want to Have Fun* (1985), *Just One of the Guys*, *Can't Buy Me Love*, *The Forbidden Dance* (1990), *Dogfight* (1991), *Clueless*, *She's All That*, *10 Things I Hate About You*, *Girlfight*, *Whatever It Takes*, *Here on Earth* (2000), *13 Going on 30* (2004), *Superbad*, *Twilight*, *Prom*, *Carrie* (2013).

18. Cynthia Fuchs wittily questioned the commonality of the "movie disease" for this and other girls' terminal illnesses, referencing notable cases: "Shades of Winona [*Autumn in New York*]-Leelee [*Here on Earth*]-Ali McGraw [*Love Story*]-and-Bette Davis [*Dark Victory*]. Come to think of it: when was the last time you saw a movie where the boy dies of a withering-but-strangely-glow-inducing illness to teach the girl an important life lesson?" *A Walk to Remember* review, *Nitrate Online*, Jan. 25, 2002, http://www.nitrateonline.com/2002/rremember.html.

19. *Moonrise Kingdom* review, Jeffrey Anderson, *San Francisco Examiner*, June 1, 2012, D3.

20. *Moonrise Kingdom* review, Todd McCarthy, *Hollywood Reporter*, May 16, 2012, http://www.hollywoodreporter.com/movie/moonrise-kingdom/review/325507.

21. Amy Best, *Prom Night: Youth, Schools, and Popular Culture* (New York: Routledge, 2000). See also Marietta Abell and Agnes Anderson, *"The Junior–Senior Prom," Complete Practical Suggestions for Staging the Junior–Senior Prom* (Minneapolis: Northwestern Press, 1936). Prom movies after *Harold Teen* (1934) not mentioned in this chapter include *Born to Gamble* (1935), *Best Foot Forward* (1943), *Sweet and Low-Down* (1944), *Junior Prom* (1946), *Good News* (1947), *A Date with Judy* (1948), *Mickey* (1948), *Any Number Can Play* (1949), and *Cheaper by the Dozen* (1950).

22. Richard G. Calo, *The First and Original Book of Prom* (Wormleysburg, PA: Awaken Sky Books, 2004), and *American Prom* (Nashville: Cumberland House, 2006).

23. Part of my argument here was published in "Buying Me Love: 1980s Class-Clash Teen Romances," *Journal of Popular Culture* 44, no. 3 (June 2011): 563–582.

24. David Ansen, *Pretty in Pink* review, *Newsweek*, Mar. 17, 1986, 81.

25. No less than four reasons have been cited for the changed ending of the film from the original John Hughes script, and from the first answer print (shown only within the studio), which had Andie and Duckie together rather than her and Blane. Some critics' theories dominated discussion for over two decades, with Bernstein offering the most common understanding: "Test audiences balked at this

outcome. They wanted to see the poor girl get the rich boy of her dreams. They didn't care about the dignity of the oppressed" (78). Similar stories have been repeated in multiple sources since then, including the 2006 DVD release of *Pretty in Pink (Everything's Duckie Edition)*, in a featurette titled *The Original Ending: The Lost Dance* that repeats the test audience response as a culprit, but also cites "Ringwald's dislike of the pairing of Andie and Duckie because she believed she had no romantic chemistry with Jon Cryer," as reported by Rebecca Taylor, http://www.dvdactive .com/reviews/dvd/pretty-in-pink-everythings-duckie-edition.html. Susannah Gora supports aspects of both explanations in her study *You Couldn't Ignore Me If You Tried: The Brat Pack, John Hughes, and Their Impact on a Generation* (Pittsburgh: Three Rivers Press, 2011), 142–151. But soon after the film's release, Nigel Floyd was one of a few critics who cited both "technical and personal reasons — no time to shoot the reaction shots of the 'richie' onlookers, and Molly Ringwald's illness in the last few days of shooting" to explain the new ending, all of which is true, but incomplete as motivations for the change. See *Pretty in Pink* review, *Monthly Film Bulletin*, Aug. 1986, 243. The most authoritative explanation comes from Jon Cryer himself, who, in a public interview with Diablo Cody in 2008, confirmed that the *initial* reasons behind the changed ending were that the original prom scene between Duckie and Andie was indeed compromised by Ringwald being sick and the reaction shots being ineffective (the first cut, he claimed, "lacked a certain oomph"), and that this "lacking" ending, when shown to test audiences, then motivated the producers to reshoot and edit the new "*Cinderella*-style closure" (my term) that now ends the film. I thank Jessica Turetz for directing me to the Cryer interview at http://news .moviefone.com/2013/03/29/pretty-in-pink-alternate-ending-jon-cryer/.

26. *Pretty in Pink* review, David Denby, *New York*, Mar. 10, 1986, 93.

27. *She's All That* review, Stephen Holden, *New York Times*, Jan. 29, 1999, C11.

28. *Prom* review, Owen Gleiberman, *Entertainment Weekly*, May 6, 2011, 46.

29. *Fast Times at Ridgemont High* review, David Denby, *New York*, Sept. 27, 1982, 50.

30. The director of *Last American Virgin*, Boaz Davidson, attained prominence in the early '80s with his "Lemon Popsicle" series from Israel, produced by the Cannon company's Menahem Golan and Yorum Globus. Jonathan Bernstein provides some background on the connection between the "Lemon Popsicle" films and *Virgin*: "Though largely unseen in America, these movies (threadbare titillation set in the fifties, executed in a style that aimed for *Porky's* but achieved Benny Hill), packed European cinemas, largely on the backs of TV-advertised soundtrack albums stuffed to the gills with early days rock 'n' roll standards. . . . Boaz Davidson used its components — sex-seeking stud, shy guy and gutbucket — as the basis for *The Last American Virgin*. But there the similarities end" (22). There were at least seven films made in the franchise until 1987, but the fact that these films were made with largely the same intentions as other American teen sex films of the time — and were so successful in Europe — raises the possibility that the increasingly sexual

representation of youth in the '80s was a more global phenomenon, an investigation of which demands further study.

31. *Risky Business* review, David Denby, *New York*, Aug. 22, 1983, 62.

32. Perhaps the truly last moanings of the '80s teen sex comedies came from the Canadian film industry, which produced *The Virgin Queen of St. Francis High* in 1987, although it had virtually zero visibility; the film followed in the cycle of "big bet" plots, with its story of a teen who wagers that he can bed his high school's most conspicuous virgin beauty. The few reviews I've been able to find on this film are also uniformly negative.

33. Shary, *Pictures of a Generation on Hold*, 160.

34. bell hooks, "White Light," *Sight and Sound* 6, no. 5 (May 1996): 10.

35. Owen Gleiberman, "Bold Before Their Time," *Entertainment Weekly*, July 21, 1995, 47.

36. Tom Doherty, "Clueless Kids," *Cineaste* 21, no. 4 (1995): 15.

37. A different *American Virgin* appeared in 2009, critical of abstinence commitments that have become popular for youth in recent years, as also seen in *Saved!* (2004), *Teeth* (2007), and *Chastity Bites* (2013).

38. For a revealing discussion of moral and literary issues in *Cruel Intentions*, see Bruce Newman, "Can't Read the Classic? See the Teen Movie," *New York Times*, Feb. 28, 1999, C13. After an abortive attempt to adapt the original film into a TV series called *Manchester Prep*, the FOX network gave the show's pilot to TriStar, which released it as a video feature titled *Cruel Intentions 2* in 2000.

39. Sharyn Pearce, "Sex and the Cinema: What *American Pie* Teaches the Young," *Sex Education* 6, no. 4 (2006): 373.

40. *American Pie* review, Jonathan Foreman, *New York Post*, July 16, 1999, 33.

41. A revealing irony about the cast of *American Pie* is that many of the male actors were so religious that they were initially concerned about the moral implications of their roles, which they ultimately found to be compatible with their beliefs by the time the film went into production. See Rebecca Ascher-Walsh, "Virgin Territory," *Entertainment Weekly on Campus*, April 1999, 10–12.

42. See a thesis that appeared shortly after *American Pie*, "No Glove, No Love: Messages About Contraception in Teen Movies," by Carolyn Stemshorn (M.P.H., University of Washington, 2001).

43. *American Pie* review, Owen Gleiberman, *Entertainment Weekly*, July 16, 1999, 44.

44. *Coming Soon* review, Amy Taubin, *Village Voice*, May 9, 2000, 57.

45. The sequels to the theatrically released *American Pie* trilogy were all titled *American Pie Presents* and followed by the subtitles *Band Camp* (2005), *The Naked Mile* (2006), *Beta House* (2007), and *The Book of Love* (2009).

46. *Superbad* review, Manohla Dargis, *New York Times*, Aug. 17, 2007, C1.

47. Jeffery P. Dennis, *Queering Teen Culture: All-American Boys and Same-Sex Desire in Film and Television* (New York: Routledge, 2006), 46.

48. Considine, 242.

49. Ibid.

50. Vito Russo offers some of the only thorough coverage of *Abuse* in *The Cel-luloid Closet: Homosexuality in the Movies*, rev. ed. (New York: Harper & Row, 1987), 273–274; see also 260–261.

51. Significant images of youth questioning their sexuality are contained in the work of Sadie Benning, who as a teenager in the late 1980s began making tech-nically crude but aesthetically rich pixelvision videos of lesbian life experiences, such as *Welcome to Normal, Me and Rubyfruit*, and *Jollies*, which have since become landmark texts of young lesbian representation. See Mia Carter, "The Politics of Pleasure: Cross-Cultural Autobiographic Performance in the Video Works of Sadie Benning," *Signs: A Journal of Women in Culture and Society* 23, no. 3 (1998): 745–769.

52. To clarify my terminology, I use the term "queer" in reference to non-heterosexual orientation in general. "Gay" is used to specify homosexual or bi-sexual characters, often but not always men, while of course "lesbian" is specific to women. "GLBT" is an acronym for gay, lesbian, bisexual, and transgendered sexual identities.

53. *This Boy's Life* (1993), which is set in the late '50s, introduces a gay teenage boy with a subtle crush on the protagonist, and while his role is rather small, the film reminds us that young same-sex attraction is not a contemporary phenomenon.

54. *Totally F***ed Up* review, Randy Gener, *Village Voice*, Oct. 11, 1994, 74.

55. *Totally F***ed Up* review, Tony Rayns, *Sight and Sound* 5, no. 2 (Feb. 1995): 55.

56. *Totally F***ed Up* review, Kevin Thomas, *Los Angeles Times*, Nov. 2, 1994, Cal-endar, 4.

57. *The Incredibly True Adventure of Two Girls in Love* review, Joe Brown, *Washington Post*, June 30, 1995, D1.

58. *All Over Me* review, Nell Bernstein, April 27, 1997, http://www.salon.com/.

59. The 1996 short feature *Hide and Seek*, by avant-garde filmmaker Su Fried-rich, testifies to this as well. The narrative considers the development of lesbian youth through narrative and documentary styles, depicting a twelve-year-old girl coming to terms with her sexual identity in the 1960s.

60. Little-known films or smaller roles by queer youth at this time include *Story of a Bad Boy* (1999), *Speed Bump* (2000), *Gypsy 83*, *Storytelling* (both 2001), *Blind Spot* (2002), *On the Downlow, Steam Cloud Rising* (both 2004), *Dream Boy, Half-Life* (both 2008), *We Are the Mods, Wrecked* (both 2009), *Anderson's Cross, Every Day* (both 2010), and *Someday This Pain Will Be Useful to You* (2011). My thanks to Richard Brown and Jonathan Lupo for suggesting many titles throughout this section.

61. *Mysterious Skin* review, Dennis Lim, *Village Voice*, April 26, 2005, 57.

62. *Mysterious Skin* review, Roger Ebert, *Chicago Sun-Times*, June 2, 2005, C1.

63. *Pariah* review, Mary Pols, *Time*, Dec. 12, 2011, http://entertainment.time .com/2011/12/28/pariah-coming-out-and-coming-of-age/#ixzz2JuVYj97o.

64. While very early films are difficult to obtain and thus synopses can be dif-ficult to verify, numerous films were made about teenage pregnancy long before

Roe v. Wade in 1973, including some dealing with abortion, such as *The Road to Ruin* (1928).

65. "Evaluation of Sexual Content in Teen-Centered Films From 1980 to 2007," by Mark Callister, Lesa Stern, Sarah Coyne, Tom Robinson, and Emily Bennion, *Mass Communication and Society* 14, no. 4 (2011): 471.

66. *Nickel Mountain* (1985) features a teenage girl who becomes pregnant and has the child, but this unusual and obscure film was not indicative of other teen depictions at the time.

67. Speaking in 1988, at the effective end of Molly Ringwald's career playing teenagers, Roger Ebert astutely pointed out her—and John Hughes's—influence on youth films of the '80s: "The movies of Molly Ringwald have been responsible for a revolution in the way Hollywood regards teenagers. Before Ringwald (and her mentor, John Hughes) there were only horny teenagers, dead teenagers, teenage vampires and psychotic crack-ups" (*"For Keeps"* review, Roger Ebert, *Chicago Sun-Times*, Jan. 15, 1988, 27). Ebert's description refers to the increasing senses of sincerity and compassion that were characteristic of many youth films in the mid to late '80s, and further intimates the subgeneric changes that would mark the more complex youth films of the era.

68. *"For Keeps"* review, Janet Hawken, *Monthly Film Bulletin*, June 1988, 174.

69. *"For Keeps"* review, Roger Ebert, *Chicago Sun-Times*, Jan. 15, 1988, 27.

70. Margaret Tally, "Reconceiving Conception: Changing Discourses of Teen Motherhood in Popular Culture," in *Bound by Love: Familial Bonding in Film and Television Since 1950*, ed. Laura Mattoon D'Amore (Newcastle upon Tyne, UK: Cambridge Scholars, 2011), 61.

71. *Immediate Family* review, David Edelstein, *New York Post*, Oct. 27, 1989, 21.

72. Leslie Harris, the writer and director of *Just Another Girl on the I.R.T.*, discusses the reception of the film in the "Teens" episode of the informative Independent Film Channel documentary series *Indie Sex* (2007), produced and directed by Lesli Klainberg and Lisa Ades, 27:25–29:00.

73. *Just Another Girl on the I.R.T.* review, Jami Bernard, *New York Post*, Mar. 19, 1993, 29.

74. *Just Another Girl on the I.R.T.* review, David Denby, *New York*, April 5, 1993, 60.

75. The mistaken-identity comedy *Mrs. Winterbourne* (1996) features Ricki Lake as a pregnant eighteen-year-old who has her baby early in the film. As with Lake's pregnant character in *Cry-Baby* (1990), the focus on the pregnancy is relatively minimal.

76. Kelly Oliver, *Knock Me Up, Knock Me Down: Images of Pregnancy in Hollywood Films* (New York: Columbia University Press, 2012), 41.

77. Sarah Hentges, *Pictures of Girlhood: Modern Female Adolescence on Screen* (Jefferson, NC: McFarland, 2006), 211.

78. See Madonne M. Miner's reading of *Sugar and Spice* as a remake of *The Usual Suspects* (1995), "Not Exactly According to the Rules: Pregnancy and Motherhood

in *Sugar & Spice*," in *Motherhood Misconceived: Representing the Maternal in U.S. Films*, ed. Heather Addison, Mary Kate Goodwin-Kelly, and Elaine Roth (Albany: State University of New York Press, 2009), 43–62.

79. In an unusual twist on the pregnant teenager story, *October Baby* (2011) is about a girl who learns she was adopted as the result of her birth mother's failed abortion attempt.

80. *Juno* review, Ty Burr, *Boston Globe*, Dec. 14, 2007, http://www.boston.com /ae/movies/articles/2007/12/14/hip_and_hysterical_juno_delivers/.

81. *Juno* review, Andrew Sarris, *New York Observer*, Dec. 4, 2007, http://www .observer.com/2007/12/maybe-baby/.

CHAPTER 6. CONCLUSION: YOUTH CINEMA INTO A NEW CENTURY

1. In 2012, three of the top ten highest-grossing American films at the box office were about teenagers: *The Hunger Games*, *The Twilight Saga—Breaking Dawn Part 2*, and the animated feature *Brave*. As this book goes to press in June 2013, studios are still planning franchises with *The Hunger Games*, *Percy Jackson*, *The Mortal Instruments*, and *Divergent* (to begin in 2014), while strong reviews and ad campaigns have not resulted in large audiences for exciting teen tales such as *The Bling Ring*, *The To Do List*, and *The Way Way Back*. Meanwhile, lower-budget and independent films provide further diversity with intriguing stories about coming of age, as in *The Kings of Summer*, *Standing Up*, *The Spectacular Now*, and *Grow Up, Tony Phillips*. Images of youth continue to thrive.

AFTERWORD

1. Catherine Driscoll, *Teen Film: A Critical Introduction* (London: Berg, 2011); *Girls: Feminine Adolescence in Popular Culture and Cultural Theory* (New York: Columbia University Press, 2002); *Modernist Cultural Studies* (Gainesville: University Press of Florida, 2010).

2. See Henry Jenkins, *Convergence Culture: Where Old and New Media Collide* (New York: New York University Press, 2006).

3. Thomas Doherty, *Teenagers and Teenpics: The Juvenilization of American Movies in the 1950s*, rev. and exp. ed. (Philadelphia: Temple University Press, 2002).

4. See my arguments in "Plastic Visibility, Visible Plasticity: On the Sexual-isation of Girlhood," in *Girlhood Studies and the Politics of Place: New Paradigms for Research*, ed. Claudia Mitchell and Carrie Rentschler (Oxford, NY: Berghahn Books, 2013), forthcoming; and "*She's All That*: Girl Sexuality in Teen Film," in *Girls' Sexualities and the Media*, ed. Kate Harper, Yasmina Katsulis, Vera Lopez, and Georganne Scheiner (New York: Palgrave, 2013), 93–108.

BIBLIOGRAPHY

Abell, Marietta, and Agnes Anderson. *"The Junior–Senior Prom,"* Complete Practical Suggestions for Staging the Junior–Senior Prom. Minneapolis: Northwestern Press, 1936.

Addams, Jane. "The House of Dreams." In *The Spirit of Youth and the City Streets*, 1909. Reprinted in *The Movies in Our Midst: Documents in the Cultural History of Film in America*, edited by Gerald Mast. Chicago: University of Chicago Press, 1982: 72–78.

Aloi, Peg. "A Charming Spell: The Intentional and Unintentional Influence of Popular Media upon Teenage Witchcraft in America." In *The New Generation Witches: Teenage Witchcraft in Contemporary Culture*, ed. Hannah E. Johnson and Peg Aloi. London: Ashgate, 2007: 113–128.

Altman, Rick. *Film/Genre*. London: British Film Institute, 1999.

Ariès, Philippe. *Centuries of Childhood: A Social History of Family Life*. New York: Random House, 1962.

Ascher-Walsh, Rebecca. "Virgin Territory." *Entertainment Weekly on Campus*, April 1999, 10–12.

Baker, David. "Rock Rebels and Delinquents: The Emergence of the Rock Rebel in 1950s 'Youth Problem' Films." *Continuum* 19, no. 1 (March 2005): 39–54.

Barson, Michael, and Steven Heller. *Teenage Confidential: An Illustrated History of the American Teen*. San Francisco: Chronicle Books, 1998.

Beck, Jason. "A Comparison of Male Athletes with Teenage Peers in Popular Teen Movies." Brigham Young University, M.A. thesis, 2011.

Behm-Morawitz, Elizabeth, and Dana E. Mastro. "Mean Girls? The Influence of Gender Portrayals in Teen Movies on Emerging Adults' Gender-Based Attitudes and Beliefs." *Journalism and Mass Communication Quarterly* 85, no. 1 (March 2008): 131–146.

Bennion, Emily. "Sexual Content in Teen Films: 1980–2007." M.M.C. thesis, Brigham Young University, 2008.

Bernasek, Eric D. "Does Barry Manilow Know You Raid His Wardrobe? Themes of Authority and Rebellion in American Movies About High School." M.A. thesis, Trinity College (Hartford, CT), 2008.

Bernstein, Jonathan. *Pretty in Pink: The Golden Age of Teenage Movies.* New York: St. Martin's Griffin, 1997.

Best, Amy. *Fast Cars, Cool Rides: The Accelerating World of Youth and Their Cars.* New York: New York University Press, 2006.

———. *Prom Night: Youth, Schools, and Popular Culture.* New York: Routledge, 2000.

Betrock, Alan. *The I Was a Teenage Juvenile Delinquent Rock 'n' Roll Horror Beach Party Movie Book: A Complete Guide to the Teen Exploitation Film, 1954–1969.* New York: St. Martin's Press, 1986.

Blumer, Herbert, and Philip Hauser. *Movies, Delinquency, and Crime.* New York: Macmillan, 1933.

Bodroghkozy, Aniko. "Reel Revolutionaries: An Examination of Hollywood's Cycle of 1960s Youth Rebellion Films." *Cinema Journal* 41, no. 3 (Spring 2002): 38–58.

Bowles, Scott. "Chloe Moretz, 13, Can Kick Your You-Know-What." *USA Today,* April 15, 2010, http://usatoday30.usatoday.com/life/movies/news/2010-04-15-chloe15_ST_N.htm.

Boyles, Deron, ed. *The Corporate Assault on Youth: Commercialism, Exploitation, and the End of Innocence.* New York: Peter Lang, 2008.

Bracke, Peter. *Crystal Lake Memories: The Complete History of "Friday the 13th."* Los Angeles: Sparkplug Press, 2005.

Brickman, Barbara Jane. *New American Teenagers: The Lost Generation of Youth in 1970s Film.* New York: Continuum, 2012.

Browne, Nick, ed. *Refiguring American Film Genres: History and Theory.* Berkeley: University of California Press, 1998.

Bulman, Robert C. *Hollywood Goes to High School: Cinema, Schools, and American Culture.* New York: Worth, 2004.

Burfeind, James, and Dawn Jeglum Bartusch. *Juvenile Delinquency: An Integrated Approach*, 2nd ed. Sudbury, MA: Jones and Bartlett, 2010.

Burt, Richard. *Unspeakable ShaXXXspeares: Queer Theory and American Kiddie Culture.* Rev. ed. New York: Palgrave Macmillan, 1999.

Callister, Mark, Sarah Coyne, Tom Robinson, John J. Davies, Chris Near, Lynn Van Valkenburg, and Jason Gillespie. "'Three Sheets to the Wind': Substance Use in Teen-Centered Film from 1980 to 2007." *Addiction Research and Theory* 20, no. 1 (2012): 30–41.

Callister, Mark, Lesa Stern, Sarah Coyne, Tom Robinson, and Emily Bennion. "Evaluation of Sexual Content in Teen-Centered Films From 1980 to 2007." *Mass Communication and Society* 14, no. 4 (2011): 454–474.

Calo, Richard G. *American Prom.* Nashville: Cumberland House, 2006.

———. *The First and Original Book of Prom.* Wormleysburg, PA: Awaken Sky Books, 2004.

Campbell, Neil, ed. *American Youth Cultures.* New York: Routledge, 2004. Previously published as *The Radiant Hour: Versions of Youth in American Culture.* Exeter: University of Exeter Press, 2000.

Canby, Vincent. "Stop Kidding Around." *New York Times*, July 23, 1972, sec. 3, 1.

Carlson, Zach, and Bryan Connolly, eds. *Destroy All Movies! The Complete Guide to Punks on Film.* Seattle: Fantagraphics, 2010.

Carter, Mia. "The Politics of Pleasure: Cross-Cultural Autobiographic Performance in the Video Works of Sadie Benning." *Signs: A Journal of Women in Culture and Society* 23, no. 3 (1998): 745–769.

Chennault, Robert. *Hollywood Films About Schools: Where Race, Politics, and Education Intersect.* New York: Palgrave Macmillan, 2006.

Cherry, Brigid. "Subcultural Tastes, Genre Boundaries, and Fan Canons." In *The Shifting Definitions of Genre: Essays on Labeling Films, Television Shows, and Media*, ed. Lincoln Geraghty and Mark Jancovich. Jefferson, NC: McFarland, 2008: 201–215.

Children's Defense Fund. *The Adolescent and Young Adult Fact Book.* Washington, DC: 1991.

Christensen, Kyle. "The Final Girl Versus Wes Craven's *A Nightmare on Elm Street*: Proposing a Stronger Model of Feminism in Slasher Horror Cinema." *Studies in Popular Culture* 34, no. 1 (Fall 2011): 23–47.

Christie, Thomas A. *John Hughes and Eighties Cinema: Teenage Hopes and American Dreams.* 2nd ed. Kent, UK: Crescent Moon Publishing, 2010.

Clark, Caroline Clayton. "Film Families: The Portrayal of the Family in Teen Films from 1980 to 2007." M.A. thesis, Brigham Young University, 2008.

Clark, Randall. "Teenage Films." *At a Theater or Drive-In near You: The History, Culture, and Politics of the American Exploitation Film.* New York: Garland, 1995: 49–76.

Click, Melissa A., Jennifer Stevens Aubrey, and Elizabeth Behm-Morawitz, eds. *Bitten by "Twilight": Youth Culture, Media, and the Vampire Franchise.* New York: Peter Lang, 2010.

Clover, Carol. "Her Body, Himself: Gender in the Slasher Film." *Representations* 20 (1987): 187–228.

———. *Men, Women, and Chain Saws: Gender in the Modern Horror Film.* Princeton: Princeton University Press, 1992.

Cohen, Michael Lee. *The Twenty-Something American Dream: A Cross-Country Quest for a Generation.* New York: Dutton, 1993.

Coleman, James. *The Adolescent Society: The Social Life of the Teenager and Its Impact on Education.* New York: Free Press of Glencoe, 1961.

Conklin, John E. *Campus Life in the Movies: A Critical Survey from the Silent Era to the Present.* Jefferson, NC: McFarland, 2008.

Connelly, Kelly. "From Final Girl to Final Woman: Defeating the Male Monster in *Halloween* and *Halloween H₂O*." *Journal of Popular Film and Television* 35, no. 1 (Spring 2007): 12–21.

Considine, David M. *The Cinema of Adolescence.* Jefferson, NC: McFarland, 1985.

———. "The Depiction of Adolescent Sexuality in Motion Pictures: 1930–1980." Ph.D. diss., University of Wisconsin, Madison, 1982.

Cook, David. *A History of Narrative Film.* 3rd ed. New York: Norton, 1996.

Cook, Pam. *The Cinema Book*. 3rd ed. London: British Film Institute, 2008.

Coupland, Douglas. *Generation X: Tales for an Accelerated Culture*. New York: St. Martin's Press, 1991.

Coyne, Sarah, Mark Callister, and Tom Robinson. "Yes, Another Teen Movie: Three Decades of Physical Violence in Films Aimed at Adolescents." *Journal of Children and Media* 4, no. 4 (2010): 387–401.

Cranon, Angela M. "Rolfe Kanefsky's Creepy Thriller Nightmare Man Already Taking Home Awards!" *Hollywood Scriptwriter* 27, no. 5 (Oct. 2007): 4–9.

Cressey, P. G., and F. M. Thrasher. *Boys, Movies, and City Streets*. New York: Macmillan, 1934.

Cripps, Thomas. *Slow Fade to Black: The Negro in American Film, 1900–1942*. New York: Oxford University Press, 1977.

Dalton, Mary. *The Hollywood Curriculum: Teachers and Teaching in the Movies*. 2nd rev. ed. New York: Peter Lang, 2010.

Davies, J. N. P. "Iatrogenic Vagina Dentata." *American Journal of Forensic Medicine and Pathology* 10, no. 3 (Sept. 1989): 269.

Davis, Glyn, and Kay Dickinson. *Teen TV: Genre, Consumption, and Identity*. London: British Film Institute, 2008.

DeGraffenreid, L. J. "What Can You Do in Your Dreams? Slasher Cinema as Youth Empowerment." *Journal of Popular Culture* 44, no. 5 (Oct. 2011): 954–969.

Denby, David. "High School Confidential." *New Yorker*, May 31, 1999, 94–98.

Dennis, Jeffery P. *Queering Teen Culture: All-American Boys and Same-Sex Desire in Film and Television*. New York: Routledge, 2006.

Dika, Vera. *Games of Terror: "Halloween," "Friday the 13th," and the Films of the Stalker Cycle*. Toronto: Associated University Presses, 1990.

———. "The Stalker Film, 1978–81." In *American Horrors: Essays on the Modern Horror Film*, edited by Gregory Waller. Urbana: University of Illinois Press, 1987: 86–101.

Dixon, Wheeler Winston. "'Fighting and Violence and Everything, That's Always Cool': Teen Films in the 1990s." In *Film Genre 2000: New Critical Essays*, edited by Wheeler Winston Dixon, 125–142. Albany: State University of New York Press, 2000.

Doherty, Thomas. "Clueless Kids." *Cineaste* 21, no. 4 (1995): 15–17.

———. *Teenagers and Teenpics: The Juvenilization of American Movies in the 1950s*. Boston: Unwin Hyman, 1988.

———. *Teenagers and Teenpics: The Juvenilization of American Movies in the 1950s*. Rev. and exp. ed. Philadelphia: Temple University Press, 2002.

Driscoll, Catherine. *Girls: Feminine Adolescence in Popular Culture and Cultural Theory*. New York: Columbia University Press, 2002.

———. *Modernist Cultural Studies*. Gainesville: University Press of Florida, 2010.

———. "Plastic Visibility, Visible Plasticity: On the Sexualisation of Girlhood." In *Girlhood Studies and the Politics of Place: New Paradigms for Research*, edited by Claudia Mitchell and Carrie Rentschler. Oxford, NY: Berghahn Books, 2013.

———. "*She's All That*: Girl Sexuality in Teen Film." In *Girls' Sexualities and the Media*, edited by K. Harper, Y. Katsulis, V. Lopez and G. Scheiner. New York: Palgrave, 2013.

———. *Teen Film: A Critical Introduction*. London: Berg, 2011.

Dysinger, Wendell, and Christian Ruckmick. *The Emotional Responses of Children to the Motion Picture Situation*. New York: Macmillan, 1933.

Edmundson, Mark. *Nightmare on Main Street: Angels, Sadomasochism, and the Culture of the Gothic*. Cambridge: Harvard University Press, 1997.

Erikson, Erik. *The Challenge of Youth*. Garden City, NY: Anchor Books, 1963.

———. *Identity, Youth, and Crisis*. New York: W. W. Norton, 1968.

Falzon, Christopher. *Philosophy Goes to the Movies: An Introduction to Philosophy*. New York: Routledge, 2007.

Ford, Richard. *Children in the Cinema*. London: George Allen and Unwin, 1939.

Forman, Henry James. *Our Movie Made Children*. New York: Macmillan, 1933.

Forman, Murray. "The 'Hood Took Me Under: Urban Geographies of Danger in New Black Cinema." In *Pictures of a Generation on Hold: Selected Papers*, edited by Murray Pomerance and John Sakeris. Toronto: Media Studies Working Group, 1996: 45–56.

Fornas, Johan. "Youth, Culture, and Modernity." In *Youth Culture in Late Modernity*, edited by Johan Fornas and Goran Bolin. London: Sage, 1995: 1–17.

Fox-Kales, Emily. *Body Shots: Hollywood and the Culture of Eating Disorders*. Albany: State University of New York Press, 2011.

Freud, Anna, Joseph Goldstein, and Albert Solnit. *Beyond the Best Interests of the Child*. New York: Free Press, 1979.

Friar, Ralph, and Natasha Friar. *The Only Good Indian: The Hollywood Gospel*. New York: Drama Book Specialists, 1972.

Friedman, Lester. *The Jewish Image in American Film*. Secaucus, NJ: Citadel Press, 1987.

Gill, Pat. "The Monstrous Years: Teens, Slasher Films, and the Family." *Journal of Film and Video* 54, no. 4 (Winter 2003): 16–37.

Gillis, John R. *Youth and History: Tradition and Change in European Age Relations, 1770– Present*. New York: Academic Press, 1981.

Giroux, Henry. "Hollywood Films and the War on Youth." In *Breaking in to the Movies: Film and the Culture of Politics*. Malden, MA: Blackwell, 2002: 45–192.

———. *Youth in Revolt: Reclaiming a Democratic Future*. Boulder, CO: Paradigm, 2012.

Gleiberman, Owen. "Bold Before Their Time." *Entertainment Weekly*, July 21, 1995, 47.

Goldstein, Ruth, and Edith Zornow. *The Screen Image of Youth: Movies About Children and Adolescents*. Metuchen, NJ: Scarecrow Press, 1980.

Gora, Susannah. *You Couldn't Ignore Me If You Tried: The Brat Pack, John Hughes, and Their Impact on a Generation*. Pittsburgh: Three Rivers Press, 2011.

Grant, Barry Keith. *The Hollywood Film Musical*. West Sussex, UK: Wiley-Blackwell, 2012.

Griffin, Christine. *Representations of Youth: The Study of Youth and Adolescence in Britain and America.* Cambridge, UK: Polity Press, 1993.

Grodal, Torben. *Moving Pictures: A New Theory of Film Genres, Feelings, and Cognition.* New York: Oxford University Press, 1997.

Gross, David M., and Sophfronia Scott. "Proceeding with Caution." *Time,* July 16, 1990: 56–62.

Hall, Stuart, and Tony Jefferson, eds. *Resistance Through Rituals: Youth Subcultures in Post-War Britain.* London: Hutchinson, 1976.

Hall, G. Stanley. *Adolescence: Its Psychology, and Its Relations to Physiology, Anthropology, Sociology, Sex, Crime, Religion, and Education.* New York: D. Appleton & Company, 1904.

Hammer, Rhonda, and Douglas Kellner. "Movies and Battles over Reaganite Conservatism." In *American Cinema of the 1980s: Themes and Variations,* edited by Stephen Prince. New Brunswick: Rutgers University Press, 2007: 107–125.

Hardcastle, Anne, Roberta Morosini, and Kendall Tarte, eds. *Coming of Age on Film: Stories of Transformations in World Cinema.* Winston–Salem: Wake Forest University Romance Languages Film Symposium, 2006.

Haskell, Molly. *From Reverence to Rape: The Treatment of Women in the Movies.* New York: Holt, Rinehart and Winston, 1974.

Havighurst, Robert. *Developmental Tasks and Education.* New York: Longman, 1948.

Hebdige, Dick. *Hiding in the Light.* London: Methuen, 1993.

———. *Subculture: The Meaning of Style.* London: Methuen, 1979.

Heller, Peter. *A Child Analysis with Anna Freud.* Madison, CT: International Universities Press, 1990.

Henne, Peter. "Teen Days That Shook the World." *Premiere,* Dec. 1999: 69–78.

Hentges, Sarah. *Pictures of Girlhood: Modern Female Adolescence on Screen.* Jefferson, NC: McFarland, 2006.

Hine, Thomas. *The Rise and Fall of the American Teenager.* New York: Harper Perennial, 2000.

Hinton, David. *Celluloid Ivy: Higher Education in the Movies, 1960–1990.* Metuchen, NJ: Scarecrow, 1994.

Holden, Stephen. "A New Rule: The Beautiful Are the Bad." *New York Times,* Feb. 28, 1999, C3.

Holtz, Geoffrey T. *Welcome to the Jungle: The Why Behind "Generation X."* New York: St. Martin's Griffin, 1995.

hooks, bell. "White Light." *Sight and Sound* 6, no. 5 (May 1996): 9–12.

Hunt, Morton. *The Story of Psychology.* New York: Doubleday, 1993.

Jackson, Kathy Merlock. *Images of Children in American Film: A Sociocultural Analysis.* Metuchen, NJ: Scarecrow Press, 1986.

Jamieson, Patrick, and Daniel Romer, eds. *The Changing Portrayal of Adolescents in the Media Since 1950.* New York: Oxford University Press, 2008.

Jenkins, Henry. *Convergence Culture: Where Old and New Media Collide.* New York: New York University Press, 2006.

Jowett, Garth S., Ian C. Jarvie, and Kathryn H. Fuller, eds. *Children and the Movies: Media Influence and the Payne Fund Controversy*. New York: Cambridge University Press, 1996.

Karlyn, Kathleen Rowe. "*Scream*, Popular Culture, and Feminism's Third Wave." In *Motherhood Misconceived: Representing the Maternal in U.S. Films*, edited by Heather Addison, Mary Kate Goodwin-Kelly, and Elaine Roth. Albany: State University of New York Press, 2009: 177–198.

Kaveney, Roz. *Teen Dreams: Reading Teen Film from "Heathers" to "Veronica Mars."* London: I. B. Tauris, 2006.

Kawin, Bruce. *Horror and the Horror Film*. London: Anthem, 2012.

Kearney, Mary Celeste. "Girlfriends and Girl Power: Female Adolescence in Contemporary U.S. Cinema." In *Sugar, Spice, and Everything Nice: Contemporary Cinemas of Girlhood*, edited by Murray Pomerance and Frances Gateward. Detroit: Wayne State University Press, 2002: 125–142.

Kehily, Mary Jane. *Understanding Youth: Perspectives, Identities, and Practices*. London: Sage, 2007.

Kelsey, Candice. *Generation MySpace: Helping Your Teen Survive Online Adolescence*. New York: Marlowe & Co., 2007.

Kendrick, James. "Razors in the Dreamscape: Revisiting *A Nightmare on Elm Street* and the Slasher Film." *Film Criticism* 33, no. 3 (Spring 2009): 17–33.

Keniston, Kenneth. "Youth: A 'New' Stage of Life." In *Youth and Culture: A Human-Development Approach*, edited by Hazel V. Kraemer. Monterey, CA: Brooks/Cole Publishing, 1974: 101–117.

———. *Youth and Dissent*. New York: Harcourt Brace Jovanovich, 1960.

Klanberg, Lesli, and Lisa Ades. "Teens" episode in *Indie Sex*, Independent Film Channel. Orchard Films, 2007.

Klein, Amanda Ann. *American Film Cycles: Reframing Genres, Screening Social Problems, and Defining Subcultures*. Austin: University of Texas Press, 2011.

Klein, Jessie. *The Bully Society: School Shootings and the Crisis of Bullying in America's Schools*. New York: New York University Press, 2012.

Langford, Barry. *Film Genre: Hollywood and Beyond*. Edinburgh: Edinburgh University Press, 2005.

Lebeau, Vicky. *Lost Angels: Psychoanalysis and Cinema*. New York: Routledge, 1995.

Lee, Christina. "Going Nowhere? The Politics of Remembering (and Forgetting) Molly Ringwald." *Cultural Studies Review* 13, no. 1 (March 2007): 89–104.

———. *Screening Generation X: The Politics and Popular Memory of Youth in Contemporary Cinema*. London: Ashgate, 2010.

Leitch, Thomas. "The World According to Teenpix." *Literature Film Quarterly* 20, no. 1 (Jan. 1992): 43–48.

Lewis, Jon. *The Road to Romance and Ruin: Teen Films and Youth Culture*. New York: Routledge, 1992.

Lincoln, Siân. *Youth Culture and Private Space*. London: Palgrave Macmillan, 2012.

Littwin, Susan. *The Postponed Generation: Why America's Grown-Up Kids Are Growing Up Later*. New York: Morrow, 1986.

Lizardi, Ryan. "'Re-imagining' Hegemony and Misogyny in the Contemporary Slasher Remake." *Journal of Popular Film and Television* 38, no. 3 (July–Sept. 2010): 113–121.

Loiry, William S. *The Impact of Youth: A History of Children and Youth with Recommendations for the Future*. Sarasota, FL: Loiry Publishing House, 1984.

Lopez, Daniel. *Films by Genre: 775 Categories, Styles, Trends, and Movements Defined, with a Filmography for Each*. Jefferson, NC: McFarland, 1993.

Mallan, Kerry, and Sharyn Pearce, eds. *Youth Cultures: Texts, Images, and Identities*. Westport, CT: Praeger, 2003.

Markovitz, Jonathan. "Female Paranoia as Survival Skill: Reason or Pathology in *A Nightmare on Elm Street?*" *Quarterly Review of Film and Video* 17, no. 3 (2000): 211–220.

Massood, Paula. "Mapping the Hood: The Genealogy of City Space in *Boyz N the Hood* and *Menace II Society*." *Cinema Journal* 35, no. 2 (Winter 1996): 85–97.

McGee, Mark Thomas, and R. J. Robertson. *The J. D. Films: Juvenile Delinquency in the Movies*. Jefferson, NC: McFarland, 1982.

McKelly, James C. "Youth Cinema and the Culture of Rebellion: *Heathers* and the *Rebel* Archetype." In *Pictures of a Generation on Hold: Selected Papers*, edited by Murray Pomerance and John Sakeris. Toronto: Media Studies Working Group, 1996: 107–114.

McRobbie, Angela. *Feminism and Youth Culture: From "Jackie" to "Just Seventeen."* London: Macmillan, 1991.

Milner, Murray. *Freaks, Geeks, and Cool Kids*. New York: Routledge, 2006.

Miner, Madonne M. "Not Exactly According to the Rules: Pregnancy and Motherhood in *Sugar & Spice*." In *Motherhood Misconceived: Representing the Maternal in U.S. Films*, edited by Heather Addison, Mary Kate Goodwin-Kelly, and Elaine Roth. Albany: State University of New York Press, 2009: 43–62.

Mitchell, Alice. *Children and Movies*. Chicago: University of Chicago Press, 1929.

Mogelonsky, Marcia. "The Rocky Road to Adulthood." *American Demographics*, May 1996: 26–35, 56.

Morey, Anne, ed. *Genre, Reception, and Adaptation in the "Twilight" Series*. London: Ashgate, 2012.

Nashawaty, Chris. "Oh, the Horror." *Entertainment Weekly*, Jan. 17, 1997: 8–10.

———. "The New Teen Age." *Entertainment Weekly*, Nov. 14, 1997: 24–35.

Neale, Stephen. *Genre and Hollywood*. London: Routledge, 2000.

Newman, Bruce. "Can't Read the Classic? See the Teen Movie." *New York Times*, Feb. 28, 1999, C13.

Nocenti, Annie. "Adapting and Directing *Election*: A Talk with Alexander Payne and Jim Taylor." *Scenario* 5, no. 2 (1999): 104–109, 189–190.

Norden, Martin. *Cinema of Isolation: A History of Physical Disability in the Movies*. New Brunswick: Rutgers University Press, 1994.

Northup, Temple, and Carol M. Liebler. "The Good, the Bad, and the Beautiful." *Journal of Children and Media* 4, no. 3 (Aug. 2010): 265–282.

Nowell, Richard. *Blood Money: A History of the First Teen Slasher Cycle.* New York: Continuum, 2011.

———. "'There's More Than One Way to Lose Your Heart': The American Film Industry, Early Teen Slasher Films, and Female Youth." *Cinema Journal* 51, no. 1 (Fall 2011): 115–140.

Ochoa, George. *Deformed and Destructive Beings: The Purpose of Horror Films.* Jefferson, NC: McFarland, 2011.

Oliver, Kelly. *Knock Me Up, Knock Me Down: Images of Pregnancy in Hollywood Films.* New York: Columbia University Press, 2012.

Olson, Scott R. "College Course File on Horror." *Journal of Film and Video* 48, nos. 1–2 (Spring–Summer 1996): 47–62.

Orenstein, Peggy. "The Movies Discover the Teen-Age Girl." *New York Times*, Aug. 11, 1996, B1.

Palladino, Grace. *Teenagers: An American History.* New York: Basic Books, 1996.

Paul, William. *Laughing Screaming: Modern Hollywood Horror and Comedy.* New York: Columbia University Press, 1994.

Pearce, Sharyn. "Sex and the Cinema: What *American Pie* Teaches the Young." *Sex Education* 6, no. 4 (2006): 367–376.

Pearson, Geoffrey. *Hooligan: A History of Respectable Fears.* New York: Schocken Books, 1983.

Peterson, Ruth, and L. L. Thurstone. *Motion Pictures and the Social Attitudes of Children.* New York: Macmillan, 1933.

Piaget, Jean, with Bärbel Inhelder. *The Growth of Logical Thinking.* New York: Basic Books, 1958.

Pichaloff, Tony, and Doug Pichaloff. *Hollywood Teen Movies: 80 from the '80s: The Good, the Bad, and the Forgotten.* New York: BookPal, 2011.

Pinedo, Isabel. "Postmodern Elements of the Contemporary Horror Film." *Journal of Film and Video* 48, nos. 1–2 (Spring–Summer 1996): 17–25.

Pomerance, Murray. "Pachyderm's Progress." In *Youth Culture in Global Cinema*, edited by Timothy Shary and Alexandra Seibel. Austin: University of Texas Press, 2007: 207–221.

Pomerance, Murray, and Frances Gateward, eds. *Sugar, Spice, and Everything Nice: Contemporary Cinemas of Girlhood.* Detroit: Wayne State University Press, 2002.

———. *Where the Boys Are: Cinemas of Masculinity and Youth.* Detroit: Wayne State University Press, 2005.

Pomerance, Murray, and John Sakeris, eds. *Pictures of a Generation on Hold: Selected Papers.* Toronto: Media Studies Working Group, 1996.

———. *Popping Culture.* 7th ed. New York: Pearson, 2013.

Quart, Alissa. *Branded: The Buying and Selling of Teenagers.* New York: Basic Books, 2003.

Rapping, Elayne. "Youth Cult Films." In *Media-tions: Forays into the Culture and Gender War*, edited by Elayne Rapping. New York: South End Press, 1999: 88–99.

Rathgeb, Douglas. "Bogeyman from the Id." *Journal of Popular Film and Television* 19, no. 1 (Spring 1991): 36–43.

Rich, Jennifer. "Shock Corridors: The New Rhetoric of Horror in Gus Van Sant's *Elephant*." *Journal of Popular Culture* 45, no. 6 (Dec. 2012): 1310–1329.

Rieser, Klaus. "Masculinity and Monstrosity: Characterization and Identification in the Slasher Film." *Men and Masculinities* 3, no. 4 (2001): 370–392.

Ritchie, Karen. *Marketing to Generation X*. New York: Lexington Books, 1995.

Robinson, Jessica. *Life Lessons from Slasher Films*. Lanham, MD: Scarecrow Press, 2012.

Robinson, Tom, Mark Callister, and Dawn Magoffin. "Older Characters in Teen Movies from 1980–2006." *Educational Gerontology* 35, no. 8 (2009): 687–711.

Rockoff, Adam. *Going to Pieces: The Rise and Fall of the Slasher Film, 1978–1986*. Jefferson, NC: McFarland, 2002; reprinted 2011.

Roddy, Nikki. *How to Fight, Lie, and Cry Your Way to Popularity (and a Prom Date): Lousy Life Lessons from 50 Teen Movies*. San Francisco: Zest Books, 2011.

Rollin, Lucy. *Twentieth-Century Teen Culture by the Decades: A Reference Guide*. Westport, CT: Greenwood Press, 1999.

Ross, Sharon Marie, and Louisa Stein. *Teen Television: Essays on Programming and Fandom*. Jefferson, NC: McFarland, 2008.

Roth, Elaine. "'You Just Hate Men!': Maternal Sexuality and the Nuclear Family in *Gas, Food Lodging*." In *Motherhood Misconceived: Representing the Maternal in U.S. Films*, edited by Heather Addison, Mary Kate Goodwin-Kelly, and Elaine Roth. Albany: State University of New York Press, 2009: 111–124.

Russo, Vito. *The Celluloid Closet: Homosexuality in the Movies*. Rev. ed. New York: Harper & Row, 1987.

Sapolsky, Barry, and Fred Molitor. "Content Trends in Contemporary Horror Films." In *Horror Films: Current Research on Audience Preferences and Reactions*, ed. James B. Weaver and Ron Tamborini. Mahwah, NJ: Lawrence Erlbaum Associates, 1996: 35–52.

Schauer, Bradley. "Dimension Films and the Exploitation Tradition in Contemporary Hollywood." *Quarterly Review of Film and Video* 26, no. 5 (2009): 393–405.

Scheiner, Georganne. *Signifying Female Adolescence: Film Representations and Fans, 1920–1950*. Westport, CT: Praeger, 2000.

Schneider, Barbara, and David Stevenson. *The Ambitious Generation: America's Teenagers, Motivated but Directionless*. New Haven: Yale University Press, 2000.

Shary, Timothy. "Angry Young Women: The Emergence of the 'Tough Girl' Image in American Teen Films." *Post Script* 19, no. 2 (Winter–Spring 2000): 49–61.

———. "Buying Me Love: 1980s Class-Clash Teen Romances." *Journal of Popular Culture* 44, no. 3 (June 2011): 563–582.

———. "Film Genres and the Cinematic Image of Youth: A College Course File." *Journal of Film and Video* 55, no. 1 (Spring 2003): 39–57.

———. "Generation Multiplex: The Image of Youth in American Cinema, 1981–1996." Ph.D. diss., University of Massachusetts, 1998.

———. "The Incredibly True Adventure of Teenage Homosexuality in American Cinema." In *Cinema and Multiculturalism: Selected Proceedings*, edited by J. Héli Hernández and Sheryl Lynn Postman. Mineola, NY: Legas Press, 2001: 97–110.

———. "1995: Movies, Teens, Tots, and Tech." In *American Cinema of the 1990s: Themes and Variations*, edited by Christine Holmlund. New Brunswick: Rutgers University Press, 2008: 137–156.

———. "'The Only Place to Go Is Inside': Confusions of Sexuality and Class in *Clueless* and *Kids*." In *Pictures of a Generation on Hold: Selected Papers*, edited by Murray Pomerance and John Sakeris. Toronto: Media Studies Working Group, 1996: 157–166. Reprinted in Pomerance and Sakeris, *Popping Culture*, 7th ed., 2013; revised as "'The Only Place to Go Is Inside': Confusions about Sexuality and Class from *Kids* to *Superbad*," 5–13.

———. "Reification and Loss in Postmodern Puberty: The Cultural Logic of Fredric Jameson and American Youth Movies." In *Postmodernism and Cinema*, edited by Cristina Degli-Esposti. Providence: Berghahn Books, 1999: 73–89.

———. "The Teen Film and Its Methods of Study." *Journal of Popular Film and Television* 25, no. 1 (Spring 1997): 38–45.

———. *Teen Movies: American Youth on Screen*. London: Wallflower, 2005.

Shary, Timothy, and Alexandra Seibel, eds., *Youth Culture in Global Cinema*. Austin: University of Texas Press, 2007.

Schatz, Thomas. *Hollywood Genres: Formulas, Filmmaking, and the Studio System*. New York: Random House, 1981.

Schwarzbaum, Lisa. "Demonic Youth." *Entertainment Weekly*, Oct. 11, 1996: 99–101.

Sellers, Christian, and Gary Smart. *The Complete History of "The Return of the Living Dead."* London: Plexus, 2011.

Semenza, Gregory M. Colón. "Shakespeare After Columbine: Teen Violence in Tim Blake Nelson's *'O'*." *College Literature* 32, no. 4 (Fall 2005): 99–124.

Siegel, Carol. *Goth's Dark Empire*. Bloomington: Indiana University Press, 2005.

Sinclair, Marianne. *Hollywood Lolitas: The Nymphet Syndrome in the Movies*. New York: Holt, 1988.

Slocum, J. David, ed. *"Rebel Without a Cause": Approaches to a Maverick Masterwork*. Albany: State University of New York Press, 2005.

Sloniowski, Jeannette. "A Cross-Border Study of the Teen Genre: The Case of John N. Smith." *Journal of Popular Film and Television* 25, no. 3 (Fall 1997): 130–137.

Snyder, Scott. "Movie Portrayals of Juvenile Delinquency: Part 1—Epidemiology and Criminology." *Adolescence* 30, no. 117 (Spring 1995): 53–64.

———. "Movie Portrayals of Juvenile Delinquency: Part 2—Sociology and Psychology." *Adolescence* 30, no. 118 (Summer 1995): 325–337.

———. "Movies and Juvenile Delinquency: An Overview." *Adolescence* 26, no. 101 (Spring 1991): 121–132.

Speed, Lesley. "Tuesday's Gone: The Nostalgic Teen Film." *Journal of Popular Film and Television* 25, no. 1 (Spring 1998): 24–32.

Staiger, Janet. "Hybrid or Inbred: The Purity Hypothesis and Hollywood Genre History." *Film Criticism* 22, no. 1 (Fall 1997): 5–20.

Stamp Lindsey, Shelley. "Horror, Femininity, and Carrie's Monstrous Puberty." *Journal of Film and Video* 43, no. 4 (Winter 1991): 33–44.

Stemshorn, Carolyn. "No Glove, No Love: Messages About Contraception in Teen Movies." M.P.H. thesis, University of Washington, 2001.

Stephens, John. "'I'll Never Be the Same After That Summer': From Abjection to Subjective Agency in Teen Films." In *Youth Cultures: Texts, Images, and Identities*, edited by Kerry Mallan and Sharyn Pearce. Westport, CT: Praeger, 2003.

Tally, Margaret. "Reconceiving Conception: Changing Discourses of Teen Motherhood in Popular Culture." In *Bound by Love: Familial Bonding in Film and Television Since 1950*, edited by Laura Mattoon D'Amore. Newcastle upon Tyne, UK: Cambridge Scholars, 2011: 47–67.

Tasker, Yvonne. "Bodies and Genres in Transition: *Girlfight* and *Real Women Have Curves*." In *Gender Meets Genre in Postwar Cinemas*, edited by Christine Gledhill. Urbana: University of Illinois Press, 2012: 84–95.

Taves, Brian (chair), Judi Hoffman, and Karen Lund. *The Moving Image Genre-Form Guide*. Library of Congress Motion Picture/Broadcasting/Recorded Sound Division report, Feb. 12, 1997.

Trencansky, Sarah. "Final Girls and Terrible Youth: Transgression in 1980s Slasher Horror." *Journal of Popular Film and Television* 29, no. 2 (Summer 2001): 63–73.

Tropiano, Stephen. *Rebels and Chicks: A History of the Hollywood Teen Movie*. New York: Back Stage Books, 2006.

Tudor, Andrew. "Genre." In *Theories of Film*. New York: Viking Press, 1973. Reprinted in *Film Genre Reader IV*, edited by Barry Keith Grant. Austin: University of Texas Press, 2012: 3–11.

Tzioumakis, Yannis, and Siân Lincoln, eds. *The Time of Our Lives: "Dirty Dancing" and Popular Culture*. Detroit: Wayne State University Press, 2013.

Umphlett, Wiley Lee. *The Movies Go to College: Hollywood and the World of the College-Life Film*. Rutherford: Fairleigh Dickinson University Press, 1984.

Vaz, Mark Cotta. *"Twilight": The Complete Illustrated Movie Companion*. New York: Little, Brown, 2008.

Watkins, S. Craig. *Representing: Hip Hop Culture and the Production of Black Cinema*. Chicago: University of Chicago Press, 1998.

Weaver, James B. "Are 'Slasher' Horror Films Sexually Violent? A Content Analysis." *Journal of Broadcasting and Electronic Media* 35, no. 3 (Summer 1991): 385–392.

Wee, Valerie. "Resurrecting and Updating the Teen Slasher: The Case of *Scream*," *Journal of Popular Film and Television* 34, no. 2 (Summer 2006): 50–61.

———. "The *Scream* Trilogy: 'Hyper-postmodernism' and the Late-Nineties Teen Slasher Film." *Journal of Film and Video* 57, no. 3 (Fall 2005): 44–61.

Weinraub, Bernard. "Who's Lining Up at Box Office? Lots and Lots of Girls." *New York Times*, Feb. 23, 1998, B4.

Whatley, Marianne H. "Raging Hormones and Powerful Cars: The Construction of Men's Sexuality in School Sex Education and Popular Adolescent Films." *Journal of Education* 170, no. 3 (1988): 100–121.

White, Armond. "Kidpix." *Film Comment* 21, no. 4 (Aug. 1985): 9–16.

Willemen, Paul. "Presentation." In Stephen Neale, *Genre*. London: British Film Institute, 1983: 1–4.

Winnicott, D. W. *The Child, the Family, and the Outside World*. Baltimore: Penguin, 1964.

———. *Playing and Reality*. New York: Tavistock Publications, 1971.

Wiseman, Rosalind. *Queen Bees and Wannabes: Helping Your Daughter Survive Cliques, Gossip, Boyfriends, and the New Realities of Girl World*. New York: Crown, 2009.

Wolfrom, Katy J. "Reel Principals: A Descriptive Content Analysis of the Images of School Principals Depicted in Movies from 1997–2009." D.Ed. diss., Indiana University of Pennsylvania, 2010.

Wood, Denis. "No Place for a Kid: Critical Commentary on *The Last Starfighter*." *Journal of Popular Film and Television* 14, no. 1 (Spring 1986): 52–63.

Wood, Robin. "Introduction to the American Horror Film." In *The American Nightmare: Essays on the Horror Film*, edited by Robin Wood and Richard Lippe. Toronto: Festival of Festivals, 1979: 7–28.

———. "Party Time or Can't Hardly Wait for That American Pie: Hollywood High School Movies of the '90s." *CineAction* 58 (Winter 2002): 2–7.

Young, Josh. "They're All That." *Entertainment Weekly*, March 12, 1999: 20–29.

Zacharek, Stephanie. "There's Something About Teenage Comedy . . ." *Sight and Sound* 9, no. 12 (Dec. 1999): 20–22.

INDEX

Page numbers in italics indicate photographs.